THE NEXT JERUSALEM: Sharing the Divided City

Michael Sorkin, editor

THE MONACELLI PRESS

Photograph Credits
page 247: Albatross Archive
page 248: Albatross Archive
page 388: By permission of the Department of Antiquities, Jordan. Photograph
courtesy of Thames and Hudson
page 396: Michael and Jane Wilson Collections
page 403: Bibliothèque Royale Albert Iᵉʳ, Brussels
page 406: Gernsheim Collection, Harry Ransom Humanities Research Center, The
University of Texas at Austin
page 411: Jewish National and University Library
page 412: Michael and Jane Wilson Collections. Courtesy Santa Barbara Museum of Art
page 415: Michael and Jane Wilson Collections. Courtesy Santa Barbara Museum of Art
page 416: Centre Canadien d'Architecture/Canadian Centre for Architecture, Montreal
page 418: Michael and Jane Wilson Collections. Courtesy Santa Barbara Museum of Art
page 420: Michael and Jane Wilson Collections. Courtesy Santa Barbara Museum of Art
page 423: Michael and Jane Wilson Collections. Courtesy Santa Barbara Museum of Art

THE NEXT JERUSALEM

Michael Sorkin, editor

Contributors

Ghiora Aharoni
Ariella Azoulay
Rasem Badran
Caroline Barat
Moustafa Bayoumi
Stella Betts
M. Christine Boyer
Joan Copjec
J.D. Dodds
Keller Easterling
Amir Sumaka'i Fink
Samira Haj
Rassem Khamaisi
Romi Khosla
David Leven
Thom Mayne
Rose Mendez
Deborah Natsios
Moshe Safdie
Mack Scogin
David Snyder
Michael Sorkin
Achva Benzinberg Stein
Jafar Tukan
Dag Tvilde
Andrei Vovk
Eyal Weizman
James Wines
Lebbeus Woods
Haim Yacobi
Oren Yiftachel
John Young
Omar Youssef
Ali Ziadah

For Peace and Justice

Contents

Preface   8

Introduction: Thinking about Jerusalem   12

Displaced Meanings / Monuments / People   22
J.D. Dodds, Moustafa Bayoumi, and Ghiora Aharoni

Hybrid City   36
Jafar Tukan

Reading Jerusalem   50
Dag Tvilde and Ali Ziadah

The New Canaanites   62
Romi Khosla

The Crescent Model   84
Rassem Khamaisi

My Winter Dreams   108
Achva Benzinberg Stein

The Subversion of Jerusalem's Sacred Vernaculars   120
Eyal Weizman

The Palestine League   146
Mack Scogin

Jerusalem SKY   152
Deborah Natsios and John Young

Parrando's Paradox: Error in Holy Lands   170
Keller Easterling

The People of Jerusalem Reordered   188
Samira Haj

A Shared City of Peace   202
Oren Yiftachel and Haim Yacobi

Civilization Center: Sketchbook for a Public Space   216
James Wines

Spaces between the Hills   224
Stella Betts, David Leven, and David Snyder

To Hell and Back: Jerusalem's Queer Center   238
Amir Sumaka'i Fink

Comments on the United Development Corporation's Proposal   260
Thom Mayne, Rose Mendez, and Caroline Barat

Jerusalem: United City, Two Sovereignties   268
Moshe Safdie

Jeruslem: Toward a City of Equals, Capital of Two States   292
Omar Youssef

A Plan for East Jerusalem   306
Michael Sorkin and Andrei Vovk

The Spectre of Jerusalem   320
Ariella Azoulay

Sour Justice, or: Liberalist Envy   338
Joan Copjec

Meditations on a New Jerusalem   354
Lebbeus Woods

Jerusalem Portfolio   368
Rasem Badran

Memories of Contention: The Sacred Stones of Jerusalem   378
M. Christine Boyer

Biographies   426

Preface

This book is the outgrowth of two conferences. The first took place in Jerusalem in 1997 and focused on the character of historic cities in the contemporary environment with Jerusalem itself a prime example. Although many distinguished architects and academics attended, including numerous Israelis, Palestinians were conspicuous by their absence.

The reasons offered for this omission were all stock occlusions: "We forgot" and "We asked and they refused" and "We were going to ask but knew that they would refuse and so we didn't"—answers that betrayed simultaneous antagonism and guilt. With my own easily purchased outsider's impatience with the lurid intractability of the conflict, I was quick to think ill of the organizers' motives.

As an urbanist, however, I was perplexed by the resistance of the "problem" of Jerusalem to ready solution. It had been thirty years since I had visited the city, and on returning I found it both familiar and transformed. Transformed by the violence, hostility, and odious everyday apartheid that characterize life there; transformed, too, by the expansive construction of the settlements that now surround it, impressive in extent but smug and domineering on their hilltops.

I was also struck by the city's smallness. Well versed in the crises of megacities and suburban sprawl, I found Jerusalem both relatively compact and strikingly uniform in its contiguities of texture and place. The city was relatively calm at the time, too, and felt accessible to me. So, as someone who loves cities both as physical and as cultural artifacts, I enjoyed my tourist's right to the city and wandered freely between East and West. Emblematic of this freedom was a single day in which I paid visits to the Church of the Nativity, the Wailing Wall, and the Dome of the Rock—a typical tourist agenda, perhaps, but personalized by bet-hedging prayers for a family member suddenly taken gravely ill.

I became frustrated with the various obfuscations and arguments used to justify the city's inequalities and with the intransigence of the professional class in the face of those inequalities. It may have been my own myopia, but in looking at the city I was impressed by the tractability of its physical problems. Questions of housing, public space and amenity, transport, or infrastructure might seem politically impossible, but the practical solutions were not obscure and the necessary resources did not seem out of reach.

My wanderings gave rise to a fantasy of amelioration, the idea that professionals—architects, planners, urbanists—might frame a view of the city that dealt simply with the idea of making it functional, beautiful, and physically generous to its inhabitants' needs.

Just getting on with this job, I thought, might amount to a strategy for reconciliation and cooperation. Indeed, if the effort devoted to action could match that devoted by all sides to expressing pieties about Jerusalem's ineffable qualities, much progress for her citizens might be made.

After speaking with a number of colleagues, I decided to organize a second conference. This one would also concern Jerusalem, but would feature professionals from both sides. It may simply have been my own mistaken faith in the religion of architecture, but I felt that there were issues that *could* be discussed outside the territory of politics. No matter the ultimate disposition of sovereignty, it seemed to me that questions of ecology, preservation, neighborhood development, open space, and so on would need many of the same answers.

In many ways, of course, this was simply a convenient fiction, for all these matters carry a strong political charge. Still, it seemed worth a try, an "objective" territory on which to search for common ground. This second conference took place in July 1999 in Bellagio, Italy, and had twenty-five participants, evenly divided among Palestinians, Israelis, and "others," mainly Americans. I asked each participant to address the gathering through the medium of some specific proposition for the physical future of the city and—as this book bears witness—many responded with plans that are remarkably specific. The mood of the conference was constructive, emotional, frank, and willing. It was tremendously interesting.

I had not sought any consensus from the conference, but was surprised at the actual convergence of views. Partly, this was due to the attendance list, which included, by definition, people who were inclined to talk and willing to accept the premise behind the invitation. But that was not the whole story: a consistent set of threads seemed to undergird many of the arguments, a a common (though sometimes grudging and covert) sense of what the urban denouement would ultimately be.

First, there was universal acknowledgment of the legitimacy of the desire for— indeed, of the existence of—Palestinian nationhood. There also seemed to be little doubt that the capital of Palestine would be called Al-Quds and would be located within the Jerusalem conurbation. In 1999 there was already much discussion of a site in Abu Dis—a town just east of the Israeli municipal boundary—as a place for the governmental infrastructure for the newborn state. This location was considered a good one not in traditional planning terms but because—given the political boundaries then in force—it could produce a fiction palatable to both sides. Israelis could claim that it was not, in fact, in Jerusalem, and Palestinians the opposite.

By the end of the conference, additional areas of informal agreement seemed clear: the need for some rational consolidation of infrastructure. The logic of a north-south transportation link along the topographic seam that defines the linear city stretching from Nablus to Hebron. The inevitability of two municipalities of potentially ambiguous territorial reach. Finally, the necessity of an open city which, by extension, raised the question of an open border between the two states. The conference ended with an unspoken but clear acknowledgment of both its desirability and necessity.

This book gathers the work of a number of the conference participants and is supplemented by the ideas of architects and writers enlisted later. These texts and proposals span a broad range of approaches, from historical and theoretical analysis to governance and organization, specific architectural and planning proposals, and speculative and notional propositions. Although by no means uniform, all move in the general direction described above; all, I hope, convey the spirit of possibility that characterized the conference; and all, I know, are predicated on a clear-eyed knowledge of the necessity and inevitability of amicably sharing this vexed but enthralling place.

Neither conference nor book would have been possible without the generous assistance of a number of people and organizations. The Rockefeller Foundation provided both the wonderful facilities of Bellagio (where the most intractable of foes couldn't help getting along) and a grant for the completion of this book. The Graham Foundation in Chicago gave me a very generous grant to cover conference expenses and to keep the project going. A grant from the Foundation for Middle East Peace in Washington, D.C., came at an opportune moment during the preparation of the book. And I owe a special debt of thanks to my dear friend Suha Ozkan, Director General of the Aga Khan Award for Architecture, whose official and personal generosity were critical to this project's success.

Jacob Kain bore the brunt of designing this book and of coordinating the gathering of a huge number of documents and images. I am indebted to him for his energy, patience, and creativity. Andrei Vovk was not simply central to our own design project but to keeping this publication (and me) going over the years. Larry Gilman was our excellent editor, performing miracles on texts written in what—for some —was a third or fourth language. Gianfranco Monacelli agreed to publish this project early and enthusiastically and I am grateful to him, Andrea Monfried, Steve Sears, and Elizabeth Kugler who forebore through a very long process.

Finally, I offer my heartfelt thanks to all who participated in this project. Perhaps the most rewarding aspect of all this is the net of individual friendships and collaborations that have arisen from the Bellagio meeting. It is here that I sense most clearly that my initial feeling about the ultimate simplicity of things was completely correct.

This book goes to press in the immediate aftermath of the events of September 11. That horrific act of terror makes the message of reconciliation essayed by this book all the more urgent and brings home to Americans an aspect of the lived lives of Palestinians and Israelis that we have been able to view with the luxury of detachment. Looking over the material gathered here one last time, I find that nothing in its feeling or analysis shifts. A just and equitable peace remains the only hope.

Back Row (left to right): Jafar Tukan, Basem Elayan, Romi Khosla, Dag Tvilde, Moshe Safdie, Andrei Vovk, Meron Benvenisti, Ali Ziadah, Suha Ozkan, Michael Sorkin, Omar Youssef, Suad Amiry, Eyal Weizman, Michael Dumper

Front Row (left to right): Rashid Khalidi, Rassem Khamaisi, Oren Yiftachel, Ariella Azoulay, Achva Stein, Maxine Griffith, Samira Haj, Joan Copjec, Christine Boyer, Lou Gelehrter, Gaetano Pesce

Introduction: Thinking about Jerusalem

Michael Sorkin

All planning is about boundaries, establishing them, inventing pathways across them. The organization of cities is based on differentiation, whether between uses, green space and built space, one neighborhood and another, areas of higher and lower density, or administrative and political districts. Such differences and the boundaries that inscribe them are critical to both the logic and the vibrancy of cities. Indeed, the accommodation of such differences is the city's reason for existence.

Of course, every difference carries a valence. The division of cities into zones of poverty and wealth or racial districts, for example, is a ubiquitous but troubling component of urban form. But not even this is simple. The difference between a neighborhood and a ghetto is not distinct, and the vitality and affinity of concentrated groups are key to identity and function in the city. Such complex negotiations are at the roots of urban personality and habit.

Jerusalem is a city in which coercions of difference have been raised to the flash-point. A mosaic of exclusion, Jerusalem constructs neighborhoods according to geographies of antagonism. Whether in the degradations of the refugee camp of Shuafat, or in the self-isolation of the Haredi in the elective ghetto of Mea She'arim, or in the colonial, disciplinary inscription of the Pisgat Ze'ev "settlement," Jerusalem has a genius for exclusivity.

Cities are propinquity engines, spatial juxtaposition machines. All cities structure the quality of interplay between their differences; in Jerusalem, collisions of difference are often violent and ugly, made visible in the open contempt between secular and religious Jews, between Israelis and Palestinians, between rich and poor, between modernity and tradition. However endemic to life in this city, this ugliness is not urbanistically necessary. In a good city, a difference need not be a barrier.

Jerusalem, a city packed very tightly, produces its discontinuities in a very small territory. And these are too often based not on logics of topography, breathing room, and architectural character but on suspicion, coercion, and contempt. Although the latter are not strictly matters of architecture, building patterns can communicate and reinforce (or contradict and dissipate) such messages. Jerusalem, riven by seams both visible and invisible, has acquired a disheartening expertise in the technologies of boundary. No city is more ardently fragmented.

Because Jerusalem's political crisis finds its ultimate expression in the idea of territory, the practice of politics and the practice of urban planning here merge. Both share an obsession with mapmaking; both seek to clarify relations of power and property through the sure dimensions of the map. Planning, with its history of classification, distribution, and organization, has become a device by which this struggle is both carried on and reified. Power understands and reproduces itself through this medium and also exercises its creativity. To the too-simple question of who plans and who benefits, a plan can also suggest and embrace nuance far beyond imagining.

In a game where all the players have hyper-developed hermeneutic traditions, reading maps and plans assumes deep significance. Every map is, of course, a distortion of the facts, and in the visual language of diplomacy and negotiation one distortion after another assumes privileged meanings. Embedded history, memory, demography, movement, and development acquire significance that becomes a lens focusing the impossibility of revision and projecting an image of inevitability.

Typical is the "Green Line" of Jerusalem, the border that divided the city into opposing territories starting in 1948. Drawn with a grease pencil, the line exceeded its abstraction and acquired physical dimension, a specific thickness. Its literal manifestation—a meters-wide stripe of territory demarcating the two sides but part of neither—itself became a territory of disputation, the site of conflicting property claims. This oscillation between the literal and figurative role of the graphical signifier has characterized conflict in Jerusalem for years. Demography rises to destiny in the act of recording. Information can never be neutral; any measurement is immediately associated with a question of rights.

The graphic and even morphological language of Jerusalem has reached a point where it cannot function, cannot even be spoken, without making some stipulation of advantage. The city thus produces a weird inversion of the goals of sound planning, which would seek to objectify the situation on the ground, resolve conflicts in space, locate construction sensitively, understand the multiple layers that underlie any site, and seek the delicate adjustment of physical conflicts and the creation of useful synergies.

In the struggle between Israel and Palestine, Jerusalem's obsessional mapmaking, whoever the mapmaker of the moment may be, is invariably reducible to a single characteristic. Whether the inquiry is into housing conditions, distribution of infrastructure, family size, or location of greenspace, invariably privileged is the depiction of ethnicity. If one semantic operation were to be imposed to force a revision away from the inevitability of conflict (the only thing most maps of the city record), it would be simply this: Let ethnic disposition arise from the reading of maps only by inference. The project of removing Jerusalem from its tragic conflicts begins with seeing the city as something other than a map of ethnic or religious differences.

This book is predicated on the idea that Jerusalem is a single city. The Jerusalem conurbation—a dense and continuous fabric from Bethlehem to Ramallah—is inescapably one physical entity, no matter how many divisions it may incorporate. Rather than taking division as a primary issue, then, this book begins from the fact of consolidation. Division into neighborhoods, districts, built space and open space, or even into enclaves of people who choose to live differently is seen here as subsidiary to this fact.

It is, however, important to be clear. This oneness is not a metaphysical construct but an ecological one. The political argument over Jerusalem consists of colliding, irreconcilable claims of ownership. That is, the question of Jerusalem—and of Palestine—has always revolved around the legitimacy of opposing claims to the same territory. Authority has been marshaled in many registers, but always seeks to establish particular rights—of return, of compensation, of ownership, of use—ultimately reducible to rights of property. These competing claims simply cannot be resolved without leaving one party or the other bereft, whatever definition of fairness is invoked.

A review of these debates reveals both the degree of difficulty of resolving them on their own terms and the possibility that a shift away from a discourse of already defined, but disputed, rights toward a recognition of every individual's political right to formulate their claims to rights—Hannah Arendt's famous "right to have rights." This would be a discourse in which the universal right to political contest—the right not to be excluded from the field in which rights are formulated—was acknowledged. For its part, planning would not work to preserve what once was, or rights already declared, but to preserve the possibility of universal access to the political process of instituting what will be.

This will mean circumnavigating or resituating the primary issues that currently impede progress:

The Record of Inhabitation

Israelis brandish the irrefutable claim that Jews preceded Muslims in Jerusalem and thus oppose the Arab claim to having been the site's inhabitants at the time of Israel's founding. These opposed claims are founded on ideas of continuity, duration, numbers, and immediacy, but the ethical foundations of any and all of these claims are a matter of apples and oranges, dependent on interpretations that must diverge by definition. While the presence of a few Jews in Hebron for a period of centuries surely has standing in establishing the right of Jews to live there, it is an enormous leap to claim that this automatically grants sovereignty over the land.

Arabs, for their part, have on their side both numbers and centuries of continuous presence on the site. Their historical presence is irrefutable and cannot be erased. The gerrymandering of municipal boundaries cannot obliterate their memories or, for that matter, the thick ecologies of their long continuities of inhabitation. Why not nurture this indigenousness for the sake of a thriving metropolis?

Introduction: Thinking about Jerusalem

The Contest of Sacralities

Jews offer passages from the Bible to affirm the sacred vibration of this place or that; Muslims respond from the Koran. This argument revolves around numbers of citations, their dates of inscription, their degree of holiness—a myriad of categories that can never be adjudicated or made comparable. In any event, recourse to theological arguments is of little use in making everyday decisions about property rights fixed in any specific territory. Such arguments may have some standing in a more general debate about the "right" to property, but offer only irreconcilable vagueness on the ground.

The contest of sacralities draws a straight line to a kind of statistical theology, a territory of permanent undecidability. But there's an up-side to theological authority, which is capable of coalescing opposites and of transcending narrow physicality. Jews insist that Jerusalem is the eternal and undivided capital of Israel. Arabs insist that Jerusalem is the eternal and undivided capital of Palestine. On the metaphysical plane, these statements are completely compatible, for Jerusalem can be both at once. Only when religion becomes a means of selling real estate is this happy potential conjuncture rendered impossible. The real problem, though, is that theological arguments inevitably squeeze out or displace the political.

Legal Ownership

The point of origin for legalistic arguments over ownership of Palestine and Jerusalem is itself religious: the notion that the territory was covenanted to the Jewish people. This will never be gainsaid as long as the site of its adjudication can only be a Jewish court which—by definition—does not recognize the standing of claimants outside its own religious authority, of "nonbelievers."

Some variation of this issue of judicial rights bedevils most secular claims of ownership as well. Property transfers conducted under the Ottoman, British, or Jordanian administrations, while bound by the legal instruments of their day, are undercut by the revised codes of successor administrations. While the rights of the inhabitants, especially those with records of payment and conveyance, have deep standing, there are precedents—based on changes in the nationality of territory; on revolutionary alterations in legal, financial, and administrative structures; and on the aftermath of warfare—that open many practical possibilities of redress.

Degree of Affection

The propaganda of sentimental attachment looms large in the discourse on whose right it is to possess the territory of Palestine. Here, in effect, is the secularization of the contest of sacralities, its expression in cultural terms. The battle of affection is fought on the field of popular songs, of poetry, of nostalgic paintings; in public demonstrations, in historically sensitive architecture, in archaeological investigations, in breast-beating, in martyrdom. In the end, all that can be agreed is that both sides hold the land and its history in strong affection.

Here, however, we see how affection for the very same thing can lead to mutual ruin; what looks on the surface like a marvelous harmony of will—what I hold dear, the other does too—introduces the worst sort of competition. But shouldn't it be possible for this double affection to lead to the competitive ornamentation of the city, to a vitalized science of water collection and energy production, to vigorous cooperation in economic activities, to the rhythmic intersection of cultural practices, and to a doubling of the delight taken in a place that both sides never cease to describe in terms of the marvelous?

Superiority of Stewardship

The trope of Arab neglect—deployed by Israelis despite the continuous and productive historical character of Arab agriculture—is augmented by the long-standing claim of Zionists and Israelis to have "made the desert bloom." These arguments, compounding error, arrogance, and racism, are daily given the lie by the Israeli uprooting of olive and orange groves for "security" reasons, by the contraction of the agricultural sector as a component of the Israeli economy, and by our renewed appreciation for the historic agricultural practices of generations of farmers in Palestine and comparable dry climates.

All arguments about superiority of stewardship would be undercut by the adoption of a more ecological view, one focused less on differences than on interdependencies. The ecological gloss—which gives priority to sustainable practices and provides a more nuanced view of the range of global biotopes—takes a view in which the fragility of the desert, rather than its hostility, becomes paramount. If there were a logical territory of cooperation, it would seem to reside precisely in the environment and its care, for natural laws would seem to know no national boundaries and thus to make everything harmonious. But desire for ecological stability can be as unreliable a foundation for a universal law as happiness is: politics is still required.

Level of Suffering

One of the most pernicious sites of national competition in Palestine is the idea that any solution of current issues must take into account the prior sufferings of the peoples of Palestine. Jerusalem is drenched in remembered miseries. Consider the Via Dolorosa, marker of the foundational pain of Christianity; the poignant abandonment of a legion of Palestinian villages as the result of Al Naqba, the "disaster"; or the innumerable human and architectural monuments to the Holocaust. This is an extremely ugly territory of competition, not susceptible to any outcome but animus.

On a cynical day in Jerusalem—and this is a city to encourage them—one imagines declaring every street a Via Dolorosa and every wall a wailing wall, taking the

Introduction: Thinking about Jerusalem

physical texture of the city and converting it into a ubiquitous mnemonic for misery. It's an ugly fantasy, however—indulged by both sides—that the only territory of commonality is extravagant grief.

Degree of Displacement by the Other

A refinement of the sweepstakes of suffering, the discourse of both Palestine and Jerusalem is colored by diasporan thinking. This entails notions of an ingathering of refugees (which grows more imperative as refugee status persists, becoming more central to individual identities) as well as special elaborations of the injustices of diasporan culture. The Jewish people are the paradigmatic diasporans, yet fail to see the irony of their own affliction in light of what they have inflicted on the Palestinians. The origin tale of modern Israel—like the origin tale of modern Palestine—begins in a historic dispersal by the other.

The expulsion of the Jews is, in effect, laid at the feet of contemporary Palestinians, whether because of actions by their ancestors or—by association—via arguments about Jewish refugees from elsewhere in the Muslim world who fled to Israel in 1948 and subsequent years. For Palestinians, it is the same. It is the other who is directly responsible for one's expulsion and for one's subjection to the perils and degradations of refugee life. Again, a spiraling game of comparisons can have no successful outcome in the adjudication of claims; it can only reinforce mutual suspicion and contempt.

The Force of Nationality

Underlying each side's claim to nationhood is a premise of exclusivity: the conversation constantly devolves into the question of whose right it is to prevail over the other. This is part of the sorry history of nationalism and is particularly fraught with ideology at the beginning of the twenty-first century, now that the nation-state seems to be under assault from forces pushing toward globalization. The conundrum lies in the simultaneous force of arguments for nationalism as an antidote to colonialism (itself the result of the rise of nationalism) and other forms of oppression and in incompatible arguments for superseding individual nationality to create a binational state. In this case, two peoples coming late to the table of states have the rug jerked out from under them—either by spurious denials of nationhood or in nominally selfless and progressive arguments for a merger of nationalities as yet too distinct.

One solution: remove national division of territory as a consideration and seek an equitable solution outside the realm of nationalistic victory, one in which all formulations of superiority are set aside, leaving a flatter set of questions about individual fairness. Although modern democratic states are constituted as guarantors of rights, nationhood can only give form to rights imagined before they are expressed in specific political practices, as the "right" of choice precedes the institution of the vote.

Indeed, even for those who eschew nationality altogether, Jerusalem could be a brilliant arena in which to practice the possibility of junction. The sublimation of territorial nationhood within the boundaries of Jerusalem via some metaphysical or diplomatic sleight-of-hand would not only give the "problem" a semantic and practical solution but provide a test case for the argument that these two nations might—in some sunny future—be merged. And where better to test this possibility than a place that has, on the one hand, eluded a shared solution and, on the other, attracted the most extravagant declarations of affection from both sides?

Looking at the City Itself

But let us begin the argument again. Or rather, let us set aside arguments that can never be settled and look to where there is consensus about tools. Although it taxes the imagination in many ways, it is possible to look at Jerusalem through an urbanist lens, a shift in perspective to at least temporarily remove the discussion from global issues of territory and justice. Metropolitan Jerusalem looms very large on the stage of world consciousness yet rather small in physical presence. The population of metropolitan Jerusalem, including Ramallah and Bethlehem, is well under one million—a city comparable in size to Portland, Oregon, or Guatemala City. Its economy is relatively modest and the average income of its inhabitants is, by world standards, neither tremendously prosperous nor particularly poor.

Jerusalem does have a large number of physical sites of global significance, monuments of both architecture and aura. The Old City of Jerusalem and the center of Bethlehem are particularly rich in texture and in individual works of architecture, works of great, even transcendent, value. Taken as a whole, however, these sites of intense quality make up only a small fraction of the area of the city. It is the curse of Jerusalem that through a pervasive metonymy the quality of these sites and their imputations of sacrality have suffused the city as a whole.

Like any city, Jerusalem embodies the memories, ghosts, and stories of countless inhabitants; but Jerusalem embodies those not only of its actual residents but also (what is perhaps more to the point) of the millions of virtual inhabitants who have for millennia cleaved tenaciously to dear fantasies of the city. These fantasies—Biblical, Koranic, and literary—have propelled an amazing array of responses, from crusades to aspirations, literary depictions, and the city's inscription in a panoply of metaphors for spirituality, urbanity, justice, and home.

The thought experiment that undergirds this essay—this whole book—is to think of Jerusalem simply as a city, not the Chosen City shining on its hills but one with all the quotidian problems of movement, recreation, employment, housing, and infrastructure that concern planners, urbanists, and architects in every city. These issues may be both ameliorated and exacerbated by looking at Jerusalem as a single urban entity.

In many ways, the city's most sacred territories present the most modest difficulties to planners. The Old City of Jerusalem is the subject of perhaps more study, measurement, and documentation per square meter than any other site on the planet, and there is widespread agreement about its physical issues, which are essentially questions of preservation, enhancement of infrastructure, and exclusion of inappropriate architecture and uses.

The great threat to the physical fabric of the Old City is the theft of its aura and its reduction to a kind of sacral Disneyland. A cruel irony of the Old City's partition into ethnic and religious quadrants is the precision with which this division replicates the conceptual organization of theme parks. The quality of a visit to the Old City is often an overwhelming experience of tourist crowds in a shopping mall where cheap souvenirs are hawked from what seems like every shopfront. This is a product of the Old City's sacrality but it is also a function of the mismanagement and neglect of its periphery, underdeveloped due to occupation and neglect on the Palestinian side and sterile and disengaged on the Israeli. The Old City is truly, like Disneyland, a corpus separatum.

Although the question of housing cannot really be separated from issues of power and the fair distribution of resources, it is nevertheless the case that the future of the city will require tremendous investment in housing replacement, improvement, and expansion. The blight and shame of the city are the refugee camps in which many Palestinians are forced to live in unspeakable conditions. Although the political origin of these places is particular, their character of misery and neglect is familiar from slum housing around the globe, as are their issues of simultaneous degradation and attachment. The tragedy of Jerusalem springs not simply from squalor and segregation but from the tremendous resources available to solve its physical problems, should its political questions be resolved.

Nothing is more symptomatic of the politicization of the housing question than Israeli settlement policy since 1967. Like the American urban renewal that was so vigorously critiqued at the same time, housing has been used as an extension of the political division of the city. The story of the Israeli authorities' efforts to ring the city with segregated suburban developments resonates with other urban issues as well. The architectural mediocrity of many of the projects is compounded by their arrogant and aggressive machismo-of-the-hilltops, well calculated to insult the excluded Palestinians.

The settlements tip the intercourse of neighborhoods into a pattern of fortified ghettos, a medieval condition. However, because this is as much a matter of intent as of form, there remains an opening to tractability. London is the classic example of a city that grew from the aggregation and interaction of separate villages, and there is no reason why Jerusalem cannot do the same. Blurring the edges of needless physical autonomy and opening the settlements to cohabitation, limited only by respectful treatment of intervening natural and social ecologies, would help accomplish this.

Perhaps more telling is the contribution of the settlements to another of the most primal issues for the growth of Jerusalem: sprawl. Jerusalem is at risk of disappearing into a continuous conurbation that might eventually run north to Nablus, south to Hebron, and west to the Mediterranean. The settlements policy has also begun to press dramatically eastward, an even more threatening development because of the fragility of the landscape it usurps there.

Clearly, the idea of growth limits—one of the liveliest debates in contemporary urbanism—tends to be short-circuited in Jerusalem by territorial politics. But continued growth will only increase destruction of the environment, strain on an already overburdened infrastructure, and submersion of the city's unique character in bland homogeneity. This risk is accelerated not only by arrogant Israeli expansionism but by indifferent planning and mediocre construction within Palestine. The post-Oslo speculative boomlet in Ramallah, to cite one example, has already had an extremely deleterious effect on a landscape far more deserving of respect and on a city in great need of both rational and poetic order.

Jerusalem, sitting at the seam between two contrasting and beautiful ecologies, might become an exemplar of humane planning and a sustainable relationship to the natural environment. Although both Israeli and Palestinian authorities have done good work in planning for the future of their own natural systems, the lack of coordination between their visions betrays the very essence of ecological thinking. One of the striking myopias of the division of Palestine is its avoidance of the region's inescapable interdependencies. This can especially be seen in conflicts over water and territorial rights, but these are only the most schematic expression of the attempt to reconfigure patterns of interrelationship into structures of isolation and difference.

No division is more myopic than that of transport. Jerusalem has reached the point in its growth where it cannot function effectively without a modern and integrated system of transportation. This is a matter rife with prospects for innovation, improvements that might distinguish Jerusalem from the frustrated metropolises of so many regions. The current system needs revision at many levels. A critical requirement, given the longitudinal configuration of the city, is dramatic improvement to north-south links at both regional and local scales. Within the city there's an obvious need to integrate bus networks, to rationalize and extend the highly efficient informal system of collective taxis, and to restrict the use of private automobiles. As a corollary, the extension and unification of disparate pedestrian networks must become a priority, as must a radical revisitation of basic public circulation modes within the city. At the moment, however, thinking seems overly locked into contemporary default solutions—heavy-rail, light-rail, bypass highways—and inadequately open to innovation. Yet given the city's singular topography, innovative thinking—which might result in modern versions of the kinds of systems built at the turn of the nineteenth century in Lisbon or San Francisco—is indispensable.

The question of infrastructure is even more straightforward and arguably—given its invisibility—even more tractable. The shit of Israelis and Palestinians already mingles in the municipal system, earthy harbinger of harmony. Issues of solid waste, creation and distribution of power, water supply, telecommunications, and other services remain, but offer the material grounds for equity and cooperation. Being quantifiable, they may evade the metaphysical savageries of the current disposition of resources. And, given the aggressive reverence that both sides claim for the city, this would seem like a ripe territory for innovation in sustainability and in minimization of impacts.

Finally, the economic character of the city—already a skein of distorted interdependencies—must be further integrated for mutual benefit. Both sides stand to profit tremendously from the enhancement of access and facilities for tourists, conventioneers, and pilgrims. Equally crucial for a city that has been a seat of learning for thousands of years is the expansion of knowledge-based industry. This begins with an emphasis on education at every level—both secular and religious—with a special emphasis on tertiary learning. University collaboration seems like a promising initiative. The kind of knowledge-based and high-tech industrial growth that might be spawned by such a collaboration would have benefits beyond raw economics, as these industries are susceptible to original and small-scale forms of organization and distribution and have potentially limited environmental impacts compared to other forms of production.

A shared Jerusalem will also derive special economic benefits from its position, as it were, between two worlds. One would expect not simply the emergence of a regional educational, touristic, and cultural center but also of a diplomatic and financial one. Clearly, this is a metropole that might quickly boom, become a magnet for investment. In particular, capital flows from the Muslim world will, given a rational reconciliation, flood the city—matched, one would hope, by an Israeli economy finally freed from militarization.

Jerusalem is in a unique position to blend modernity and tradition to create a global model of cooperation, economic innovation, and sustainable environmental practice. As a paradigm of the kind of social mosaic that will increasingly characterize the world's cities, Jerusalem might well become a laboratory for spatial practices that mediate the autonomy of individuals and of groups and for the cooperation of cities and nations. As a purely physical matter, this presents very little difficulty.

Perhaps architecture can help.

Displaced Meanings/Monuments/People

J. D. Dodds, Moustafa Bayoumi, and Ghiora Aharoni

Displaced Meanings J. D. Dodds

John Donovan: It's day after day, it's funeral after funeral, it's a grinding life in refugee camps for Palestinians going on 52 years. It's a constant obsession with security for the Israelis since the day their nation was born. And if an American president is offering a way out, then why not take it? Why not, to take the Israelis first, why not give the Palestinians sovereignty over this tiny sliver of land that the Jews call the Temple Mount if it will bring peace? It's 1/25th the size of New York's Central Park. It's already under a degree of Muslim control. Why not, for the sake of peace, make the damn compromise?

Joel Singer: Well, the funny thing is that it is sometimes easier to resolve issues that are not symbolic, that are real issues, than it is to resolve those symbolic issues. It is . . . more difficult to deal with dreams than with the reality.[1]

[1] *Nightline*, ABC News. Broadcast Wednesday, January 3, 2001. www.abcnews.go.com/ Sections/Nightline.

Among the decisive moments in the conflicts over Jerusalem that began in 2000 was the visit in September of then Likud party leader Ariel Sharon to the Dome of the Rock, accompanied by about 1500 heavily armed Israeli soldiers. The provocative visit by the well-known hard-liner, whom many Palestinians held personally responsible for the death of Palestinian refugees in Lebanon, fueled both paranoid rumors and rational fears of the loss of the holy site. Israeli defense forces, gathered for the anticipated demonstration, fired rubber-coated steel bullets; Palestinian demonstrators threw rocks. Seven months later, the bloodshed has not abated, and Sharon's visit can be seen as a catalyst for the escalating strife that led to his own election. This level of fighting hadn't been seen in Jerusalem since 1996, when plans to construct an archaeological tunnel beneath the Dome of the Rock sparked fears among Palestinians that the integrity of the monument was in peril. In a desperate struggle over land, security, and the repatriation of the dispossessed, it is the possession or the peril of a site "1/25th the size of New York's Central Park" that spirals Jerusalem into deadly, desperate violence.

The assumption of an ancient bipolar struggle in Jerusalem—of an immutable historic opposition of Muslim and Jew extending deep into the city's medieval past—is an image fetishized in American tradition, and within this mythic discourse the site of the Temple Mount and the Haram al Sharif becomes Jerusalem's fetishized body.

The Euro-American West has profited from identifying itself as a cool and rational outsider, mediator to a lawless feud between two desperate populations. In this mythic imagining, the struggle between Palestinian and Israeli for a place, for land, is transformed instead into an inevitable clash between Jew and Muslim. Opposition is configured as essential to the parties involved, immovable in history except for the intervention of this stable, disinterested outsider. This ahistorical image of a city's passion is marked for most outsiders by a single frozen media vision. The physical site of the Western Wall and the Dome of the Rock has only been contested since 1948, and yet for most, the Haram/Temple Mount is now the stable image of this cherished myth of the inevitable opposition of Muslim and Jew. In a world in which a single video clip brands a city, and a pair of images polarizes it, the Dome of the Rock and the Western Wall have come to be the physical embodiment of this opposition, as if these monuments' histories were immediately intertwined: as if the Temple had long ago been destroyed to accommodate the Dome.

When such powerful markers of an urban landscape—the ones that root a people to a place and a land—absorb this facile brand of hopelessness and inevitability, they have the power to make corrosive myths become concrete. And when these same monuments are conduits of memory for communities that coexist, exposure to reductive and essentialist ideas about religion and ethnicity can seem to rewrite monumental histories and inscribe on the urban fabric new polarized meanings that concretize the reductive myth of inevitable opposition.

How do you heal a city fabric physically rent by myth? In this tentative interaction, we explore three personal strategies. Ghiora Aharoni proposes displacing the key monuments themselves; moving them to smaller communities as centerpieces for new plural populations; loosing them from the polarized meanings they draw into Jerusalem. Their place is taken by housing for the resettlement of dispossessed Palestinians in a plural, undivided Jerusalem. Moustafa Bayoumi begins the rebuilding of authentic identities in a pilgrimage through the separate narratives of pain and dispossession that must begin among all parties before healing can occur. This dialogue is given a site through the repatriation of Jerusalem's Palestinians, and it takes place in a city untangled from the divisive symbols the monuments had become. I propose, finally to bear witness to an urban history unvoiced in Jerusalem's monuments today; the memory of a city acted upon by multiple forces, but one in which Jews and Muslims were rarely opposed before this century. The reclamation of this part of history can be a powerful tool for defying hopeless and reductive myths of ethnic interaction, for constructing a plural future in a complex city.

It can accomplish this in part by revealing the role of the West in the dismemberment of Jerusalem. The West—this fictive image of a vast, objective, enlightened world force over which the United States hovers like enveloping greenhouse gases—has always been the third party in Jerusalem's travail, a third party intent on exteriorizing Israeli and Palestinian identity from its fold; intent on concretizing the unspeakable anguish of a contemporary conflict into historical essentialism. What those powerful opposed images of monuments fail to remind us is how present this third party has always been; how essential the "West" is and was to the fragmentation of coexistence in Jerusalem. First Rome, then medieval Europe under the Roman church, then European-American alliances: the West was first Jerusalem's ravisher and now is its voyeur.

Long before Islam, it was in fact the very prototype of the unified West that would destroy the Temple, in a struggle not about ideology or religion, but about land, economy, and authority. It is Rome that would make the Temple Mount—on which the Second Temple had stood for nearly six centuries—a site of contention in which religion and hegemony intertwined. Herod's Temple, the opulent rebuilding of the Second Temple constructed by Zerubbabel, was destroyed on August 28 in the year 70 of the Common Era, part of the brutal destruction of Jerusalem that followed a revolt of subjected Jews in 66. Josephus tells us that the Romans poured "into the alleys" and "massacred indiscriminately all they met, and burnt the houses with all who had taken refuge within."[2] It was Romans, over half a millennium before the birth of Islam, who dismantled the Temple; by 135 Hadrian had replaced it deftly with a temple to Jupiter and a statue of himself. Jerusalem was rebuilt as the Aelia Capitolina, and Jews were prohibited by law from living in, or even visiting, the holy city.

2 Hershel Shanks, *Jerusalem: An Archaeological Biography* (New York, 1995), 175.

After the fourth century the universal Roman religion would become, with occasional interruptions, Christianity. The Temple Mount would garner the power of mythic absence. Jerusalem's great Roman monument becomes the Holy Sepulchre, which is built at the site of the forum, absorbing the Roman center of power. The Temple Mount is left in shambles, as if to confirm Christ's prophecy; its ruins now signify the triumph of a Christian Empire over a polarized, exiled Judaism.

When the Arabs took Jerusalem in 638, the primary political struggle, then, was between them and the Byzantines, or between Muslims and Christians in the mythic sense. Jews, who had been banned from the city, shared with Christians legislated rights and protection under the Islamic law that they could never have hoped for under Byzantine rule. Under the Umayyads, the law prohibiting Jewish settlement in the city was revoked and, in Bahat's words, "The respect accorded the Jews by the Caliph Omar was a thorn in the flesh of the Christians."[3] The reintroduction of Jewish population "in turn revived the religious disputes between Jews and Christians," Nasser Rabbat reminds us. In these the Muslims "preferred, and even adopted, the Jewish viewpoints."[4] The Byzantines called themselves Romans; they saw their rights over Jerusalem as extensions of Empire, and its sanctification. The alliance between Jews and Umayyad Muslims posed a threat to every assumption of Byzantine authority over the city, and revealed the persistent hegemonic impetus of official Christian anti-Semitism. This was the atmosphere in which the Dome of the Rock was built on the site of the destroyed Temple.

3 Dan Bahat, *The Illustrated Atlas of Jerusalem* (Jerusalem, 1990), 83.

4 Nasser Rabbat, "The Meaning of the Umayyad Dome of the Rock," *Muqarnas VI* (1990), 16.

The Dome of the Rock was not a mosque when first constructed, nor did it originally possess the association with Muhammad's Night Journey that it retains today. Built in addition to the Al Aqsa mosque, it was a commemorative building, which, as Grabar and others have demonstrated, showcased Umayyad power while at the same time reinforcing the common traditions that bound Jews, Muslims, and Christians.[5] Its Koranic inscriptions articulate the place of Jesus and Mary in Islam, while warning against the deification of Christ. Mount Moriah itself was recognized by Muslims as a

5 These meanings were first explored by Oleg Grabar, who must be seen as the foundational author of the interpretations offered here: "The Umayyad Dome of the Rock in Jerusalem," *Ars*

Orientalis 3 (1959): 33–62;
The Formation of Islamic Art,
(New Haven, 1973), 48–67;
*The Shape of the Holy: Early
Islamic Jerusalem* (Princeton,
1996).

6 Rabbat, "The Meaning of
the Umayyad Dome of the
Rock," 14–16.

7 John H. Hill, "Crusades
and Crusader States to
1192," in Joseph Strayer, editor, *Dictionary of the Middle
Ages*, vol. 4 (New York), 33.

8 Hill, 36.

9 Nurith Kenaan-Kedar,
"Symbolic Meaning in
Crusader Architecture,"
Cahiers Arqueologiques, 34
(1986), 109–17.

spot sacred to God and as the site at which Solomon built his "Holy House." Indeed, associations with David, Solomon, and Abraham were accepted and monumentalized here, and there is some suggestion that the Rock was sacred to Jews in Jerusalem before it was embraced by this great dome. Rabbat has shown in fact that the choice of site for the Dome of the Rock was made with particular attention to Jewish sources.[6] In this moment, then, some of the most significant alliances in Jerusalem are between Jews and Muslims. The Dome of the Rock—far from being a physical vestige of polarization—emerges as a significant document of that alliance.

It is once again the West that tears at this fabric of coexistence: once again in search of land, and once again the Temple Mount is at the heart of the urban drama. The First Crusade was initiated by Pope Urban II, with the stated purpose of liberating the pilgrimage sites in the Holy Land, though there is little evidence that pilgrims fared worse in Seljuk Jerusalem than under the Byzantines.[7] In fact, the Crusades channeled a violent society; a feudal system in need of additional lands; genuine piety; and an ambitious papacy into the appropriation of the eastern Mediterranean in a staggering act of expansion. In Jerusalem the effect was the violation and dismemberment of the city: Crusaders consolidated their power over the urban fabric through the massacre of most of the population, young and old, of a city that was supposed to be an earthly metaphor for Paradise. "The ensuing slaughter," one scholar remarks, "was recorded by Christian clerics who looked on the destruction of the enemy as the will of God."[8] For the first time since the Roman massacre of the first century, ethnic partition in Jerusalem was effected as a means of securing land and power: Muslims and Jews were forbidden to settle in Jerusalem. Here, it was the papacy, playing at Rome, that polarized.

The power of the extraordinary buildings on the Haram al Sharif/Temple Mount was such that the Crusaders, instead of destroying or replacing them, reconfigured their histories and appropriated them for the benefit of the new Christian hegemony in a kind of Reactive Adaptation. The Dome of the Rock was determined to be actually the "Temple of Solomon," which had been somehow deviously appropriated by the Muslims; and the Al Aqsa mosque became the "Palace of Solomon," also allegedly disguised for the centuries of Islamic rule.[9] They were linked to the now rebuilt Holy Sepulchre by ceremonial processions that ritually acted out Crusader possession of the city, and the inscription of Christian exegesis upon it. The Temple Mount was thus coopted by the Crusaders, who wove its buildings into a fictive cosmic history from which Islam had been expelled. Since Jews were no longer permitted to live in the city, the Solomonic references served only Christian cosmic discourse, and so buttressed Crusader possession of the city and lands. Chained to the Holy Sepulchre now by ritual and myth, the buildings of the Temple Mount/Haram al Sharif were cleansed of the rich, complex histories and plural character that had been retained under Islamic hegemonies. They would now serve a uniquely Christian worldview, as well as the design of the Catholic Church to rule once more over the lands that were the Roman

Empire. This possession of Jerusalem—both the terrestrial and the heavenly—continued to be acted out in architectural copies throughout Europe, as Ousterhout has demonstrated time and again.[10] The Crusaders had sewn up heaven and earth through the reconfiguration of a single city.

It is, then, the mythic West that polarized the Temple Mount, that has made it a site in which the ancient acts of betrayal and defilement are ritually reenacted. When the city fell again into Muslim hands, the interaction of Jews and Muslims resumed. Neither ideal nor utopian, society in Jerusalem nevertheless became constructively plural in this resumed coexistence. Decimated in the Crusader period, the number of Muslims and Jews in Jerusalem grew under the Mamlukes, who encouraged immigration. When the Jewish population of Spain was eradicated by the genocidal acts of the Castillian-Aragonese Conquest, including the Inquisition and the infamous fifteenth-century Expulsion, many Spanish Jews immigrated to Palestine and were received in Jerusalem. More came via Istanbul after the ascendancy of the Ottomans. Reforms enacted under Egyptian rulers in the nineteenth century made life for non-Muslims more equitable than before, and for a while the Jewish population of Jerusalem and its suburbs grew again under an Islamic hegemony.

The events that have poised the Haram and Temple Mount as superposed, opposing markers in the urban landscape—that have now locked Palestinians and Israelis in a death hold—did not begin with the advent of Islam in Jerusalem. They were initiated with the Balfour Declaration: with intervention, once again, of the third party, in the form of Britain, the concurrent heir to the notion of a Western Christian Empire. Indeed, the colonial notion of entitlement to a place not one's own, to entirely having one's way with a city and its people, is consistent with Rome's treatment, and medieval Europe's treatment, of Jerusalem since the beginning of the Common Era. Just as European anti-Semitism—gestated during years of papal hegemony—spawned the Holocaust, it was in some part the West's persistent, arrogant anti-Semitism—Europe and America's reluctance to receive Jewish refugees following the Second World War—that facilitated the final colonization, without regard for its indigenous inhabitants, of Jerusalem and Palestinian lands.

The new colonial struggle that has ensued—the one perceived as an essential battle between Muslim and Jew—is to some degree the creation of that imperial and callous act. The old exile of Jews and the new exile of Palestinians are each the work of the "West"; wounds inflicted, since the destruction of the Second Temple, by the heirs of Rome. The parts played by today's heirs to this tradition—American leaders playing mediators, or harbingers of Western civilization—obscure the chilling fact that their aggrandizing "mission civilisatrice" depends on the continued opposition of the polarized parties for its rhetorical power. Jerusalem today is indeed the one remaining political stage on which leaders like Bill Clinton might embody the West as a kind of Christian Roman Emperor. The Dome of the Rock and the Western Wall are now their battered props in the bloody drama unfolding on the Temple Mount, on the Haram al Sharif.

10 For instance, "Flexible Geography and Transportable Topography," *The Real and the Ideal Jerusalem in Jewish, Christian and Islamic Art: Jewish Art* 24 (1997), 393–404.

Displaced Meanings/Monuments/People

Displaced Monuments Ghiora Aharoni

The struggle over Jerusalem is monumental in many senses of the word, and most often, the struggle is for possession of the city's key religious monuments. The Christian, Jewish, and Islamic monuments have fetishized Jerusalem, and for many, the security and control of monuments such as the Wailing Wall or the Dome of the Rock have become the central metaphor for the complex aspirations of Israeli or Palestinian national identities. But can the city of Jerusalem be reduced to a handful of holy places? The power, the tension provided by these monuments in undeniable, but is Jerusalem unimaginable without them? I propose to rethink Jerusalem by dislocating its holy monuments. In this new spiritual geography, the Dome of the Rock is relocated to Nablus, the Wailing Wall to the mountains of Safed, and the Holy Sepulcher to Nazareth. Each monument can carry on its spiritual mission in a less politically charged location, while in Jerusalem, a new urban fabric may emerge. For instance, with no Wailing Wall in Jerusalem, the plaza in front of it is superfluous. Begun in 1967 to monumentalize the holy site by bestowing it with a ceremonial grandeur, the plaza can be replaced with its pre-1967 condition: a dense pattern of housing that reminds us that Jerusalem is a city for people as well as ideologies.

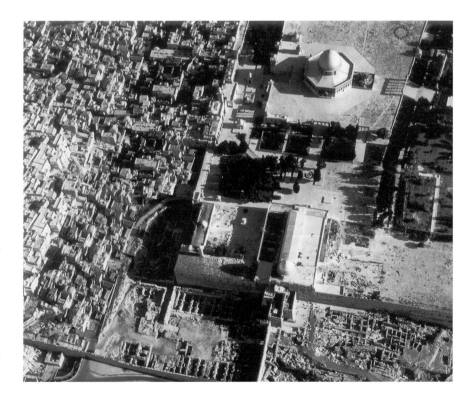

A residential neighborhood expands into spaces currently occupied by the Wailing Wall Plaza.

Dome of the Rock relocated to Acre

Displaced Meanings/Monuments/People

Wailing Wall relocated to the mountains of Safed

Dome of the Rock relocated to Nablus

Displaced People Moustafa Bayoumi

There seems to be something in the locality which makes one feel that Jerusalem is no ordinary place, whether we regard its past or its future.[1]

For a colonized people the most essential value, because the most concrete, is first and foremost the land: the land which will bring them bread, and above all, dignity.[2]

1 E. W. Blyden, *From West Africa to Palestine* (London: Simpkin Marshall & Co., 1873), 199.

2 Frantz Fanon, *The Wretched of the Earth*, trans. C. Farrington (New York: Grove, 1968), 44. Observations by Frantz Fanon writing in the midst of the Algerian war against French colonization.

Connecting the physical with the metaphysical, Fanon links dignity with land. These are not novel musings. The philosophical connection of humanity with dignity reaches far back, dating at least to Kant, and finds contemporary expression in the first article of the Universal Declaration of Human Rights, a heroic document rescued from the horrors of the Second World War. "All human beings are born free and equal in dignity," it states. But Fanon's contribution comes in warning us against seeing dignity as a mere abstraction. "As far as the native is concerned, morality is very concrete,"[3] he repeats, and that morality can only be expressed by a recovery of the land. The contest against colonialism is a concrete struggle for human dignity.

3 Fanon, 44.

What is the nature of this fight? Action and reaction. Force confronting counterforce. Violence breeding violence. And out of oppression springs the inexhaustible thirst for liberty. This is the Manichean struggle that Fanon ascribes to the colonial situation, where the colonizer and the colonized depend on each other, each defined by the other. "For it is the settler who has brought the native into existence and who perpetuates his existence," writes Fanon, who further explains that the colonial exploitation of the settler exhibits its "totalitarian character" by painting the native as a sort of quintessence of evil.[4] "On the logical plane," Fanon continues, "the Manicheism of the settler produces the Manicheism of the native. To the theory of the 'absolute evil of the native,' the theory of the 'absolute evil of the settler' replies."[5] Thus two narratives—the colonizer's and the colonized—inscribe themselves within each other under Fanon's scheme, yet they see themselves as surviving in a drama of "reciprocal exclusivity."[6] We would be remiss, however, if we did not note how Fanon's description above carries a temporal notion: "The Manicheism of the settler *produces* the Manicheism of the native." The narratives may appear reciprocal, but they are not equivalent. They are, moreover, germane to the future of Jerusalem.

4 Fanon, 36, 41.

5 Fanon, 93.

For centuries, European anti-Semitism tore at the dignity and livelihood of the Jewish community by preventing their connection to land and property ownership and by committing terrible and violent acts of religious hatred. This horrific history, culminating in the Nazi genocide, propelled the idea of Jewish self-preservation as a

6 Fanon, 39.

7 Chaim Weizmann, *The Letters and Papers of Chaim Weizmann*, vol. 1 (London: Oxford University Press, 1968), 28.

8 Theodor Herzl, *Zionist Writings: Essays and Addresses*, trans. H. Zohn, vol. 1 Jan. 1896–June 1898 (New York: Herzl Press, 1973), 67.

9 Herzl, 31.

10 Herzl, 30.

11 Quoted in Joseph Massad, "The 'Post-Colonial' Colony: Time, Space, and Bodies in Palestine/Israel." *The Pre-Occupation of Post-Colonial Studies*, ed. Fawzia Afzal-Khan and Kalpana Seshadri-Crooks (Durham: Duke University Press, 2000), 315. Found in *The Complete Diaries of Theodor Herzl*, ed. Raphael Patai, trans. Harry Zohn, vol. 4 (New York: Herzl Press, 1960), 1361.

12 Herzl, 30–31.

prime value. Here, then, the logic of tying one's dignity to land was paramount. It became a moral imperative, so that Chaim Weizmann could write that, with the establishment of a national home, the Jewish people "would cease to be *morally the homeless*, however small our home may be."[7]

In this sense, we would be right to consider Jewish longing for a homeland as that of a colonized people seeking concrete dignity, in Fanon's phrase above. As Jews suffered under the brutality of the internal colonization of Europe, desire for nationhood found expression in the late-nineteenth-century movement of Zionism. And just as Fanon describes colonial expressions for liberation as caught in a Manichean world of absolute opposites, Zionism understands its essence as deriving from the deep hatreds of anti-Semitism. Consider how Theodor Herzl describes the reason why nationalism applies to the Jewish people: "A nation is a historical group of people who recognizably belong together and are held together by a common foe."[8] Or, on another occasion, Herzl writes, "In us Jews the force we need is created by anti-Semitism."[9] Thus, Zionism as a liberatory nationalism is born out of a Manichean struggle.

Tragically for the Palestinians, however, Zionism discovered its power not only in its foe of European anti-Semitism but also in its ally of European colonialism. It became a displaced Manicheism, where the native inhabitants of Palestine suffer the wounds of this displacement. Operating within a colonial frame, Zionism transfers its desire for land and dignity outside Europe. Before the decision to settle Palestine—in total disregard for the local inhabitants—Zionism sought its fulfillment in Uganda, Mozambique, and Argentina. ("Is Argentina or Palestine preferable?" asks Herzl in an 1896 editorial. "We shall take what we are given and whatever is favored by the public opinion of the Jewish people."[10]) In commenting on his meetings with Joseph Chamberlain, Herzl writes in his diaries, "If I could show him a spot in the English possessions where there were no white people as yet, we could talk about that."[11] The significance of this need be noted, for Zionism began not as a religious movement but as a secular-national one, propelled by colonial attitudes of bearing the burden of a white civilization to a backward population. "We would serve as an outpost of civilization as opposed to barbarism. As a neutral state we would retain a connection with all of Europe, and Europe would have to guarantee our existence," explains Herzl.[12] The colonized becomes colonizer, and the Manichean narrative ever more complicated.

To say that Zionism was unconcerned about the native population of Palestine is to utter an understatement of heartbreaking proportions. For the complications surrounding the question of Palestine revolve around the unforgettable fact that the escape from European anti-Semitism—later in boatloads of sad, pitiable refugees—meant concomitantly the creation of another refugee population, forcibly uprooted, violently displaced, and now—at 3.7 million registered refugees, according to the UN—waiting out their fate in a wretched existence extending now over fifty years.

Victims become victors, and the vanquished change places in a struggle for dignity and land and self-preservation.

To think through the conflict between the Palestinians and the Israelis means to understand that land—not religion, not symbols, not ethnicity—is the principal issue. It demands that we see that this is not a theological quarrel extending back centuries; rather, it requires us to think through the connection between home and dignity universally. Dispossessed of their land and of their national aspirations by another people seeking theirs, the Palestinians thus become, ironically, the latest victims of European anti-Semitism at the hands of the victims of anti-Semitism. In a tense drama of self-preservation, the Israeli state terrorizes the Palestinians, convinced that the Palestinians are dedicated to its destruction. If Zionism requires a foe, anti-Semitism, to propel it forward, it creates it in its construction of the Palestinians, a people whose society has been—and continues to be—ravaged. Conversely, the Palestinians respond to destruction by resistance, terrorism, and confrontation. An ever-widening circle of violence erupts, seemingly sprawling out of control. Each, however, is forever now inscribed into the other's narrative. Their fates are linked. No narrative of the Jewish people can be complete without a reckoning of Palestinian suffering. Likewise, the historic pain of the Jewish people is now an essential element of the story of the Palestinians as a people. Each narrative depends on the recognition of the other, but again, not in a function of reciprocity. Zionism produced the reality of the Palestinians, not the other way around. The question for the future remains whether a single narrative can be mutually agreed upon that can weave together the land and dignity in a pattern based on mutual recognition and respect, on tolerance, inclusivity, equality, and tolerance, or whether the reciprocal exclusivity of the Manichean world will force a future of separation, exclusion, fear, hatred, and partition.

No city exercises the imagination like Jerusalem. And as the West Indian traveler Edward Wilmot Blyden observed, in the latter part of the nineteenth century, as European colonial control was seeking its influence there, this is no ordinary place, but one teeming with history and of unknown future. When I visited the city in 1994, I was struck by the tension evident everywhere. The furtive existence of the Palestinians, proud but clenched. The seeming ease of the Jewish population to travel the city, but constantly on watch, afraid of what will turn up around the corner. A single eggplant slipping off a rickety hand-pulled cart could upset this delicate balance. Lone settlers in starched white shirts arrogantly patrol the Old City and brazenly bear arms at their sides. ("The settler pits brute force against the weight of numbers. He is an exhibitionist," Fanon observes.[13]) Pilgrims and tourists gaze with outside eyes, confused or willfully oblivious to the daily tensions and humiliations of life in the city.

Jerusalem, it is often claimed, is in the most difficult of difficult fixes—the drama of the conflict between Palestinians and Israelis. The competition between sacred

13 Fanon, 53.

narratives intrudes on any compromise, it is said, and compromise is not the stuff of religion anyway. Dodds' introduction to our essay can put to rest some of these facile assumptions, for the city of Jerusalem—while often visited by bloodshed—does not know only violence and exclusion. It is a city with an enormous multicultural past—Canaanite and Jebusite, Hebrew and Hellenic, Roman, Byzantine, Christian, Muslim, Arab, Ottoman, British, Palestinian, and Israeli. The competing historical claims over the city simply cannot cancel out the histories of others in its place.

Furthermore, to configure the debate around Jerusalem solely in the terms of religious rights to history and worship is to deny the fact that there can be no solution to the question of Jerusalem without a resolution to the Palestinian refugee problem. Undoubtedly, Jerusalem contains within its thick walls connections to various sacred pasts, but the city also consists of a recent past and continuing present of dispossession. It is often forgotten that over 30,000 Palestinians lived in what is today called West Jerusalem before fleeing or being expelled from their homes in spring 1948. Several months later, 2,000 Jewish residents were forced to leave their homes in East Jerusalem.[14]

After the 1967 war, the Israeli authorities, in breach of international law, immediately took measures to expand the borders of the ancient city and continued dispossessing the native Palestinians. "The area from Ramallah in the north to Bethlehem in the south, [and from] Ma'ale Adumim in the east to Mevasseret [an Israeli suburb of Jerusalem] in the west is one metropolitan area," explains Moshe Amirav, former Jerusalem city council member.[15] "Greater Jerusalem," as it is called, now juts glaringly into the West Bank, virtually breaking the contiguity of that land and complicating any future agreement, perhaps forever. Encircled by dull and obtrusive high-rise buildings ("surrounding the city like the old crusader castles," in the words of Karen Armstrong[16]), "Greater Jerusalem" comes into being only by the expropriation of a half million *dunums*, or 12 percent of the West Bank. The struggle for the land continues.

Thus, the contest for Jerusalem is not only a competition for holy sites, but is first and foremost a question of borders. Does the question of Jerusalem circulate around the borders of the corpus separatum of the partition plan? The armistice line from the 1948 war? The borders of the city immediately following the 1967 war? The expropriated and enlarged "greater Jerusalem"? When we speak of Jerusalem, of which Jerusalem do we speak?

Inside the old borders of East Jerusalem, the facts are not any easier. In 1967, the Palestinian population of East Jerusalem comprised about 70,000 people, with the only Jewish residents in the area being found on French Hill. By 1994, the Palestinian population had enlarged to 155,000, while the Jewish population had exploded to 168,000 settlers. Jewish settlements in East Jerusalem appear in areas originally planned for Palestinian commercial and industrial growth, destroying

14 Edward Said, "Keynote Essay," *Jerusalem Today: What Future for the Peace Process*, ed. Ghada Karmi (London: Ithaca Press, 1996), 3–4.

15 Quoted in Geoffrey Aaronson, "Israeli Settlements in and around Jerusalem." *Jerusalem Today: What Future for the Peace Process*, ed. Ghada Karmi (London: Ithaca Press, 1996), 80.

16 Karen Armstrong, *Jerusalem: One City, Three Faiths* (New York: Ballantine, 1996), 412.

Palestinian sustenance and increasing the deliberate pauperization of Palestinian life in Jerusalem.[17] Some Israelis recognize the deliberate strategy to disenfranchise the Palestinian East Jerusalemites. To take 1992 as an arbitrary example, "Palestinians made up 28 percent of the city's population [East and West] but received between 2 and 12 percent of the budget in the various city departments [urban development, education, sports and social activities, housing, social services, road construction]," explain Amir Cheshin and Avi Melamed, former aides to Jerusalem's mayor Teddy Kollek.[18] East Jerusalem thus increasingly appears as the architectural equivalent of the Manichean world, a world of compartments based on absolutes, that Fanon previously described. Here is Fanon:

> The zone where the natives live is not complementary to the zone inhabited by the settlers. The two zones are opposed, but not in the service of a higher unity. Obedient to the rules of pure Aristotelian logic, they both follow the principle of reciprocal exclusivity…. The settler's town is a strongly built town, all made of stone and steel. It is a brightly lit town; the streets are covered with asphalt, and the garbage cans swallow all the leavings, unseen, unknown and hardly thought about. The settler's feet are never visible except perhaps in the sea; but there you're never close enough to see them. His feet are protected by strong shoes although the streets of his town are clean and even, with no holes or stones. The settler's town is a well-fed town, an easygoing town; its belly is always full of good things…. The town belonging to the colonized people… is a place of ill fame, peopled by men of evil repute. They are born there, it matters little where or how; they die there, it matters not where, nor how. It is a world without spaciousness; men live there on top of each other, and their huts are built one on top of the other. The native town is a crouching village, a town on its knees, a town wallowing in mire.[19]

And here is Cheshin and Melamed's description of East Jerusalem:

> In north Jerusalem, for instance, new villas and apartments of the French Hill neighborhood are just several dozen meters away from Issawiya, where the stench from freely running waste is only now being brought under control with the construction of a sewage system. There are few paved roads in Issawiya, no sidewalks, and no parks. Municipal and state funding for such projects was never allocated to Issawiya. Driving up Rehov Lohmei Hageta'ot (Ghetto Fighters Road), passing French Hill's small shopping plaza, and then heading down toward the villages of the Tzamaret Habira section of the neighborhood, no signs are needed to show you that you have left a Jewish area and entered an Arab one. And what makes it obvious has nothing to do with differences between the more traditional Arab and more modern Jewish building styles. At the Tzamaret Habira gas station junction, a well-paved road with sidewalks and shrubbery leads toward the Jewish homes; the road leading to Issawiya is full of potholes, and narrows to barely one lane as it nears the village.[20]

Such policies are undertaken by the municipality of Jerusalem and the Israeli state in a concerted effort to force the removal of Palestinian life from Jerusalem.

17 Tim Llewellan, "The Stolen City," *Jerusalem Today: What Future for the Peace Process*, ed. Ghada Karmi (London: Ithaca Press, 1996), 97.

18 Amir Cheshin et al., *Separate and Unequal: The Inside Story of Israeli Rule in East Jerusalem*, (Cambridge: Harvard University Press, 1999), 25.

19 Fanon, 39.

20 Cheshin et al., 19.

21 See, for example, Yael Stein, *The Quiet Deportation Continues: Revocation of Residency and Denial of Social Rights of East Jerusalem Palestinians,* trans. Zvi Shulman (Jerusalem: HaMoked B'tselem, 1998).

This is not even to mention the continuing land expropriations, house demolitions, deportations, and identity confiscations that continue to this day (and are regularly reported by B'tselem, an Israeli human rights organization[21]). To this cycle of violence, the response too often is useless and immoral terrorism, where Israeli civilians too suffer and die innocently. But the chain of violence cannot be broken by more dispossession and more pain. Only inclusion and accountability can begin to delimit a possible future together.

The increasing sacralization of the conflict between the Palestinians and Israelis threatens the future of the city and the prospects of both peoples. Resolution of the conflict between the Palestinians and the Israelis rests not on lording over each other's places of worship but on recognizing the pain and sacrifice that is tied to the struggle over the land. To this effect, Ghiora Aharoni has envisioned, in total fancy of course but with a political point in mind, that the religious sites be removed and placed elsewhere in the land. In their place, we need to memorialize the city in other ways, remembering the dispossessions, quite literally, by putting the body back together. In early June 1967, for example, almost a thousand Palestinians were thrown out of their ancestral homes in the Haret El-Maghariba section of the Old City for the vast plaza constructed in front of the Western Wall.[22] Their past is deliberately hidden, obstructed, and forgotten by the memorialization of another narrative, a single manifestation of how the brute facts of Palestinian dispossession are excised from the official historical narrative of the state of Israel. For this, Ghiora Aharoni's imaginings of replacing this area with housing for returning refugees opens a dialogue for a right of return. Denying this discussion can produce a prospect built only on narrative and physical separation, leading us down the road to greater exclusivity, symmetrical opposition, and a lousy, foreboding future full of further vilification and violence.

22 See Donald Neff, *Warriors for Jerusalem* (New York: Simon & Schuster, 1984), and Michael C. Hudson, "The Transformation of Jerusalem: 1917–2000," *Jerusalem in History,* ed. K.J. Asali, (Brooklyn, N.Y.: Olive Branch Press, 2000), 270.

Jerusalem, then, can only be secured as a city with a future if an openness is forthcoming that involves the recognition that both people are inextricably linked with each other and that they both now have the need and the right to exist on shared land (whether in a singular secular state, a bi-national federation, or two fully autonomous states). But the recognition needs to extend further, for the Israelis must be willing to recognize that their state came into being by the catastrophic destruction of another society. Both sides must assure each other of their needs for self-preservation, neither at the other's expense. And the right to free religious practices for all must be guaranteed, never at the exclusion of the other. Jerusalem, the holy city, has too rich a past and too important a future for it to be a city of any one faith. It must be made to stand for justice, freedom, and equality, not for exclusion, racism, and dispossession. It must allow us to live, not lead us to death. And as such it cannot be a city for Christians, Muslims, or Jews, but ultimately, must be catholic in its grace.

Hybrid City

Jafar Tukan

Introduction

When Michael Sorkin first invited me to the gathering that occasioned the writing of this paper, and revealed to me the reasons for it—primarily "to promote a conversation among design practitioners, the kind of conversation that must eventually take place in a peaceable environment when it finally becomes possible to implement meaningfully collaborative plans for sharing a space we all revere"—contradictory emotions surged within me. Jerusalem is a place I love; its memories, climate, topography, and urban texture are a part of me. It would be wonderful, I felt, to engage in an effort, an experiment, that focuses on Jerusalem. The list of invited participants was also most interesting. Several of them were known to me personally or through their outstanding achievements, so the rest, I assumed, would be a good match. A dialogue with such a distinguished group was an opportunity not to be missed.

Yet the legacy of twenty years of total isolation between Israel and its neighbors and of thirty years of occupation has bred many negative realities. These form barriers not only of preconceived impressions but of irreversible facts on the ground—facts of political, economic, and military power. Most especially, there has been the intense settlement program (uniquely for Jews) in and around Jerusalem.

Zones of possible
development

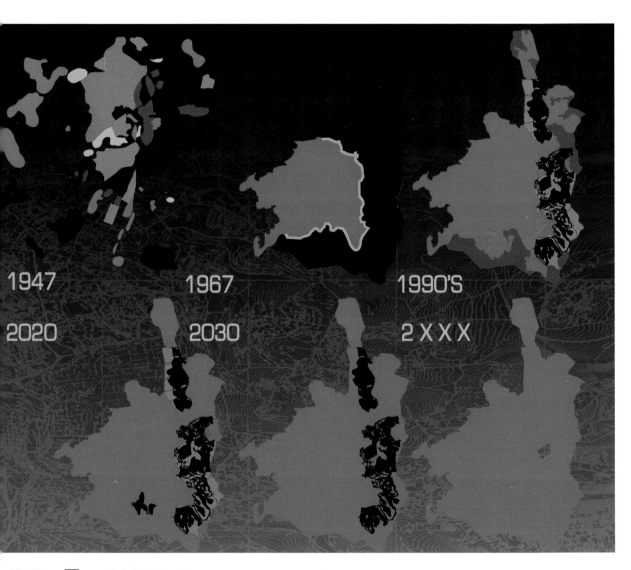

1947 1967 1990'S

2020 2030 2 X X X

RED CITY

■ Muslim Neighborhoods
▨ Jewish Neighborhoods
▨ Muslim-Jewish Neighborhoods
▨ Arab-Christian Neighborhoods
▨ British Security Zones
▨ Green Areas
▨ Unplanned Area

So to invite a Muslim professional totally isolated for many years from the urban and political life of Jerusalem to discuss what can be done for Jerusalem with Jewish scholars and professionals deeply involved in the city's contemporary issues seemed absurdly inadequate to the real problem—particularly given that participation in this gathering required the preparation of an urban-planning proposal for Jerusalem. It seemed a simplistic response not only on the practical level but on the psychological level, for while our Israeli counterparts have come to terms with the present status of Jerusalem as the eternal capital of the state of Israel and accepted this as an established fact, we Muslims and Christians of Palestinian descent have not and cannot simply accept a situation imposed by political, economic, and military force. In short, my participation seemed implausible.

However, Michael took the trouble to pass through Amman for a very brief and (I am sure) most exhausting one-night stop, and I had the pleasure of discussing the event with him. Obviously he was most convincing.

To get to know one another is always a step in the right direction. To exchange views with people who uphold human values beyond those of politics and material power may lead to common understanding, and the consolidation and diffusion of such understanding may be a deterrent to the forces of extremism.

As an architect, I have not had much chance to get involved in extensive urban design and to experience a more diverse set of problems than that which an architect encounters in designing a building. This exercise has offered me a wonderful opportunity to get out of the routine of day-to-day architectural design based on limited concerns, to deal with a wider and less determinate program, a theoretical exercise with an unlimited margin of freedom. For the first time, I have been my own client.

Jafar Tukan

Personal History

I was born in Jerusalem in 1938 and lived there for two years before moving to Nablus. I continued to visit relatives in Jerusalem—all of Jerusalem—until 1948. Between 1948 and 1967, however, only a part of Jerusalem was accessible to me. Visiting Jerusalem after 1967 was a totally different experience.

The memories of Jerusalem I retain from before 1948 are happy ones. The rocking horses at Freeman's, a shoe shop in Ben Yehuda St. (Jewish owner), toys at Zananiri's in Mamila (Christian owner), and a variety of sweet delicacies in shops in the Old City (Muslim owners). A bosomy Jewish woman used to breast-feed a cousin of mine whose mother did not have enough milk in her breasts. We moved freely all over the city. To me, at that time, "Cinema Rex" sounded like the ultimate in high tech.

A few years before 1948, Jewish underground movements intensified their violence and a dark cloud began to loom over Jerusalem. Movement within the city became less free until the city was divided in 1948.

While East Jerusalem continued to grow slowly, in the West—across the wall and the no-man's-land strip—rapid high-rise growth was taking place, totally unlike anything in the Jerusalem we knew.

In June 1967, the Israeli army took over East Jerusalem, tore down the wall, and "unified" the city. Though an administrative and physical union occurred, Jerusalem's ethnic divisions not only remained but deepened.

In the early years of the occupation of what was called the West Bank (the part not yet included in Israel), the agony of defeat was slightly mitigated by the fact that Palestine was physically reconnected and I could go to Haifa, Jaffa, Nazareth, and Safad, places I had heard of as part of my homeland but never had a chance to visit.

Crossing the border from Jordan grew more difficult with the increase of Palestinian guerrilla activities, which, while substantially ineffective and mostly suicidal, gave justification for indiscriminate and humiliating Israeli policies affecting Palestinian visitors from across the river and also for those alienating forms of collective punishment and other retaliatory acts that led to the Palestinian popular uprising in 1987. While the uprising led to the Oslo accord in 1992, it also, over five turbulent years, increased the distance between the Jewish community on the one hand and the Muslim and Christian communities on the other. It also depressed the economic, educational, and social conditions of the latter communities to unprecedented levels.

The Oslo accord, which in the beginning promised coexistence and peace, suffered from a series of setbacks, including an unprecedented acceleration of the construction and expansion of Israeli settlements around Jerusalem and in the West Bank. Palestinians like myself, who hold an I.D. issued by Israeli authorities through the Palestinian Authority, are the only people in the world who have to change four vehicles going home and five vehicles going out to a distance of less than 100 km.

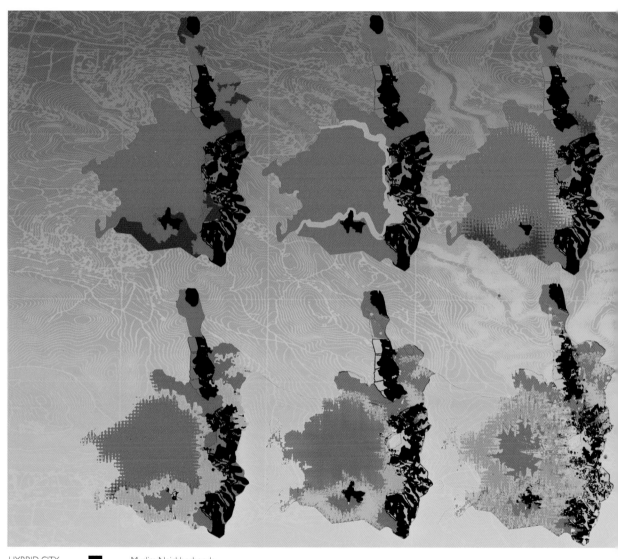

HYBRID CITY

- ■ Muslim Neighborhoods
- ▨ Jewish Neighborhoods
- ▨ Muslim-Jewish Neighborhoods
- ■ Arab-Christian Neighborhoods
- ▨ British Security Zones
- ▨ Green Areas
- ▨ Unplanned Area

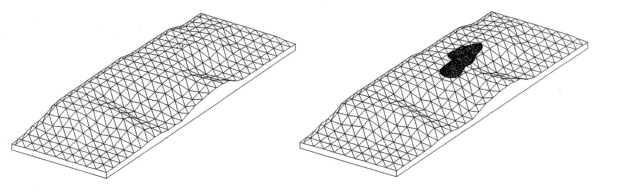

Planning Policy in Jerusalem at Present

A study prepared by Ir Shalem shows that

of the total area of East Jerusalem prior to expropriation, approximately 7.3% only is available for residential construction and approximately 0.6% for commercial and industrial construction. The remaining areas are zoned for various needs that do not enable private sector exploitation or are unplanned areas. Consequently, less than 8% of the area of East Jerusalem is available to the Moslem and Christian Palestinian sector for any kind of private sector development. [1]

1 From Ir Shalem, *East Jerusalem: The Current Planning Situation, A Survey of Municipal Plans and Planning Policy* (1995), 6.

The pattern of expropriation and settlement in and around East Jerusalem reveals an intention to segregate areas of Muslim and Christian concentration from one another within the municipal boundary of Jerusalem and to encircle them with a continuous wall of Jewish residential settlements within the limits of greater metropolitan Jerusalem, separating them from other Muslim and Christian villages and towns further east. These policies may freeze development in Muslim and Christian areas, preventing them from accommodating increasing population and forcing the overflow of people to abandon Jerusalem. It is also possible that these areas will get squeezed out of the city by pressure from West Jerusalem to the west and Jewish settlements to the east, north, and south.

It appears from the maps that every space in East Jerusalem has been mapped, labeled, and either commodified for present capital investment or claimed by the state and expropriated for political goals.

Background to the Present Project

The political uncertainty that engulfs the status of Jerusalem has resulted in extreme tension among the different communities living there. Religious politics have not only distanced Muslims and Christians from Jews but even created tension between secular and Orthodox Jews. Thus, although the physical and administrative division of Jerusalem has been eliminated, a deeper and more complex division has been created. At this moment there are two physically distinct and isolated sectors in the city,

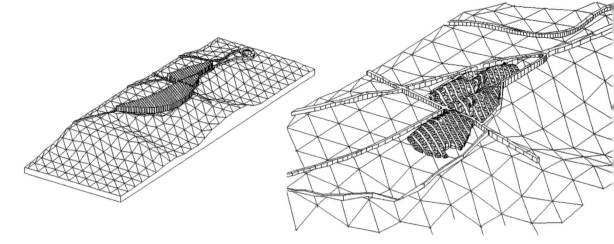

and if no genuine effort is made to rectify this division there may soon be three such sectors.

As Machiavelli says in *The Prince*:

> Anyone who becomes master of a city used to being free and does not destroy her can expect to be destroyed by her, because always she has as a pretext in rebellion the name of liberty and her old customs, which never through either length of time or benefits are forgotten, and in spite of anything that can be done or foreseen, unless citizens are disunited or dispersed, they do not forget that name and those institutions.[2]

2 Niccolo Macchiavelli, trans. Daniel Donno, *The Prince* (New York: Bantam Books, 1981), 24.

Jerusalem will always be claimed by the three faiths with equally strong arguments. Each has at some point seized control of Jerusalem by military force and lost it to another by military force, that is, through pain, death, and fire, creating an awesome heritage of hate.

Is it conceivable that we, the Palestinians of the three faiths, can agree that Jerusalem in particular and Palestine in general have had enough of war, death, and hate? Can we admit that no one faith can have full and permanent control? Can we all accept the otherness of the others? Can we start thinking about and working toward the goal of sharing Palestine with love, dignity, and equality, making it worthy of its ancient epithet, "a land flowing with milk and honey" (Exodus 3:8), and of the teachings of the three faiths about love?

It is here, I believe, that our efforts should be focused. In our capacity as architects and planners and with the help of the specialists in other areas of life we should aim at initiating projects that can help make Jerusalem not only a united city but an integrated city—projects that can help bridge the social, economic, and human abysses that divide us.

Our country is now sectioned horizontally and vertically under the pretext of security. It needs new political and security concepts, not military but multi-dimensional security, a security based on common interests: economics, water, environment, education, and freedom for all. Enhancing mutual recognition and familiarity is the basis of my proposal.

Jafar Tukan

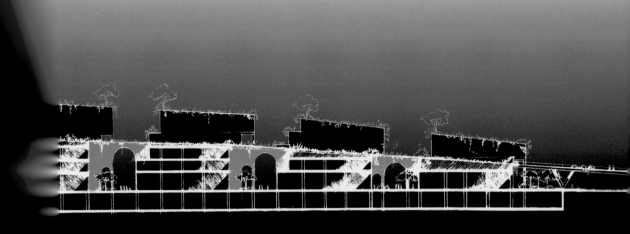

The Proposal

General Location

My proposal identifies lines of intensity that seem to follow what used to be the actual wall and no-man's-land of 1967. Some expropriated lands separating Jewish settlements from those of Muslims and Christians shall not be developed as residential areas, but as areas for the activities that can bring people together. To maximize contact between presently separate communities, this space shall be striated directionally so as to generate attraction between the two communities, drawing into itself people from both sides and engaging them in mutually beneficial activities.

Commercial activity, combined with a central major transportation node, may restore Jerusalem from bipolarity to concentricity.

Selected Site

A flat peak can be identified fairly close to the train station and west of it along the Bethlehem road. This site is substantially flat. Its northern part is triangular and about 75,000 m². Its southern part is rectangular and about 90,000 m². It falls between predominantly Jewish Talpiot and predominantly Muslim and Christian Sur Baher, Abu Tor, and Jabal Al Mukabber.

Land Use

Jerusalem now consists of predominantly Jewish West Jerusalem and what used to be predominantly Muslim and Christian East Jerusalem, the latter surrounded and severely divided by extensive areas expropriated and hurriedly built up into high-density, exclusively Jewish residential areas.

In multi-ethnic societies, ethnic groups tend spontaneously to create segregated residential communities. Therefore, my proposal will avoid primarily residential development. Some of the common interests mentioned earlier will determine the nature of the proposed development.

The virtual wall that now separates the Jewish settlements from Muslim and Christian areas needs to be transformed from a line to a space, a space in which all three communities are brought together by economic forces generated by environmentally conscious transportation and commercial nodes. The latter may include

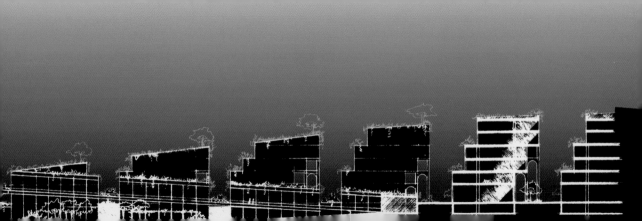

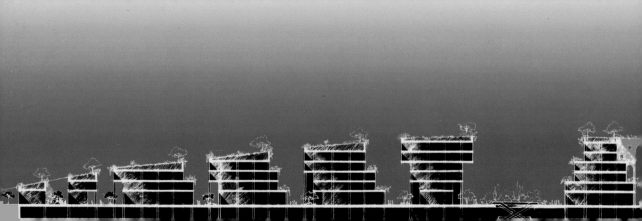

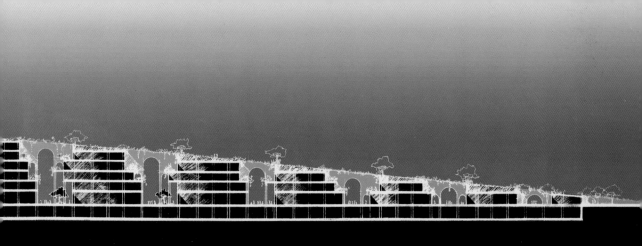

Section

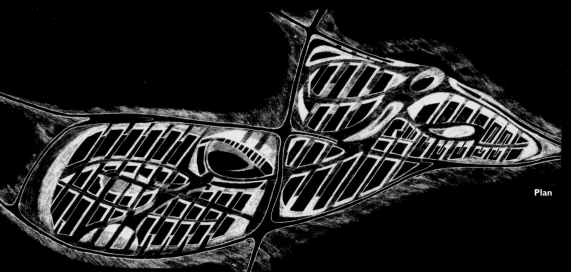

Plan

Conclusion

Jerusalem is not just a museum of holy places. It is primarily a place to live, and a beautiful one too. Conflict has turned it into a place where God is used, not worshiped. Only by getting to know each other—only by using our social and cultural differences as means of enrichment rather than justifications for isolation and segregation—only thus can Jerusalem be restored as a wonderful home for life. This is not merely a naive dream; it is possible, because Jerusalem has been one city before and can be so again for all its citizens, if we can generate enough pressure to make the politicians on both sides leave God alone, stop using Jerusalem for political ends, and make this city a home for all of us once again.

Jerusalem should be managed by wisdom, not politics.

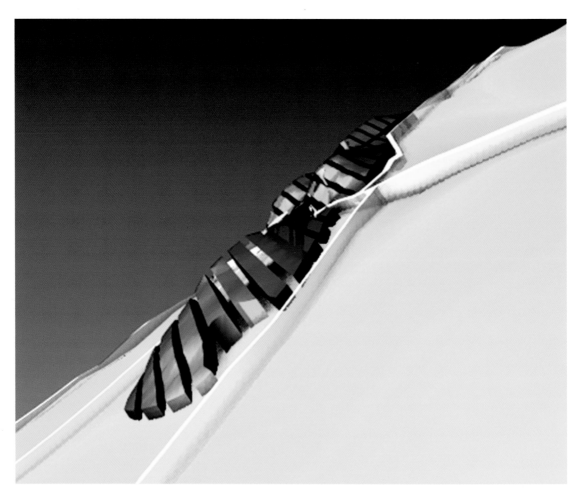

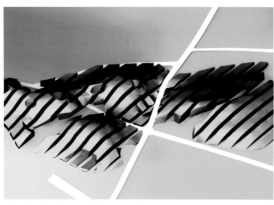
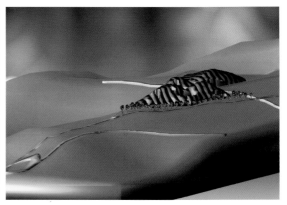

Hybrid City

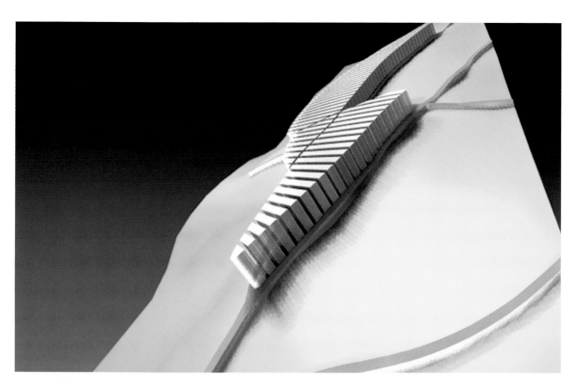

Reading Jerusalem

Dag Tvilde and Ali Ziadah

Introduction

An implicit aim of the conference that we attended in Italy in 1999, the occasion of this book, was to envision Jerusalem as one city where Israelis and Palestinians might peacefully coexist. However, given developments after the Oslo Accords and the ongoing frustrations felt by Palestinians, we decided to challenge this approach and to examine the possibility of a divided city. Later political developments seem to have validated our decision.

As we two have distinct cultural, political, and religious backgrounds and so are affected by the realities of Palestine in highly unequal ways, this essay is more an attempt to discover a common understanding than the proclamation of a single point of view. It is also the result of analyzing documents, of talks and discussions, of travels and observations of the city. The situation in Jerusalem—which includes restricted access for Palestinians—has forced us to depend more on available documents than we would have liked, with limited possibility to verify their accuracy. But the resulting picture is still, we think, a clear one.

How does one go about visualizing a future for Jerusalem? One approach is to produce utopian fantasies—to imagine possibilities out of reach today. While such visions do help us understand what might be gained by a change of attitudes, the political situation discourages the idea that such visions have, in themselves, the power to produce change. If we are to help the inhabitants of the region overcome the hatred that has infected it for so long, we must work with credible visions rooted in a recognizable reality. Therefore, in "Reading Jerusalem," we attempt to visualize the reality that has been created by the ongoing conflict.

Yet there are many perceptions of the "reality" of Jerusalem. Indeed, the city is so saturated with religious beliefs and historical narratives that it is as much an idea as a city of stone. To many people, Jerusalem is more a concept than a physical territory. The conflict over the city is thus a struggle for spiritual ownership, a contest of

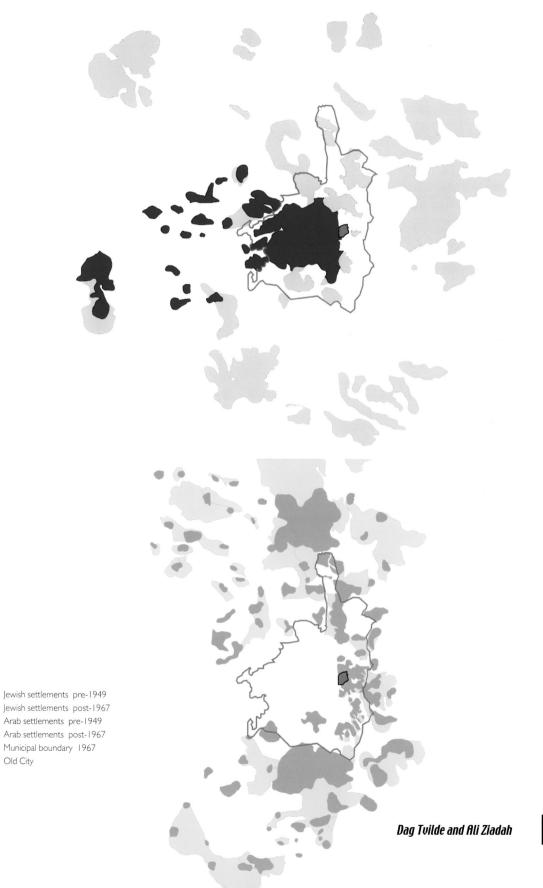

Jewish settlements pre-1949
Jewish settlements post-1967
Arab settlements pre-1949
Arab settlements post-1967
Municipal boundary 1967
Old City

Dag Tvilde and Ali Ziadah

memories and sacrifices. In this sense, it is difficult to define the "reality" of Jerusalem. Demagoguery is often used to create new "realities," thus obscuring the fact that the conflict over Jerusalem is also a question of occupation, politics, borders, and international law; of land ownership, refugees, and human rights.

We do not believe that planning as such can bring a solution to the current conflict in Jerusalem. It is all too well known that planning can be used as a political tool, as it has been used in the occupied territories of the West Bank and in Jerusalem—especially the latter, where planning has been used to boost Israeli settlement, confiscate land, and neglect infrastructure in Palestinian areas. Only in the context of a fair political solution can planning can play its role as a tool for development. A fair political solution, in turn, depends on the understanding and knowledge of the realities on the ground.

The Division of Jerusalem

The myth of the "unified city" has generated, or become, a new reality. Slogans such as "Never again a divided city" or "No new Berlin Wall" both assume and reinforce the notion that Jerusalem is one city and that only Palestinian hard-liners want to "divide" it. This notion persists even though the "division" of the city was first made by the Israeli occupation of West Jerusalem in 1948 and even though its "unification" come about only through the Israeli occupation and annexation of East Jerusalem in 1967. Although both acts were violations of international law, even Israeli leftists and liberals have adopted this new reality of Jerusalem as one city, and they take it for granted that this undivided one city would be to the benefit of all its inhabitants. By doing so they support the assertion of the historical and religious right of a "unified" Jerusalem, thus stigmatizing all supporters of a divided city as being against peaceful and healthy development.

Few Palestinians share these attitudes. Their decades-long experience of the "unified" city has not been a pleasant one. Even the most generous Israeli promises of sharing the city are perceived by most Palestinians as really meaning, "We have what we have and we will 'share' what you have." A sophisticated system of Judaization has expelled generations of Palestinians and destroyed the credibility of all such promises. Even a radical change in the Israeli political scene, such as might clear the way for a joint "democratic" governance of the city—which is not likely to happen—would not necessarily lead to a just and dignified solution. The economic and educational imbalances between the two parties would produce an unbalanced community, a community in which Palestinians would occupy the lower position. Today, almost the only areas open for further development are those of the Palestinians in East Jerusalem. These areas exert a continuous attraction for "natural growth" for those Israelis who claim ownership of the whole city.

Jerusalem is divided today, not only economically, socially, and ethnically but by

■ (dark)	Jewish settlements pre-1949
■ (light)	Jewish settlements post-1967
■ (medium gray)	Arab settlements pre-1949
■ (light gray)	Arab settlements post-1967
—	Municipal boundary 1967
⬩	Old City

Dag Tvilde and Ali Ziadah   53

an invisible border that people hardly cross: The traffic system in the region of Jerusalem is totally divided, with only a few roads used by both sides. Practically no taxi driver will take you from the West to the East. About the only thing that keeps Jerusalem from being a totally divided city is that one half rules, represses, and neglects the other.

Many arguments can, of course, be made against the division of Jerusalem. Perhaps the most important is that division would injure the existing, "integrated" economy of the city. However, this integrated economy has, in the eyes of many Palestinians, been created by occupation and has destroyed the independent Palestinian economy. They claim that time is now needed to give the Palestinians a chance to build up both their economy and their identity.

A second argument, advanced by many liberals on both sides, is that the long-term development of the Middle East lies naturally in the direction of a secular union, making the declaration of a Palestinian national state an anachronism. However, the federation of the Middle East into something like the European Union is a long-term dream without credibility among most of the region's inhabitants. A federation can be created only by equal partners, not by occupiers and occupied. And to quote a Czech colleague speaking just before the vote on a separation of the Czech Republic and Slovakia, "Even though everyone knows it is not logical in relation to economy and contemporary European development, [separation] is a historical necessity."

Yet there are many divided cities where the inhabitants cross the border every day—Geneva, for instance. In cities close to the Norwegian-Swedish border, people go shopping every day on the other side and may have their weekend houses in the other country. Where there is peace, a border is not a problem.

Traditional Palestinian road, north-south

The Transformation of Jerusalem

One might be tempted to overlook many injustices and humiliations for the sake of a vision of Jerusalem that seems feasible in the long term. An idea of the future can survive many on-the-ground realities if it is strong enough. However, there are some facts that have to be taken into consideration in any new vision.

An accelerating transformation of Jerusalem is taking place. The unbalanced development of East and West Jerusalem has been made possible by systematic neglect of Palestinian institutions and infrastructure, bans on construction, and restrictions on movement. At the same time, investments are about to turn the center of West Jerusalem into a modern business and tourism district. There is another, even more powerful force at work: a new rigorous schema of the city is being implemented, leading to dramatic interventions in the territorial structure. This is the result of an intentional, specific plan and has a crucial impact on the transformation of Jerusalem. To better explain this, we must first examine urban transformation in general.

——— Israeli roads (constructed)
- - - Israeli roads (proposed)
——— Municipal boundary 1967
◧ Old City

Jenin

Nablus

Tel Aviv

Ramallah

Jerusalem

Bethlehem

Hebron

— Tel Aviv–Dead Sea axis (Israeli)
Jewish communities
— North-south axis (Palestinian)
Palestinian communities

Israeli regional road system connecting the West Bank to Jerusalem. While waiting for negotiations on the Palestinian status of the West Bank, a coherent Palestinian area becomes an illusion.

Reading Jerusalem

Urban Transformation

Cities reflect the societies that build them; and just as all societies undergo more or less continuous change, so cities are in constant flux. These transformations may consist of slow, organic changes in the urban fabric. They may also result from brute-force interventions by some ruler—"planned" interventions.

However it happens, urban transformation is rarely a smooth and harmonious process. Thus the city does not have a simple texture, but reflects the complexity of its history. Even so, it is possible to some extent to decompose the city into layers with internal coherence. The urban fabric consists, to begin with, of physical structures reflecting functional, economic, and social relations. These structures and relations are variously exposed to change, transforming at different speeds and to different degrees.

It is possible to model the urban texture as a hierarchy of layers ranked according to their susceptibility or resistance to transformation. Parameters such as symbolic value, relationship to power, economic significance, and prestige determine to what degree structures are reinforced, altered, or broken down by certain interventions. Some structures are "weak," that is, extremely vulnerable to intervention (e.g., poor neighborhoods), whereas others strongly resist even dynamic transformations of the total urban texture (e.g., buildings of high symbolic value).

Regional-scale structures are among the strongest generators of urban transformation, and tend to develop independently from the rest of the urban texture. These structures are often developed by governments or strong economic interests. Typical are regional highways, which generate new business corridors and malls but may corrode existing networks by draining the city center and acting as barriers to chop up preexisting urban patterns.

In Jerusalem, the dramatic interventions in the structure of the city require a new concept of the city itself. To frame this new understanding of Jerusalem, we introduce a general descriptive model for studying the impacts of urban transformation.

The Facts on the Ground

Facts have been created on the ground that dramatically limit the possibilities of development for Palestinian areas in and around Jerusalem. This has without doubt been intentional.

Since the Oslo Accords of 1994, the Israeli government has increased the building of settlements and security roads in the occupied territories. These violations of the Accords have been designed to create a new reality before a final agreement can be worked out, a reality that will survive any changes of administration. The aim has been to transform the West Bank into a structure of Israeli installations tightly connected to Jerusalem. This is accomplished step by step, risking a manageable level of national and international reaction at each increment. No explicit plan has ever been made public, but such a plan obviously exists and has efficiently fragmented the Palestinian parts of Jerusalem and the West Bank into an incoherent landscape with no prospect of further development. The goal has been to forestall a "two-states solution" with a "too-late solution."

The main feature of this plan is a network of regional highways (rhetorically named "security roads") connecting the settlements around Jerusalem and on the West Bank:

- a ring road and radial roads closing the "Great Jerusalem" ring of Israeli settlements.

- a grid of regional roads connecting the settlements on the West Bank to one another and cutting connections between the traditional Palestinian villages and towns along the ridge of the West Bank.

- a regional axis road from Tel Aviv to the Dead Sea connecting the settlements and cutting the Palestinian presence into two pieces.

These roads are constructed exclusively for Israelis and are hardly accessible from any of the Palestinian territory that they cross. All junctions with the Palestinian road system are controlled by heavily guarded checkpoints.

The result is predictable: The main structure of the Palestinian territory—the traditional road along the ridge connecting the main towns and villages to Jerusalem—is cut into pieces. Movement between built-up Palestinian areas is restricted to an intricate back-road network. The Israeli regional superstructure thus strangles the West Bank, transforming the linear Palestinian development along the ridge into scattered fragments between Israeli roads and settlements. The traditional development along the ridge has been the backbone of the Palestinian economy, but now it suffocates slowly as communications and natural growth are cut off. Since a coherent geographic area with a functional infrastructure is necessary to economic synergy, the Palestinian areas have no prospects of healthy development.

On the other hand, a regional road network connecting urban centers tends to generate territorial expansion. This is the main intention of the well-defined Israeli masterplan for Great Jerusalem and the West Bank. The effects of the Israeli network on the Palestinian linear structure on the ridge, on the traditional rural structure, and on the relationship between the built-up areas and their institutional and historical context are obvious. They are turned into fragments, like pieces of broken glass scattered in the interstices of the expanding Israeli regional superstructure.

A Vision for Jerusalem

The conflict over Jerusalem has involved continuous dispute over the definition of the city. Ethnicity and boundaries have been particularly key issues. Censuses and statistics

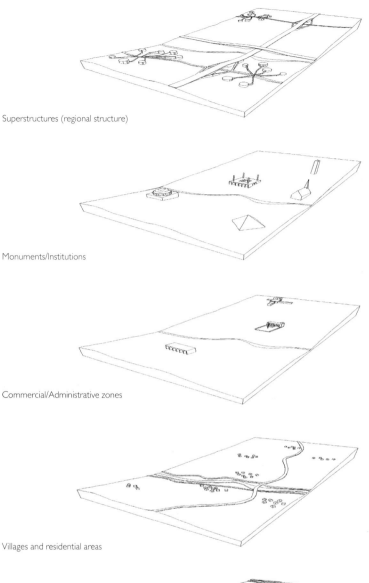

Superstructures (regional structure)

Monuments/Institutions

Commercial/Administrative zones

Villages and residential areas

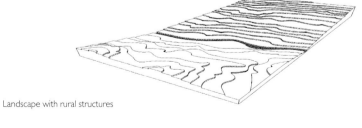

Landscape with rural structures

One can read Jerusalem as a hierarchic order of physical layers, each contributing differently to urban transformation. The higher a layer's place in the hierarchy, the more it tends to generate new structures; the lower its place, the more it tends to degenerate existing structures.

Dag Tvilde and Ali Ziadah

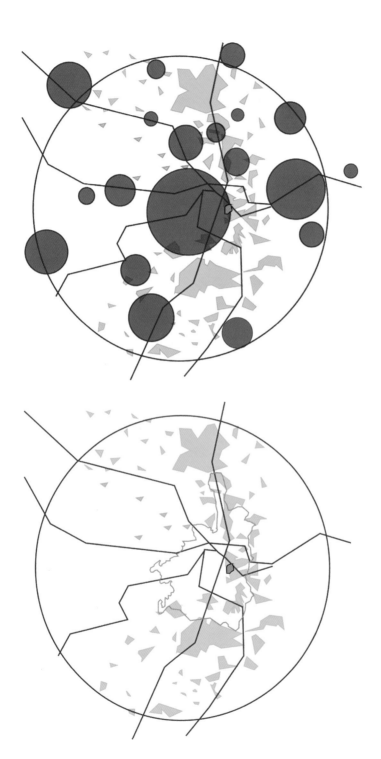

Diagram showing Palestinian
communities as fragments
stitched in between Israeli
installations

● Jewish communities
▨ Palestinian communities
— Road network

Reading Jerusalem

have been used to evaluate the ethnic composition of different parts of the city and to justify various borders. A favorite statistical strategy has been to manipulate demographic figures in order to claim this or that ethnic group's right to the city. Another has been to link symbolic identity to different parts of the city, justifying various suggestions for a segregated city and attempts to encapsulate the conflict within the confines of ethnic neighborhoods. However, a viable vision for Jerusalem cannot restrict its idea of the city to a few symbolically loaded areas. It must take into account that Jerusalem is part of a geographic, economic, and historical region from which its development is inseparable. In the same way that the autonomy and sovereignty of Gaza are illusory if seen as separate from the surrounding region, the subsections of Jerusalem have to be part of a coherent regional structure if they are not to end up as underdeveloped ghettos.

Focusing on ethnic neighborhoods may therefore be compatible with a political "art of the possible," but can also become a rhetorical substitute for a peace process. The idea of creating stability through "ethnic autonomy" has few successful historical precedents anyway, and tends to divert attention from the irreversible realities that are being created. The facts that have been and are being created on the ground in the whole region cannot be neglected in any discourse about the future of Jerusalem.

Conclusion

Jerusalem is increasingly a regional city. Therefore, to ensure development of Palestinian areas, their structural integration with Jerusalem is crucial. The Old City and its environs are the core of the Palestinian areas and so will be the generator of any Palestinian development. Both historically and structurally this coherence is of vital importance. Whatever long-term political solution appears, it must preserve a potential for structural development in these areas. What is more, partition of both Jerusalem and the West Bank cannot be successful if it does not deal with the Israeli superstructure. Previous negotiations have dealt with percentage of and regulations of land use of Palestinian areas. In order to support Palestinian development, however, it is necessary to reinforce the historical linear structure along the ridge. This means strengthening the *infrastructure* along the ridge. Years of successive demolition of Palestinian infrastructure have made the need for a more efficient and ecological transportation system apparent. One obvious move would therefore be to construct public transport (railway/metro) connecting the most important Palestinian religious, administrative, and financial nodes along the ridge. We stress these features not solely for functional and economic reasons. The Israeli installations in the occupied territories have a strong symbolic value of the arrogance of the occupier, in garish contrast to the restrictions on movement of the occupied. Accessibility within the Palestinian areas is finally also a question of dignity.

The New Canaanites

Romi Khosla

Introduction

This is an unusual architecture book. Its oddity lies in the fact that so many distinguished people should be contributing ideas for a city that is so small. Yet it is one of
the wonders of Jerusalem that it receives a share of world attention totally dispro-
portionate to its size. Until a couple of years ago I myself had no interest in
Jerusalem; ironically, I was dropped into the city to work for eight months deep
inside the cluttered and constrained ministries of the Palestinian National Authority.

Around the world, ethnic conflicts are not all that different. The fear, barbarities,
atrocities, and compassion have an uncanny similarity. The point is to propose solutions to these conflicts. My own proposal is about design and how design can
influence the future of conflicting communities. It concerns the whole of Palestine
and Israel. I shall need all three of the communities that inhabit this land to gener-
ously overlook my errors of detail and the seeming amateurism with which I have
interpreted material from original and secondary sources obtained through official
and unofficial contacts. I have interpreted things in my own way.

I have at least based my arguments on facts collected on the ground; these I
refer to as evidence for want of a better word. My proposal is not a part of the system of emotional justifications and beliefs that govern the day-to-day affairs of both
the Palestinians and Israelis, and so I would prefer to regard it not as a construct of
my own mind so much as a natural outcome of the evidence.

Background of the Proposal

Historical Context

The context of this proposal is defined by two events that occurred outside the Middle East and before its internal confrontations became so apparently impossible to resolve. The first is the brutal behavior of a certain state government in the Second World War, which defined a new low for state repression. Because the Nazi state apparatus reached such an extreme condition of barbarity, subsequent state barbarities have seemed almost acceptable. As Eric Hobsbawm has explained, military atrocities have become a regular part of the rule of law.[1]

1 Eric Hobsbawm. *The Age of Extremes: The Short 20th Century History 1914–1991* (India: Viking Press, 1994).

The second event was the Cuban Revolution of 1960. This triggered a new set of phenomena—radical students, revolutionary groups, guerrillas in the jungles and deserts, the IRA, Hezbollah, Hamas, Taliban, the Red Brigade, Che, Carlos, and so many more. The global consequences of these two events have become inseparable from the belief systems of Palestine and Israel.

Background

Throughout my eight months of wanderings in the beautiful landscape of Palestine it was difficult for me not to feel a fool. I could see at every turn the approaching darkness of sunset, and in this twilight the whole region spinning out of control. This spin confuses one at first. It seems difficult to locate its source. Every discussion, every argument, ends up against a wall with no place to take the first step toward finding one's way out. Neither the Israelis nor the Palestinians will concede an inch. Whatever is given in discussions and stiffly reluctant handshakes abroad is taken back when the leaders return home and address their fanatical supporters.

In some ways my proposal is extremely ambitious—yet not in its technical goals, for it posits, in the end, little more than a railway train that is to stop at some rather special stations. Its ambition is not part of the whoopee of Architecture, but the ambition, rather, of fools, those fools who see, staring them in the face, the need for a whole new reality to prevent the spiritual destruction of one of the great places of the world.

The route of the proposed train and the stations at which it is to stop are envisioned at the center of an ideology that proposes justice, integration, and interdependence rather than cruelty, apartheid, and the illusions of independence. This train is conceived to bypass those grandiose forms of assault and robbery—exploitation and colonialism.

Another ambition of the proposed train is to exploit the architecture of multilayered, multifunctional stations. Religious fanatics might see such concourses as subverting their portrayals of space and time as exclusively religious in character and rhythm. If so, they would be correct. The concourse is indeed a secular space whose activity is regulated by the arrival of trains. As passengers alight, its many   activities are activated. This is an alternative to the religious control of public space, where rhythms are determined by prayer times. This leads to antagonism because each religious chronotype must continually be defended; the same time is claimed by different religions for their prayers.

Significant architectural efforts need to be made in spaces where ancient conflicts are destroying the future. Modern architectural proposals can provide alternatives to hastily sketched military solutions. Military solutions diminish all other solutions and ideas, for they forestall all efforts to probe any dimensions other than antagonistic ones. Even the most sophisticated army remains ill-equipped to integrate; it is educated to disintegrate. Military solutions are the most destructive products of the technology of the modern state.

This proposal is presented as a catalyst for reconciliation, reconstruction, and an alternative future. Without articulating a new manifesto, it does propose to intervene on behalf of social democracy for the newly emerging dual citizenship of the larger territory anciently called Canaan. It may be seen as an opportunity for the battered ship of Modernism to dock at a port reminiscent of the home yard where social concerns first welded its hull together. It advocates reconstruction of the illusions and the frustrated dreams that keep Palestinians and Israelis apart. Its emphasis is not on nation-statehood but on common citizenship in a natural region. That is, it assumes integrated cohabitation by the populations of Palestine, Israel, and eventually Jordan as separate states within a larger nation called Canaan. It treats these contiguous territories as one geographical and economic region divided only by the madness of colonial cartography. Its titular reference to history exposes dormant potentials and lost identities—though using history to define lost identities may be seen as antagonistic by both the Palestinian and Israeli communities, especially the latter. For if Jerusalem is the third most holy city for the Muslims (after Mecca and Medina), it is also the first and last city for the Jews. They do not accept the earthly events that form the narrative of Jerusalem. They do not accept easily that historical events have brought the Arabs to Jerusalem to stay. This imposition of an imagined Biblical history on the real terrestrial history of Jerusalem inevitably leads to antagonism between celestially ordained events and those recorded by history and archaeology. For their part, the Arabs do not recognize the powerful influence of the Biblical narratives on the Jewish imagination, an influence etched on the memory of the Jews and stirred and reinscribed with every ceremony and ritual.

Political and territorial reconciliations need a deep economic logic; they cannot spring from abstract notions of peace or from merely written accords. The underlying logic of economic integration can enrich generations of inhabitants and create vested interests among the participating communities. Enrichment and development are greater incentives than military treaties. Round-table conferences of military

Satellite map of Israel and Palestine showing the route of the proposed train across a united Canaan.

Image of train traveling
across the desert
landscape.

First phase of the exca-
vated site with skylights
over the underground
Jerusalem station.

advisers and the territorial fragmentations that result are retrograde ways to build the future, their pretensions to everlasting peace doomed.

Solutions are, of course, being intensively searched for by many who refuse to accept a permanent state of antagonism between the Palestinians and the Israelis. Edward Said is perhaps one of the most important proponents of a reevaluation of the relationship between the two communities. Below, I examine Said's proposal for reconciliation, including the preconditions described by him, and propose alternatives to his views. His advocacy of a common Palestinian-Israeli history and education, syncretist citizenship, and merged identities is questioned. Instead, I propose a shared economy with the encouragement of distinct characters for each community. I explore the dangers of defining separate identities and instead propose character and potential as the creative source material that needs development. I refuse to accept the viability of a separated Palestine and Israel and argue that their gradual integration is the only economically viable alternative to setting up pretentious Lilliputian national state economies.

Said, in his first talk in Israel, said that that country was moving toward apartheid. Nobody in the surrounding Arab region wanted the Palestinians; they were treated like refugees in their own land and in surrounding lands. In Egypt, Said noted, Palestinians had to report to the police every month. They had been robbed of their own land, something the Israeli occupiers knew only too well. He quoted Moshe Dayan, who said once: "There is not one place in Israel that did not have an Arab population." Even so, the Palestinians persisted in dreaming about returning to a pre-1948 situation. Israel, in the meanwhile, was engaged in a campaign of misinformation, mopping up all the space that could be used for alternative views. Everybody distorted the future. Said also observed that the Israeli military machine was imposing a synthetic nationalism while Arafat continued to rule with the "ludicrous trappings of a Head of State."

"Whatever happened," Said asked, "to the common regional history of this place? Perhaps the dialectics of separation is exhausted. Now let us adjust to the disagreeable home that we have." His message was clear: though surrounded by tottering regimes and pulled and pressured by American exertions, this region had better find its own solutions, solutions from within its own resources and communities. According to Said, the direction toward a common future was clear. Quoting Raymond Williams, Said declared that the only hope lay in merging the separate identities of the Palestinians and Israelis into an "emergent composite identity." It was, he said, imperative to merge the two histories of the region into a common one: one people, one history, a composite future.

The unanswered question is whether history is really relevant for the formation of this new identity. It seemed to me, coming from a rich and wrinkled civilization of multilingual and multireligious identities, that Said's argument was advancing at sonic speed and assuming the unfolding of events beyond my comprehension. He was appealing to the Palestinians to accept the connections between those historical and literary imperatives that formed Israel and the Holocaust that devastated the Jews in Europe. In turn, the Jewish community should recognize its perpetration on the Palestinian community of the Naqba, the great expulsion, of 1948. I understood Said's proposal as a kind of Desmond Tutu-style truth-and-reconciliation process of healing between the Palestinians and Israelis.

To fulfill Said's impassioned plea for a common history would require scholarly effort on a scale that might be difficult to achieve in the time needed to slow down the region's suicidal spin. Dovetailing three thousand years of archaeology, Biblical texts, and contemporary events into a single joint seems very daunting. Both communities use history as an arsenal. There are too many available versions of the region's history. Archaeological evidence, religious texts, and political agendas are mixed and matched to create attractive patterns that bear no resemblance to reality. How far back should one go to find a common beginning to the history of the region, a point that both communities could accept as a beginning?

It remains to be seen whether it is possible to achieve reconciliation between Palestinians and Israelis by forming an "emergent composite identity"—a kind of secular, suprahistorical new citizen. It seems, on the face of it, a fine intellectual concept. There is something unavoidably seductive about the concept of identity. It seems a smooth way to counter the new internationalism and global homogenization. Yet it is fraught with problems. Identity is a recently manipulated phenomenon in nation-building, a contemporary concept that has been synthetically forged as an aggressive defense mechanism and drenched in blood and tears. The construction of the present Palestinian and Israeli identities is linked irrevocably to both communities' Diasporas—or rather to the way their identities *ought* to be defined.

Any efforts at reconciliation should take into consideration Bakhtin's vision of cultural encounter in opposition to that being advocated by Said. (Bakhtin's concept is theoretical, not framed specifically around the Palestinians and Israelis.)[2] He explains that in each culture, the past has potentials that remain hidden and unrealized. Further, the presence of an adjacent, alien culture inevitably leads to a culture's asking new questions about itself; each culture discovers itself through the eyes of the other. The ensuing dialogue does not result in a merger, mixture, or blending of the two cultures into one. Each retains and reinforces its unity and uniqueness while both are enriched. Said's proposition for a new syncretic citizen seems, on these terms, unrealizable. The quest for reconciliation is actually the quest for two separate potentials, each unique, each dependent on the other for realization.

I contend that the leads given by Edward Said in his lecture cannot be followed up because they are based on the idea that is not possible to move beyond the elementary problems that imagined history has imposed on both communities. The

2 M. M. Bakhtin, "Otvet na Vopros Redaktsii Novogo mira," in *Estetka Slovesngo Tuorchestva* (Moscow: Iskusstvo, 1979).

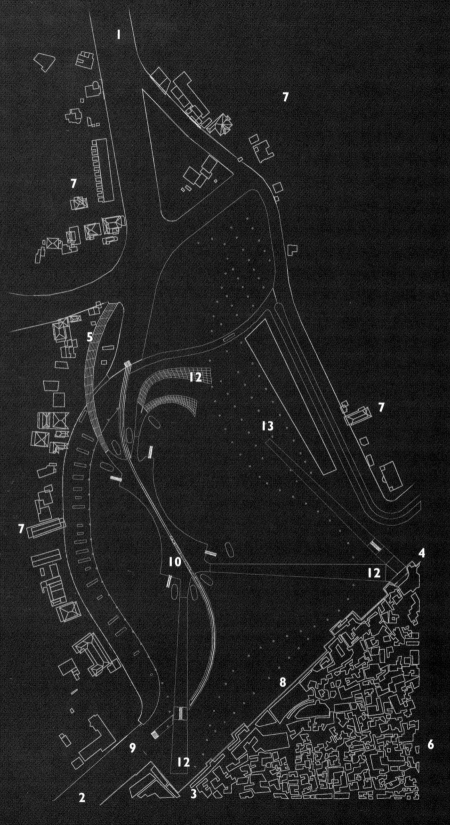

1 To Nazareth
2 To Bethlehem
3 Jaffa Gate
4 Damascus Gate
5 New Jerusalem
6 Old Jerusalem
7 Existing Fabric
8 Wall
9 Suleman Street
10 Platform
11 Bus Interchange (Below)
12 Ramps Down from Train
13 Concourse Below

alternative history that one might hope archaeology would put together is compromised by its dependence on the Biblical texts, which are used to make the giant leaps in time that are needed to connect the evidence from digs.

Bakhtin's notion of blending the separate characters and potentials of the Palestinians and Israelis into a more stable, mutual interdependence is the only way out. And the economic sector is the only sector in the lives of these two nations that can realistically provide such a state of interdependence. It is this sector that can provide a context in which rapprochement can be considered and in which the world community can participate.

It is, in my view, not possible for either Israel or Palestine to exist as stand-alone nations. The economic wealth of the divided territories of Palestine can only be harnessed for the benefit of the people if the entire land is considered to be a composite, whole, and integrated territory. Yet the region's economy is presently regulated by military dictates. No semblance of democracy in Israel can conceal the parasitic nature of the laws that the Israeli military has arbitrarily imposed on the Palestinian areas. Indeed, the Israeli army has devastated the economy of Palestine. Some 1,500 military laws now regulate economic life there.

Furthermore, the Oslo Accords have been accepted by the Palestinian National Authority, which is controlled by returnees with dreams of ruling a nation-state. This accord has reduced the hill territories of Palestine into an archipelago of reservations between which people and goods may travel only at the pleasure of Israeli troops.

To see the landscape of Palestine as having economic potential thus requires a major shift in how this land is imagined, represented, and divided up by both communities. Its redemption as either the Holy Land or an idyllic Promised Land has no relevance to its future; nor does its place in the Arab Dream as a land of gardens and tiled houses inhabited by happy Palestinians. This landscape's potential, strangled by martial law, cannot be realized through pilgrimages and tourism. One needs to accept the whole landscape of the entire territory to even begin the dialogue of possibilities. To attain such a geographical understanding one must look beyond the artificial political boundaries of recently born nation-states. To utilize any landscape for survival and for the accumulation of wealth one must look at the region as a whole; economic potential is closely allied with geographical features. In the region under consideration, these features are (1) the coastal zone, (2) the central uplands, and (3) the valley of the Jordan River (the Ghor). These three zones are the keys to the future of Palestine and Israel.

The fertile coastal zone consists of a plain which varies in width from five to forty kilometers. Its soils include clay, gravel, and sand. The uplands of Samaria and Judea consist of a series of mountain clusters that rise up to nine hundred meters above the surface of the Mediterranean. These latter are the lands that more or less define the imagined and negotiated territories of the Palestinian nation. While the land of Samaria is open and full of fertile valleys, the land of Judea is essentially composed of limestone and rock.

The third zone, the Jordan River valley, is part of the Palestinian dream of a homeland contiguous with Jordan. In this territory Israel has established a string of settlements. It has identified upland locations for these settlements that effectively block any clear, unbroken territorial flow from Palestine to Jordan. This desert rift valley, irrigated by the waters of the Jordan River as it runs below sea level into the Dead Sea, is cordoned off with two barbed-wire fences that are patrolled by military jeeps round the clock.

While these three zones have remained constant, considered as units of landscape, their exploitation by the Israeli military has transformed the region's irrigation and transportation. Consider the urban and agrarian settlements of the coastal lowlands. The flat lands have been reclaimed and their areas of light, sandy soil have been organized into large, efficiently run, capital-intensive farms. The northern and southern coastal lowlands have been connected by highways. The farmlands have been connected with the irrigation system of the National Water Carrier, which takes water from the Sea of Galilee to the Negev desert. Because of the large investments made by Israel in urbanization, transportation, and irrigation, the coastal zone functions as a single economic unit.

In contrast, the central uplands occupied by the Palestinians have been devastated by physical, political, and economic fragmentation. Today both Samaria and Judea are relatively barren. Soil erosion was once countered by terracing the land with rough limestone walls. These terraces still cover the hills of Palestine but are sadly neglected today as the area's agricultural economy spirals downward. Terracing increased the productivity of the land and provided a livelihood for the many habitations that once dotted the region. Apart from providing a series of level surfaces for agriculture, the terraces trapped runoff water from rainfall. This water seeped into the ground and built up the aquifers that underlie the hills. These hills are where the maximum precipitation in the region takes place; in ancient times, before terracing diverted the water to the aquifers, it used to run off and flow to the lowlands, where it formed swamps. The territory today defined as Palestine thus sits on the major aquifer resource for both Israel and Palestine—yet this aquifer is the state property of Israel, as defined by laws discussed above.

The post-1948 pattern of exploitation of the coastal zone has significantly altered the economy of Palestine in at least two ways. First, the occupation and exploitation of the coastlands and lowlands has stabilized under Israeli management. The process of urbanization has produced suburbia along large lengths of the coast. The Arab population in the coastal zone has been encouraged to reinhabit the remains of some of the villages that it had inhabited during the pre-1948 period. I recently visited Akko and Jaffa, two such villages primarily inhabited by Palestinian

Jerusalem Station with the roof covering removed.

Arabs, which had been "conserved." Akko still has its own historical morphology, though I could not help but sense a ghettoized isolation. This was apparent from the affluent housing developments that surrounded the place. Jaffa has been converted from an affluent Arab town into a suburb of Tel Aviv. Here, in the suburb parks in the heart of Jaffa, built over the ruins of demolished houses, green lawns provide Arabs with images of how life could be lived within an Israeli reservation.

I propose to look at just one sector of the economy—water—to illustrate the nature of the problems that need to be overcome to restore balance to the economies of Israel and Palestine. I argue that Israel is destroying the character and potential of its own economy, which instead of being a balanced, regional economy has become an unbalanced, parasitic one. In so arguing I will move closer to the substance of my proposal, the central concern of which is the restoration of balance in the economy and in the development of the resources of both the Palestinians and the Israelis.

The land of Palestine is for the most part sandy and rocky. Water is crucial for sustaining life and is central to the accumulation of wealth. Three military orders issued for the West Bank (described further below) have effectively captured the water resources of the Palestinians. The background of this seizure is as follows: in 1949, Israel consumed less than 20 percent of its renewable water resources. This had increased to 95 percent five years later. Within thirty years, water consumption in Israel had exceeded the renewable supply. Water, along with the land it can irrigate, is the key to prosperity in the region, and so, after fifty years and several wars, Israel has extended its control over all the water resources of Palestine and Israel.[3]

Water scarcity has made Palestine (like many other Arab countries) deficient in food crops: olives, fruits, grapes, and wheat. One feature of the archipelago of reservations imposed on the Palestinians by the Oslo Accords is that water cannot be transported from one area to another. The instrument of control is the Mekorot Company, which is an Israeli water monopoly. Under Israeli law Palestinian owners cannot tap or use water without permits. All Palestinians have to receive their water supply from Mekorot. Thirty-five percent of the Palestinian economy is agriculture-based, compared to 3 percent of the Israeli economy.

In order to diffuse this antagonism, it will be necessary to work toward utilizing the agricultural potential of the mountainous area under which the major aquifers of the region lie. Water is required for exploring the full productive potential of this region and would need to be transported across the territory from north to south to enable a regeneration of this entire zone. It is therefore a crucial element in the project proposal.

The aquifer is a crucial economic resource. Yet it is being diverted. Its use for watering the extensive lawns and golf courses of the coastal zone cannot be regarded as anything but antagonistic, particularly given that over 80 percent of the ground water of Palestine is taken by Mekorot.

3 _Israeli Obstacles to Economic Development in the Occupied Palestinian territories_ (Jerusalem Media & Communication Centre, 1994), 16.

Jerusalem Station with translucent roof

It is disturbing that while the European Economic Community, the United States, the World Bank, and other donors are pouring aid into the Balkans for "structural reform," none of the money pledged to Palestine—ten times more per capita than the sum earmarked for the Balkans—seems clearly marked for "structural reform." In identifying the economic sectors of Israel and Palestine for integration and interdependence, this project therefore has a specific thrust. It is part of a structural reform process for a country that needs radical surgery, not saline drips. If the Palestinian economy has been distorted by its imbalances and lack of hinterland and market, the Israeli economy is equally imbalanced. Distortions in the Israeli economy have been caused by excessive exploitation of cheap labor from Palestine and by the import of capital.

The political geography of Israel has a grossly underdeveloped and distorted Palestinian economy located in its midst. Furthermore, the rich, perfumed economy of Israel is surrounded by other underdeveloped economies in the throes of political and social instability. Israel's mortal fear of the dormant competitive abilities of the Palestinians is thus fueled by its social, political, and economic isolation. Lebanon, Iraq, Jordan, Saudi Arabia, Syria, and Egypt have not yet formed an economic union, but if they did so and extended this to a military union, Israel's dream of living in peace would seem somewhat on the edge of a nightmare.

When I was working on projections for the future demand for schools, I was surprised to see the 1997 population statistics. Graphed, these statistics resemble a pyramid whose base comprises persons up to four years old. This promises to place an enormous number of people onto the labor market in fifteen years, which is disturbing because if the agricultural land of the West Bank has been forcibly dried up, current Israeli policies will ensure that the working population of Palestine is reduced to degraded poverty in that time.

The Proposal
Intervention in the political, social, economic, and architectural situations in Palestine and Israel is proposed.

A The Political Proposal
It is proposed that the part of the ancient Levant variously called Palestine or Israel in the twentieth century should be called Canaan in the twenty-first. Its citizens are to be Canaanites and will dwell in two separate states, Palestine and Israel. Canaan would be a federation of the states of Palestine and Israel (à la United States), with one national capital in Jerusalem and two separate state capitals, Ramallah and Tel Aviv. (This idea was not invented by me, of course—it has been the declared position of the Indian government for many years: one nation, two states.) This would define the wider context for implementation of this proposal.

B The Social and Economic Proposal

This proposal advocates social separation and economic integration. It advocates development of the character and potential of each community as a separator of the Palestinians and the Israelis. The unique character and potential of each community contributes to the integrated economic activity of United Canaan, a single economic territory. The question of Jordan's membership in Canaan is left open, although it is my view that it should be integrated into the United Canaan economic system.

C The Architectural Proposal

The architectural proposal has three subcomponents—Connectivity, the Mesocity, and the Concourse.

Connectivity

The existing road network in the land that will become United Canaan has been laid out in a way that isolates Palestinians and Israelis from each other. The roads connecting the towns and villages of Israel are virtually closed to Palestinians, who only travel on them at great risk of interrogation. The roads that connect the Palestinian towns and villages bypass the Israeli roads or else pass through the fortified checkpoints of the Israeli army. A third category of existing roads links the Israeli settlements that have mushroomed on the West Bank. These are open only to Israelis. I propose a railroad project that will cut across these ridiculous barriers.

This consists of a fast train to link the port of Haifa on the Mediterranean coast to Tiberias on the shores of the Sea of Galilee by a crescent-shaped route via Nazareth. From Nazareth the track runs south, linking key Palestinian towns to Israeli towns to form a continuous single market. It then proceeds to Jenin, Nablus, Jerusalem, Bethlehem, Hebron, and Beersheba, where it turns east and ends at Gaza. The train is for the commuters and goods of Canaan, and, equally significant parallels a new national water carrier that will bring the water from the desalination plants of Haifa, the Sea of Galilee, and the aquifers of the West Bank, and distribute it to the water-starved agricultural terraces of the West Bank and the deserts of Negev. The train track and the water carrier are integrated; the carriages run atop the water-carrying tube. Each station on this track is a secular space that will encourage new economic, social, and political activities.

A new connectivity thus links all the important towns of the West Bank to towns in Israel. Old roads could become local links or even fall into disuse. In fact, two parallel movement systems to traverse United Canaan from north to south are proposed. The first travels along the coastlands and is already well developed within Israel as a road and rail system. The second is the proposed rail system, which will travel through the uplands, connecting communities and economies and integrating them into the United Canaan infrastructure.

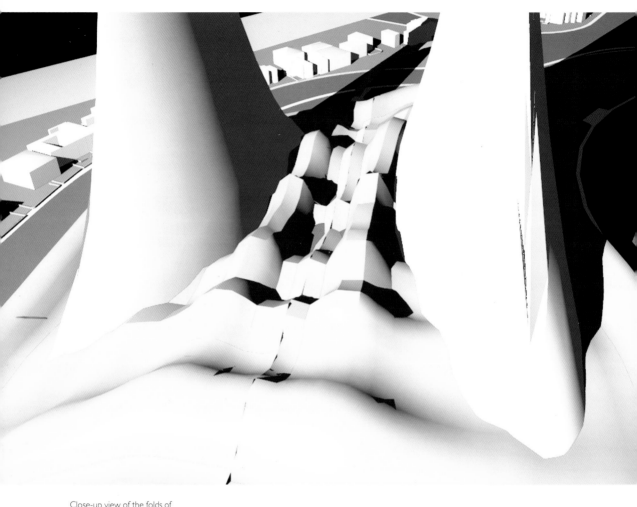

Close-up view of the folds of
the roof cover.

The New Canaanites

As mentioned above, the rail bed shall be an integrated water and carriage carrier. While the carriages connect the economy of manpower and produce, the water carrier connects and irrigates the wasting lands of the West Bank. The water will be taken from three sources: the Sea of Galilee, the aquifers, and the new desalination plants yet to be built in Haifa. This new water carrier will enable a balancing of the consumption of water in United Canaan.

The Mesocity

Old Jerusalem belongs to the Arabs. New Jerusalem belongs to Israel. The Ottoman city walls neatly define Old Jerusalem's boundaries. New Jerusalem is well settled around a city center full of boutiques and includes endless stretches of suburbia that are being created to try to balance the population statistics so that the Jewish population appears in the census as the major population. Between the two lies a fuzzy space, a buffer zone in which both communities fear to implement radical change. If they did it might start a riot, because it would shift the imagined lines of control and give advantage to one or the other of the two contenders.

My proposal, however, is not just about spatial planning. To me, Jerusalem is not exclusively important for the prosperity of United Canaan; it is but a link in the chain. Jerusalem needs to be a mop that absorbs the aggressive energies of two civilizations that are bent on clashing with each other, Arab Christians and Muslims on one side and Jews and Latin Christians on the other. The proposed railway station concourse is to do some of the absorbing. Its users are the inhabitants of the mesocity—Arabs, Jews, Orthodox and Latin Christians. The mesocity is the intermediate world between the macrocity and the microcity. The word *meso* is from the Greek *mesos*, or middle. I have coined *mesocity* to mean the city of temporary stability, the city whose spaces and forms mediate between the pressures of the micro-level world of individual citizens and the macro-level world of civic order, written rules and regulations, and so on.

The macrocity is ruled by the state and is planned by professionals for the people. Physical planning processes bring the written laws and regulations of the state to the citizen's front door and seek to plan all aspects of their life and behavior outside that front door. The macro process is thus a planned, written process, while the meso process is an autonomous, oral, self-adjusting process that ebbs and flows in usage and function.

The mesocity is the realm in which community relationships and public life interact with the private worlds of community members. It is the repository of the deep oral culture of a community. It acts in a city but does not try to know it. It talks about a city but it does not try to write it. A mesocity space is a space inhabited by people of diverse cultural origins who have been brought together into a synergetic relationship that depends on mutual integration without homogenization and without obsession over "origins" (thought necessary to define identity). It is a space where the rubbing together of polycultures initiates new creative activities and where the distinction between the modern and the traditional is difficult to make out and where the regulations of the macro authority are suspended and redundant.

Mesocity space is not a mere extension of the written orders and spatial patterns of a city. It is a space dominated by the personal use of the community, a space where multiple operators act reciprocally, almost ignoring the macro system. One or both of the following are probably true:

- People's prevailing relationships and common understandings have to do with the technical, not the moral, order, with administrative regulations and business and technical convenience.

- The cities of Canaan are populated by people of diverse origins removed from the indigenous seats of their cultures. They are cities in which new states of mind, following from these characteristics, develop and become prominent. These new states of mind are indifferent to or inconsistent with, or supersede or overcome, states of mind associated with local cultures and ancient civilizations. The intelligentsia of these cities are not the literati, but those who express their creativity in the spoken word, the oral tradition.

Yet all the planning exercises envision a future for Jerusalem that is about the written tradition. New Jerusalem is already, in a sense, a city of literati. The macrocity bulldozes and codifies local culture and replaces it with a written, macro moral order. The mesocity, in contrast, carries the evolution of local cultures into the contemporary world without fear of the modern. The mesocity remains equidistant from religious and municipal dictates.

The proposed station concourse is a mesocivic space. It carries forward local cultures, it enhances character and potential, it absorbs the antagonisms of macro moral orders. It is constrained only by the technical order of the space enclosure and the train. Within these bounds it swirls, motivated by the inevitable integration of interdependent communities, each with its unique commercial and cosmic concerns. It is a space of oral cultures and their unlimited ability to adjust continuously to contemporary needs.

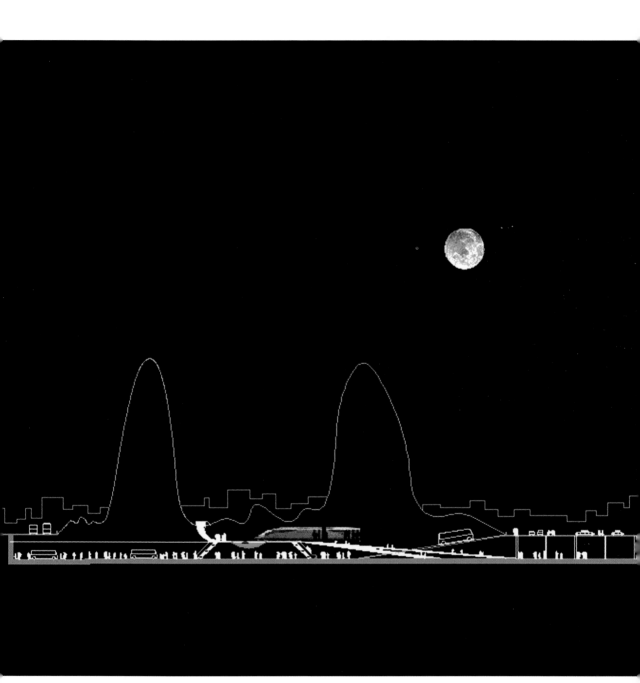

Section through station

The New Canaanites

The Concourse

The triangular site outside Damascus Gate is in the buffer zone between the Israeli city of New Jerusalem and the Arab city of Old Jerusalem. The Israeli city, to reiterate, is a macrocosmic city of written cultures. Here the moral order of Zion has been codified into a series of rules and regulations that preclude the emergence of ever-changing moral orders from the collaborations and negotiations of citizens interacting with each other and adjusting to their mutual needs. The Arab city, on the other hand, is a mesocity of oral intellectuals, of an oral culture that will not codify the moral order of its citizens into written rules and regulations. Here the community meshes its activities not according to imposed functional forms but on the basis of permissiveness, tolerance, and a level of mutual adjustment that is of a high order.[4]

This proposal would create within the triangular site outside Damascus Gate site a large covered space—a transport concourse—into which the mesocivic activities of the Old City and of other locales could flow. The train line, its platforms, and its intercity connections provide the technical order of the space, along with the associated bus station. This concourse is a space in which the mesocity swirls with activity, an activity whose moral, social, and ethical order is governed by its users. Exits are provided on both sides of the rail line. The platform to the west connects to the New Israeli Jerusalem and to the bus station and its ordered shops. From the platform to the east, passengers exit on the concourse level, into the excitement and activity of mesocivic Jerusalem where kabobs, games of chess, and pirated CDs jostle for attention. This is the space where the fishermen of Tiberias bring their catches, where olives from Nablus are on sale, where the grapes of Hebron compete with those of Beersheba. Such stations shall, as mentioned above, also exist at Haifa, Tiberias, Nazareth, Jenin, Nablus, Ramallah, Jerusalem, Bethlehem, Beersheba, and Gaza.

The challenges of surviving as a collective of civilizations cannot be met by accepting solutions to economic and social prosperity that have been devised by military persons. Their role in providing any sort of harmony is doomed by the very nature of their own professionalism in destroying options and simplifying them to straitjacket surrenders and treaties. I am aware that the difficulties of trying to solve the crisis in Israel and Palestine by using the army on one side and a dubiously democratic system on the other side cannot be wished away. However, the proposal described here is aimed at emphasizing the need for a creative solution to problems that are not as deeply political as they are economic. Canaan must be united if it is to come out of the whirlwind that is currently sucking the region into a black hole—not the stable black hole of astronomy, held together by gravity, but one doomed to explode.

4 Robert Redfield and Milton Singer, "The Cultural Role of Cities," *Economic Development and Cultural Change* II (1954), 43–73.

Aerial view of station

THE CRESCENT MODEL:
A Planning Framework for Jerusalem/Al-Quds

Rassem Khamaisi

Population Increase

It is possible to increase the population both through positive immigration and natural population growth. In fact, government policy encourages population increase through financial incentives to Jewish immigrants to Jerusalem.

Average Family Size
3.2 persons per family

Introduction

The conflict over Jerusalem has negatively affected its natural and balanced development. This conflict is increasing Israel's influence and control over Jerusalem; in return, Israel is weakening Jerusalem's structure, its ability to survive and prosper. It is eroding Jerusalem's ability to balance its available natural resources with its ability to develop them, and is creating an imbalance between population and available housing.

Inspection of existing Israeli plans for Jerusalem reveals that they have been devised to secure Israel's control over Jerusalem. The objectives and methodology of such plans do not take into account the development requirements of all Jerusalem's residents. Rather, they have been devised to ensure Israeli interests by demographic and political means.

In the action-reaction style of the Palestinian-Israeli conflict, the Palestinian side has tried to ensure its interests in Jerusalem by reacting to Israeli initiatives; however, the Palestinians' political, economic, and social conditions have made their efforts less successful. Both sides are battling for survival in Jerusalem, yet differ in their understanding of "survival" and in their methods for achieving it. Israel occupied Jerusalem and continues to consolidate its presence there in accordance with a colonialist understanding of "Jewish historical rights." It presents its continued occupation and

**Demographic Structure:
Ages 65 and over**

10 %

**Demographic Structure:
Ages 0–19**

38 %

5.6 persons per family

3.5 %

50 %

settlement of Jerusalem as part of the battle for Jewish survival as such, historically and globally threatened. Meanwhile, the Palestinian side is under occupation, and, for it, "to survive" means to successfully resist displacement and subjugation.

Given this two-sided situation, planning the urban and functional structure of Jerusalem is not an easy task. Nevertheless, the object of such planning is to undermine this very mentality by contributing to the development of a Jerusalem viewed by everyone as theirs. Such planning must include administrative and political arrangements for fulfilling some interests and requirements of both parties, though it cannot give each party everything it wants; it must be based on mutual concessions. Even so, planning may enable Jerusalem to pass from an era of conflict to the proper enjoyment of its special spatial, climatic, residential, cultural, and religious assets.

This study examines planning concepts for the spatial and functional development of Jerusalem. It considers existing structure and current trends and tries to devise strategies for creating an international city in which all can live in dignity, prosperity, and peace, a city in which the natural and physical space is balanced, distinctness is preserved, and prosperity and sustainable development are guaranteed.

These concepts have come out of an International Peace and Co-operation Center (IPCC), planning process for fitting Al-Quds to Palestinian needs in the wake of a peace agreement between Palestinians and Israelis. In addition, the model suggested in this study can guide physical planning in the current period. Below, I will first present a general analysis of the existing spatial structure of Jerusalem. Later, I will present the proposed planning concept for the spatial development of Jerusalem.

Factors Considered in the Suggested Plan

Seeking an international status for Jerusalem is not a new idea. In fact, Jerusalem already possesses international status thanks to its religious uniqueness. What we (the developers of the current plan) seek to add is an international economic, cultural, and service status. This can be attained through establishing theaters, exhibitions, museums, and headquarters for international companies and firms; hosting international activities and conferences; and establishing international universities and research centers. There is no doubt that developing Jerusalem in this way can have positive effects on its economic base and regional and international status; however, we reaffirm that Jerusalem must not lose its uniqueness. Indeed, that uniqueness is the basis for improving its international status.

Any planning study must consider several factors shaping urban spatial and functional structure. Some of these factors are constant, so planning must be adjusted to suit them; others can be changed via planning or by structural or political adjustments. The following is a brief overview of ten factors that must be taken into consideration in planning the urban space and the functional structure of Jerusalem.

52 %

1 The Existing Situation

Jerusalem was one city before 1948 and a divided city between 1948 and 1967. In 1967 Israel occupied East Jerusalem and annexed West Jerusalem. Today East Jerusalem is still under Israeli occupation and is divided into at least two subcities or communities. The tables in the margins summarize the diversity between the Palestinian part of Jerusalem (East Jerusalem) and the Israeli part (West Jerusalem).

2 Religious Status and Historical Inheritance

Jerusalem's religious status is unique, and the hill on which the city first appeared 5,000 years ago is still its center and the heart of its spiritual and religious glamour. Throughout this long period different civilizations have settled in Jerusalem, leaving behind cultural and historical inheritances that must be taken creatively into consideration by planners.

3 Planning in a Transitional Period

Jerusalem is currently undergoing—as usual—a process of transition, not only at the political level but also at the social, economic, and cultural levels. This requires of planners a vision that enables the groups undergoing transition to bridge their gaps, to talk in the language of one urban space and of one multifaceted functional and cultural structure.

4 Climate

Jerusalem's location gives it a fluctuating climate, for it lies at the border of the moderate Mediterranean Climatic Zone and the warm Semi-Desert Climatic Zone. Thus the western rims of the Mount of Olives and Al-Masharef Mountain tend to enjoy a temperate climate while their eastern rims have a hot desert climate. A similar climate may not be enjoyed by any other city in the world.

5 Preexisting Plans

Several city plans have been devised for Jerusalem since 1918. Some of these have been ratified and are still in operation. Any new plan must take these into consideration, whether by adoption, addition, or adjustment. The planning concept proposed in this study, will not take as given the schemes currently operational on the local and regional levels; rather, new concepts will be proposed for the sake of treating old planning deficits.

6 Changing Political Scene

The planning of any city usually can assume a fairly clear vision of its political future; however, in Jerusalem one can be sure only of change. This might mean repartition or other political arrangements having direct effects on the evolution of urban space and functional structure.

Individual's Legal Status

Citizenship + Residence

Residential Neighborhoods

Israeli only

Population Density

1.1 persons / room

Resident

Mixture of Israeli
and Palestinian

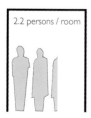

2.2 persons / room

7 Variable Social and Ethnic Structure

There are three basic social and ethnic groups in Jerusalem: the Palestinians, the secular Jews, and the religious Jews. These groups are subdivided into secondary social and cultural groups, each of which seeks to develop an urban and functional space different from the other. This social structure—variously divided between a foreign immigrant society and an indigenous local society, a rural society and an urban society, a religious society and a secular society, a Palestinian society and an Israeli society—directly affects the urban spatial and functional structure of the city.

8 Civic and Functional Hierarchy

The hierarchy of Jerusalem's civic and functional centers is a direct outcome of its partition and annexation in the wake of many wars.

9 Ensuring Regional and International Status Without Losing Distinct Attributes

The city's ability to feed itself and to attract economic and functional development depends on its status in the regional and international economy. Jerusalem must, therefore, be transformed from a peripheral city—a secondary center—to a primary regional and international center. This transformation must, however, occur compatibly with the city's uniqueness, ensuring continuity of local social life. One attribute (economy) must not be developed at the expense of the other (special character).

10 Geographic and Spatial Location

The geography of Jerusalem must be taken into consideration on two levels. First is the city's topographic situation: Jerusalem evolved on the southern tip of a hill inclined eastward and is surrounded from the south, west, and east by valleys overlooked by the Old City. The original hill extends toward the north and northwest and is overlooked and protected by the Mount of Olives and Al-Masharef Mountain. The extension of the hill along a north-south axis, the existence of valleys penetrating the hill, and the sharp inclination from the Mount of Olives and Al-Masharef Mountain toward the east form impediments that must be taken into account by planners.

In addition to its topographic situation, Jerusalem's location at the heart of Palestine and along various regional and national axes increases its importance. Jerusalem lies on the historical road axis linking Nablus to Hebron, which forms the backbone of urban growth in Palestine and links Palestinian cities from Jenin in the north to Al-Thahrieh in the south. In addition, Jerusalem lies at the middle of another axis, that linking the regional centers of Amman and Tel Aviv. The medieval European belief that Jerusalem is the center of the world is not far off, in a sense, given its location at the juncture of three continents and of the axes that link all Palestine together.

Guidelines for the Proposed Plan

We conducted an overview of Jerusalem and its environs and concluded that much of its existing urban and functional character is not the outcome of directed planning; some development has prioritized the creation of facts on the ground over proper planning. We also found that planning concepts devised during the British Mandate continue to affect Jerusalem's image and structure. Yet Jerusalem's expansion and its physical continuity with the surrounding cities on the north-south axis (from Ramallah to Bethlehem) and on the east-west axis (from Mivaseret Zion settlement to Ma'ale Adumim settlement) must be considered in any proposed plan. Therefore, planning proposed by this study will seek to do the following:

- Balance the development of the city proper and its rural hinterland in a way that enables the hinterland to support the center instead of merely depending on it, thus creating a coherent marriage between the urban bloc and the surrounding rural space.

- Protect the possibility of a continuous integrated cultural plurality in the urban space.

- Ensure a balance between Jerusalem on the economic and social levels. Preserve and enhance Jerusalem's international status on the religious and cultural levels, utilizing the latter to help Jerusalem to become an international city on the economic level.

- Focus on East Jerusalem without ignoring West Jerusalem.

- Take into consideration various political solutions and arrangements that may affect the future of Jerusalem, while preserving the city's distinctiveness.

- Build on Jerusalem's distinct characteristics while introducing modern urban planning and management ideas.

- Meet residents' needs for housing, economic and social services, and infrastructure.

- Conserve available natural resources and Jerusalem's cultural inheritance.

Before describing the proposed spatial planning concept for Jerusalem, several points must be clarified and assumptions made explicit. Our starting point will be Jerusalem as functional open city with free movement of goods and people; the capital of two states, Palestine and Israel; a city with a Palestinian and an Israeli hinterland. The political and administrative border between the city's two parts will be the pre-1967 border.

Housing Patterns

Public; a person can buy or rent an apartment; with an architectural pattern comprising several floors and with proper infrastructure made available before the house is inhabited and with only partial participation by the resident.

Planning Methodology

Directing, developing, and initiating; with a strong relationship between planning and implementation; financial resources are made available for the implementation of plans.

Housing Planning

Full planning for the neighborhood and issuance of building permits for the entire neighborhood. Takes into consideration the services in and to the neighborhood.

How Housing is Provided

Through public and governmental initiative and financing (in some areas by associations or individuals in the framework of "Build Your Own House" project), but all on governmental lands.

Private; with an open architectural pattern up to two floors; without adequate infrastructure, roads, sewage, and drainage. This infrastructure is made available after the house is inhabited and at the owner's expense.

Regulating, controlling, and hindering; without any relationship between planning and implementation; without providing financial resources for implementation.

Individual building permits issued without any consideration of the neighborhood or the services.

Through self initiative and financing on privately owned lands.

Jerusalem evolved from the nucleus of the Old City, which stands on the tongue of a relatively flat hilltop surrounded by other hills and mountains. This hilltop is the physical point from which Jerusalem began to expand to the surrounding hills, which, though extensions of the Old City, form distinct physical and spatial units. Some of these units are so distant that it is not possible to see the Old City from them: for instance, Beit Hanina, Shu'fat, and Al-Issawieh. Additionally, some of these units differ from the Old City in terms of their climate, especially those on the eastern side of the Mount of Olives and of Al-Masharef Mountain, as well as the Anata area in the north and Al-Sawahreh, Al-Gharbieh, and Sour Baher in the south.

East and West Jerusalem thus currently extend over various physical units separated from each other by mountains, hills, and valleys. This physical structure directly affects our planning concept, as we will propose numerous land uses and variable development strategies for Jerusalem as it is defined today, from Kufr Aqab in the north to Jabal Abu Ghneim in the south.

Jerusalem residents differ in nationality, ethnic origins, religion, political affiliation, and level of urbanization. This multiplicity, especially the variability in ethnic political affiliations (most basically, the Israeli-Palestinian split) directly affects the urban structure of Jerusalem. Furthermore, the Israelis are divided into secular Israelis and religious Israelis. Each of group has distinct urban characteristics. Therefore, functional partnership must be created in some areas while discouraged in others. Demographic variability requires elastic planning solutions that consider each group's needs while prioritizing Jerusalem's interests as a unique city; participation must be voluntary, not compulsory.

The last masterplan prepared for both East and West Jerusalem was completed in 1968, and the last plan prepared for East Jerusalem alone was completed in 1963, during the Jordanian era. Detailed plans prepared later for the Arab neighborhoods and Israeli settlements built on and adjusted these plans. However, the Palestinian neighborhoods in Jerusalem are currently being developed without clear planning. There is a need to devise a general image of Jerusalem, taking into consideration the planning space of Jerusalem proper and its surroundings and including both the Palestinian and the Israeli residents. It is obvious that continued urban development in Jerusalem without a spatial plan will continue to be fragmented and unbalanced; therefore, the spatial planning concept proposed below seeks to do the following:

- Stop urban fragmentation.

- Encourage balanced urban growth in Jerusalem, Ramallah, and Bethlehem.

- Maintain the diversity of the landscape.

- Restore cohesion and balance between built-up areas and green zones.

Assumptions

The following is a brief overview of the assumptions on which this planning concept depends. The inapplicability of any one of the following assumptions would not necessarily mean that the planning concept was unsuitable; rather, the proposed planning concept could be adjusted.

Social and Cultural Assumptions

- The social and cultural plurality of each social and national and ethnic group in Jerusalem shall be accepted; the partial separation of these groups on national and ethnic grounds shall continue.

- The Israelis shall continue to be concentrated in the western sector of Jerusalem and the Palestinians in the eastern sector.

- The process of urbanization in Palestinian society shall increase; religious conservatism in Israeli society shall dwindle.

- The social and cultural differences between the different population groups shall begin to accommodate, yet each group shall retain a sense of distinct identity.

Demographic Assumptions

- In 2020 the population within Jerusalem's current municipal boundaries shall increase to about one million people, approximately 42 percent of whom shall be Palestinians.

- Jerusalem District shall attract positive Palestinian immigration to Jerusalem and the surrounding villages, especially in the northern area.

- Residents shall not be forcibly moved on a national or ethnic basis.

- The population growth rate shall decrease for both Palestinians and Israelis.

Recreational Areas and Playgrounds

Largely available as parks, public gardens, theaters, cinemas, and closed and open playgrounds for all sorts of athletic activities.

Development of Residential Neighborhoods

Planned and directed to occur on governmental land, the majority of which was confiscated from Palestinians.

Consumption Culture and Spatial and Functional Behavior

Tends to the contemporary capitalist consumption pattern; high spatial mobility for both the resident and the consumer. Operates in accordance with the modern world pattern and tries to imitate the American pattern.

Inheritance From and Continuity With the Past

New city alongside the Old City. Began in the middle of last century without cultural, religious, archaeological, and historical inheritance and continuity.

Absent except the religious center (the Holy Sanctuary), markets, a small theater with limited resources and activities, and limited inappropriate playgrounds.

Spatial Assumptions

- The urban space and the functional structure of Jerusalem cannot be planned in isolation from the area that is functionally and administratively affiliated with the city.

- Internal regional relations shall be established between the Palestinian and the Israeli areas on the one hand and Jerusalem on the other. In addition, regional relations shall be established between Jerusalem and urban centers such as Amman, Cairo, Tel Aviv, Damascus, and Beirut.

Randomly and arbitrarily, on private lands.

Political Assumptions

- Jerusalem is an open city, undivided by walls or barriers.

- Jerusalem will be the capital and the seat of government of two states: Israel and Palestine.

- Jerusalem is run by two municipalities: an Israeli municipality running the Jewish neighborhoods in West Jerusalem and a Palestinian municipality running East Jerusalem. The two municipalities are in cooperation and partnership with each other.

Tends to be traditional; limited resources and functional spatial mobility. Operates in accordance with the Third World pattern.

Economic Assumptions

- Economic growth shall continue for both Palestinians and Israelis, with Palestinians tending to catch up.

- Jerusalem, including Ramallah and Bethlehem, shall form an international "world" and a regional city as well as forming the national center of Palestine.

The high concentration of religious, historical, archaeological, and cultural centers and architectural patterns that have developed throughout history gives Jerusalem cultural inheritance and urban continuity.

Existing Urban Structure as a Starting Point

Our analysis and description of the urban space and the functional structure of Jerusalem reveals the following:

- The Palestinian urban space has developed linearly along the Old City road from Sour Baher in the south to Kufr Aqab in the north.

- The growth of some Palestinian villages and Israeli settlements as "satellite cities" affiliated with Jerusalem and dependent on it has been uneven in terms of size, form, development process, and degree of linkage with Jerusalem. The satellite cities form a radial urban pattern around Jerusalem and are connected to each other via a network of roads.

- Jerusalem is currently a dual urban and functional space. Duality in this space is based on Palestinian versus Israeli affiliations. Although some Palestinian neighborhoods are physically connected to Israeli settlements, they are functionally and ethnically separated from them. This separation affects the patterns and shapes of the urban masses in the space. Both this and the administrative fragmentation of the urban space into several Israeli and Palestinian local authorities have contributed to a dual, unevenly balanced metropolis.

- The urban space that extends from Bethlehem in the south to Ramallah in the north and from Lifta in the west to Maale Adumim settlement in the east is characterized by various urban densities separated by valleys and green zones.

- Differences and gaps in the availability of services and infrastructures affect neighborhoods on an ethnic/political basis.

- The different urban areas and masses are functionally diversified. This situation evolved on the Israeli side in accordance with a planning policy. On the Palestinian side, however, it evolved randomly, in response to the challenge of Israeli-imposed limitations and of guided and unguided market forces, and is therefore incoherent and unbalanced.

- The Palestinians lack housing and job opportunities, services, and economic development.

- Development has occurred without concern for the city's distinct character.

- Jerusalem has the potential to become a "world" city.

- Jerusalem's image is associated with the political conflict that threatens its residents and visitors.

Relationship to the Cultural, Physical, and Functional Space

Planted in the space and imposed on it; result is fragmented and strange.

Social and Economic Transformations

Industrial and civic society trying to apply the capitalist system in its behavior.

Individual's Monthly Income

The income of the head of the family is medium to high. Usually there are two sources of income in the family and the family size is small to medium. Individual's average monthly income is high and equals nearly 960 shekels.

Concentration of Commercial Activities

Commercial activities are concentrated inside a main center and secondary neighborhood centers with a clear and integrated hierarchy.

Gradually growing through the space and developing a suitable balance with it.

Agricultural society undergoing a process of urbanization; trying to bypass the industrial phase to the services phase.

The income of the head of the family is low; therefore, an individual's average income is low as the family size is large. Individual's average monthly income is nearly 420 shekels.

Commercial activities are distributed inside the neighborhoods and along the roads without a clear hierarchy.

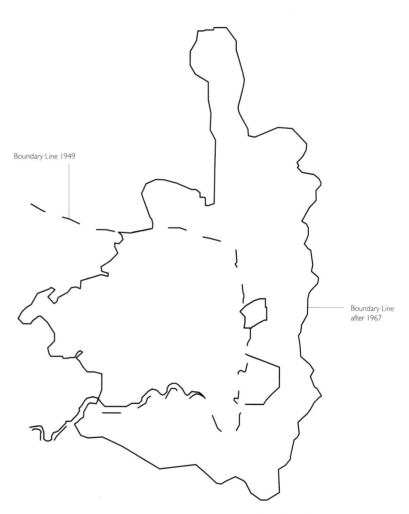

Boundary Line 1949

Boundary Line after 1967

General map of Jerusalem boundary during different periods.

Aims of Urban Planning

The following is a brief summary of the aims of urban planning for the Jerusalem area.

- Jerusalem shall become a unique capital for two states (Palestine and Israel), enjoying cohesion, equality, and plurality. *Cohesion* means freedom of movement for all peoples, goods, and values; *equality* means arriving at a situation whereby East Jerusalem's residents can enjoy the same opportunities enjoyed by those of West Jerusalem; *plurality* means the coexistence of groups having different and diverse cultural, religious, and social characteristics.

- An urban area shall be created in which all residents live in harmony, experience social justice and a stimulating environment, and become politically and economically productive.

- The Old City shall be preserved and the quality of life in it improved, making it an axis of growth and uniqueness in Jerusalem. The Old City must be linked to the different sites around Jerusalem, and shall form a living museum and core of inspiration for the city's development.

- Jerusalem's physical infrastructure and human resources shall be improved while protecting its cultural inheritance and religious values.

- Jerusalem shall be enabled to join the network of "world" cities through the reinforcement of its existing cultural and religious significance and through modernization of its tourist services and information and other industries.

- Jerusalem shall be made a center for conflict resolution and the exchange of knowledge.

- The enjoyment of Jerusalem's natural scenery and climatic diversity shall be facilitated.

- Political and administrative arrangements shall be made to guarantee stability.

- Approximately 120,000 additional residential units shall be constructed in and around Jerusalem.

Labor Sectors

The majority of workers work in economic sectors requiring relatively high skills, especially in the services, education, health, and advanced industries sectors.

Functional Continuity with a Hinterland

Strong hinterland and encouraged continuity with it to enforce the connection between the center and the hinterland.

Industrial Zone

Four integrated industrial parks having varied specializations. Clear separation between workshops and factories on one hand and service and residential centers on the other.

Infrastructure

Developed and constantly maintained even in the Jewish settlements in East Jerusalem.

Most workers work in low-wage economic sectors, construction, and primary industries not requiring high skills.

Spatial and Urban Planning Concepts

The various theoretical models of urban development have been a source of inspiration for our planning concept for Jerusalem. In the past, the urban structure in Jerusalem has been influenced by masterplans advocating one or more of these models—linear, radial, grid, and ring—but these plans have changed with time. Presently, the Israeli model favors the radial pattern. The question is: What pattern or patterns should our planning concept choose? In order to answer this question it is necessary to consider the components of the concept itself.

Components of the Planning Concept

Weak hinterland and controlled functional continuity with it.

- The Old City, including its walls and gates, is the heart of Jerusalem. Its walls will be converted from a barrier to a "crystal crescent" separating the Old City from its urban and functional surroundings. The gates of the crystal crescent will form points of entry to Jerusalem and to the linking paths to its surrounding space.

- The Old City and the area surrounding it shall continue to have special urban characteristics, ensuring a breathing space surrounding the Old City and giving it special centrality.

- The proposed crystal crescent will break up urban continuity between the center of Jerusalem and the peripheral cities and secondary centers that surround it.

Nonexistent, but there is a workshops area in Wad El-Joz and mixed workshops and residential areas.

- Administrative and functional service centers shall be developed within the space defined by the crystal crescent.

- A diversity of building densities within the larger urban space shall be specified with reference to the comparative advantages of each area.

- Natural resources shall be preserved; the physical surroundings of each location shall be a central factor directing the density and height of construction.

- A balanced relationship between the current axes of spatial development in Jerusalem shall be assured.

Underdeveloped and deteriorated; completely absent in some areas; limited maintenance in the Palestinian neighborhoods.

- A road network ensuring continuity between the different parts of Jerusalem and between Jerusalem and its surroundings shall be constructed.

Basic Planning Concepts for Jerusalem

The primary visual symbols of the three monotheistic religions that consider Jerusalem to be holy are the six-pointed star, the cross, and the crescent. These symbols have formed a source of inspiration for the proposed urban structure. The Old City may be seen as a sun from which rays of different thicknesses emerge on two axes, forming a cross. These two axes are the two main roads along which Jerusalem's urban development extends linearly. This pattern of development does not extend indefinitely, as it meets the "crystal crescent" described above and a larger crescent separating Jerusalem from the surrounding cities and penetrated by a set of functional "open gates" (to be described below). Our planning concept seeks to complete the crescent that surrounds the eastern sector of Jerusalem, making a complete circle surrounding both East and West Jerusalem and having the Old City as its center.

The "crescent" planning concept merges three planning geometries: the linear or longitudinal, the radial, and the ring or concentric. It takes the Old City as its center and the new "gates" as the entrances of the outer crescent. In contrast to this pattern is the "star concept," which merges the linear or longitudinal urban pattern with the radial pattern. The star concept would also take the Old City as a central point and spread toward the periphery. Around the rays of this star the transportation network and the urban structure would evolve.

Evaluation: Crescent vs. Star

In order to choose one of these two planning concepts (the cross pattern being already part of the urban structure) we sought to determine which is more conducive to the objectives we have proposed for Jerusalem. Figure 1 records the marks given to each planning concept on a 1–10 scale, with 1 = "not realizing the objectives" and 10 = "realizing the objectives in an ideal manner." This table demonstrates that the crescent (or crescents) pattern is better able to realize our planning objectives. Therefore, we will now focus our attention on this planning pattern, which considers Jerusalem's gates as one of its basic components.

The crystal-crescent concept offers a new direction for the development of Jerusalem. This concept considers Jerusalem's new gates as entrances to the crystal-crescent area, that is, to the heart of the metropolis and to Jerusalem District. It is believed that intensification of development in the heart of metropolitan Jerusalem can complement the unity of the Old City bloc while consolidating Jerusalem's unique image. The new gates in Jerusalem's outer crystal crescent parallel the seven gates in the Old City walls.

The pattern of the crescent is not new to the region. The historic Fertile Crescent concept, for example, refers to Iraq, Syria, Lebanon, Jordan, and Palestine. Moreover, the crescent represents the beginning of the month in the Hebrew and

The inner crescent

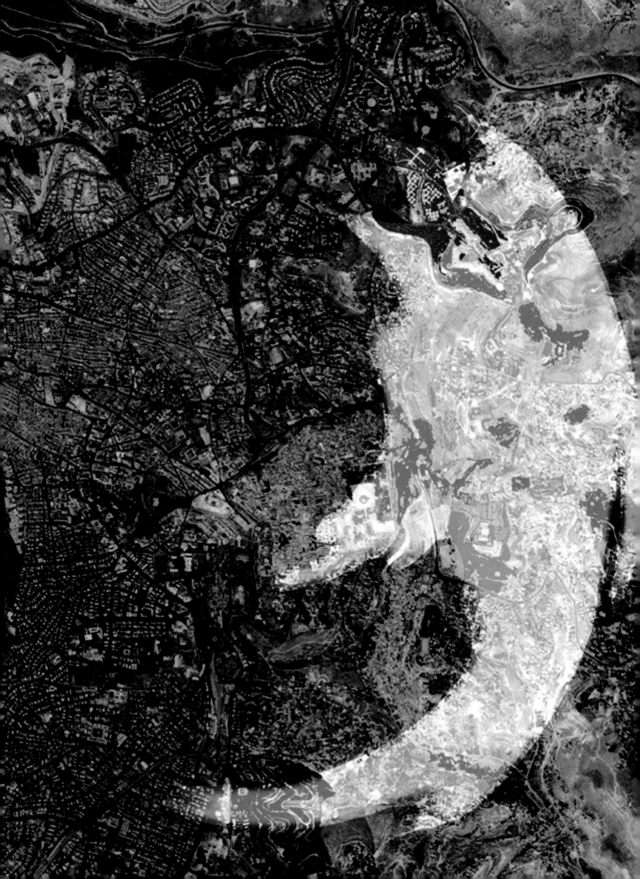

the Muslim (Hijri) calendars and is viewed as a symbol for the beginning of a better future. The proposed image of the crystal crescent takes into consideration the geographic, historic, symbolic, religious, and spatial background of the crescent and seeks to exploit its significance in the surroundings of Jerusalem, especially around the Old City.

It might be thought that we are proposing a green belt that would form a barrier surrounding Jerusalem and preventing its expansion. What we are proposing is rather the allocation of an area of transition or transformation between the building patterns of Jerusalem and those of the surrounding cities. This transitional belt or buffer zone would have a very low housing and population density; housing would be confined to areas already built up. We also propose the establishment of certain assets—parks, playgrounds, green recreation areas, cemeteries, car parks, an airport—within this buffer ring. Such activities need open space and can relieve the continuity of the urban blocs. This barrier shall be characterized as "green" by virtue of its high density of trees and green fields and low density of houses.

The proposed green crystal crescent shall form an open space paralleling the intensive urban growth of Jerusalem, a green space or urban lung for the metropolis. Meanwhile, the crescent around the Old City shall preserve its urban and spiritual status. Such a pattern would shift the area's urban growth pattern from a linear grid to an integrated concentric pattern that builds unity, balance, equality, and integration.

From a functional point of view, the crystal crescent and open gates shall give Jerusalem an open heart at the center of metropolitan area, thus pointing to the beginning of a new era in Jerusalem. There is a strong reciprocal relationship between a city's heart and its hinterland; the more developed a city's hinterland, the stronger the push for development and expansion at its heart. At the same time, increasing the population of Jerusalem and upgrading its economic and administrative status from a peripheral city to a regional and an international center should lead to the expansion of the center toward the peripheries, intensification of economic and administrative activities at the center, suburbanization of the residents toward the periphery, and transformation of economic and other activities. This process, the slipping of urban activities toward the periphery, has already taken place in other metropolitan cities and shall take place in Jerusalem as well.

The crystal crescent shall determine the distribution of functions within the urban space and shall contribute to dividing Jerusalem on functional bases. The nucleus of the city remains the Old City, whose distinguishing characteristics must be preserved. The Old City's housing, economic, and functional activities must be revived, even while its functional role is limited to tourism and religion. Nevertheless, the continuation of housing in this area requires some development of services and economic activities within it.

The Crescent Model

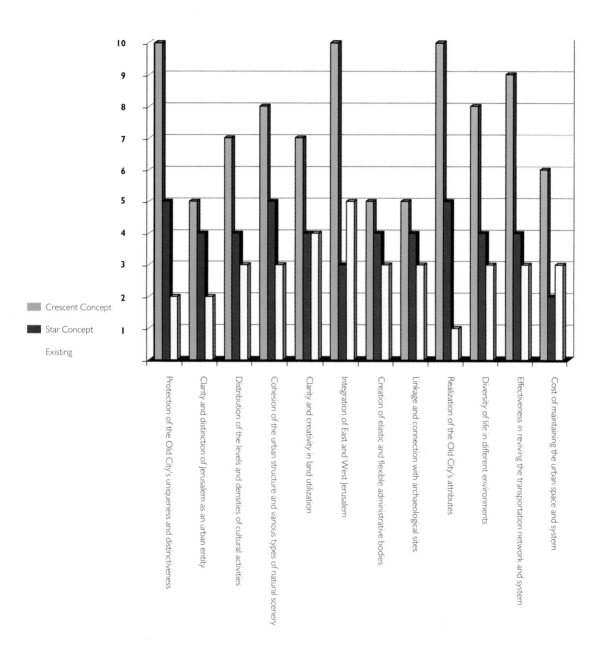

Key:
- Crescent Concept
- Star Concept
- Existing

Chart categories (x-axis):
- Protection of the Old City's uniqueness and distinctiveness
- Clarity and distinction of Jerusalem as an urban entity
- Distribution of the levels and densities of cultural activities
- Cohesion of the urban structure and various types of natural scenery
- Clarity and creativity in land utilization
- Integration of East and West Jerusalem
- Creation of elastic and flexible administrative bodies
- Linkage and connection with archaeological sites
- Realization of the Old City's attributes
- Diversity of life in different environments
- Effectiveness in reviving the transportation network and system
- Cost of maintaining the urban space and system

Figure 1
Evaluation of spatial planning concepts for Jerusalem

The rest of the area inside the first crescent—excluding the Old City itself—shall be allocated for cultural, social, and administrative activities, including symbolic government buildings connected with the functional structure of the Old City. Housing development shall continue in this area, but the establishment of high-rise buildings shall be prohibited because they would make it impossible to see the Old City proper from many locations. Meanwhile, in the area between the first and second crescents, urban, commercial, housing, administrative, and governmental activities shall develop. This area could see higher housing densities; high-rise buildings could be built here provided that they do not block existing views of the Old City. Thus the Old City shall be the point of orientation. We do not favor the establishment of high-rise hotels or public buildings inside the Old City parcel.

The area outside the outer crystal crescent, including the rest of Jerusalem District and the surrounding peripheral cities, must complement the heart of Jerusalem without repeating or competing with it. We view Jerusalem, its district, and the cities surrounding it and forming urban continuity with it as one urban unit. The aim of the crescent zone is to distribute functional and urban roles across this unit. The urban space of Jerusalem shall be divided into functional spatial blocs, each enjoying special characteristics and comparative advantages. Those blocs form components of a whole, balancing that whole and giving it strength and diversity without destroying the uniqueness of its core—the Old City.

The implementation of the crystal crescent zone must not be confined to the eastern sector of Jerusalem; it must include the western sector. In spite of the functional duality that might tend to arise in Jerusalem as the capital of two states, West Jerusalem is already the center of some economic and administrative activities that can complement those in East Jerusalem. Therefore, West Jerusalem can give East Jerusalem strength and enable it to compete with other national and regional cities.

Image of the Gates
The proposed gates along the outer boundary of the crystal crescent zone will link Jerusalem to the surrounding cities. These gates could conceivably be closed or converted to checkpoints, as at present (when nine Israeli checkpoints have been established on the roads leading to Jerusalem) or prior to 1850 (when the Old City's gates were closed at night). However, we are not proposing checkpoints—which act as barriers to movement and development—but rather open gates around which functional activities would be concentrated in order to reflect transition from one area to another. Functional activities could be either constructed or natural; for example, they could include a soccer stadium near Jaba'a village at the entrance of Jerusalem, a commercial center at the entrance to Jerusalem from the direction of

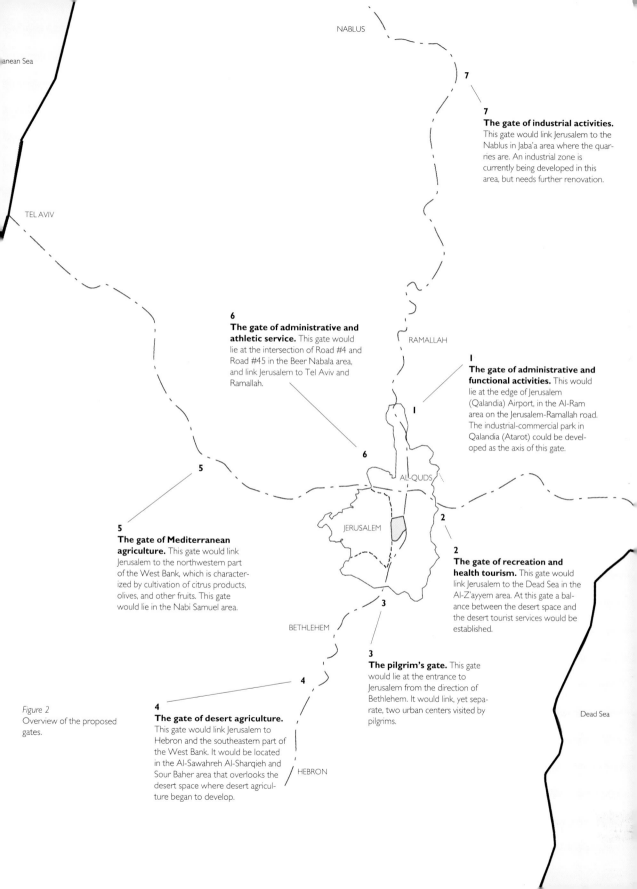

NABLUS

ranean Sea

7

7
The gate of industrial activities.
This gate would link Jerusalem to the Nablus in Jaba'a area where the quarries are. An industrial zone is currently being developed in this area, but needs further renovation.

TEL AVIV

6
The gate of administrative and athletic service. This gate would lie at the intersection of Road #4 and Road #45 in the Beer Nabala area, and link Jerusalem to Tel Aviv and Ramallah.

RAMALLAH

1
The gate of administrative and functional activities. This would lie at the edge of Jerusalem (Qalandia) Airport, in the Al-Ram area on the Jerusalem-Ramallah road. The industrial-commercial park in Qalandia (Atarot) could be developed as the axis of this gate.

1

6

5

AL-QUDS

5
The gate of Mediterranean agriculture. This gate would link Jerusalem to the northwestern part of the West Bank, which is characterized by cultivation of citrus products, olives, and other fruits. This gate would lie in the Nabi Samuel area.

JERUSALEM

2

2
The gate of recreation and health tourism. This gate would link Jerusalem to the Dead Sea in the Al-Z'ayyem area. At this gate a balance between the desert space and the desert tourist services would be established.

3

BETHLEHEM

3
The pilgrim's gate. This gate would lie at the entrance to Jerusalem from the direction of Bethlehem. It would link, yet separate, two urban centers visited by pilgrims.

4

Dead Sea

Figure 2
Overview of the proposed gates.

4
The gate of desert agriculture.
This gate would link Jerusalem to Hebron and the southeastern part of the West Bank. It would be located in the Al-Sawahreh Al-Sharqieh and Sour Baher area that overlooks the desert space where desert agriculture began to develop.

HEBRON

Ramallah, a tourist center at the entrance to Jerusalem from the direction of Bethlehem, and an open tourist center at the eastern entrance to Jerusalem. Therefore, the proposed open gates would represent points of transition or transformation from one type of construction, one set of functional activities, to another, giving those coming to Jerusalem a distinct impression of having entered the city. Similarly, each of the Old City's gates gives to those who enter through it a distinct sense of arrival. We would like the open gates to convey to those entering East Jerusalem/Al-Quds some of the feeling of spirituality and uniqueness that a person has upon entering the Old City or first seeing the Holy Sanctuary and the Dome of the Rock.

Proposed Planning Concept

We have evaluated various plans for Jerusalem and chosen concentric development utilizing the crystal-crescent pattern for the urban and functional form of Jerusalem as the concept that will direct the proposed plan.

The mission of the proposed planning concept can be summarized in the following points:

- The Old City shall remain the heart of Jerusalem, the core of its urban and functional formation.
- Planning shall begin from the existing structure of Jerusalem and its district. It shall aim at adjusting the existing situation while preserving Jerusalem's distinctiveness.
- The urban originality of Jerusalem shall be modernized through the proposed functional gates, which parallel the literal gates of the old Jerusalem.
- Jerusalem's religious status shall be reinforced. Jerusalem shall also attain national and international centrality as an economic and urban heart.
- Jerusalem and its district shall be divided into integrated urban and functional blocs that exist in unity and balance.
- An elastic urban structure shall be created that gives individuals and commercial and administrative institutions the choice to settle in it.
- The current urban and geopolitical impediments and limitations shall be overcome for the sake of the city's future.

The Crescent Model

Main Elements of the Planning Concept

The following is a brief summary of the elements of the proposed concept (in no particular order):

- The Old City within the wall is to be revived.

- The crystal-crescent zone is actually defined by two crescents, one surrounding the Old City and the second surrounding Jerusalem and forming a buffer separating it from the various urban extensions of Jerusalem District and from the surrounding cities.

- The new gates are to be located at the outer boundaries of the crystal crescent zone, on the main roads connecting Jerusalem to surrounding cities.

- The expansion of cities or the establishment of new cities through the expansion of villages shall take place outside the crystal-crescent zone.

- The Old City parcel includes the Old City influence area, the crystal crescent surrounding the Old City, the western sides of the Mount of Olives and Al-Masharef Mountain, Silwan, Ras Al-Amoud, and Al-Thawri.

- The current axis of urban growth extends along Nablus-Jerusalem-Bethlehem road.

- The rural area outside the crystal crescent comprises the desert area and villages that extend from Al-Sawahreh Al-Sharqieh in the south along the eastern sides of the Mount of Olives and Al-Masharef Mountain to Mukhmas village in the north. This also includes the agricultural villages to the northwest of Jerusalem.

- West Jerusalem is a diverse urban unit distinct from East Jerusalem.

- Diversity of housing densities shall create balance and cohesion between an urban space that feeds itself and has a dense bloc structure, on the one hand, and grid growth, on the other. In order to create these balances, the proposed planning concept advocates distributing housing densities and heights of buildings inside the urban space so as to create diversity and balance between the urban environment and its functional structure. Figure 3 illustrates the proposed distribution of densities according to the different urban environmental blocs. The proposed averages of building heights aim at creating organized, cohesive, and integrated skylines. However, it is possible for distinct buildings to form orientation points within the urban blocs, that is, landmarks or functional nodes, provided that they do not compete with or block the buildings that represent the heart of Jerusalem—the Holy

Sanctuary and the Dome of the Rock in the Old City parcel.

It would be premature to enter into the design details of the urban masses in this context; however, we hope to do so in the future. Concerning the relation between functional structure and urban space, we believe in distributing functional activities according to the comparative advantages of each planning bloc. Nevertheless, we proposed the establishment of centers of services and economic and administrative activities within the urban space.

The Plan

The planning concept comprises three factors: image, value, and function. The image of the crescent concept has been discussed extensively above; below, value and function are considered further.

Value

In the proposed crystal-crescent concept the crescents area, especially the external crescent, represents a value that balances the grid- and radial-type urban growth of Jerusalem by creating an ecologically unique area at the level of the metropolitan urban space. This area must be refined to produce a balanced urban environment that can feed and preserve itself and prevent the formation of a pressurized urban environment.

The crystal-crescent concept allows development and growth through the establishment of an integrated, hierarchical transportation and roads network. It encourages circular, grid, or radial urban growth, depending on the planning unit.

Function

The Old City area, the crystal crescent, and the functional "open" gates form the central components of our proposed planning concept. This concept seeks to develop Jerusalem as a regional, national, and international center. This requires the establishment of international functions and activities within the middle region of the crystal crescent. These would include the following:

- Local government center. Jerusalem is currently the capital of the Hebrew state and will be the capital of the Palestinian state. As Jerusalem is already an Israeli government city, a Palestinian governmental city forming an urban mass inside the urban space must be established. This mass must include several governmental buildings, either concentrated in one area or distributed over East Jerusalem. Such buildings can be outside the Old City parcel area except the Parliament, the Presidential Palace, and the Supreme Court of Justice, which should be located inside the Old City parcel in an area overlooking the Old City due to the symbolism of such a linkage.

The Crescent Model

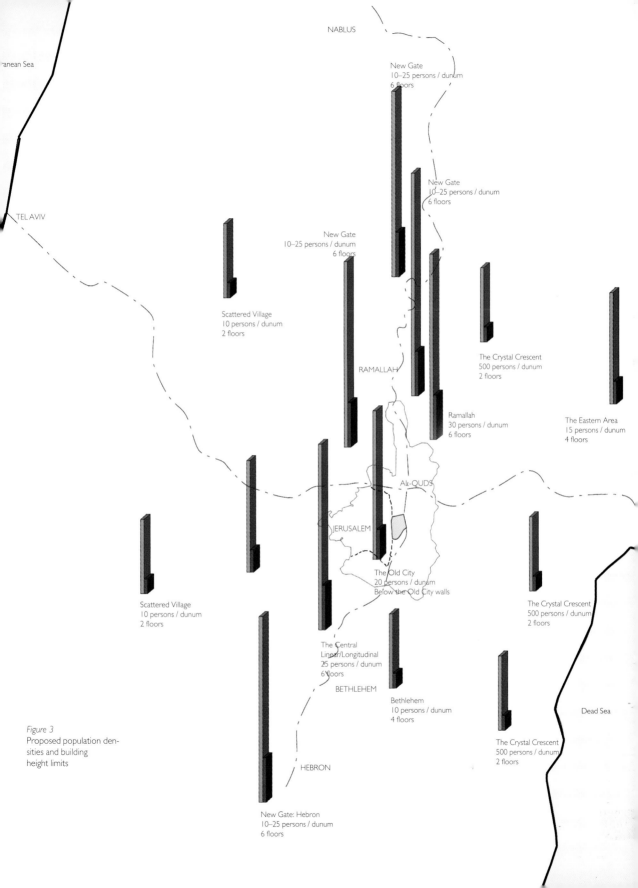

NABLUS

New Gate
10–25 persons / dunum
6 floors

New Gate
10–25 persons / dunum
6 floors

ranean Sea

TEL AVIV

New Gate
10–25 persons / dunum
6 floors

Scattered Village
10 persons / dunum
2 floors

The Crystal Crescent
500 persons / dunum
2 floors

RAMALLAH

Ramallah
30 persons / dunum
6 floors

The Eastern Area
15 persons / dunum
4 floors

AL-QUDS

JERUSALEM

The Old City
20 persons / dunum
Below the Old City walls

The Crystal Crescent
500 persons / dunum
2 floors

Scattered Village
10 persons / dunum
2 floors

The Central
Linear/Longitudinal
25 persons / dunum
6 floors

BETHLEHEM

Bethlehem
10 persons / dunum
4 floors

Dead Sea

Figure 3
Proposed population den-
sities and building
height limits

HEBRON

The Crystal Crescent
500 persons / dunum
2 floors

New Gate: Hebron
10–25 persons / dunum
6 floors

- Jerusalem (Qalandia) Airport. This shall supply air transport services to all of metropolitan Jerusalem. A part of the airport shall be located inside the crystal crescent, while the other part (including the accompanying service and industrial buildings) shall be located in the adjacent industrial and service area.

- A metropolitan athletic center shall include a football stadium and playgrounds.

- Metropolitan industrial parks shall be distributed along the boundaries of the crystal crescent in Qalandia (Atarot), Jaba'a, and Hizma.

- A commercial belt shall be developed along which metropolitan commercial activities are distributed. This belt starts at the heart of the Old City and runs along the north and south axes. In addition, commercial centers shall be established throughout the metropolitan space.

- A health center and a national university hospital shall provide health services to the residents of Jerusalem in particular and to those of Palestine in general. This complex shall include health research centers and facilities for holding international conferences.

- International research centers in resolution of ethnic, religious, and sociopolitical conflicts shall be established. Such centers, like the Al-Tantour Center, shall also hold international conferences.

- National museums and theaters shall provide cultural services to Palestine and the surrounding region.

- Functional centers will form around the gates, as described above.

- The crystal-crescent area shall include green zones, nature reserves, and recreational areas in order to preserve the distribution of land uses and the skyline in the space surrounding the city.

- Residential areas shall differ in their quality, density, and height.

Strategic Planning Issues for the Jerusalem Area
The following is a brief summary of issues affecting implementation of the crystal-crescent and functional-gates concepts.

- The Palestinians may promote the proposed planning pattern through official and unofficial means. They must take initiative and increase awareness.

- The Palestinians may discuss the proposed planning concept with the Israeli authorities and Israeli politicians.

- Increased national and international awareness of planning considerations in Jerusalem must be sought.

- The new pattern must be promoted by professionals and academicians, politicians and ordinary people, a local and international information campaign; they shall organize design competitions, hold detailed planning festivals, and prepare graduate-level projects for university students.

- Work must be coordinated with Israeli institutions and authorities for the sake of developing selected projects in ideal or representative locations.

- The support of international donors must be gained.

- An information campaign is needed that aims at stopping Israeli actions and activities that contradict the proposed planning concept, such as the expansion of settlements. For example, the Palestinians must work on stopping the expansion of Ma'ale Adumim settlement in order to protect the proposed eastern gate.

Warnings

During the preparation of this planning concept we conducted interviews and meetings with a large number of individuals having various roles and responsibilities. We found that any idea concerning Jerusalem can receive two completely contradictory interpretations. For example, there are some who see the crystal crescent as a means of separating Jerusalem from its Palestinian hinterland, and therefore as a tool suiting Israeli policy. I would like to emphasize that our planning concept does not promote this separation. On the contrary, it seeks to ensure Palestinian demographic, economic, and institutional growth inside the crystal-crescent space and therefore to increase Palestinians' linkage with Jerusalem.

Moreover, the existence of Israeli settlements outside the Jerusalem area and outside the crystal crescent does contradict the planning concept since the future of those settlements has not yet been determined. Although those settlements have been established in violation of international law, they are currently exist and any planning concept must discuss short- and long-term scenarios involving their continued existence. We suppose that the near political future will involve political separation between Israel and a Palestinian state and will therefore lead to decreasing Israeli settlement in the Palestinian land. Nevertheless, we do not suggest the removal of the Jewish residents from their settlements; they may continue to live in the settlements under the Palestinian state.

It is important to point out that our planning concept presents scenarios but does not make policy. It depends purely on professional considerations and does not assume adherence or advocate a certain political position. We are presenting it to decision makers as one alternative for urban planning in Jerusalem. We know that any planning solution has political dimensions and implications, but the current planning concept has been, to the best of our ability, devised and proposed in a professional, nonpolitical manner.

My Winter Dreams

Achva Benzinberg Stein

The people who reside in Jerusalem, regardless of their religious or political affiliations, relate to the land ideologically. That is, their connection to the land is determined by the agricultural origins of their faiths and by the continuous upholding of traditional principles of natural resources exploitation. The value of the ecosystem as a whole for sustaining life—or even the economic, cultural, and aesthetic importance of maintaining a diverse landscape—has barely reached public consciousness. Fauna and flora, soil and water are viewed as assets to be manipulated and utilized for immediate human use only. This view, tragically, is the only belief equally shared by nearly all, regardless of place of habitation, gender, age, religion, or race.

True, many scientists and laypeople are interested in maintaining nature preserves. However, these places are located outside the urban area. The environment consists of species large and small, many of which are seemingly insignificant. Bacteria, algae, lichen, mosses, insects, and rodents are all necessary for the functioning of an ecosystem. However, we have waged war on all species, most of which we have deemed to be neither important nor useful. Even in created gardens these life-forms are banished and viewed as hazardous. Under certain laws governing hygiene—laws that are, by the way, scientifically unfounded—restrictions have been put on raising domestic animals or letting certain plants grow in the city, leading to a situation where many species that were once the companions of human habitation have disappeared. People in the Middle East have yet to learn to live harmoniously, not only with themselves and their neighbors, but with the living world around them.

In the city, designed gardens and parks are the most common places available for interaction with nature. The form and content of these gardens are based on socioeconomic and aesthetic concepts borrowed from Western Europe and the United States, and are solely devoted to recreation. Furthermore, the quantity of water required to maintain the palette of exotic plants thought desirable by most people is incongruent with the local climate and with the character of the soil. The Middle East, part of the cradle of the hydrological civilizations, has forgotten the lesson of their destruction, despite large-scale unearthing of the past and despite the pride invested in archaeological and historical findings by both Israelis and Palestinians. As in

most other urban locations, they live in a parasitic relationship to their surroundings, wastefully sucking scarce resources from the countryside and returning them polluted by-products.

For generations the occupations of Jerusalem's inhabitants have been tied to those religious, educational, and governmental institutions that dominate the life of the city. As a result, the upbringing of each new generation places a heavy emphasis on the continuation of political and religious ideology and on their symbolic outgrowths, rather than on the preservation of life.

In this city people forget that there is life outside their minds, that they are part of a fragile web of life suspended in a delicate balance, a web that includes all the species that share the earth with us.

Years ago, while I was riding with my father from Tel Aviv to Jerusalem, the taxi driver got into minor traffic accident with another car, which was driving at excessive speed. As usual, everyone got out and started shouting. The taxi driver reproached the careless driver, calling him *ocher Israel* (one who hates and destroys the people of Israel). The driver screamed that the taxi driver had no right to call him such names because, he said, "I will die for my country anytime." My father shot back: "It won't hurt you to learn to live for your country for once."

I was about nine. It was the first time that the concept of learning to live had been raised, and the meaning of the commitment to die for the country had been questioned. The old road that we have all been speeding down together for so long has not led to an understanding of the value of life. It has been based on the values of power and control, on doctrines and ideal solutions which, when uttered publicly with the right rituals, can send people off to kill one another while those who orchestrate the dance of death remain unaffected.

This thinking is perpetuated in our children. We program them to believe in uni-dimensional solutions to every problem, to believe that the temporarily mighty and the ragingly disaffected are either wrong or right. The few books I have read on the "question of Jerusalem" have only strengthened my belief that all those who claim that they speak objectively for either side are fanning the flames of an ideology that can yield only hate and destruction.

We are witnessing a dark time for Jerusalem now. Every possible road toward destruction and collision has been cleared and opened. Every shred of hope is buried under a mountain of religious and political propaganda.

The Israeli poet Yehuda Amichai wrote in his poem "Tourists":

Once I sat on the steps by a gate at David's tower. I placed my two heavy baskets at my side. A group of tourists was standing around their guide and I became their target marker. "You see that man with the baskets? Just right of his head there's an arch from the Roman period. Just right of his head." "But he is moving, he's moving!" I said to myself: redemption will come only if their guide tells them: "You see that arch from the Roman period? It's not important: but next to it, left and down a bit, there sits a man who's bought fruits and vegetables for his family."[1]

[1] In Yehuda Amichai, trans. by Glenda Abramson and Tudor Parfitt, *Poems of Jerusalem* (Riverdale-on-Hudson: The Sheep Meadow Press, 1988).

When asked to present some of my projects in Jerusalem, I hesitated and pro-
crastinated. I could only offer a pictorial view, not designed projects, and only for the
Israeli part of Jerusalem.

I also hesitated because I had not realized, in the past, that I was stepping
behind architects and builders who straighten traffic patterns and "re-create" historical streets, who construct commercial housing ventures for rich expatriates and
provide for the well-to-do. These projects reflected the habit of providing fait
accompli solutions (*uvdot bashetach*), which, while they may seem to help politicians
achieve their aims, have meant pain and destruction for the people of Jerusalem. In
addition, they have cheapened the meaning of history and sold the city to the highest bidders. The speculative rationale has become the basis of action, that rationale
itself based on the presumed importance of commercialism and on the worship of
the golden calf (*egel paz*).

My Jerusalem is the old Israeli (West) Jerusalem, the area where the Jewish population created a new city, where they live, study, shop, and pray. I still carry with me
the memory of the city before the flag of "Gold, Copper, and Light." was raised.
There I used to visit relatives and there, later, I worked, siting housing (*shikunim*) and
designing parks. I loved the Jerusalem of olive groves, Aleppo pines growing on limestone, and thin mountain soil. I loved early spring, when anemones dotted the sides
of the roads and where cyclamen would pop out from between the rocks or in the
spaces between the buildings. I loved to touch the stone walls of the old buildings,
real stones on small-scale structures, not the thin veneer found on high-rise buildings

that falsely recalls the construction traditions of the past. I loved the snow that came once every few years and covered the city with a white blanket, giving us permission to leave our car stuck in the middle of the road and walk slowly back home. I recall the small-town atmosphere where the butcher knew who would buy his "white meat" (pork) without squealing on him to the authorities, where one could find real bread, dark and heavy with lots of wheat seeds during the week, light and sweet for the Shabbat. That Jerusalem retained evidence of my family's contribution to the building of the new city in the form of a few cast-iron manhole covers carrying our family name, installed by my grandfather before 1940. (Palestinians who knew my family from that time told my father that some were still to be discovered in the Old City of Jerusalem.)

Since I have been away from battlefields, my muses could whisper more loudly in my ear that dreaming and imagining another Jerusalem is far more rewarding than seeing the reality of the situation. "The flowers of spring are winter dreams related at the breakfast table of the angels," said Kahlil Gibran. Then let the angels seed my winter dreams in Jerusalem's marginal land, the vacant lots, the discarded gardens, all the urban waste places. There lies my "urban ore." These sites are the opposite of the "pedigree garden" or the "political landscape"; they are the living and nonliving entities that have not been deemed useful and thus have not been imprisoned in the straitjacket of existing culture. These sites are the locations of my hopes and dreams. Maybe here a completely new road can be delin-eated—a road paved with small-scale gestures and few overt lessons. And maybe, while we mark a new path illuminated by daily facts, by our con-nection to the natural physical world, we can teach ourselves to coexist with our neighbors, to enjoy work as much as play, and to reexamine women's traditional and nontraditional roles.

With so many places of religious worship, war monuments, archaeological restoration projects, political institutions of justice and fame, maybe we can afford to create specks of light and beauty (*nekudot chen*) that people can find along their daily route to and from their regular destinations. Places dedicated to the conservation of life. Places protected from the bulldozers, from the pens and the drafting pencils of the grand planners, places that resist unnecessary development. Maybe we can create spaces for men, women, and children to live their everyday lives in spite of our educated concepts of beautification. Maybe these specks of living systems can help children grow up more tolerant, less aggressive, and more observant of the life around them. Such qualities may better prepare them to live with others.

Can we find a location for the animals, the insects, and the unimportant plants, sites where the caper and the hyssop growing in the Wailing Wall, feeding birds and butterflies, are allowed to expand everywhere? Can we let standing pools in the winter remain as places where tadpoles develop into frogs and toads, where the turtles are permitted to procreate without being stoned to death by children who have never seen wildlife except in the zoo or on TV? Can we consent to let trees be reduced to dust by termites? Can we let the swallows build their nests and the spiders build their webs and catch their prey without being attacked by cleaning brooms? Can the so-called weeds grow unchecked so that native animal species have sustenance? Why build a virtual reality in our machines when better lessons can be learned faster from even a managed landscape?

Can people create small gardens where they cultivate vegetables, flowers, and herbs—not in faraway places that they can only visit by car or bus, but all around, all over the city? Can we watch hens and roosters, and feed goats and milk them? Can we see rabbits procreate, geese and ducks multiply? Can we restore some respect for physical labor as opposed to grandiose development plans and business schemes? Can we learn some patience and respect for life by simply watching it grow, rather than by observing it in fast-forward through the lenses of our machines? Is it possible to bring up a new generation that is interested in its actual place of living, not just in its ideas about that place?

Can we reincorporate water-harvesting measures into the urban structure, as we have incorporated solar panels into housing design? Can we create a system of underground cisterns, finding additional ways to capture surface water during the rainy season? Can we divert wastewater to purification ponds and retention basins? Can we spend some time saving resources rather than consuming more and more? Is it possible to understand the power of the wind and its relation to our energy needs? In ancient Jerusalem, houses were cooled naturally. Is the old system of passive cooling truly dead, or it is just missing in action in the war that the Brutalists and the Functionalists have been fighting on the battleground of modern architecture?

The Hebrew word for city is a feminine form. Jerusalem is especially so. All our writers and poets, from Biblical times to the present, have used endearing female terms when referring to Jerusalem. The predominance of male ideas and values, however, designates Jerusalem as a male place. Even the gardens, which should be designed for the use of all young children, favor the aggressive boys, the old men, and those who are in charge of taking care of the young. There are very few places where females, especially young ones, can have a place of their own. No place is assigned to them. The loss of traditional female social support is evident not only here, but throughout the daily activity of the city. Have knitting, embroidering, weaving, exchanging advice on healing and cooking—all the occupations of the "nurturing arts"—been denigrated to such a lowly position that we cannot consider them part of our urban culture? Or can we reestablish the value of informal feminine exchanges and activities, encourage the allocation of physical spaces for these activities on a par with the space allocated for men's activities?

Can the city of Jerusalem learn to be more inclusive, more ethnographic than ethnocentric, less bound by middle-class pretensions in its aesthetic understanding of place? Is it possible that the more we think about the conservation of nature and of resources, the more we will seek to preserve knowledge about the management of daily life? Can Israeli Jerusalem learn to live in peace within its own boundaries, learn its limitations, become mature enough to let others live in the conditions they choose?

Peace is a long process, and can be sustained only by generations following a slower road, one based on a different approach to life. I still dream that a new breed of people may develop in this city. I still dream that we can provide some of the conditions needed for a healthy physical and mental environment. I believe that many people on both sides have cherished longings similar to mine.

I trust that more meetings shall occur among those who dream as I do. When this happens, we will agree to discard the narrow vision "that exalts the busyness of the ant above the singing of the grasshopper" (Kahlil Gibran). I also hope that we will considered the maintenance of life, the conservation of resources, and the nurturing of our environment as our most precious mis-

sion, and will not "claim that [we] can draw the line between necessities and luxuries." (Kahlil Gibran). I hope that we will not disregard the voice of the few (like myself) who sit upon a cloud and do not see the boundaries line between one country and another. Clouds begin by floating above us, but they also reach the earth in form of rain, giving birth to the seeds and continuing the cycle of life. When we have more such dreams, maybe we will be able to construct a meaningful partnership between the Israeli and the Palestinian in Jerusalem.

I believe that learning to live together starts by trying to live better oneself. Collaboration begins apart. Therefore, I hope that someone in the Palestinian part of the city will construct her own personal dream, depicting her people's everyday needs. Not in anger, but in the spirit that for years has typified both nations, the spirit of survival by living.

The Subversion of Jerusalem's Sacred Vernaculars:
Four New Planning Tools for a Holy Environment

Eyal Weizman

The frontiers of conflict in the Middle East run through the center of Jerusalem, fragmenting its urban fabric, creating and exacerbating religious, political, national, cultural, and ethnic differences. As a consequence, a series of enclaved neighborhoods are juxtaposed that are estranged from and incompatible with one another. Their interweaving and overlapping frontiers form invisible boundaries that enclose individual territories which operate according to religious or national laws. It is within these territories that the different urban vernaculars of Jerusalem are formed.

The term *vernacular*, beyond its use to refer to the traditional style of a locality, relates to a mode of architectural production that is less designed then evolved, in which the built environment is formed according to the demands of commonplace needs and local culture. The most widely perceived Jerusalem vernacular is that of a cliché pastoral Mediterranean hill-town, as generated by the local topography, materials, and weather. However, Jerusalem's many other vernaculars are the material and formal products of other traditions, born out of an evolutionary process that has developed along the city's ever-changing religious, political, national, cultural, legal, and financial realities.

A vernacular condition relies on the relation between a *boundary*, a *territory*, and a *law*. The *law* is that which defines the use of the *territory*; this law could be civil, religious, normative, or merely a behavioral etiquette. The *boundary* is the edge beyond which a certain kind of urban coherence ends. This edge could be material or immaterial, perceived or imperative. The marking of a boundary applies the authority of a law to a territory, which, in return, manifests in its urban fabric the consequences of that law. The constitution of a boundary reveals the limits of a law, and its characteristics reflect both the nature of a territory and its relation to its neighbor.

The strength of a vernacular condition depends on the vigor with which environmental forces act upon urban territories. In Jerusalem a fundamentally extreme national and religious environment creates a strong vernacular condition. The city could not escape a controlled and dictated development and, instead of growing according to the urban logic of its needs, has been swept along by the ever-changing political desires of its rulers.

In a strongly vernacular environment, architectural and urban intervention may take place within the straitjacket of preexisting constraints or else seek ways to act against environmental conditions, and change them.

Recreating Jerusalem—
an Eruv line connecting
homes in Brooklyn, New
York.

Could Jerusalem's strong vernacular conditions be stretched, subverted, relaxed, broken, or transgressed so that the city may develop to the benefit of all its inhabitants?

This essay tries to answer this question by recounting four separate episodes, each describing a different urban vernacular and each revisited in proposals. Transformation of the urban vernaculars of Jerusalem thus becomes the means by which change can be made in the city. Jerusalem is a strange city, full of unique situations and bizarre daily realities. These form the background.

Boundary and Transgression: Tracing the Eruv of Jerusalem[1]

1 Coauthored with Manuel Herz; based on "Between City and Desert," *AAfiles* 34 (Spring 1998).

Besides its complex political edges, Jerusalem is surrounded by a boundary that defines not its municipal border, but the geographical limits of one of its religions. The Eruv—a metal wire stretched over high poles—encapsulates the Jewish parts of the city, and prescribes a different religious use mode within it.

The path of the Eruv cuts across the varied fabrics of the city. It follows the eastern wall of the Old City and crosses at its northeastern end into a deep valley. It then climbs up Mt. Scopus and passes beside the Hadassah hospital. From there it follows the new road leading to the Jewish hilltop enclave neighborhoods of Pisgat Zeev and Ramot, and after encircling them it turns southward again, following the other side of the same road, avoiding the Arab neighborhoods to the left and right of it. For a while it follows Tel Aviv Road, then leaves it to go around Ein Kerem and the other Hadassah municipal hospital. It proceeds along a dirt road that passes by the construction sites of the controversial Har Homa neighborhood. From there it crosses a disused British-era railway station and turns into Gilo Park, across from the Hebron road. For a few hundred meters, it runs parallel to the fence of Kibbutz Ramat-Rachel, an enclave within the municipal boundaries of the city, following it around the Peace Forest, then proceeds along the edge of the Arab neighborhood of A-Tur and back to the Old City walls.

This path describes only the current Eruv; the Eruv is a mobile frontier that is always being rerouted to encapsulate every newly built Jewish neighborhood in the city. The path of the Eruv marks therefore the momentary state of the city's Jewish neighborhoods. The Eruv of Jerusalem is about 100 km long, but its metal wire, the only necessary element of its construction, weighs no more than 80 kg.

Urban boundaries that
demarcate the Eruv
in Jerusalem.

Along its path the Eruv boundary manifests itself in different ways. Beyond its presence as a series of poles strung with wire, the Eruv, like a giant-scale act of urban bricolage, incorporates and uses the existing boundaries and urban scars of Jerusalem: fences, walls, concrete decks, metal handrails, rock faces, house facades, a water reservoir, a railway line, a deep valley to mark its boundary, saving the use of poles and string. These elements could be considered parts of an Eruv boundary, according to laws described in the Talmud, on the single condition that they be higher or deeper than 1 meter. Seeing the city as an object, the Eruv reinterprets and reuses its props and imbues them with another meaning.

The Eruv is actually a construction—of poles and wire—or a rereading of existing boundaries, undertaken to change the religious definition of the area within its circumference. For believing Jews, it marks the transition of the area it encapsulates from the public domain (*reshut harabim* in Hebrew) to the private domain (*reshut hayahid*) during the Sabbath. The Eruv thus temporarily turns the city into an overgrown Talmudic "home." The laws that define and regulate the behavior and prohibitions in one's home, different in most cases from the laws that govern outdoors, apply thereafter in the public domain. The erection of the Eruv boundary redefines the territory within it and consequently changes the sets of laws that apply to it.

This symbolic transformation of a public domain into a private domain is based on a semiotic chain described in the Eruv treatise in the Talmud: In order to turn the city into a "home" it suffices to build a roof over it. To signify a roof it suffices to build a continuous wall. A wall could conceivably have any number of doors. To signify a door it suffices to build a crossbeam. The crossbeam can be made of any material of any thickness, as long as it is capable of withstanding an ordinary wind; thus, a wire stretched over thin poles suffices. The Eruv of Jerusalem indeed consists mostly of a wire stretched over a series of metal poles. In order for the Eruv to be complete and applicable, however, it is essential that a continuous, undisturbed circumference be achieved.

When the continuous boundary has been achieved, the public domain is considered a "roofed" area and is thereafter defined as a private domain according to the Talmudic law. A part of the city becomes, for the period of one day every week, one single home.

The Subversion of Jerusalem's Sacred Vernaculars

Eruv line recently moved
to include new construction

stone wall

army barrier

fence

army barrier

Tel Aviv road

Eruv on both sides
of the road

fence

reservoir

fence

fence around
YAD VASHEM
Holocaust museum

cliff edge

KIDRON valley

stone wall of Old City

fence of Peace Forest

fence of
HADASSAH hospital

housing walls

fence of an
olive orchard

fence along
dirt road

fence along
railway line

fence of kibbutz
RAMAT-RACHEL

fence along
dirt road

channel way

The boundary of the
Jerusalem Eruv encloses and
defines the Jewish parts of
the city, separating it into a
religiously defined "inside"
and "outside." The Eruv
expands whenever the
municipal boundary of
Jerusalem is enlarged or
when a new Jewish neighborhood is added to the city. It is
thus a flexible entity that
marks at any given moment
the geographical extent of
the expansion of Jerusalem's
Jewish neighborhoods.

Eyal Weizman

Eruv line (marked yellow) following the wall of the Old City of Jerusalem.

Both by the introduction of signifying elements and by the designation of existing physical elements as signifiers, apparently absurd situations are created: the city becomes a private space, urban elements become walls and doors. All such references are visible and comprehensible only to those people for whom the Eruv is an important amenity, and invisible to those for whom it means nothing. This constitution of a boundary by minimal, strategic intervention acts to appropriate and subvert an existing set of laws in a given territory, rather than to replace those laws with another, newer set.

The impetus to erect an Eruv is the difference between the laws that apply to private domains and those that apply to public domains. Since the Talmudic laws of the private domain are more lenient there is a real benefit in redefining the public domain as private so that the more lenient laws will be made applicable there. Specifically, movement and the carrying of objects on the Sabbath are severely restricted on the public domain by laws specified in the Bible and the Talmud, but are not restricted in the private domain. This prohibition on carrying is expanded to include the use of walking sticks and wheelchairs, the pushing of baby carriages, and even the carrying of house keys. These prohibitions severely limit the movements of elderly people, parents of small children, and the disabled. The Eruv is erected to relax this harsh law; a method of circumventing the religious territorial prohibition by the redefinition of the outdoor territories. By changing the definition of a territory it changes the law that applies to it—carrying becomes permissible within the Eruv's circumference, as everything within its perimeter is considered one's home. (The Eruv has earned its Ashkenazi nickname, the "magic schlepping circle.")

Reconsidering the existing definitions of urban territories, the Eruv shifts the current notion and meaning of the private and the public in the urban landscape. The public space is not the space of exchange and activity but a restrictive space of limitation. It is the private which becomes the space of liberation and interaction.

A parallel definition of spaces and domains is thus developed. The privatization

The Subversion of Jerusalem's Sacred Vernaculars

of the territory surrounded by the Eruv does not entail ownership; the space is private in terms of religious law, but is still public in terms of civil law.

As an urban apparatus the Eruv thus structures and permits a more lenient urban attitude than that originally defined by the law. The urban consequences of this leniency are pronounced visibility and presence in the public space of groups within the religious community that were previously excluded from that space. An important point about this leniency is that it comes from the same legal tradition that imposed the prohibition in the first place. 2

2 This essay is indebted to the beautifully sensitive work of the French artist Sophie Calle, who upon her visit to Jerusalem in 1996 traced both the boundary and the concept of the Eruv of Jerusalem. Sofie Calle, *L'erouv de Jerusalem, actes sud,* 1996.

Could the Eruv become a model for more general and perhaps secular urban attitudes in Jerusalem?

According to the approach promoted by the Eruv, the potential to generate urban change lies in particularities that are already embedded in the urban status quo. This mode of intervention is not revolutionary, but transgressive. If a revolutionary act implies the replacement of one set of laws with another, a transgressive act seeks in the existing legal order its potentials, contradictions, and loopholes. It challenges and manipulates this very stuff to create a new urban reality through the rereading of an existing vocabulary.

The Eruv demonstrates that without the need for an overwhelming physical intervention, an act of naming has the power to create a new urban reality, while leaving the existing fabric intact. This technique of naming rather then changing, separating, or constructing is an economical device that could offer elegant solutions to longstanding political problems.

Jerusalem's complex web of cultures, legal entanglements, and political constraints could offer the material for such manipulations and potentials within which new situations could be conceived. This approach will therefore aim at the very heart of its urban problems.

Manufacturing Sacredness
The stones that clad Jerusalem are to a great extent quarried in Israeli-occupied areas around Jerusalem.

The Subversion of Jerusalem's Sacred Vernaculars

Storrs' Stare of Medusa: The Jerusalem Stone Bylaw

Jerusalem is literally a city built upon rock. From that rock, cutting soft but drying hard, has for three thousand years been quarried the clear white stone, weathering blue-grey or amber-yellow with time, whose solid walls, barrel vaulting and pointed arches have preserved through the centuries a hallowed and immemorial tradition.
—Sir Ronald Storrs, Acting Military Administrator of Palestine (November 1918 to March 1919) and Military Governor of Jerusalem (December 1917 to July 1920)

The external walls of all buildings shall be constructed of stone unless the approval in writing of the Jerusalem District Building and Town Planning Commission has been first obtained.
— Jerusalem Town-Planning Ordinance, 1936

3 The stone demanded by Jerusalem bylaws arrives from quarries in the vicinity of Jerusalem and Bethlehem. The geological formation of the indigenous Cretaceous and Tertiary rocks belongs to the Turonian period and consists mainly of limestone, dolomite, and sometimes chalk. The texture particular to the stone's surface is caused by the abundance of marine carbonate sediments. On the emotional effect of this stone we can learn from a typical text for the marketing of Jerusalem stone:
Regardless of faith— Christians, Moslems or Jews— Jerusalem is the holiest city for all. "Jerusalem Stone" is a precious stone, carved from holy mountains of Jerusalem. The beauty and texture of the stone with its pink and purple shades is a wonderful masterpiece of nature.
—Jerusalem stone, Moshe Aizenman

Perhaps Jerusalem's best-known bylaw is the one enacted in 1918 by the first British military governor of the city, Sir Ronald Storrs, soon after he started his term in office. The first urban bylaw of the British Mandate in Palestine required square, dressed natural stone—Jerusalem stone[3]—for the facades and visible external walls of all new buildings constructed in the city. This historic bylaw, later confirmed by the Jerusalem District Building and Town Planning Commission in 1936, determined the image of Jerusalem more than any other law, bylaw, or program devised by the authorities over the subsequent eighty years.

Storrs was the officer in command of the battle for Jerusalem in General Allenby's army. So deep was his admiration for Jerusalem, fueled by romantic and religious zeal, that while fighting the Ottoman army, and subsequently taking Jerusalem off their hands, he issued an order stating that none of Jerusalem's buildings could be destroyed during the battle. Storrs' aim was to protect the Holy City as he imagined it, and repel all threats to its "hallowed and immemorial tradition." During the time of his rather peaceful reign, the city's growing poverty on the one hand and its rapid expansion on the other threatened to overrun its image much more than the potential destruction of war. Within the city walls, mud, cheap wood, and tin constructions were common in poorer areas, giving parts of the city the look of a shantytown, and although a more rapid expansion of the city, coinciding with the local emergence of concrete and the International Style, did not take place before the 1920s, new, mainly Jewish neighborhoods built outside of the city walls posed a visual threat to the visual basin of the Old City.

By enacting the bylaw calling for the stone finish, Storrs sought to regulate the city's appearance, to resist time and change. He could not have realized that by dressing Jerusalem in a single architectural uniform, he in effect created the conditions for its excessive expansion, self-replication, and sprawl as a single entity.

In the context of contemporary Jerusalem, the stone does more than just fulfill an aesthetic agenda of preservation: it defines visually the geographic limits of Jerusalem and more important—since Jerusalem is a holy city—marks the extent of its holiness.

The idea of Jerusalem as the City of God, and thus as a holy place, is entrenched in Judeo-Christian belief. In their Diaspora, Jews started yearning for a city that became in their imagination increasingly disassociated from the reality of the physical site.[4] Jerusalem itself became holy rather than a place containing holy sites.

If the city itself is holy, then, in the contemporary context, the totality of its buildings, roads, vegetation, infrastructure, neighborhoods, parking garages, shops, and workshops is holy. A special holy status is reserved for the ground. And if the ground is holy, its relocation as stones from the horizontal (earth) to the vertical (walls), from the quarries to the facades of buildings, transfers holiness further. As Jerusalem's ground paving of stone climbs up to wrap its facades, the new "ground topography" of holiness is extended.

When the city itself is holy, and when its boundaries are constantly being negotiated, redefined, and redrawn, holiness becomes a planning issue.

Shortly after the occupation of the eastern, Arab part of the city during the Six-Day War of 1967, the municipal boundaries of Israeli Jerusalem were expanded to include the Palestinian populated eastern parts as well as large empty areas around and far beyond them. (The municipal area of Jerusalem grew from 33.5 square kilometers in 1952 to 108 square kilometers in 1967.[5]) These "new territories" annexed to the city, designed as "reserves" for future Israeli expansions, were required to comply with Storrs' bylaw—their buildings to be clad in stone, preserving the traditional and familiar Jerusalem look—turning suburban neighborhoods, placed on remote and historically insignificant sites far from the historic center, into "Jerusalem," and thus participating in the city's sacredness.

The holy status, felt psychologically and defined visually in the stone, places every remote and newly built suburb well within the boundaries of "the eternally unified capital of the Jewish people."[6] Like the Gaze of Medusa, Storrs' law petrified new construction in new neighborhoods, suburbs, and settlements: shopping malls, kindergartens, community centers, synagogues, office buildings, electrical relay station, sports halls, and housing were covered in stone, and as far as the stone facades were extended, the holiness of Jerusalem sprawled. Holiness, as Meron Benvenisti writes, is a very political matter: "From the moment a particular area is designated as part of the Holy City, it comes under Jerusalem's religious laws, whose sole objective is to strengthen the spiritual ties between Jews and their sacred city."[7]

4 Under the prophet Zacharia of the Babylonian Diaspora, Jerusalem is first referred to as a metaphysical city—an ideal place and an earthly reflection of the heavenly kingdom. It is there that a relationship between the boundaries of the city and its sacredness is established.

1 And I lifted my eyes and saw, and behold, a man with a measuring line in his hand!

2 Then I said, "Where are you going?" And he said to me, "To measure Jerusalem, to see what is its breadth and what is its length."

3 And behold, the angel who talked with me came forward, and another angel came forward to meet him,

4 and said to him, "Run, say to that young man," Jerusalem shall be inhabited as villages without walls, because of the multitude of men and cattle in it.

5 For I will be to her a wall of fire round about, says the LORD, and I will be the glory within her.

6 Ho! ho! Flee from the land of the north, says the LORD; for I have spread you abroad as the four winds of the heavens, says the LORD.

7 Ho! Escape to Zion, you who dwell with the daughter of Babylon.

5 Facts based on: Chosen Maya, Shahar Naama, ed., *Statistical Yearbook of Jerusalem* No. 16, 1998 (Jerusalem: The Jerusalem Institute for Israel Studies and the Municipality of Jerusalem, 1999).

The Subversion of Jerusalem's Sacred Vernaculars

The establishment and growth of Jewish neighborhoods in areas beyond the 1967 border extended the application of Storrs' stone bylaw into areas far from the city center. Population migration to the eastern parts of the city had diluted the western center.

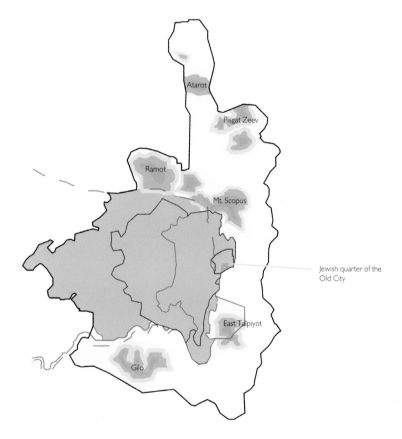

Atarot

Pisgat Zeev

Ramot

Mt. Scopus

Jewish quarter of the Old City

East Talpiyot

Gilo

Jerusalem's present municipal boundaries under Israeli sovereignty.

The armistice line of 1949. The de facto border between the western Jewish part of Jerusalem and the eastern Palestinian part until 1967.

Eyal Weizman

Manufacturing Sacredness
Stone cladding factory in
East Jerusalem.

The Subversion of Jerusalem's Sacred Vernaculars

6 Common pre-election political statement in Israel.

7 Meron Benvenisti, *City of Stone: The Hidden History of Jerusalem* (London: University of California Press, 1996), 52.

8 Benvenisti, 51.

Jerusalem did not grow and develop naturally. After the 1967 war the expansion of Jewish neighborhoods into Arab lands to the north and the east was designed to ensure the impossibility of a geographical redivision of the city into two distinct parts, Arab-Palestinian and Jewish. The fact that the new hilltop neighborhoods were located according to this political and strategic logic, rather than according to urban logic, has created a disaster on a colossal scale. The new neighborhoods demanded an ever-increasing paving of roads and an expensive network of infrastructure while their placement in remote locations left large empty areas between them and the historic city center.

The optimal boundaries of Jerusalem were not determined according to the criteria of economy or scale or efficiency of service delivery to its citizens, but in conformity to nationalist parameters. The bare hills and populated suburbs were conscripted to the internal and external political struggle, and from the moment they were declared part of the city, they were imbued with sanctity.[8]

In Plan No. 64 of the 1955 Israeli-devised Jerusalem masterplan, relating still only to the areas within the 1967 borders, the city classified zones in which the use of stone was required to varying degrees, depending on their historical value and relative "holiness." The historic city, the Old City, and the neighborhoods around it were required to have the most comprehensive use of stone cladding—on all visible planes of the building. In areas beyond the historic center the law became more lenient and allowed other materials to varying degrees on facades, while the industrial areas, which were built farthest from the then municipal boundaries of Jerusalem, were completely liberated from the use of stone. After the 1967 war, however, there was a change of policy.

The new suburban hilltop neighborhoods built beyond the 1967 lines, on areas annexed to the city, are located farthest from the center and describe the outermost circle. Nonetheless, the stone regulations that apply there are as strict as those called for in the city center. The symbolic center has been relocated to the periphery, leaving vast gaps in the urban fabric inbetween. The relocation of the center to the periphery was not only a symbolic move—the city inhabitants themselves, wary of the congested, multicultural, and disputed city center, opted for the ethnic, cultural, and social homogeneity of the periphery, leaving the city center divested of Jewish dwellings. Approximately 188,416 Jewish people migrated within Jerusalem between 1990 and 1997, more than half of them from the center of the western city to the new periphery.[9] These in-town migrants, seeking the aura of Jerusalem in its suburbs, have transplanted its holiness along with its stone.

9 Maya Chosen et al., 10.

The Jerusalem stone cladding has a different meaning for each of the groups that make up the diverse city. For the Palestinian Arab, stone is a traditional local construction material; for the Israeli Jew, it is imbued with the city's holiness. Whereas the Palestinians use stone as a matter of fact, for the Israeli builder, stone coating is required and specified by law. In this context the 1955 masterplan grants another important concession and incentive: Unlike other claddings, the stone, sometimes as thick as twenty-five centimeters, is allowed to project outside of the building envelope, thus occupying, on occasions where the building line corresponds with that of the street, public ground. The law acknowledges the fact that this cladding performs an important public function, and since public signs are meant to occupy public ground, the stone was allowed "to invade" the street.

The extension of the city's "holiness" to the new suburbs was conceived as part of an Israeli attempt to generate widespread public acceptance of the newly annexed territories, otherwise viewed as a political and urban burden. Whatever is called Jerusalem, by name and by the use of stone, lies at the heart of the Israeli consensus that "Jerusalem shall not be redivided." The cladding of buildings in stone is an architectural ritual whose repetition attempts to fabricate a collective memory serving a nationalistic agenda.

Jerusalem, as a name, as an idea, and as a city, has great influence on the psyche — a city that was always perceived as an idea rather than as concrete and earthly reality has no boundaries besides those in the mind. Thus the stone functions to connect the transformed geographical reality of Jerusalem with the ephemeral idea of the heavenly city. This politically conscious use of geographical identity relies heavily on stone as a signifier to call forth the image of a mystic past. The public acceptance of the expansion of Jerusalem is made possible by the replication of its "character" and "feel." The spectator is left incapable of drawing the boundary between the city and its idea, between its earthly geographical reality and a sense of sanctification and renewed holiness epitomized in the salvation of the ground.

Although originally conceived to protect and preserve an aesthetic status quo, Storrs' stone bylaw was extended by Israeli policy makers beyond the performance of mere aesthetic purposes. By visually defining the geographic limits of the city and marking the extent of its holiness, it has been made into a politically manipulative and colonizing architectural device.

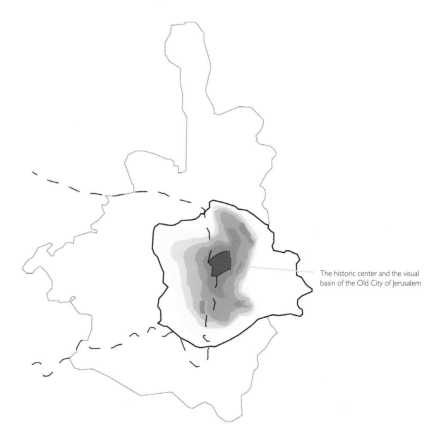

The historic center and the visual basin of the Old City of Jerusalem

Stripping Sacredness
Redefining the extent of the city's holiness by a gradient use of stone intensifying toward the Old City and its visual basin. This proposal leaves the Jewish bedroom suburbs out of the new boundaries of Jerusalem and asks for the return of the land to its original owner.

Urban Jetlag: Time Zone Regulation for Jerusalem

If dealing with space in Jerusalem is a political endeavor, time—the other manifestation of reality—could not escape a heavy-handed political intervention either. Ultra-Orthodox political parties, with strong grips over a succession of governments in Israel, manage more often than not to impose their laws on the rest of the country. Daylight saving time, a common practice in every modern nation, when applied in Israel will require observant Jews to wake up an hour earlier for their morning prayer, as the time of worship is defined by celestial composition rather than simple clock time. As winters near their end, long deliberations in parliament confirm a postponed implementation of daylight saving time as a part of a political compromise. The clocks are eventually moved forward a month after the rest of the world in late spring and back a month earlier in early autumn. Palestinians observe their own time, exclusively under the control of the Palestinian Authority and in tune with the rest of the world.

Although still under Israeli sovereignty, the Palestinians in Jerusalem abide by the Palestinian clock, manifesting by their use of time their civil difference and their rejection of the legitimacy of Israeli rule. Thus, during two months, in late spring and in early autumn, Palestinians and Israelis in Jerusalem live in different time zones. Time in Jerusalem is greatly defined by the city's strict licensing regulations. The opening times of shops and pubs, the operation and closure of institutions, banks, public transport, define the city's sense of time.

During the two-month time-zone shift, the use of time is differentiated by staggered sequencing of radio and television broadcast, opening times of schools and businesses, transport, and services—a temporal abnormality that creates bizarre and fantastic havoc in the city.

A Palestinian father could wake up to send his children to school and have another full hour before commencing work in the western side of the city. Israeli taxi drivers have to amend their schedules, according to differences in rush hours in the eastern part of the city.

Can urban time zones be used as tools in the urban planning of Jerusalem?

This situation borne out of a political-temporal dispute opens up the potential for the use of time zones as an effective tool in Jerusalem's urban planning. Time zoning, in effect, creates temporal shifts in the geographical application of existing diurnal time-based urban regulations. The use of time zones in the city transgress these regulations, thus affecting mainly the application of licensing laws without changing the original law.

Time zone boundaries, despite being immaterial, assign in their path a defined territory, with a designated mode of action. Time regulates one's activities and the way in

The multiplicity of urban time zones varies time use throughout the city and serves the needs of the many international communities in it. It allows for the coexistence of the different modes of living demanded in contemporary cities.

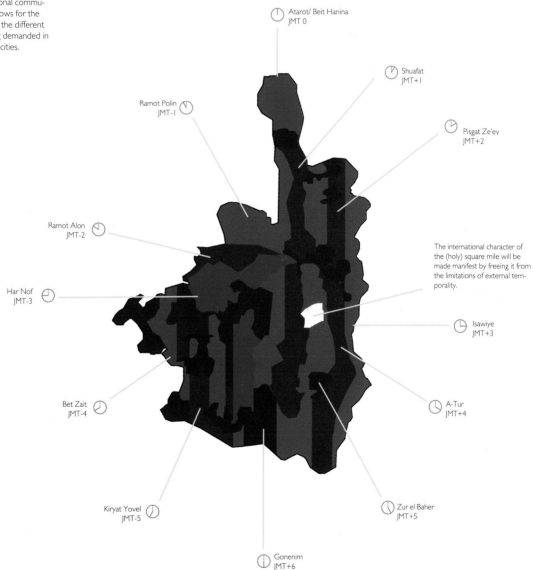

Atarot/ Beit Hanina
JMT 0

Shuafat
JMT+1

Ramot Polin
JMT-1

Pisgat Ze'ev
JMT+2

Ramot Alon
JMT-2

The international character of the (holy) square mile will be made manifest by freeing it from the limitations of external temporality.

Har Nof
JMT-3

Isawiye
JMT+3

Bet Zait
JMT-4

A-Tur
JMT+4

Kiryat Yovel
JMT-5

Zur el Baher
JMT+5

Gonenim
JMT+6

which space is used. Without the need for further physical manifestation, these boundaries have a great effect upon daily life within the spaces they define. The introduction of the time zones allows for the coexistence of contradicting modes of living within the city.

An eventual division of the city between Palestinians and Israelis into two capitals leaves the character of the boundary between the two parts to be defined. The use of urban time zones will have the effect of un-synchronizing the city instead of separating it physically, creating an organizational shift while leaving the city intact. This situation creates an integrative rather than an exclusive urban relationship. Different urban time zones become interdependent, as each inhabitant can equally benefit from services operating in the other zone, at times when these services may be closed in one's own zone of living. This could be regarded as an extension of an already existing situation in Jerusalem by which the secular inhabitants of the western city escape the siege of Sabbath imposed on entertainment and businesses into the eastern city where business operate as usual. Or the Palestinians, who upon their Friday holiday can shop in the western city.

Time in Jerusalem could indeed be more adaptive and responsive, its boundaries mobile and dynamic, changing in reaction to the city and its needs.

Tax H(e)aven: Sectional Masterplanning

The location of the heavenly datum line —"the roof of Jerusalem"—the limit above which earthly Jerusalem stops and the heavenly city begins, has been the subject of obsessive theological debates throughout the centuries and between the different religious groups that have inhabited and worshiped in Jerusalem. Defining the heavenly ± 00.00 was not purely a theoretical or theological question; indeed, this limit bore a strong planning implication, for it was to become the cap on height that would define the city's vertical growth.

Christians found the datum height in the line that follows the horizontal pole of the original wooden cross—Jesus' head hangs in heaven while his tormented body remains on earth. That same datum height, they claimed, could be retraced from the cross of the Holy Sepulchre. (Proposals for limitations on construction height at the datum line were common during periods of Christian rule of the city) Muslims, on the other hand, conceived of the line as the point on the rock from which Muhammad leapt into his nighttime journey to heaven. That claim put them in a rather awkward position as the Temple Mount, on which this rock is found, occupies topographically the lower part of the Old City. The implication of the Muslim position was reflected in their building policy as the rulers of the city, and created one of the most apparent and bizarre of Jerusalem's vernaculars. Everything lower than the plain of the datum was considered *gehenem*—Arabic for hell—and thereafter

The Subversion of Jerusalem's Sacred Vernaculars

SEZ_datum

The Subversion of Jerusalem's Sacred Vernaculars

treated with less care, while everything over it was made glamorous. Eventually this line was made manifest in the physical fabric of the city. (As the theological debate unfurled, the question of how high to build in Jerusalem remained the last evidence of its existence.)

For the Jews this line, defined by the Eruv, followed the natural topography of the city. The Eruv defines a roof by constituting a boundary. The boundary, which encircles the city, extends one meter over the ground, but signifies a roof twelve meters over that. A complex geometrical shape, stretched like a tent from poles following the height of the topography, defines the roof of the earthly city and the ground topography of heaven.

The debate of the datum remains one of the most bizarre recordings of religious masterplanning, but when speaking about the section in terms of planning contemporary Jerusalem, the idea of the heavenly datum becomes a serious matter for consideration. The datum line, when secularized, could bring masterplanning to the section.

But where could such a line be useful in terms of urban planning?

Israeli Jerusalem is losing its population: 16,000 people left the city in 1997.[10] Jerusalem is one of the poorest cities in the country, in which the percentage of housing by far exceeds the business and employment capacity of the city. (In 1997 commercial and office construction amounted to a mere 9.1 percent of all new construction, while residential construction stood at 71.7 percent, and public a mere 8 percent.[11]) There are far too many housing units built in Jerusalem and far too few businesses. Employment is concentrated mainly within the public sector, and the private sector is relatively small. Jerusalem needs business, business requires a business district, and a business district requires stimulation.

A Special Enterprise Zone (SEZ), usually defined by the suspension of taxes, primarily VAT, was considered to promote this goal and precipitate the development of a vibrant sector of service industry. But when it came to be conceived, the question of its location became mired by physical, religious, and political constraints.

Where will the SEZ take root? Each party involved would like to possess it and drain its benefits.

The definition of the SEZ in plan (on the X/Y axis) leaves the Z axis free to repeat the programs applied on plan and extrude the single use of business along the whole building envelope. Jerusalem is a city sectorialized along its plan, and homogeneous across its sections. The string of enclave neighborhoods that make up the city are semi-autonomous and, in most cases, ethnically and programmatically homogeneous.

10 Maya Chosen et al.

11 Maya Chosen et al.

Since inner-city migration leaves vast areas of empty floor space in the city center, these floors could become the new territories to be used by the SEZ. Master-planning can no longer rely on the plan alone, as the problem of Jerusalem lies in its homogeneous sections.

The marrying of two urban policies—the Special Enterprise Zone and the ancient datum line—will bring business into the section of the city. The datum height, a plane floating over the city, defines the spatial limits of the SEZ and affects those stories, throughout the city, hit by it. The invasion of the SEZ into every building in the city will encourage business functions to replace the functions already there, or fill the evicted spaces.

The plane of the datum height may pass over a building, through it, or under it, depending on its height relative to that of the topography. Along the way it activates cellars, floors, and attics, creating air rights. (The difference between the highest and lowest point of the city is 240 meters.[12] The average tolerance of topography is only about sixty-five meters.)

12 Maya Chosen et al.

The distribution of business functions throughout the city will be homogeneous, as each building, wherever it is located, will possess its "special floor" of business. By using Sectional Masterplanning, the SEZ is made integral in the fabric of the city, changing the programmatic composition of neighborhoods and the inner dynamics of single buildings rather than colonizing new territories.

The problem of defining a location, between or within each of Jerusalem's eastern or western parts, is thus defused.

Other datum heights could create different legal horizons—a plane of public functions (in a desperate lack of ground space), governmental offices (still occupying too expensive and overrepresented real estate), health clinics, religious institutions, and so on.

Conclusion

Jerusalem's urban vernaculars are more than just traditional styles of locality, but particular urban situations that evolved out of the city's political and religious particularities. The four episodes epitomize the city's problems but also its uniqueness, heterogeneity, and even its potential. Religious idiosyncrasies form the urban reality and daily life in Jerusalem and are apparent in almost every aspect of its planning. Although the episodes are based on religious urban strategies, the proposals attempt to divorce the religious reference from its mode of action, and offer them as techniques that could inform new strategies for Jerusalem.

The Eruv is a model for a Talmudic mode of intervention that acts territorially to circumvent the legal medium in which it operates. Within its circumference a

The TDR, or Transfer of Development Rights, is a system of spatial relocation of building rights for cases in which these rights could not be actualized. The unconsumed space is transferred and traded through a special Air-Rights Bank.

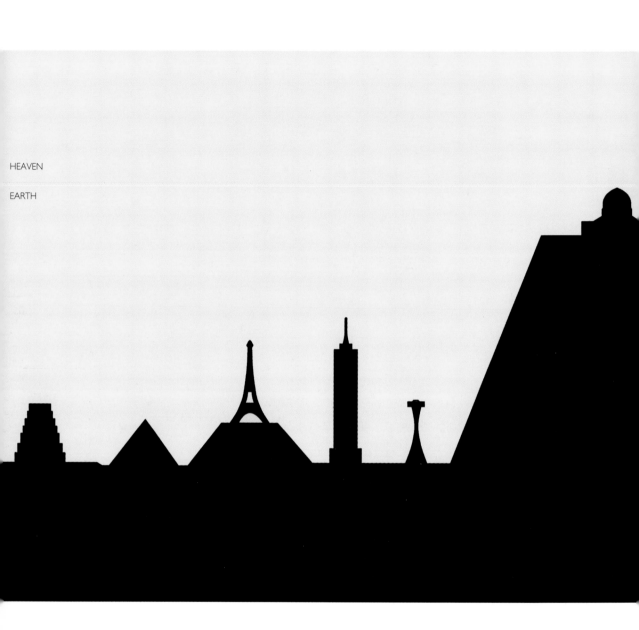

HEAVEN

EARTH

The Subversion of Jerusalem's Sacred Vernaculars

series of otherwise forbidden urban behaviors is thereafter tolerated. The Eruv demonstrates the way in which the constitution of a boundary can redefine a territory and thereafter change the law that applies to it. The three other episodes, taking the Eruv as a model for the strategies they propose, show the potential of similar modes of action. The episodes offer different ways to divide Jerusalem by manipulating boundaries, redefining territories, subverting urban territorial codes, thus affecting the very vernacular conditions of the city.

A new reading of Storrs' stone bylaw sees the stone cladding of building in Jerusalem as the repetition of an architectural ritual, aiming at the fabrication of a collective memory for the strengthening of a nationalistic agenda. The proposed manipulations to Storrs' law abuse the sign to define anew the boundaries of the city. Time zoning implies a sequenced, rather than a coherent, dictated, and absolute mode of action within a territory. Its conception as the transgression of time-based urban regulations, such as licensing laws, attempts to enrich the city programmatically and to create a separation, that is systematic rather than physical in nature while leaving the city intact.

If the three previous episodes propose changes to the organization of the plan of the city, the SEZ datum line promotes the creation of territories along the urban section. By applying different laws to the section, difference is brought into the depth of the city and into the inner composition of buildings.

Manipulation of existing urban situations (rather than the application of new strategies) could promote the creation of new urban vernaculars, capable of writing anew the hierarchy of the city. This proposed mode of action aims to diversify and enhance urban life, to maintain difference while breaking down the one homogeneous power structure that characterized the contemporary condition of Jerusalem.

If the city is an apparatus that can generate cultural and political change, it is the city that must be acted upon. The proposals therefore try to reinvigorate the mundane structures of urban life and realities in Jerusalem, blurring observation and invention to demand that we act with vigor to create an open, free, and diverse urban environment. This approach aims thus at the heart of Jerusalem's urban problem.

The Palestine League

Mack Scogin

How might two conflicting cultures enthusiastically
sponsor the raw and uncompromised coexistence of their
differences in a civil and mannered way?

What strategy can bring people from a longstanding
tradition of cross-cultural hate, suspicion, and intolerance
into a merit-based, competitive society of fairness and
mutual respect?

And what possible role could architecture play in
answering these seemingly unresolvable questions—
in resolving issues that arguably threaten the very existence
of humankind?

The answer:

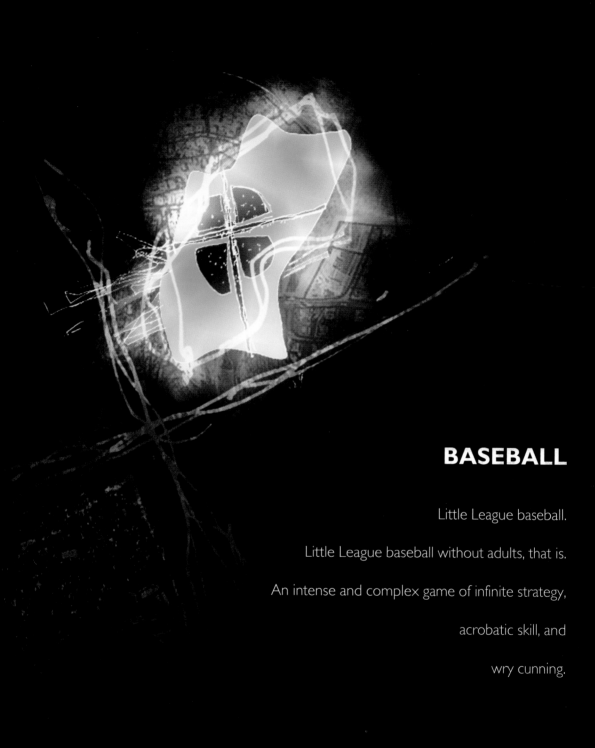

BASEBALL

Little League baseball.

Little League baseball without adults, that is.

An intense and complex game of infinite strategy,

acrobatic skill, and

wry cunning.

A Game

- of simultaneous, choreographed teamwork and nonviolent, lonely, isolated individualism.

- with no time limit, forever changing, governed by subjective rules played on a field with no prescribed overall shape or size, and involving a multiplicity of variable velocities and trajectories.

- of statistics, endless statistics; of finite, precise dimensions and split-second timing.

- played by and with the innocence of youth.

- where the managers and coaches for some reason dress in uniform like the players, and communicate with them through a prearranged set of hand signals and body gestures.

- where the very best player on offense is expected to fail in 70 percent of his or her efforts while the same player on defense is required to be almost perfect in execution.

- requiring long periods of excruciating patience and emotional control punctuated by spontaneous bursts of unbridled emotional energy and physical effort.

- where you can "pick people off," strike someone out, hit a foul ball, line drive or grand slam, steal a base, balk, execute a squeeze play, run someone down, sacrifice an out, have a designated hitter or clean-up man—all without the least bit of violence or bodily harm.

- where a woman, man, girl, or boy of slight stature and average strength can compete with the largest and strongest of players.

- full of superstition, ritual, and tradition; with occasional and sometimes spectacular moments of luck and spontaneity.

- that can be played night or day in almost any weather condition beside rain, sleet, snow, or bitter cold.

- of great grace and finesse, often decided by miniscule differences of performance and strategy.

- played, ideally, on a magic carpet of perfectly manicured dirt and grass—a place that somehow, with or without the presence of players, has everything to do with universal beauty, serenity, and potential.

- that is not traditionally played in the Middle East.

I propose that a prototypical Little League baseball complex comprising four playing fields oriented north, south, east, and west be constructed on an elevated structure accessed by a series of ramps and inclined elevators: a tabula rasa. This semi-permanent structure would be the first of many installed in cities that are centers of political and cultural conflict throughout the world, such as Sarajevo, Bosnia; Pristina, Kosovo; Beirut, Lebanon; Srinigar, Kashmere; Belfast, Northern Ireland; Kigali, Rwanda; Bujumbura, Burundi; Lhasa, Tibet; Kinshasa, Democratic Republic of Congo; and Khartoum, Sudan.

The goal is to create a new beginning: a new reference point of common understanding that allows for the peaceful pursuit of individual identity within a collective framework of intense competition.

The strategy is to isolate the youth of the present generation—the innocent—and to give them a new challenge: a game. A game that their parents have little knowledge of or affinity toward. A game that allows the youth total freedom to negotiate their individual and collective excellences. Lessons learned from the common struggle to gain knowledge, obtain expertise, and perform under pressure within a prescribed and understood code of behavior would over time, I believe, transfer to the larger realities of everyday life.

The proposed site is at the northeast corner of Jerusalem's Old City: at the intersection of the Muslim sector, the Old City, and modern Jerusalem: at the intersection of Sultan Suleiman Street and Derech Yericho Street.

The rules at the beginning are simple:

- No adults: only the innocent participate.

- Games are played only at night, so the field's north, south, east, and west orientations have no advantage, but do retain their symbolic meaning.

- The field is entirely of grass—an abstraction.

- The foul lines, diamond, and batter's box are outlined in chartreuse-dyed calcium carbonate.

- The players maintain the field (grass) during the day.

- There are two outs per inning, four strikes, and four balls.

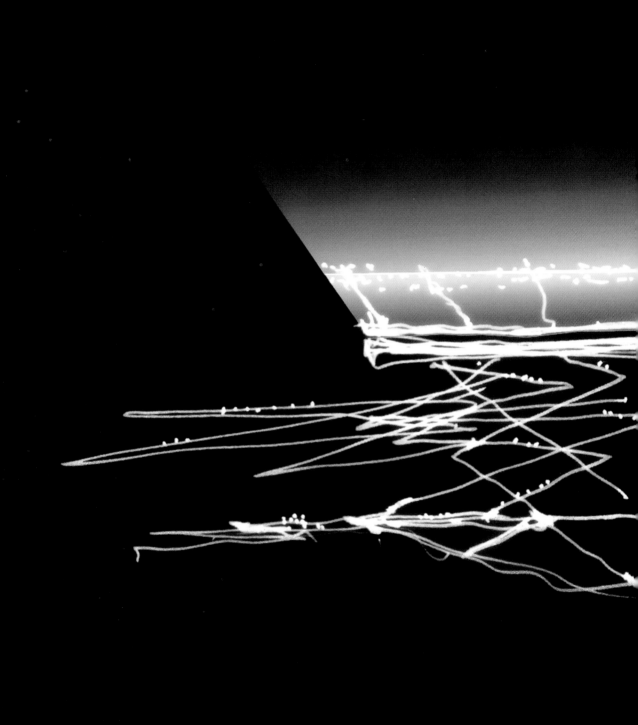

Jerusalem SKY

Deborah Natsios and John Young

Jeruslem SKY's Web-based series of hyperlinked image-maps explore the application of dual-use technologies in migratory bird conservation practices. The online archive is underpinned by Cryptome.org and Cartome.org, whose extensive collections of documents focus on issues of intelligence, encryption, dual-use applications, privacy, and other civil liberties concerns. Jerusalem SKY is linked to the man-made city: Real-time data relating to avian migrations will be uploaded to online databases after being collected at scattered rooftop bird-banding stations manned by volunteers from diverse communities across the city.

Bird's-eye-view perspectives of Jerusalem construct the city along the pilgrim's spiritual horizon, a vertical axis whose vanishing points converge into sanctified sky—the allegorical airspace of Jesus' and Muhammad's respective ascensions. The ancestral soffit absorbs the city's ecstasy and agitation, a vanishing sky-dome camouflaged by atmospheric boundaries that evaporate and recondense by the hour, product of capricious windspeeds and turbulence that whip layers of cumulus, altostratus, and cirrus into impermanent cosmology and fleeting projections of earthly desire. Such is the point of view, for instance, of the Lucas Brandis map of Palestine (Lubeck, 1475), as the cartographer—circumscribed by depictions of the blowing winds—overflies the holy city seen far below, embedded in undulating, verdant topography.

Jerusalem's migratory birds are pilgrims of the upper sanctuary. They soar on thermal currents high above escarpments of the rift valley, plying transcontinental flyways that link northerly breeding sites with southerly wintering grounds. Aerodynamic itineraries have bridged the land masses of Europe, Asia, and Africa for countless millennia, confirming Jerusalem's ecological centricity within a triadic balance of continental powers, a balance that coincides, as it happens, with the emblematic claims of Heinrich Buenting's trefoil of 1581, or the tripartite structure of such T-O mappaemundi as the Augsburg of 1472—the medieval schema that represented the world as a disc with Jerusalem at its center, separated from Asia, Africa, Europe by waterways configured in a T shape.

Each spring and autumn, a half billion migrant birds navigate the skies above Jerusalem by their own ancient compasses, tracking magnetic fields, star rotation, and the sun, escaping terrestrial confinement just as in the Bible and Qur'an, where birds are associated with transcendent themes of purification, absolution, and sacrifice. The man-made city remains inexorably linked to the avian nomads that populate its canopy, notwithstanding the transcendent altitudes of their empyreal habitat. When diasporic birds like the sparrow, eagle, santa colomba, and quail descend to roost or feed on flat roofs below, they leave faint vapor trails that link their skyborne infra-structures to the stone city's upturned ribs and bones. All across Jerusalem, rooftop refuges receive vagile birds intertwined in vaporous rays of first light, sundown, and penumbra.

In the past half century, new surveillance and imaging technologies have super-seded bird's-eye views of the city, at the very same time that avian migrants have suffered the increasing violence of birdstrikes—catastrophic collisions between species like white pelicans, griffon vultures, black kites and the mechanized high-tech birds that are recent colonists of both low- and high-altitude migration routes. Aviation casualties resulting from birdstrikes have far exceeded those of modern mili-tary campaigns. The unforgiving physics of high-velocity impacts amplifies the body mass of projectile birds, converting supple wingbeats into a destructive force meas-ured in tons, forging a debris alloy of crushed beaks, scapular feathers, and aluminum shards.

Violence is a meticulously engineered byproduct of airborne visualization tech-nologies that support the ongoing surveillance of the city. Reconnaissance aircraft, unmanned drones, profiling radars, and surveillance satellites corroborate military doctrines of command, control, and communication with new remote sensing and imaging products, culling data from systematic regional coverages to plot a totalizing, expropriating transparency: the scientific cartography of an asymmetric balance of power and the policing of the man-made city's disputed borders. Infrared radar chan-nels offer night visibility; panchromatic systems cue colors of the visible spectrum; and ultraviolet spectrometers, microwave radiometers, hyperspectral instruments, and image-enhancement techniques provide diagnostic tools for imagery analysts versed in the phenomenology of observables, who will identify the exploitable con-tours of contested urban topography.

Migrant birds populate a secular sky reinvented by meteorology and climatology through military hardware and software that encode real-time data—millibar and iso-bar in thrall to national security priorities that supplant prophecy with "forecasts" and vision with "visibility," eschewing the airborne pilgrim's progress. This is the sky of contemporary battlespace and triumphalist war games, where artificial intelligence intercedes with simulation scenarios and new algorithms for *dies irae* under the rubric of "total air supremacy."

Strict regulatory mechanisms limiting the dissemination of high-resolution satellite imagery emerged in the 1960s, a regime of restrictions that underscored geospatial imaging's military role in maintaining dominance through reconnaissance, intelligence gathering, strategic planning, and precision targeting. Jerusalem's public record, its civic mirror, was rendered opaque as contemporary aerial views were suppressed by redactions and inscrutable encryptions, as imagery intelligence—IMINT—was degraded by international covenants, shutter controls, blackouts, data quality reduction, and time-delayed transmissions.

Since the 1990s, global market forces and democratizing principles called for new information transparency through "open skies" policies, "open source" acquisitions, and "dual-use" applications. These initiatives introduce beneficial civilian applications for technologies originating in national security contexts. High-resolution satellite imagery—real-time digital data with resolutions of less than one meter—is being declassified. Commercial orbital "birds" are being granted licenses making their imagery increasingly available on the open market, with potential benefits to environmental studies, agriculture, urban planning, seismic monitoring, storm and flood control research, natural disaster mitigation, and large-scale humanitarian relief efforts. Jerusalem SKY, a Web-based project being developed by Natsios Young Architects, supports migratory bird conservation efforts by extending the transparency of "open skies" initiatives to the project's own information architecture. The digital image-maps presented below are proposed new bird's-eye views of Jerusalem—in the form of graphical user interfaces that are orientation maps for SKY's open architecture. The synthetic image-maps are hypermedia portals accessible to the growing online public worldwide—the student, amateur, refugee, scientist, detainee, or citizen with access to the World Wide Web. Icons embedded within SKY's digital image-map narratives are hyperlinked to allow connective access to myriad online knowledge systems relating to bird migration, geospatial imaging, and conflict resolution—including databases, metadata, and multimedia presentations of sound, video, and still images.

SKY's hypermedial transparency expands the narrow scope of formalist visualizations of the city—those photogenic consumer products of the tourism and nostalgia industries. SKY views probe the more complex imagery spectrum captured by multilayered sensor technologies and information systems, including those scanning beyond the range of the human eye—the multispectral, hyperspectral, and ultraspectral.

Most important, the SKY project will function as an augmented reality system by directly linking its Web-based architecture to actual sites in the built city—specifically, Jerusalem's expansive landscape of flat rooftops. It is proposed that the city's flat roofs be adapted as seasonal bird ringing (banding) stations, equipped with mistnets, calipers, scales, and other instruments of the banding process, in which birds are tagged using small leg-bands—part of a data-collection technique crucial to the study of migratory movements, routes, behaviors, and survival.

Jerusalem's network of rooftop landscape fragments will be transformed into a working laboratory as well as seasonal urban staging post, where birds pause to feed and roost before continuing intercontinental journeys. The rooftop system is to be manned by a diversity of building residents and community volunteers throughout mixed quarters of the city, who will use wireless cell phones to uplink survey data to shared online databases. The urban model of scattered rooftop collection sites parallels the World Wide Web's distributed connectivity. It encourages a more broadly inclusive network for participatory data sampling than is currently available at the Jerusalem Bird Observatory ringing facility, narrowly sited on one acre of parkland in an exclusive, politically compromised zone located between Israel's Knesset and its Supreme Court.

Jerusalem SKY's new bird's-eye views of the city have emerged out of regional conflict-resolution initiatives precipitated by birdstrike hazards. Catastrophic birdstrikes—symptom of unresolved spatial conflict between militarized airspace and transboundary avian flyways—are being mitigated through innovative remediation that relies in part on national security technologies. Today, migration conservationists are tracking and mapping their mobile subjects using what was once the exclusive paraphernalia of war—real-time surveillance radar warning systems, satellites, unmanned military drones, motorized gliders, and satellite intercept radio transmitters.

The appropriation for civilian use of technologies developed in the context of geopolitical surveillance and political control has compelling implications. Those are explored through SKY's key links to *Cryptome.org* and *Cartome.org*, Natsios Young's online archive of documents relating to the apparatuses of surveillance and political control—including hardwares and softwares that enable encryption, steganography, and geolocation—their uses, their exploitable vulnerabilities, their implications for civil liberties and the space of a new public domain.

In appropriating dual-use technologies for migratory bird conservation practices, Jerusalem SKY subordinates pernicious surveillance to the knowledge-based act of seeing Jerusalem anew. Viewed from an aerial habitat constructed out of the recurring rhythms of transboundary migration flows, the specular city mirrors back the knowledge of emancipated pilgrims.

Yellow Wagtail | Purple Heron | Night Heron | Greenback Heron | Merlin | Spotted Redshanks | Cattle Egret | Hooded Wheatear | Rede Poo

JERU

Species of Sahato-Sindian arid zone. Total: 33 species

Species of etated Pale the (including t rate and warm-temperate zones). Total: 57 species.

Cairo 29° 5

Riyadh 24°

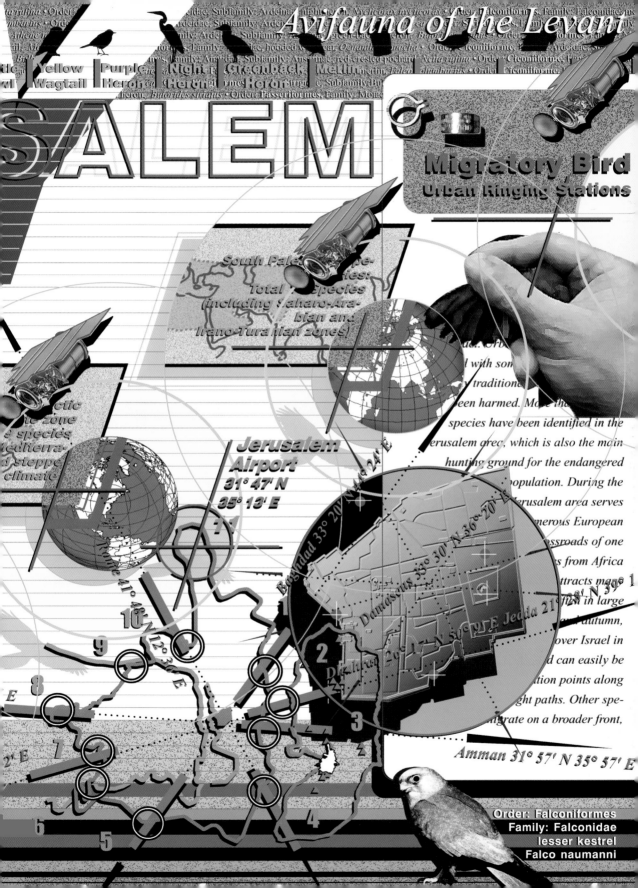

Avifauna of the Levant

SALEM

Migratory Bird
Urban Ringing Stations

Yellow Wagtail · Purple Heron · Night Heron · Greenback Heron · Merlin

South Palearctic species:
total species
(including Saharo-Ara-
bian and
Irano-Turanian zones)

arctic
zone
species
Mediterra-
steppe
climate

Jerusalem
Airport
31° 47' N
35° 13' E

...d with som...
...traditiona...
...een harmed. More th...
species have been identified in the
erusalem area, which is also the main
hunting ground for the endangered
population. During the
erusalem area serves
merous European
ssroads of one
s from Africa
ttracts ma...
...in large
autumn,
over Israel in
can easily be
tion points along
ght paths. Other spe-
...grate on a broader front,

Amman 31° 57' N 35° 57' E

Order: Falconiformes
Family: Falconidae
lesser kestrel
Falco naumanni

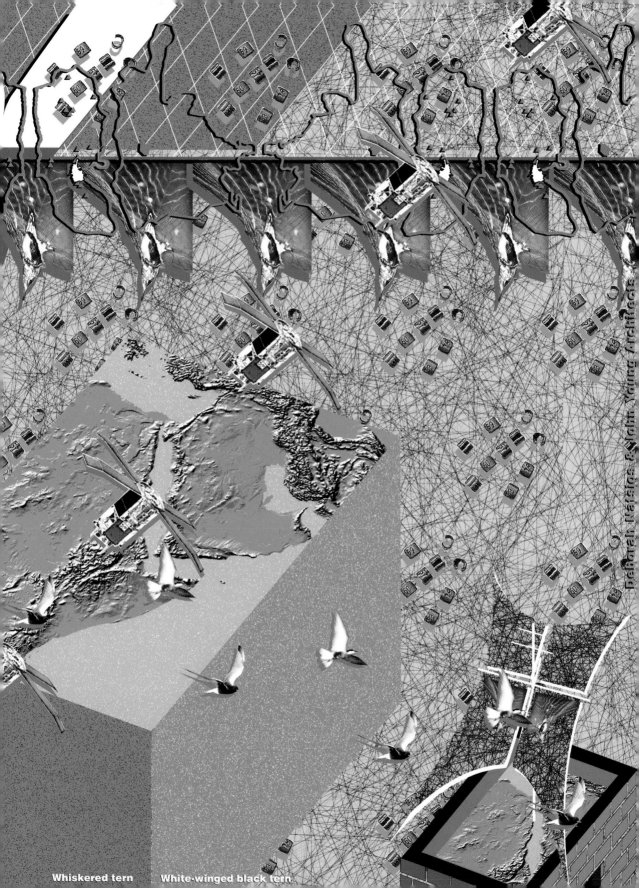

Whiskered tern   White-winged black tern

Bahrain Nakajo & John Young Architects

ROOFTOPS

jerusalem

3

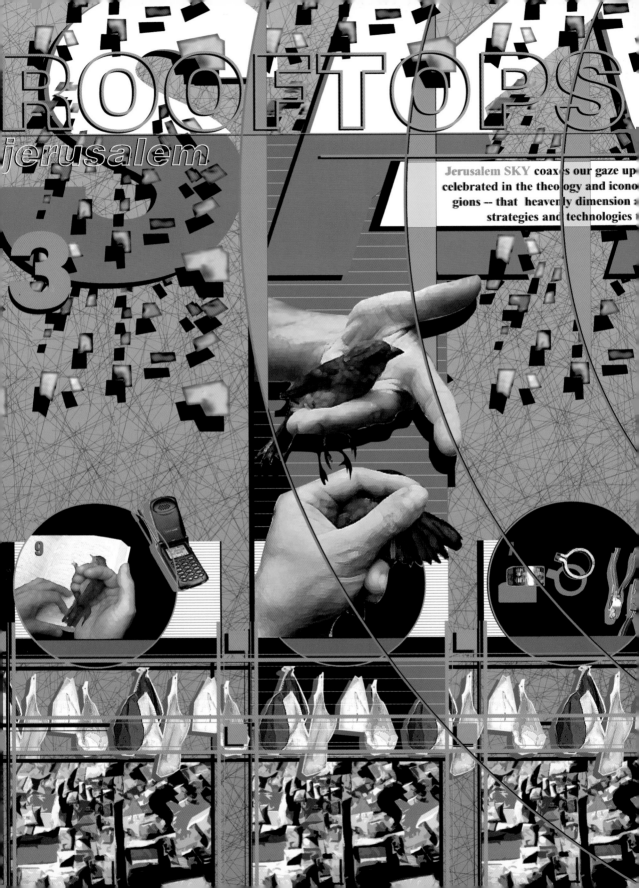

Jerusalem SKY coaxes our gaze up
celebrated in the theology and icono
gions -- that heavenly dimension a
strategies and technologies t

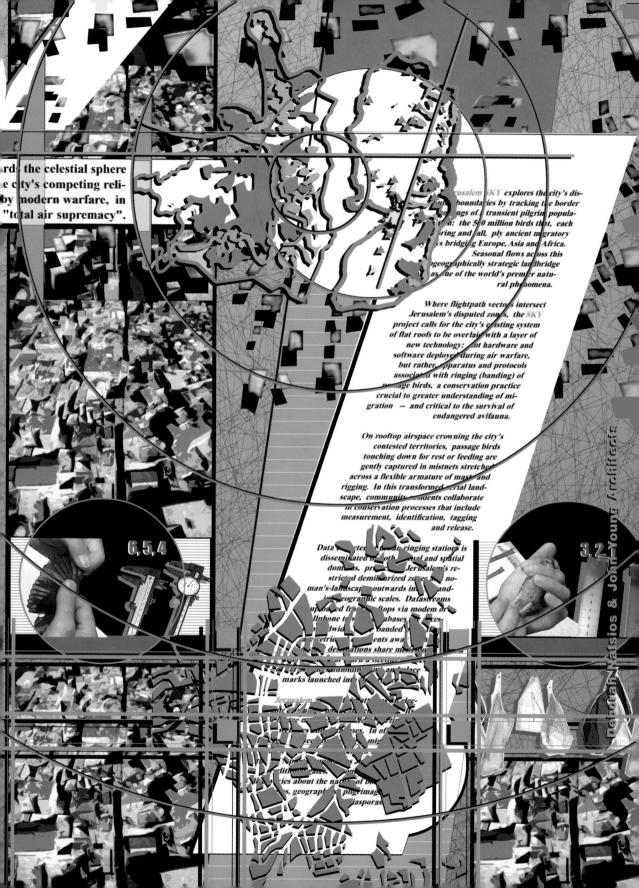

...rds the celestial sphere
...e city's competing reli-
...by modern warfare, in
"total air supremacy".

...rusalem SKY explores the city's dis-
...ut... boundaries by tracking the border
...ngs of a transient pilgrim popula-
...n: the 500 million birds that, each
...ring and fall, ply ancient migratory
...s bridging Europe, Asia and Africa.
Seasonal flows across this
...geographically strategic landbridge
...as one of the world's premier natural phenomena.

Where flightpath vectors intersect
Jerusalem's disputed zones, the SKY
project calls for the city's existing system
of flat roofs to be overlaid with a layer of
new technology: not hardware and
software deployed during air warfare,
but rather apparatus and protocols
associated with ringing (banding) of
passage birds, a conservation practice
crucial to greater understanding of migration -- and critical to the survival of
endangered avifauna.

On rooftop airspace crowning the city's
contested territories, passage birds
touching down for rest or feeding are
gently captured in mistnets stretched
across a flexible armature of masts and
rigging. In this transformed aerial landscape, community residents collaborate
in conservation processes that include
measurement, identification, tagging
and release.

Data collected at our ringing stations is
disseminated in both virtual and spatial
domains, pricing Jerusalem's restricted demilitarized zones in no-
man's-landscape outwards into expanding geographic scales. Datastreams
uploaded from rooftops via modem or
cellphone to web databases services...
...lwid... ...banded... ...
...retried... ...ents awa...
...destinations share misinfo...

6,5,4

3,2

...marks launched in...

Jerusalem...

...ries about the na... of b...
...s, geograph... pilgrimag...
...iasporas...

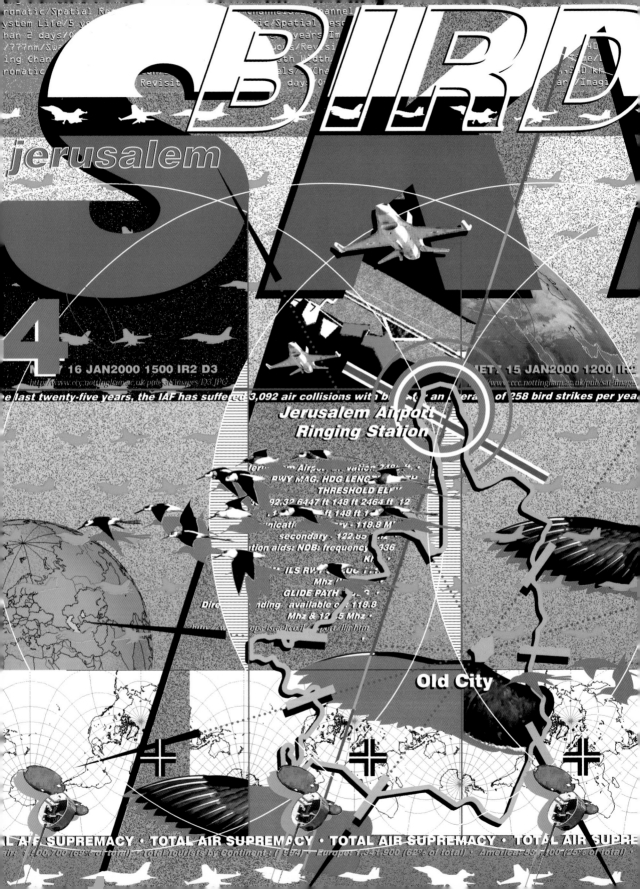

STRIKE

MET7 14 JAN2000 1900 IR2 D3   MET7 13 JAN2000 1330 IR2 D3   MET7 12 JAN2000 1600 IR2 D3

http://www.ccc.nottingham.ac.uk/pub/sat-images/D3.JPG   http://www.ccc.nottingham.ac.uk/pub/sat-images/D3.JPG   http://www.ccc.nottingham.ac.uk/pub/sat-images/D3.JPG

an aircraft lost to bird strikes present a whole other count.)

Deborah Natsios & John Young/Architects

TOTAL AIR SUPREMACY • TOTAL AIR SUPREMACY • TOTAL AIR SUPREMACY • TOTAL AIR SUP

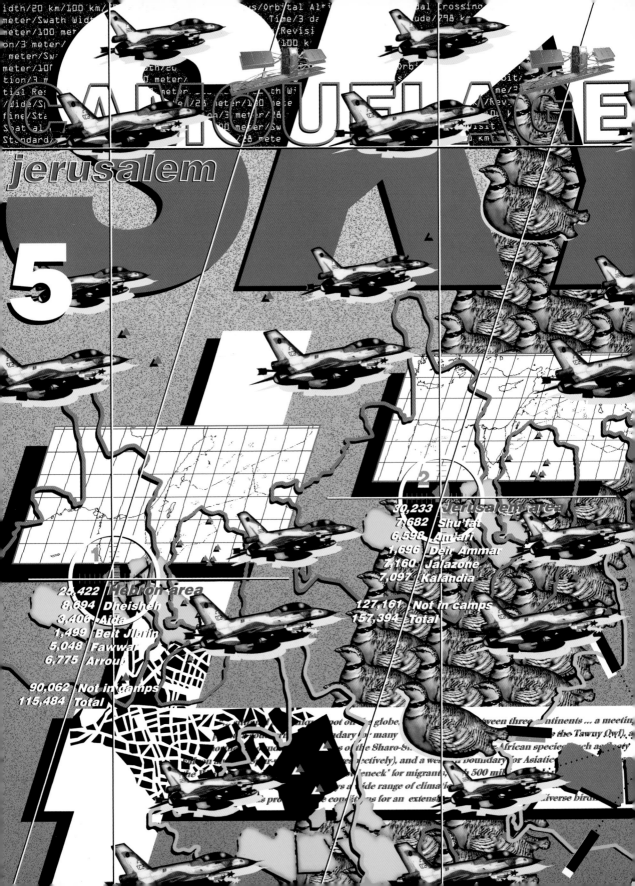

25,422 Hebron area
8,094 Dheisheh
3,406 Aida
1,499 Beit Jibrin
5,048 Fawwar
6,775 Arroub

90,062 Not in camps
115,484 Total

30,233 Jerusalem area
7,682 Shu'fat
6,598 Amari
1,696 Deir Ammar
7,160 Jalazone
7,097 Kalandia

127,161 Not in camps
157,394 Total

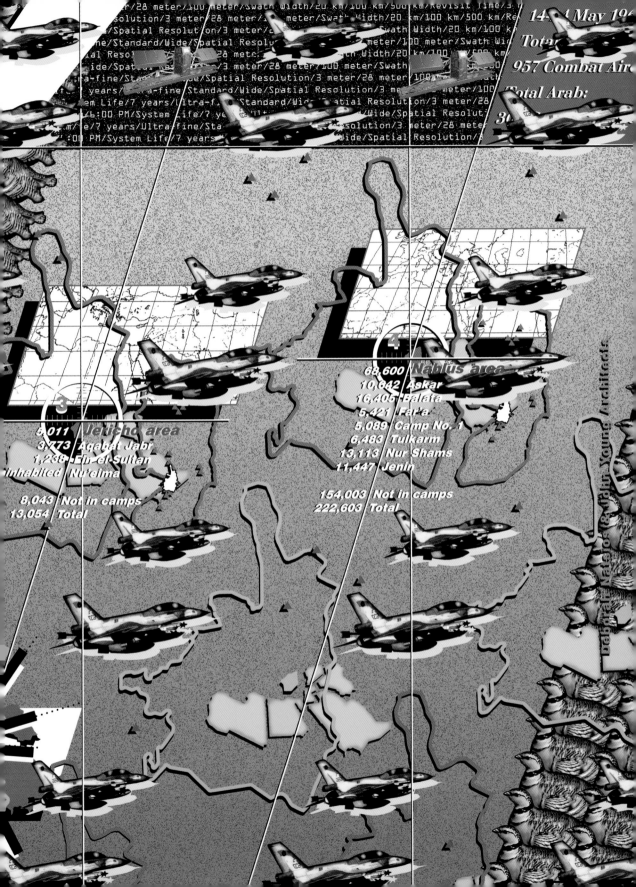

/28 meter/100 meter/Swath Width/20 km/100 km/500 km/Revisit Time/1
solution/3 meter/28 meter/ meter/Swath Width/20 km/100 km/500 km/Re
Spatial Resolution/3 meter/28 meter/ meter/Swath Width/20 km/100 k
ine/Standard/Wide/Spatial Reso th Width/20 km/100 km/500 km
al Resol /3 met 28 mete 8 meter/100 meter/Swath
ide/Spa es solution/3 meter/28 meter/100 meter/Swath
ra-fine/Stan /Spatial Resolution/3 me meter/100
years/ a-fine Standard/Wide/Spatial Resolution/3 meter/28
em Life/7 years/Ultra-f Standard/Wide/Spatial Resolution/3 meter/28
e/7 years/Ultra fine/Sta solution/3 meter/28 meter
01 PM/System Life/7 years Wide/Spatial Resolution/

14-4 May 19
Total
957 Combat Air
Total Arab:
3

68,600 Nablus area
10,042 Askar
16,405 Balata
5,421 Far'a
5,089 Camp No. 1
6,483 Tulkarm
13,113 Nur Shams
11,447 Jenin

154,003 Not in camps
222,603 Total

3 Jericho area
8,011
3,773 Aqabat Jabr
1,238 Ein el-Sultan
Inhabited Nu'eima

8,043 Not in camps
13,054 Total

Deborah Natsios (& John Young Architects)

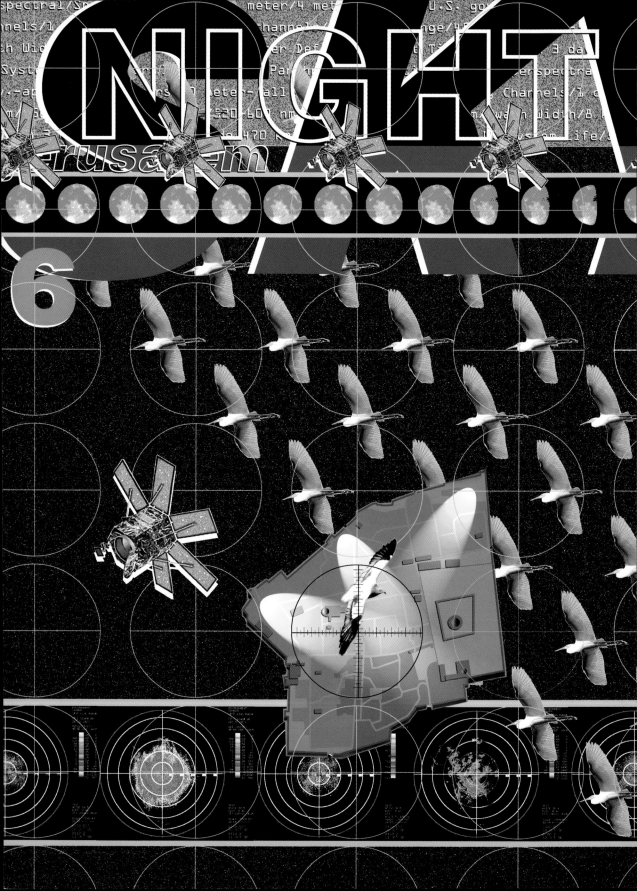

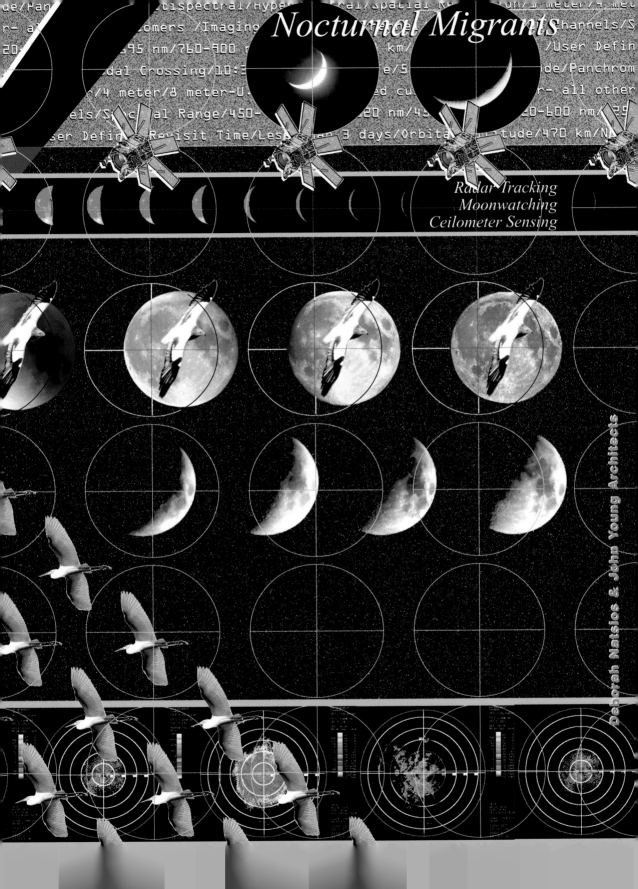

Nocturnal Migrants

Radar Tracking
Moonwatching
Ceilometer Sensing

Deborah Natsios & John Young Architects

RAPTORS

**Lesser
Spotted Eagle**
*Aquila
pomarina*

**Levant
Sparrowhawk**
Accipiter brevipes

**Steppe
Eagle**
*Aquila
nipalensis*

**Steppe
Eagle**
*Aquila
nipalensis*

Black Kite
*Milvus
migrans*

jerusalem

Watchpoints: 7 Suez, 8
Eilat, 9 Kuwait

Autumn

Old City

Spring

points: 10 Straits
z, 11 North Yemen
12 Bab-el-Mandeb

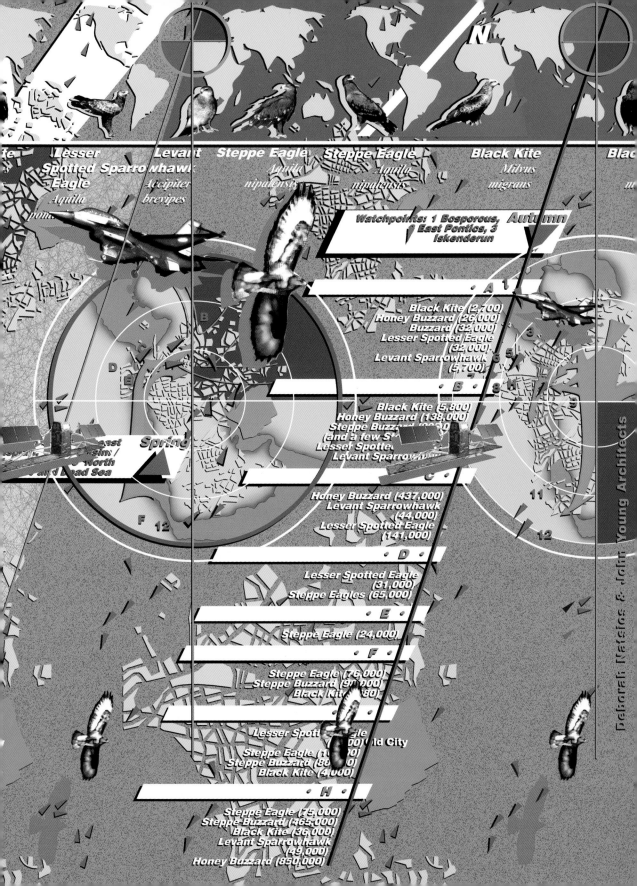

Parrando's Paradox: Error in Holy Lands

Keller Easterling

In game theory, Parrando's Paradox claims that although two losing games played independently will always lose, two losing games played alternately may generate a winning streak.[1] Switching between games, like the small repetitive supports of a ratchet, seems to prevent downward movement or losses. Since two games when cross-referenced seem to multiply intelligence, Parrando's Paradox encourages a gamble with losses that would generally be considered unproductive.

1 Sandra Blakeslee, "Paradox in Game Theory: Losing Strategy That Wins," *New York Times*, 25 January 2000.

Many organized systems, from games to electronic circuitry to genetics, behave in ways that run counter to our common notions of order and efficiency. Messy redundancies, generally thought to inhibit streamlined organization, multiply possibilities for trial and error; accidents broaden the base of responses because they introduce new information that the system needs to grow. Losses, accidents, inversions, jokes, and tricks, whether they appear as exceptional conditions or a staple crop, introduce extrinsic information—error that makes organizations robust.

Yet we try to contain error, to prevent it from disrupting our logical proofs. We even treat it as the destined antithesis that proves the assumed conclusion. Or we impose some means of returning error to a determinate system, calling it part of a chaotic, epigenetic, or entropic order, something that will stay in the family of the whole. Error is "the original sin of the technical object."[2] Error is the Fall, the obstacle that must be overcome to achieve knowledge and holiness. We pretend that the family generates all of the ingredients in the world, even error. Even Satan is, of course, part of the family and the completion of its holiness.

2 Paul Virilio, "Surfing the Accident," *The Art of the Accident: Art, Architecture and Media*, ed. Andreas Broeckmann et al. (Rotterdam: NAi/V2 Organisatie, 1998), 30–45.

Jerusalem has always incubated segregated losing games. Each game supports a destined circular story of published rules and covenants, and each separate game continues to lose. This text and its accompanying figures carefully misreads Mark Twain, juvenilia, Holy Land web sites, and the Bible, searching Jerusalem for sites of naturally occurring error and for losing games that sometimes win.

Children

Jerusalem presents with all of its wounds and grudges preserved, impacted, and expanding, inducing sympathetic distress in all who come in contact with it. It stores every biblical conundrum of the Old or New Testament about hatred and hierarchy, or about success that can come only at the expense or exclusion of others; about kings, tribes, or brothers chosen to receive slightly more or less property or intelligence so that they can then be compared to each other for the rest of their lives. These stories continuously circle very real desires to secure a place, or to be recognized in a place where the rules for qualifying as worthwhile information are constantly shifting. Jerusalem also preserves the compulsion to step over the line slightly and provocatively, and to strike preemptively and irreversibly. Its complicated sectional architecture creates additional slight overlaps and infringements to irritate its wounds. Any sectional slice through this city reveals a thick cartoon of claims, overlaps, and memorializations, all preserved as separate destined stories. Any section bristles with relics like those of a child: buried dolls and rocks and bones, marked with crude plaques and hyperbolic tales. It is a living museum devoted to the common love of hatred and entrenchment, to the comfort of immeasurable martyrdom.

Mark Twain's statement that Jesus might forego the Second Coming if it would involve revisiting Jerusalem was already an old joke—reliable fill for the professional humorist, probably when Clemens was tired of being funny. Twain toured the Holy Land in 1869, when most of the slapping, hitting, and rock throwing was between Christian pilgrims of different sects. *The Innocents Abroad*, his account of this quest and other travels, is messy, racist, and quickly written, yet one reads every word, hoping he will not stop, wishing for his companionship in any situation involving religiosity and wondering if by some haphazard placement system he might be one's personal company in heaven or hell. In guidebook parlance and fake King James English he parodies "Presbyterian Palestine" and the evenhanded gravity of every one of its incessant highlights and every square inch of its dust. Twain's feigned reverence for the terribleness of God and his obedience to all claims of authenticity and every linear sequencing of fairy-tale history effortlessly reveals its fraudulence:

> *The tomb of Adam! How touching it was, here in a land of strangers, far away from home and friends and all who cared for me, thus to discover the grave of a blood relation . . . I leaned upon the pillar and burst into tears . . . And I—I—alas, I did not live to see him. Weighed down by sorrow and disappointment, he died before I was born—six thousand brief summers before I was born. But let us try to bear it with fortitude. Let us trust that he is better off where he is. Let us take comfort in the thought that his loss is our eternal gain.*[3]

In the Holy Land today, children make up the majority of the population. Adults shape their minds with leading questions that order and arrange a virtual architecture more important even than the physical architecture of the city. In Palestinian summer

3 Mark Twain, *The Innocents Abroad* (New York: Viking Press, 1974), 422, 486.

camps, commandos teach children war games and other terrorist tactics.[4] Israel's religious Web sites are often structured to quiz children on a particular version of Jerusalem's history—teaching orthodoxy through rhymes and catechism. Virtual universities teach biased histories of a destined sequence of actions based on ancient promises, conveniently omitting most of the conflict of the last few decades. Rendered in worn parchment with burnt edges, digital buttons conjure spin about celebrities like David and Solomon (two characters who desperately need handling). Children must be shaped not only because of their innate fierceness, but also because an unshaped mind might imagine some kind of lateral interpretation of the stories—might imagine a way around the trouble. By making errors, by introducing contradictory information, such a mind would spoil a comfortable and familiar losing game.

Children are good at the miracles of error, proving that it is everywhere, even when one is desperately trying to exclude it. Twain loved juvenile writing, and collected examples of misspoken language and malapropism. He once even published a Portuguese-English dictionary supposedly authored by one "Pedro Caroleno," a magical book of double-talk any page of which has the power to completely indispose the reader with screaming laughter. Indeed, a whole genre of underground literature is devoted to such material. The richly erroneous phrases found, for example, in responses to history-test essay questions or the off-color gaffes found in the weekly church bulletin are but two of countless sources. This material cannot be contrived; it exists as naturally occurring extrinsic information that appears, by a series of wonderful accidents, even when the author is earnestly trying to stay within official structures and rules. Jesus' followers were the twelve decibels. David was talented at playing the liar. Solomon, one of David's sons, had 300 wives and 700 porcupines. The epistles are the wives of the apostles. One of the opossums was St. Matthew, who was also a taximan.[5]

Family

The Bible's stories about God, David, and Solomon in Jerusalem are written as if by a child: wordy digressions filled with error and extraneous circumstance that only occasionally remember where they left off long enough to provide a few rules and genealogies before going about a fight whose origins are impossible to trace. At intervals the clanking and moaning of battle give way to moments of moral and ethical reconciliation. Caught in freeze-frame, mid-grimace and stranglehold, with knife poised for another decapitation and knobby club drawn high, the Bible characters fall silent. As the last muffled clanks are heard offstage, they bow their heads in prayer and meet with God. These heroes congratulate themselves for knowing that they have done something wrong. Their sin makes them more adorable, almost innocent,

4 John F. Burns, "Palestinian Summer Camp Offers the Games of War," *New York Times*, 3 August 2000.

5 Anders Henriksson, "A History of the Past, Part II," *The Wilson Quarterly*, Winter (1999). Excerpted in *Harper's Magazine*, April 2000, 20–23.

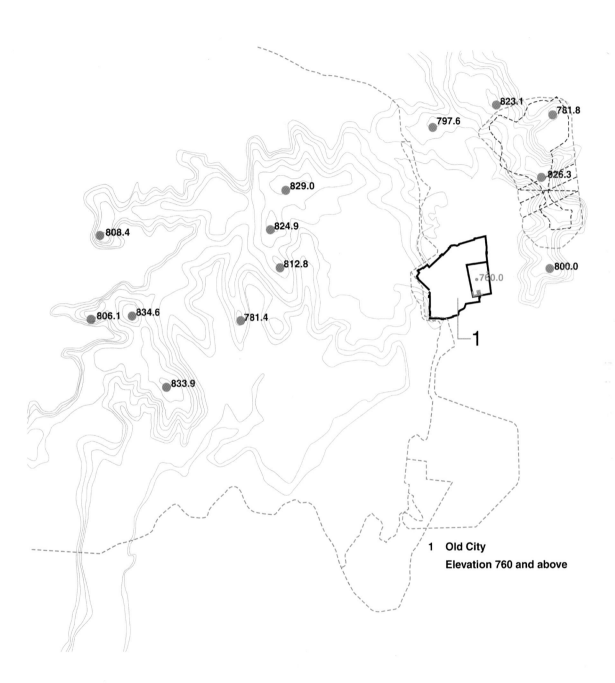

823.1

781.8

797.6

826.3

829.0

808.4

824.9

812.8

800.0

.760.0

806.1   834.6

781.4

1

833.9

1   Old City
Elevation 760 and above

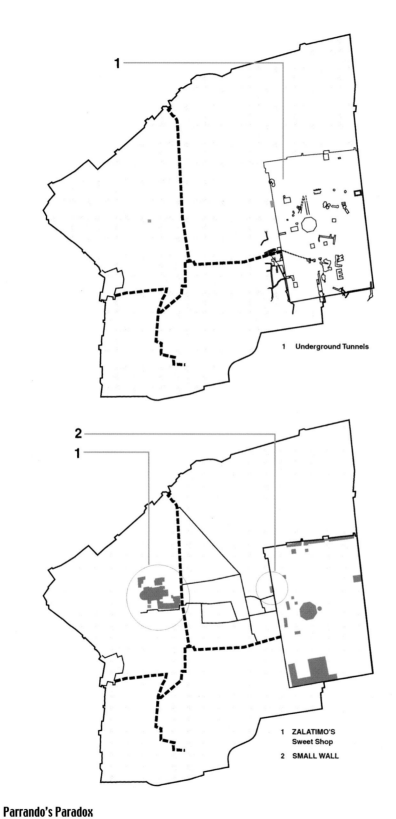

1   Underground Tunnels

1   ZALATIMO'S
     Sweet Shop

2   SMALL WALL

as they admit to being naughty and vulnerable. They have conformed by sinning in a way that precisely defies God's laws. God claims to have washed and recuperated his poor foundlings, and then he reminds them what they owe him for the service. Bible scholars get very excited over these moments, expressing their amazement that they can be nourished by these passages while dropping the hint that this nourishment is only possible because of their own powers of appreciation and their insightful infantilizing of the god in the story. The giant revelation is that these moments show a god who is learning to be a father! These are the bargains, the handshakes at the negotiating table that make a family; this is peace making and growth in the Holy Land.

Because it records error and circumstance, however, the Bible is, nevertheless, a book of truth. The official script speaks of ethical soul-searching and political reconciliation in a learning community that is revising its family organization, but the Bible chroniclers are more accurate than that and more honest than any of its characters, including its god. With simple-minded thoroughness they provide additional information and detail, telltale signs that another scene is being played offstage, outside the neat whole that is tied up by the moral of the story. Often arriving after the climactic moralizing, a stray sentence or two tells us that concurrent with this epiphany, David commits a hundred more grisly atrocities for no apparent reason or buys a new wife for one hundred Philistine foreskins. These records provide accidental evidence of a parallel system, of some other kind of deal that is propelling the story, a cold-blooded subtext about material and political gain outside the übermorals that God whispers in the author's ear. Ethical demonstration always accompanies the next shuffling of power between father and child, with both concealing what they have up their sleeve, the next ten moves in the game, the unspoken rules about the way the world works. While the covenants are proclaimed aloud, a series of silent hand signals informs the anointed ones about bonuses that will accrue when the others, the interlopers, are discarded. The hand signals instruct the children of the god-father in concealing, dominating, and surviving by manipulating extra information. One final hint from God: when necessary, use an epic nostalgic story of love to drown out the offstage noise.

God and his family cannot, however, admit information that disrupts their own tautological structure. Exotics must go. Error must be eliminated. In some larger pattern of contemplation, the Bible stories sit alone as little knots of trouble or even as marks of stalled or vestigial intelligence, because they do not recognize the contradictory evidence that is accidentally recorded within them. It sometimes seems that multiple games are being played, instructions even offered on how to play both ends against the middle; but that bargain always seems to return allegiance to a single game. The craft of the underhanded tactic is powerful, but all of this crafty intelligence is applied to repeating the structure rather than to growing it. Extrinsic information that might strengthen the game is eliminated to make it appear that one god's game is winning. While some are clever enough to coax a little success out of the odds, most are left trying to play by the official rules—rules that cannot, however, win against the tactics of players who play at more than one game.

Animals

Old and New Testament tales tell of recycling enemies, reconciling family, consolidating games, and making groups whose geometry is responsive to Euclidean formations (four opossums, twelve decibels). The structure is a weak one and must be continually shored up. The fight must be continually adjudicated. Tribes slaughter each other in valleys, or other spaces that return onto themselves. The Bible is not exactly a traveling story. Both Twain and Melville (more accomplished global travelers than almost anyone today) commented on the Holy Land's small size and how tedious it was that, given its size, it should contain so much history. Twain often compared the Holy Land to the American world of broad, long rivers and gigantic fields of crops, where the prodigal son never came home. He told his readers that nineteenth-century Jerusalem could be circumnavigated in a very few minutes by a "fast walker" and that Jesus did everything he did in the space of a typical county.[6]

In his fiction Twain often sent boys out to investigate the world, to move through it collecting contradictory evidence and different species of intelligence. Some people organize their minds with arborescent structures, but Twain's boys have minds of grass.[7] These sinners are propelled by their curiosity about how the world works, a world outside their families. They operate in river landscapes as collectors of extensive information. In Jerusalem, Twain's boys would have had the curiosity to dig up relics and grisly details, but they also would have had the courage and common sense to walk away from its neurotic self-involvement.

Twain seemed to put his boys in danger when he sent them out to meet Satan in *The Mysterious Stranger*. Twain's Satan was beguiling, and although he inverted the very structure of their lives, the boys loved him. Set in Austria during the witch hunts of the sixteenth century, *The Mysterious Stranger* tells the story of a series of senseless, tragic deaths, deaths of people close to the boys. Like the Bible's brief pauses in action for ethical demonstration, the "moral sense" that would condemn those supposedly practicing witchcraft was an endless source of amusement for the Stranger. Equally absurd, for him, were attempts to understand the chance happenings of sickness or death as predestined. Twain's Satan claimed that a moral sense was just another of God's clever ruses, to impose ethics on his followers so that He could have none. This was the common architecture of leadership. These were the usual privileges. The Bible tells us so on every page of the fight for Jerusalem and the story of demigods David and Solomon.

6 Twain, 486.

7 Gilles Deleuze and Felix Guattari, *A Thousand Plateaus: Capitalism and Schizophrenia* (Minneapolis: University of Minnesota Press, 1987), 15.

Parrando's Paradox

Lazar Beniamino Not., 22 Hillel Jerusalem TEL : 972-2-6240495 - Noam Dr. Meir, 12 Beit Hadfus Jerusalem TEL : 972-2-6518880 - Shoshani Moshe, 5 Avraham G
Jerusalem TEL : 972-2-6791186 - Weil Zeev & Naomi, 18 Hillel Jerusalem TEL : 972-2-6251729 - Zahi Eitan, 11 Strauss Jerusalem TEL : 972-2-5388190 - Zandberg
54 Netiv Hamazalot Jerusalem TEL : 972-2-5833390 - Zaretsky Hana, 33 Yafo Beit Yoel Jerusalem TEL : 972-2-6244128 - Zaretzky Aharon, 33 Yafo Yoel House Jerus
TEL : 972-2-6244128 - Zarfati Aharon, 7 Aminadav Jerusalem TEL : 972-2-6720280 - Zarfi Yoram, 33 Yafo Beit Yoel Jerusalem TEL : 972-2-6222727 - Zarzewski Yosef
19 Hamelech David Jerusalem TEL : 972-2-6250670 - Zecharia Shabtai, 97 Yafo Jerusalem TEL : 972-2-6246660 - Zedkiyahu Sasson, 5 Schatz Jerusalem TEL : 9
6245360 - Zefet Yaron, 216 Yafo Jerusalem TEL : 972-2-5000077 - Zeiger Meir, 24 Canfei Nesharim Jerusalem TEL : 972-2-6536360 - Zel, Goldberg & Co., 31 N
Hadkalim Jerusalem TEL : 972-2-5715030 - Zentler Emanuel, 23 Hillel Jerusalem TEL : 972-2-6243020 - Zentler - Goldschmidt & Co., 23 Hillel Jerusalem TEL : 9
6243020 - Zidan Suhiir, Shechunat El Ram Jerusalem TEL : 972-2-5740227 - Zieskoyt Maintenance Services Ltd.,1 Arlozorov Ramat Gan TEL : 972-3-6730
A.A.A. Ariel, 9 Anussei Mashhad Talpiot Jerusalem TEL : 972-2-6716603 - Guarding Services Ltd, 109 Harav Kook Kiryat Motzkin TEL : 97
8714123 - A. Lavie Ltd, 24 Ha'oman Talpiot Jerusalem TEL : 972-2-6428187 - B. A.M. Northern Services Ltd.Ashmoret, 8 Hataasiya Ind. 2
Talpiot Jerusalem TEL : 972-2-6711715 - Avishar Security, 28 Pierre Koenig Jerusalem TEL : 972-2-6798755 - Aviv Personnel Services Ltd
King George Jerusalem TEL : 972-2- Gdalya, 5 Hatzfira Jerusalem TEL : 972-2-5612316 - Zigler Eliyahu, Not., 2 Hillel Jerusalem TEL : 972-2-6235986 - Zilber
Aristoblus Jerusalem TEL : 972-2-6246291 - Zinger Anat, 18 Hillel Jerusalem TEL : 972-2-6251729 - Zinger Shalom, 36 Keren Hayesod Jerusalem TEL : 972-2-5633
Zinn Barry Michael - Notary, 4 Hillel Jerusalem TEL : 972-2-6256127 - Zitrum Ohad, 25 King George Jerusalem TEL : 972-2-6221414 - Zo'abi Samar, 48 Haneviim Jerus
TEL : 972-2-6257249 - Zohar Tamar, 18 Hillel -Jerusalem TEL : 972-2-6251729 - Zur Dr. Michael, 8 Davidson Jerusalem TEL : 972-2-6790821 - Zur Yehuda, 5 Hillel
Jerusalem TEL : 972-2-6222424 - Zvi Yonatan, 8 Keren Kayemet Jerusalem TEL : 972-2-6244162 - Zwebner Roni, 4 Mapu - Jerusalem TEL : 9
6245567 - Barak Veyofi, 237 Haahot Yehudit Jerusalem TEL : 972-2-6762487- Ben Hemo Jerry, 14 Aliyat Hanoar Jerusalem TEL : 972-2-5714
Cleaning Services Ltd., 10 Hamelech David Jerusalem TEL : 972-50-230227Cohen Aharon, 5 Hanered Ir Ganim Jerusalem
6247878 - Abas Aasi, 23 Hillel Jerusalem TEL : 972-2-6235482 - Abeles Amnon, 55 Hashivaa Beit Shemesh TEL : 972-2-9911280 - Abir Eli, 8 Bnei Batira Jerusalem
972-2-6785591 - Aboriya Eimon, 24 Ben Maimon Blvd. Jerusalem TEL : 972-2-5669525 - Abou Taama Jamal, 4 Salah A-Din Jerusalem TEL : 972-2-6286027- Abo
Yosef-Not., 23 Ben Yehuda Jerusalem TEL : 972-2-6234745 - Abouhoff & Co., 24 Canfei Nesharim Jerusalem TEL : 972-2-6527771 - Abrahami Amir Not., 6 Arist

LAWYERSJerusalem TEL : 972-2-6252252 - Abrahamson Ephraim & Co., 16 King George Jerusalem TEL : 972-2-6245881 - Abrahamy Eliezer - Not., 3 Haim H
Givat Mordechai Jerusalem TEL : 972-2-6789421 - Abramovitz Avi, 4 Balfour Jerusalem TEL : 972-2-5635112 - Abramowitz Ben Zion, 5 Eliash Jerusalem TEL : 9
6254242 - Abramowitz Dov, Technology Park Manahat Malha Jerusalem TEL : 972-2-6490649 Abramzon Arieh & Hava, 6 Shmuel Hanagid Jerusalem TEL : 972-2-625
Abu-Ata Ibrahim, 20 Salah A-Din Jerusalem TEL : 972-2-6285353 - Abu Ghosh Muna, P.O.B 51919 Jerusalem TEL : 972-2-6276086 - Abu Gosh Muhamed Ibrahim Neja
El Zahara Jerusalem TEL : 972-2-6272265 - 972-2-6410285 - Contracting Services Ltd., 8 King George 2nd Floor Jerusalem TEL : 972-2-6259214 - Di
Cleaning, Maintenance & Polish Ltd., 14 Meshiv Menahem Jerusalem TEL : 972-2-5377486 - Elia, P.O.B 13129 Jerusalem TEL : 972-2-65668
Globus, 17 Keren Hayesod Jerusalem TEL : 972-2-623687 - Kalinix Sara, 3 Abulafia Jerusalem TEL : 972-2-6247313 M.A - Abu Hadir Ma
Salem, 2 Abu Ubeida Jerusalem TEL : 972-2-6283860 Abu Hilal Walid, 3 Shchem Rd. Jerusalem TEL : 972-2-6287477- Abu Labda Majad, 5 Sultan Suliman Jerusalem
972-2-6286847 - Abu Lafi Anwar Fuad, P.O.B 51830 Mt. of Oives Jerusalem TEL : 972-2-6261407 - Abu Toama Jamal, 23 Hillel Jerusalem TEL : 972-2-6235482 - Ac
Ronit, 13 Shmuel Hanagid Jerusalem TEL : 972-2-6259653 - Adato Giora, 12 Shlomzion Hamalka Jerusalem TEL : 972-2-6255033 - Adetto Mordechai, 2nd Floor Jerus
TEL : 972-2-6250227 - Adler Eliahu, 16 King George Jerusalem TEL : 972-2-6259333 - Adler, Meser, Rivlin, 18 Shlomzion Hamalka Jerusalem TEL : 972-2-6251431 - A
Zvi, 36 Keren Hayesod Jerusalem TEL : 972-2-5633205 - Agron Amos, 22 Hahistadrut Jerusalem TEL : 972-2-6245292 - Agaloni Dror, 34 Ramban Jerusalem TEL : 9
5670760 - Aharoni Meir, 2 Ben Yehuda Sensor Bldg. Jerusalem TEL : 972-2-6250108 - Aini Yigal, 5 Hillel Jerusalem TEL : 972-2-6222424 - Albaranes Samuel, 11 Beit H
Givat Shaul Jerusalem TEL : 972-2-6527255 Albek-Fleischer-Schuster Notaries, 5 Nahum Heftzadi Beit Olef Givat Shaul Jerusalem TEL : 972-2-6595544 - Albek
Jerusalem TEL : 972-2-6595544 - Albom-Petel Yael, 12 Snunit Maasseret Zion TEL : 972-2-5333096 - Alon Ibrahim, 10 Salah A-Din East Jerusalem TEL : 972-2-6273
Alicia Lerner, Tzora TEL : 972-2-9908450 - Almi Mofid, 9 Ibn Sina Jerusalem TEL : 972-2-6282902 - Alon Daniel, 2 Ben Sira Jerusalem TEL : 972-2-6252524 - Alon Mor
King George Jerusalem TEL : 972-2-6255350 - Alon Yosef, 38 Keren Hayesod Jerusalem TEL : 972-2-560000 - Altbauer Yohanan, 10 Shlomzion Hamalka Jerusalem
972-2-6255848 - Alvan Zion, 10 Ben Yehuda Jerusalem TEL : 972-2-6246017 - Amiel Shlomo, 8 Strauss Jerusalem TEL : 972-2-5387227 - Amiras Leon, 2 Hillel Jerus
TEL : 972-2-6252206 - Amit-Kohn Uzi, 24 Ben Jerusalem Ltd., 4 Mordechai Hayehudi Jerusalem TEL : 972-2-6780761 - Mikud Security Guardin
Cleaning Svc. Ltd., 24 Canfei Nesharim Jerusalem TEL : 972-2-6511333 - Mizrahi Itzik, 28 Eliyahu Salman Jerusalem TEL : 972-2-6253552 -
Design, 23 Nisan Jerusalem TEL : 972-2-630073 - Or Habarak, 11 Bnei Batira Jerusalem TEL : 972-2-6799888 - **HOUSEKEEPERS** Polish
Ltd., 21 Ein Gedi Jerusalem TEL : 972-2-6333 - Reitline, 9 Nissenboim Jerusalem TEL : 972-2-6512530 - Sherutei Clalit Ltd., 40 King Ge
Jerusalem TEL : 972-2-6259704 - Shomron Maimon Blvd. Jerusalem TEL : 972-2-5669525 - Amit Shmuel, 14 Saadia Gaon Jerusalem TEL : 972-2-5632
Amnon Lorek, 31 Hillel Jerusalem TEL : 972-2-6239239 - Amsalem Shlomo, 24 Ben Maimon Blvd. Jerusalem TEL : 972-2-5669525 - Amster Yaacov & Co., 216 Yafo
Gates Jerusalem TEL : 972-2-5000077 - Anati Ibrahim Mohammed, 4 El Hariri Jerusalem TEL : 972-2-6250786 - Ansbecher Elisheva, 18 King George Jerusalem TEL : 9
6250410 - Arad Boaz, 32 Ramban Jerusalem TEL : 972-2-6662211 - Arad David - Not., 3 Washington Jerusalem TEL : 972-2-6257080 - Arad Moshe, 8 Hillel Jerusalem
972-2-6258898 - Argov Moshe, 23 Ramban Jerusalem TEL : 972-2-5665511 - Argov Ofer, 23 Ramban Rehavia Jerusalem TEL : 972-2-5665511 - Argov Ziona, 23 Ra
Rehavia Jerusalem TEL : 972-2-5665511 - Ariel Yaacov, 2 Ben Yehuda Jerusalem TEL : 972-2-6233431 - Arnon Yigal & Co., 31 Hillel Jerusalem TEL : 972-2-6239
Arnon Yosef-Carmeli Ariej, 9 Coresh Jerusalem TEL : 972-2-6245245 - Aron Richard, 12 Moshe Hess Jerusalem TEL : 972-2-6236971 - Arshid Sami, 9 Ussishkin Jerus
TEL : 972-2-5618574 - Artman Rami, Not., 24 Canfei Nesharim Jerusalem TEL : 972-2-6541944 - Asher Rogal & Co. - Notary, 23 Hillel Jerusalem TEL : 972-2-6248
Ashkenazi Avinoam, 13 Harav Herzog Jerusalem TEL : 972-2-5619772 - Ashkenazi Avraham, 10 Hillel Jerusalem TEL : 972-2-6254829 - Ashkenazi Yoel, Kiryat M
Jerusalem TEL : 972-2-6511037 - Ashkenazi Zvi, 13 Harav Herzog Jerusalem TEL : 972-2-5619772 - Ashraf AbedElkaddar, 2 Ben Yehuda Jerusalem TEL : 972-2-6252
Asli Walid, Salah A-Din Jerusalem TEL : Cleaning & Security Services Ltd., 97 Yafo Clal Center Jerusalem TEL : 972-2-6232829 - Silver Clea
Services, 3 Moshe Hess Jerusalem TEL : 972-2-6231991 - Ty Security Cleaning Services Ltd, 216 Yafo Jerusalem TEL : 972-2-5372
972-2-6283150 - Assa Aharon - Not., 6 Ben Yehuda Jerusalem TEL : 972-2-6251095 -5300130 - Atia Shalom, 5 Narkis Jerusalem TEL : 972-2-6231485 - Attali Shalom
Yafo Jerusalem TEL : 972-2-5381954 - Atzmon Avinoam, 43 King George Jerusalem TEL : 972-2-6247669 - Atzmon Matityahu, Not., 4 Aristoblus Jerusalem TEL : 9
6234020 - Atzmon Menahem, Not., 4 Aristoblus Jerusalem TEL : 972-2-6232029 - Auda Abed Allah, 1 Bab El Amud Jerusalem TEL : 972-2-6288517 - Autrabenger Ba
13 Mesilat Yesharim Jerusalem TEL : 972-2-6243161 - Avi-Isaac Dan & Co., 34 Hatayasim Jerusalem TEL : 972-2-5635161 - Aviad Ezra, 14 Coresh Jerusalem TEL : 9
6234187 - Avidani, 13 Mordechai Ben Hillel Jerusalem TEL : 972-2-6231111 - Avidani Isaac, 13 Mordechai Ben Hillel Jerusalem TEL : 972-2-6231111 - Avigail Von-Kre
5 Even Israel Jerusalem TEL : 972-2-6242818 - Avimor Yaakov, 23 Ramban Rehavia Jerusalem TEL : 972-2-5665511 - Ashkenazi Yoel, Kiryat Moshe Jerusalem TEL : 9

Twain's Satan, however, unlike the Biblical Satan, is not an errant part of the whole. He is an animal, but not the beast. Most Bible animals have to be domesticated or herded in pairs to mimic married couples, and they cannot be worshiped in brazen images. Mentions of exotic animals like whales or pelicans are only glorious accidents. In *The Mysterious Stranger*, Twain sets an episode around a dog that is being viciously beaten by two boys. In their crude hierarchy the dog is beneath them. They beat the dog so badly, "just for nothing—just for pleasure," that the dog's eye comes out.[8] Yet Twain's boys love the dog, and the dog looks to Satan for comfort. Satan replaces the dog's eye and understands his voice—the language of another species. The two chat for a while with the dog's head in Satan's lap while the boys look on with intuitive understanding. This Satan is not a poodle, a domesticated animal; he is no single animal but one of many animals. He is a point of translation to another population of creatures. He is a distributed mind. There is a world of comfort and solution in difference that is everywhere, unattached and free-floating. Twain's Satan is not a son of God or the cause of sin that requires the father's forgiveness, but productive error, the means by which to think around the moral tautologies of ostensive Bible stories—stories designed to continually recycle privilege to only a few. The boys had nothing to fear from this Satan.

8 Twain, 672–73.

> *But the Holy Land brought out all our enthusiasm. We fell into raptures by the barren stones of Galilee; we pondered at Tabor and Nazareth; we exploded into poetry over the questionable loveliness of Esdraelon; we meditated at Jezreel and Samarai over the missionary zeal of Jeehu—we rioted—fairly rioted—among the holy places of Jerusalem.*[9]

9 Twain, 486.

Architects

In the Bible stories, the demigods, or the first and second leads, may appear to possess exotic intelligence, but they are loyal to their insider heritage and when pressed will always run to it for cover. God provides one of these impostors of the exotic every once in a while to simulate a broad open world within what is really the closed loop of the game. Solomon was beautifully educated, an expert in diverse species of plants and animals. He also had exotic sexual tastes for women not in the family—women who enticed him into incense burning and idol worship. They were all the more desirable for being forbidden, and all the more dismissable when it was time to return to the script. Solomon was a bit of an operator—after all, he married the *Pharaoh's daughter*, not just an Egyptian, but the Pharaoh's daughter. He was one of the only sexualized charismatic figures in a culture that often officially denied this form of beauty. Indeed, Solomon was always a little too cool for the Bible—so much more tasteful and erudite than his humble, violent father, David. He was in charge of the official architecture, the temple, the monument to God that pretended to be a world in itself. Solomon was an architect, a member of a conservative profession that likes to play the aesthete.

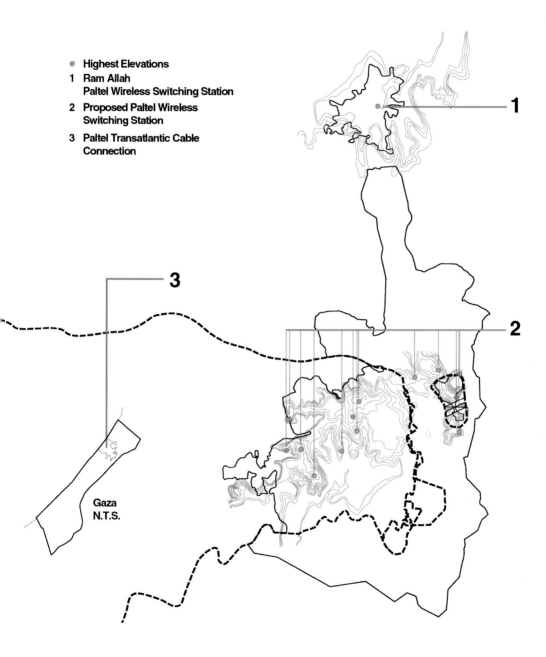

- **Highest Elevations**
1. **Ram Allah**
   Paltel Wireless Switching Station
2. **Proposed Paltel Wireless Switching Station**
3. **Paltel Transatlantic Cable Connection**

1

3

2

Gaza
N.T.S.

In "Solomon's Wise Judgment," as some editions of the Bible title this familiar story, two women were fighting over a baby (I Kings 3:16–28). The women, called "harlots" in the story, were also both new mothers. One child had died in the night and both women claimed the living child. The Bible says that God had given Solomon wisdom, and that in his godlike wisdom he threatened to slice the child in half to determine which one was the real mother. The real mother would not allow the baby to be killed; the false mother would not protect a baby that was not hers. It was so very smart and everyone was so impressed that they "feared" Solomon.

How easy it would be for a child to misread the usual Sunday-school illustration; to be suspicious not of the two harlots but of the arrogant man in the golden robes who has commanded that a razor-sharp sword be raised over a crying baby. How easy it would be for a child—or someone else who gets things wrong—to make this error. Before Solomon cut the hearing short, there was so much information in the story of the two prostitutes and the baby that they both wanted so badly, so much present and so much more needed, but he swiftly returned the focus to his own career. To this day, Solomon graciously accepts accolades from thousands of Sunday-school children, still with false modesty bowing deeply and waiving applause for his holier-than-thou theatrics. Was he wisely parodying the violence of his society? Or was he the violent one, not only because of his suggestion about slicing the baby, but because both women were a joke for him, a pawn in his larger game, like his exotic concubines or the Pharaoh's daughter? Like a pop star or demigod in closed society, Solomon was indeed an image of God.

Solomon was like so many peacemakers and planners who propose that others learn to share. God not only gave Solomon wisdom but he also gave him "forty thousand stalls of horses for his chariots, and twelve thousand horsemen" (I Kings 4:26). Even now, he remains a Jerusalem celebrity who does not have to share this spot with anyone. Like Solomon, the patient magistrates wearing beautiful clothes who summit over the Middle East, as if presiding over squabbling children, offer paternal advice: try a little harder to share and get along. These elegant men actually propose that the next *corpus separatum* will work, when it is nothing more than a blunt instrument that does not reflect the principal activities of the physical or social organization. Armed with the simple tools of planimetric geometry, these efforts continually reinforce the notion that national sovereignty and personal well-being reside in terrestrial territory.

Planners and architects also make poor peacemakers, since we too have a difficult time understanding site as a stratified condition that may exist in a section extending from subterranean regions to outer space. We have few tools for describing site as an active organizational condition and few instruments for identifying unorthodox opportunities in a complex context—sites that are active agents rather than mere properties or areas. Architects are interested in organizations that can be

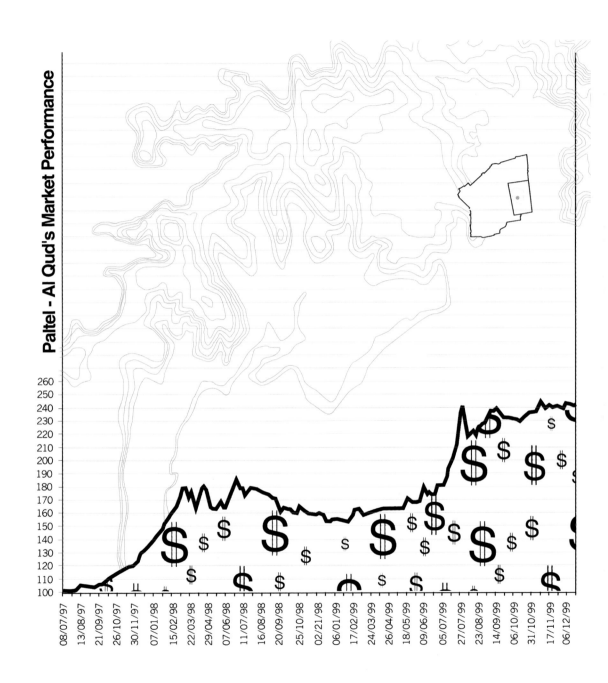

described with geometry and with orthographic projections—methods that will, however, never record the real intelligence of an organization, the space of its practices, its rejuvenating errors or its winning moves. Architects do their its best to harvest, contain, and plan error by *designing* urbanity. Fooled by complexity, they assume that a more intricate game is not a losing one, but by designing their complex game they have assured that it will lose. We merge and reconcile all games into one, pretending that we have been given Solomon's wisdom to author just the right division, the most beautiful line, the single most complex organization. The most advanced of the architects chant the non-cadastral, but often in a way that returns temporal and logistic architectures to a controllable aesthetic. Like God's exclusive family, we learn to play multiple games in support of the architecture of career, but rarely apply that intelligence to an architecture of unpredictable interplay between multiple sites.

Signals

The world marvels that the fight over Jerusalem could come down to ineffable desires for sovereignty. Not really understanding desire, we look for ways to appease it, substitute for it, sublimate it, or explain it in terms of the heroic logics of family. The desire to possess the Holy Land is not, however, the cause of the deadlock. Both sides will only succeed by wanting more, not less. Desire cannot be sampled, nor dreams confined to allegiances. That direction only returns the story to the anointed family and the horrible hierarchy of individual careers or tribes. Fueled by error and wishful thinking, the continual expansion and multiplication of sovereignty is a productive desire.

Cities succeed when they make a deliberate gamble with exceptional conditions, allowing themselves to amass an excess of circumstance, error, and contradictory evidence. They collect so many enemies and losing games that things start to go their way. Jerusalem naturally harvests huge crops of error. If allowed, it could acquire more and more enemies to diffuse the primary battles. If boundary lines must be drawn (and they must), the lines may be drawn on many different strata, in many different games at once, interdependently. To draw them in the terrestrial stratum only is to play a single, losing game that does not manipulate the actual material of sovereignty in the Middle East which may exist in terrestrial, orbital, virtual, religious, and political strata.

Sunday-school illustrations of Solomon or of a cloying, phony, crying Jesus might just as well be replaced by a chart or alphabet of signs and glyphs. Like an enlarged version of the pocket-sized cards circulated by the deaf, the chart would instruct us about silent hand signals—winks and nods, shoves and pushes, slapping and hitting, martyred trudging—code for the confidence game of the Biblical deity and his fierce

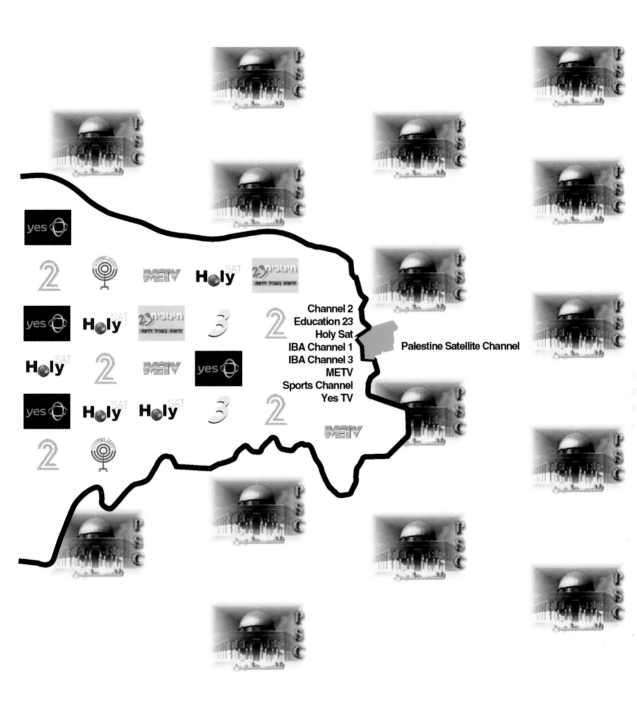

Channel 2
Education 23
Holy Sat
IBA Channel 1
IBA Channel 3
METV
Sports Channel
Yes TV

Palestine Satellite Channel

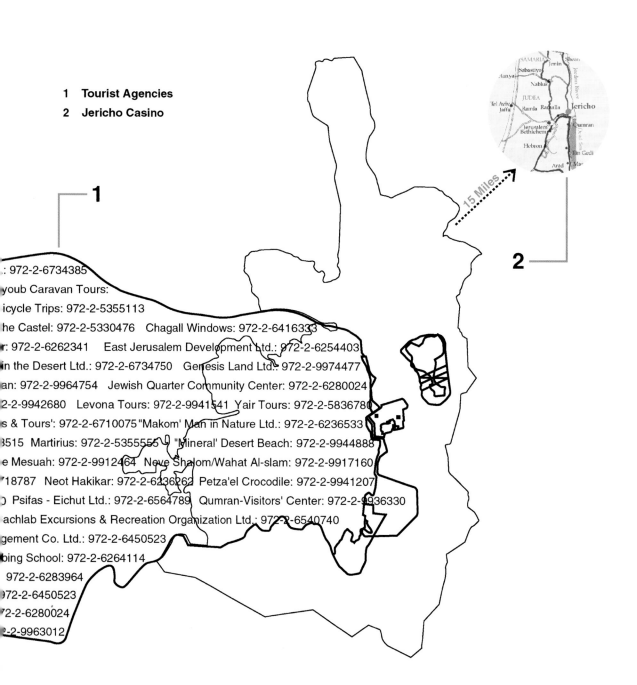

1   **Tourist Agencies**
2   **Jericho Casino**

1

2

15 Miles

: 972-2-6734385

youb Caravan Tours:

icycle Trips: 972-2-5355113

he Castel: 972-2-5330476   Chagall Windows: 972-2-6416333

r: 972-2-6262341   East Jerusalem Development Ltd.: 972-2-6254403

in the Desert Ltd.: 972-2-6734750   Genesis Land Ltd.: 972-2-9974477

an: 972-2-9964754   Jewish Quarter Community Center: 972-2-6280024

2-2-9942680   Levona Tours: 972-2-9941541 Yair Tours: 972-2-5836780

s & Tours': 972-2-6710075 "Makom' Man in Nature Ltd.: 972-2-6236533

3515 Martirius: 972-2-5355555   "Mineral' Desert Beach: 972-2-9944888

e Mesuah: 972-2-9912464   Neve Shalom/Wahat Al-slam: 972-2-9917160

'18787 Neot Hakikar: 972-2-6236262 Petza'el Crocodile: 972-2-9941207

) Psifas - Eichut Ltd.: 972-2-6564789   Qumran-Visitors' Center: 972-2-9936330

achlab Excursions & Recreation Organization Ltd.: 972-2-6540740

gement Co. Ltd.: 972-2-6450523

bing School: 972-2-6264114

972-2-6283964

)72-2-6450523

2-2-6280024

2-2-9963012

family of crafty half-wits. It could be labeled: "God's plan for us all." But for suspicious children or for Twain's boys or for other people who always get things wrong, this would be just the first of many cards in a series. There would be more and more cards behind that first one, each containing the moves of a different game, god, language, font, calibration—an incomplete series that feeds interplay and the excesses of resourcefulness. Each game would be error and exception to the other.

Notes

The accompanying documents record extra information, organizational attributes, and unconventional sites in Jerusalem. There is nothing of importance in any single site or document, only in the interplay between them. They do not provide instructions about how to unify or divide Jerusalem but rather about how to multiply it and the sites of adjustment and desire within it.

Jerusalem might already contain the ingredients of its own relief. Every conquest and seizure creates exceptional conditions, often sectional conditions that accidentally violate planimetric jurisdictions. There are sectional braids of jurisdictional lines—involutions within which the space of one enemy is nested in the territory of another. A sweet shop opens onto what is left of an old entrance to the Church of the Holy Sepulchre; a portion of the Wailing Wall is intertwined with an Arab house whose owners provide an outside light to assist Jews in reading their prayers. Like Gordon Matta-Clark's Fake Estates, in Jerusalem, the hilariously numerous lines of separation are all subject to mathematical exception. There are tunnels beneath them and topography that rises above them. The newest Palestinian villages in East Jerusalem and the West Bank cheat the mapmakers since, however distant they are, their topography allows them to possess a view of the Dome of the Rock.

Sprawl, too, is a beautiful source of error, though the architects and other players of losing games long to control it. It contains the means to expansion and annexation and trade-offs between new economies. It provides territory within which to make distinctions between religious and political sovereignty.

When an Israeli or an Arab gives their household help a ride home or gives them access to the other's segregated legal system, the winnings grow exponentially, not because anyone is consciously attending to their overt moral duty to share, not because the patient magistrates are declaring the city to be a "mosaic," but because playing between two games wins and because populations, rather than concentrated authorities, generate change over a broader surface.

Israel controls most licenses and satellite microwave frequencies, but PALTEL, a Palestinian company, has recently been granted a license to operate a wireless telephone network called JAWWAL. The network models elastic sectional boundary conditions and large fields of property and activity defined by a population. It exists within an enormous section marked not only by invisible signals and extraterrestrial satellites but also by switching stations in Ramallah and Gaza that are entirely dependent on high elevations in the terrain or access to transatlantic cable. JAWWAL makes clear the possibility that hilltop sites, most controlled by Israel, might be valued not only according to ancient covenants, but in shares of PALTEL stock.

Every employment agency or tourist center, every satellite that broadcasts another trashy television show, adds some new information to the mix. Jericho hosts global tourists as well as Israeli businessmen who are gambling alternately between two games: Israel's new Silicon Valley industry and Jericho's new casino just across the border.

Jerusalem is also multiplied in virtual and intangible forms. The only way that Twain, for instance, could reconcile the hype about the Holy Land with the reality he saw was to declare that it must have been a dream, no evidence of which he could discover. *Jerusalem 30* A.D., a living amusement community that is to be built near Midland, Texas, is not the only theme park reconstruction of the city.[10] And with every university appointment of an Arab scholar, the Arab diaspora plants a literature of Palestine, a dream of Palestine, in the minds of readers and students around the world.

Losing games played alternately might begin to amass circumstance, interdependence and, potentially, winning profits. These suggested plays offer an explicit architecture with an explicit landscape field, but with effects that are anything but planned. They do not define a recursive game, but rather the means to error and extensive information—access to millions of silent signals and advantages for good or evil.

10

www.j30ad.org/
www.architectureweek.com/2000/0906/tools_1-1.html (Architecture Week's coverage of a virtual-Jerusalem project)
www.imaginevr.co.il/vrjerusa.htm (a virtual Jerusalem tour)
www.kotelkam.com/ (live video of the Wailing Wall)
www.md.huji.ac.il/vjt/ (another virtual Jerusalem tour)
www.virtualjerusalem.com/ (a virtual Jewish community)

All accessed February 13, 2001.

The People of Jerusalem Reordered

Samira Haj

Introduction

For nearly a century now, the battle for Jerusalem has been fought partly on the terrain of demographics. The conflict has been consistently over statistical "facts"—over whose counting is essentially right, whose ideologically distorted. But what if we shift the terrain of argument altogether, understanding "statistics" as an inherently political process—one constitutive of social orders, not simply reflective of them? In this sense statistics, as Cooper and Stoler would argue, are "not just part of a wider battle, but a conflict over the nature of the battlefield itself."[1] I want to pursue this line of reasoning by making two points: First, I argue (following a well-developed tradition of philosophical and historical thought regarding statistics and governmentality) that statistics are generative of possibilities of governance and thus are constitutive of new forms of political practice and control over time. Second, I contend that while the statistical labels attached to groups and the names associated with people (e.g., Muslims, Jews, Christians) may not change over time, what these categories *mean* changes. This is because labeling and naming, like other conceptual and ideological acts, do not occur in a vacuum but inhabit a social setting within which they happen to unfold. Accordingly, to base claims on the efficacy of numbers without considering the social settings within which those numbers evolved is conceptually wrong and leads not only to misapplication but to the misappropriation of the numerical "kind." My intention is to shift the terrain of discussion over who can conjure up purer numbers (and so has "rights" to Jerusalem) by pointing out that the literature of "facts" is itself a product of historical processes, not the other way around. Unless we recognize and understand the historical processes undergirding these facts and numbers, it will be difficult even to imagine the creation of Jerusalem into an open space with equal access and equal rights for all.[2]

1 F. Cooper and L. Stoler, *Tensions of Empire* (Berkeley: University of California Press, 1997), 13.

2 Both Israelis and Palestinians have made their "rightful" claim to Jerusalem and to Palestine/Israel by crunching numbers and bidding for "truer" facts. A few such works are: I. Abu Lughud, ed., *The*

Transformation of Palestine (Evanston: Northwestern University Press, 1971); J. Abu Lughud, "Demographic Consequences of the Occupation," *Occupation: Israel over Palestine*, ed. N. Aruri (London: Zed Books, 1984); Justin McCarthy, *The Population of Palestine*, (New York: Columbia University Press, 1990); Y. Ben Arieh, *Jerusalem in the 19th Century: The Old City* (New York: St. Martin's Press,1984) and *Jerusalem in the 19th Century*, (New York: St. Martin's Press, 1989); Kimhi and Hyman, "Demographic and Economic Development in Jerusalem since 1967," ed. Kramer, *A Socio-economic Survey of Jerusalem 1967–1975* (Jerusalem: Jerusalem Committee, 1978).

Facts and Numbers in the Struggle for Jerusalem

The demographic profile of Jerusalem is one of the principal points of contention between Palestinians and Israelis today. Both sides assume that demographic dominance is key to the negotiations over the future of Jerusalem. Due to this, statistics (as in the social survey of people and landscape) play a special, if not unique, role in the struggle over Jerusalem. But what makes statistics such an apparently reliable source of knowledge? It is, I suppose, that statistics, as a numerical form of knowledge, are thought to provide an *objective* (rather than a *subjective*) vision of the world we inhabit. Widely used in the social sciences, statistics are regarded as unbiased thanks to their essential characteristics (especially their numeracy) and thus capable of offering a more accurate measurement of social reality. What about statistical studies of Jerusalem? Do existing classifications and enumerations of the city's population convey an empirical, hence accurate, vision of reality? Meron Benvenisti, a leading Israeli social scientist, appears, quite frankly, unconvinced. In his book *City of Stone* he says:

> One must regard general statistics on Jerusalem as a political statement rather than a reliable measure of the pertinent parameters that can stand up to analysis. The Israelis, cognizant of the importance of statistics and proficient at manipulating them, invest a lot of effort in their publication; and the fact that it is they who are in control and who have access to scientific institutes with great stores of experience and expertise forces Israel's political opponents to rely on the statistical data they [the Israelis] provide. . . . Thus, statistics, especially demographic statistics, serve as ammunition for the ultimate argument in the debate over Jerusalem.[3]

3 Meron Benvenisti, *City of Stone: The Hidden History of Jerusalem* (London: University of California Press, 1996), 173.

According to Benvenisti, statistics are incessantly mobilized in "support of certain political positions." Israeli Jews invoke the power of numbers to claim Jerusalem as theirs; they use statistics to demonstrate that "Jews are and have always been the majority" in Jerusalem. The Palestinians, in response, dismiss these numerical claims as "manufactured," "unreliable," and "distorting." These numbers, they insist, are founded on "contrived" borders that deliberately include Jewish neighborhoods and conspicuously exclude those of the Palestinians.[4] Summoning their numbers from the same Israeli "objective raw data," Palestinians verify that they are the majority within a more "balanced" map of Jerusalem that includes the highly populated Palestinian areas of East Jerusalem. Jewish demographic superiority, they add, has been achieved artificially by redrawing the borders of East Jerusalem after 1967 with the intention of excluding certain densely populated areas in the hinterland of Jerusalem.[5] The Palestinians' more nuanced map presumably follows more closely Michael Dumper's suggestion that an "accurate" map of Jerusalem should correspond to the city's topography and maintain its "residential and economic integrity."[6]

4 Benvenisti, 173–74.

Michael Dumper, nonetheless, is as skeptical of the existing numbers and their

5 Whereas the densely populated villages of al-Ram, Dahiya al-Barid, Bir Nabal, Beit Hanina, Azarriya, and Abu Dis were excluded from the newly drawn municipal borders of 1967, "their *lands* were included and subjected to expropriations and zoning restrictions." M. Dumper, *The Politics of Jerusalem since 1967* (New York: Columbia University Press, 1997), 56. Emphasis added.

interpretation as Benvenisti. In *The Politics of Jerusalem Since 1967*, Dumper warns us of the highly politicized quality of demographic analysis of Jerusalem:

> *Methods of enumeration and definition of subject areas can be used to lend weight to one political perspective or another, and the researcher has to be constantly vigilant in determining how and why a particular figure is offered. The categories in Israeli popula-tion statistics of "Jew" and "non-Jew," an illustration of the general Israeli policy of not recognizing Palestinians as a distinct people, also has the effect of blurring the demo-graphic profile of the Palestinian Arabs since not all non-Jews are Palestinian Arabs.[7]*

Both authors describe the prostitution of statistics in the game of politics; both argue that statistics on Jerusalem are overdetermined by political interest, which mars their objectivity.[8] It is true that any demographic representation of Jerusalem is highly politicized; my reservation about this line of analysis, however, pertains to statistics as a potentially *extra*-ideological measure of social reality. To assert that statistics can be employed as an ideological instrument implies that there can be a non-ideological use of statistics, and that "objective" and non-ideological statistics reflect the world as it is.

I want to put forward the idea that statistical knowledge as a modern form of representation is much more than a reflective measure of social reality and that its uses are more generative than ideological. Statistics, as Joan Scott's work on nineteenth-century France documents, create and produce attitudes and ideologies.[9] Through the "power of naming"[10]—the power of categorization, description, and labeling—statistical representation does not simply measure social reality, but actually contributes to its making. For instance, census-taking—the social-statistical operation *par excellence*—does more than simply count people; it reshapes people's percep-tions of themselves and the world they inhabit. As the philosopher Ian Hacking has put it, statistics "make up" people.[11]

Before going any further, it is important to point out that statistics, as a technol-ogy for classifying and enumerating, is a recent invention. We take for granted that statistical aggregates such as area, population, sex or gender, family types, gross domestic product, national debt, and so forth are identifying features of territories, and are used to represent territorial entities in this way. However, statistics have not always enjoyed this position; it became a powerful mode of representation only with the rise of the nation-state in Europe and America in the late eighteenth and early nineteenth centuries. Statistical knowledge, as the historian Silvana Patriarcha points out, is predicated on the idea that the nation needs to be objectively known in order to be effectively governed.[12] More precisely, as Ian Hacking explains in his article "Bio-power and the Avalanche of Numbers," the discourse of statistical numbers and numerical enumeration first arose in the Napoleonic era out of specific practical needs arising from imperial expansion. In the nineteenth century statistics became a

6 Dumper, 61–62.

7 Dumper, 55.

8 According to Benvenisti: "The utilization of numbers, which are by nature 'objec-tive' lends credibility to data that are shaped by values held by those publishing them, and these value-laden data are in turn used to pro-vide confirmation and backing for politically dic-tated politics." Benvenisti, 173.

9 Joan Scott, "Statistical Representations of Work: The Politics of the Chambers of Commerce's Statistique de l'industrie à Paris, 1847–48," *Work in France: Representations, Meaning, Organization, and Practice*, S. L. Kaplan and C. J. Keopp, eds. (London: Ithaca Press, 1986), 353–63.

10 The term is taken from P. Bourdieu, "The Social Space and the Genesis of Groups," in *Theory and Society* (1985), 723–44. Bourdieu argues that "the categories of perception of the social world are . . . the product of the internaliza-tion, the incorporation, of the objective structures of social space." Bourdieu, 728.

11 The analytic framework of this paper has been informed by the work of Ian Hacking, especially "Making Up People" in *Reconstructing Individualism*, T. Heller, M. Sosna, and Wellbery, eds., (Palo Alto, Calif.: Stanford University Press, 1986) 222–36; "Biopower and the

Avalanche of Printed Numbers," in *Humanities in Society* 5 (1982), 279–95; and *The Social Construction of What?* (Cambridge: Harvard University Press, 1999), 1–125.

12 See S. Patriarcha, *Numbers and Nationhood: Writing Statistics in 19th Century Italy*, (New York: Columbia University Press, 1996). See also T. Porter, *The Rise of Statistical Thinking* (Princeton: Princeton University Press, 1986).

13 The notion of bio-politics of population and statistics as a transformative agent of human life (bio-power) is Michel Foucault's and is discussed more fully in his *History of Sexuality*, vol. 1 (New York: Vintage Books, 1980).

14 Arjun Appadurai, "Number in the Colonial Imagination," in *Modernity at Large: Cultural Dimensions of Globalization* (Minneapolis: Minnesota University Press, 1996), 116.

15 Appadurai, 130.

widespread practice, encouraged by the emergence of the welfare state and the adoption by bureaucrats and reformers alike of the Benthamite principle of good government for the "greatest happiness of the greatest number." Statistics were initially concerned with the deviant and the socially marginal—the poor, the criminal, the homosexual, the mad—but by the end of the nineteenth century were extended to the management of the entire population. The idea had become firmly implanted that a centralized modern state could not survive without making enumeration a central technique of social control.[13]

Statistics proved to be as decisive a technique of control in the colonies as in the metropolis—with a difference. Statistical classifications, as Arjun Appadurai has pointed out, "had the effect of *redirecting* important indigenous practices, by putting different weights and values on *existing conceptions of group identity*, bodily distinctions, and agrarian productivity."[14] Appadurai, a scholar of colonial India, points to three differences between the operations of the census in the metropolis (Britain) and in its colonies (India). The census in Britain was primarily "territorial and occupational," whereas in the colony the census was "ethnic or racial." In Britain enumeration was largely concerned with sociological matters; in India, it became linked to the politics of communitarian representation, that is, of government not of (or by) citizens and individuals but of collective communities imagined as inherently unique. And lastly, Appadurai adds, while the census in the metropolis "reserved its most invasive investigation to the socially marginal," in the colonies the entire population was envisioned "as different in problematic ways." Conceptualizing the colonized as

> *aggregations of individuals whose bodies were inherently both collective and exotic . . . sets the stage for group difference to be the central principle of politics. Linking the idea of representation to the idea of communities characterized by bio-racial commonalities (internally) and bio-racial differences (externally) seems to be the crucial marker of the colonial twist in the politics of the modern nation-state.*[15]

In light of this, I want to suggest that statistical investigations of Jerusalem are not only performing a work of ideological and political legitimation but are contributing to the production of new forms of political practice and control. In the case of East Jerusalem, the practice of statistics-gathering is itself an important element in the practice of governance; as such, when it "reflects" the social order it is representing a social and political order that it is also in the process of constituting. Statistical knowledge has been crucial to the nature of Israeli governance, a reflection of a social reality crucial to the form of colonial rule that Israelis would develop. In this sense, statistical knowledge has actively contributed to the making of a Jewish Jerusalem and has actively participated in the creation of a hierarchy of power premised on privileging Jews over any other group. Statistics, far from merely enumerating the population of Jerusalem, have been a force in producing strife. Through an assortment of labels and classifications predicated on the separation of the "identical" and the "different," accompanied by legal and social practices premised on this separation, "Israeli Jews" and "Palestinian Arabs" have been encouraged to act upon their national and religious differences. To put it simply: Through practices aimed at making sense of the population in terms of national and religious types, that population has been *reconstituted* and *reinforced* (if not created) as one defined by national and religious difference. I dispute the commonly held view that religious strife is inherent to the region. While it is true that Jerusalem has endured many conflicts throughout its history, the issues, terms, and concerns underpinning these conflicts change over time. In order for us to arrive at a more nuanced understanding of the violence afflicting the area today, we first need to place its contemporary conflicts in the social setting that helped produce them.

Keeping this in mind, I turn now to analysis of the Jerusalem censuses and attempt to demonstrate that the production of statistical knowledge is not a matter of passive data collection but is, rather, generative and interventionist. When I say that statistics are productive of identity, I use the term *productive* to mean that statistics, like other modes of representation, not only report reality but supplement it. Before I go any further, I want to stress that whether the census statistics are objective, contestable, or questionable is not the central issue. Of central concern is *how* they have become indispensable to Israeli governance of Jerusalem and instrumental in shaping the values and practices of its entire population. Specifically, I want to highlight how classification of the population of Jerusalem, postulated on the separation of Muslim Arab from Christian Arab, of Jew from non-Jew, and so on, has contributed to the creation of a hierarchy of "rights"—rights that reinforce difference and enhance antagonism across national and religious lines. To put it differently, the classification of the population by religious and national or ethnic types produces a hierarchy of power, an ethnocratic reality that essentially recognizes only the Jews as legitimate members of the nation and thus both engenders and reinforces the Palestinian-Jewish rift.[16]

Statistics and the Production of "Kinds"

Religion is a key criterion for the social classification of the population of Jerusalem. In the censuses taken in 1967 and 1983, the population inside and outside the Old City was principally divided in terms of various religions and their denominations. There are tables upon tables enumerating the population of Jerusalem under the primary category of *religion*. One table classifies the population by "religion, sex, quarter and sub-quarter," another by religion and age, a third by "religion and sub-quarter"—and the list goes on. Thus, the population of the Old City is presented as an aggregate of diverse religious collectivities, as, for instance, Muslims, Jews, and Christians (divided into Greek Orthodox, Armenian Orthodox, Greek Catholics, and Roman Catholics).

16 Ethnocracy is a form of ethno-nationalism, "a political movement which struggles to achieve or preserve ethnic statehood" (Yiftachel, 364). Ethnonationalism combines, according to Yiftachel, the two political principles of the sovereign state and ethnic self-determinism. He defines Israeli ethnocracy as "the attempt to Judaize the land [of Palestine] in the name of Jewish self-determinism," which, he also argues, is the crucial point of contention between Jews and Palestinians. Yiftachel defines an "ethnocratic" regime as one that is "neither authoritarian nor democratic" since "such regimes are states which maintain a relatively open government, yet facilitate a non-democratic seizure of the country and policy by one ethnic group. Ethnocracies, despite exhibiting several democratic features, lack a democratic structure. As such, they tend to breach key democratic tenets, such as equal citizenship, the existence of a territorial political community (the demos), universal suffrage, and protection against the tyranny of the majority." (Oren Yiftachel, "Ethnocracy," *Constellations*, vol. 6, no.3 (1999): 364.

17 *East Jerusalem Census of Population 1967* (Jerusalem: Central Bureau of Statistics and Jerusalem Municipality, 1968), preface. See also Table 3, 6.

This is how the census report of 1967 put it:

> *East Jerusalem was divided into three regions—the old city within the walls, the northern quarter outside the walls and the southern quarter outside the wall. Each of these quarters was subdivided into sub-quarters and groups. The old city quarter, for example, was subdivided into quarters that run along religious sects, Christian quarter, Muslim quarter and Jewish quarter and Armenian quarter. The four parts of the old city, which traditionally are considered to be separate quarters, were for reasons of historical piety each regarded as a sub-quarter, although the population of three of them was not big enough to warrant this.*[17]

Counting the population of Jerusalem by religion is not an invention of the Israelis. It was done under the British and even took place under the Ottomans before them. My point, however (to be elaborated below), is that categories do not exist in an empty space. They unfold within a social material setting, a matrix of institutions, laws, policies, and practices. In other words, although the categories *Christian, Jew*, and *Muslim* might remain verbally the same, their import is different in different periods. And just as a Christian, Jewish, or Muslim identity is contingent on context, so the census process takes place under different regimes with different governing concerns. For example, a key Israeli governing concern after the 1967 war was how to render Jerusalem a national space for Jews, a space where Christians, Muslims, and others are tolerated but excluded from sharing physical space with or having the same rights as Jews. As such, Israel's prime concern in managing the population of Jerusalem was how to extend to East Jerusalem the ethnocratic regime privileging Jews over all other national or religious groups which had already been put into effect within the pre-1967 borders of Israel.

This plan was effected by means of a variety of policies and practices, including the following: (a) Four to five thousand Palestinian Arabs were evicted from their property to reestablish an enlarged historical "Jewish Quarter." These Arabs were forced to take up residence outside the municipal boundaries of Jerusalem, thus increasing the proportion of the Jewish population in Jerusalem. (b) In the "northern door-latch" project, Arab land was expropriated in order to reconnect Jewish West Jerusalem to the small enclave of Mount Scopus in the northern part of the city, which had been cut off from West Jerusalem in the aftermath of the 1948 war. (c) A thousand acres northeast of the city were expropriated to yield a new neighborhood connecting two Jewish communities, Neve Ya'acov and French Hill, in order to create territorial continuity between those two Jewish neighborhoods.[18] Further examples abound, but there is no need to repeat what has already been documented by both Dumper and Benvenisti.[19]

Besides strategies targeting the creation of a Jewish majority, the Israeli administration adopted measures toward the creation of a hierarchy of rights predicated on

18 See Dumper, 169–80.

19 Dumper, chapter 6; Benvenisti, chapter 4.

religious difference. An accommodationist policy was adopted toward Christian Palestinians. For example, the Israelis practiced a non-interventionist policy in the internal administration of the Christian denominations and granted special privileges to their clergy that included tax exemptions. They pursued a more aggressive policy toward the Muslims, as demonstrated by their forceful interference in the internal affairs of the *waqf* administration and the *Shari'a* courts, the eviction of *waqf* tenants in the Maqhribi quarter, and in the takeover of historic landmark homes of leading Muslim families.[20] While there are various explanations behind these different policies, they are immaterial to my argument. These measures contributed to the creation of a differentiated hierarchy of rights which in turn helped to create a rift between the Christian and Arab Palestinian communities.

Governance through difference not only helped to create discord among the Palestinians, it also gave the Israelis a space in which to insert and further valorize their control over Jerusalem. However, the Israelis did not encounter an open terrain for political domination. Palestinian Arabs proved capable of circumventing and undermining some Israeli policies and practices. The "Arabization" of the higher-echelon Christian clergy, for instance, helped to alleviate some of the resentment within these communities, since it helped to circumvent further selling and renting of lands to Israeli agencies.[21] In other words, Israeli governing practices founded on religious difference produced political resistance to the creation of a Jewish Jerusalem.

Religion, however, has not been the only key category in the social classification of population under the Israeli regime. Jewish identity is another prevailing category in the enumeration of the population of Jerusalem.[22] The 1995 census of Jerusalem, for example, added the classifications of "Jew" and "non-Jew" already in effect within Israel proper. Accordingly, tables upon tables on the future population of Jerusalem; the sources of its population growth; and the age, gender, occupation, and distribution of its populations are utilizing the categories "Jews" and "non-Jews" (occasionally "Jews" and "Arabs and others"). Although as national markers these categories are intended to distinguish Israeli Jews from Palestinian Arabs, the designation of Palestinians as a non-national group ("non-Jews") has facilitated yet another key governing policy: Palestinian Arabs are denied a distinct national identity.

In sum, identifying Palestinian Arabs as *Christians, Muslims,* and *non-Jews* is more than a principle for organizing census information on Jerusalem; it is an effective tool for social intervention and for inserting Israeli governing strategies and practices that inscribe these differences more profoundly. This is evident in the adoption of the "mosaic theory," a stratagem for turning Jerusalem into a Jewish city.

What is the mosaic theory? As has been amply documented, from 1964 to 1993, to make Jerusalem a unified Jewish city was the overarching goal of both the Israeli government and that of the administration of Teddy Kollek, the city's mayor.[23] Immediately after its occupation East Jerusalem was annexed, its Arab governing

20 Dumper, 184–97. The Israelis continued a policy practiced under both the British and the Ottomans. Yet the Israelis pursued this policy for fear of antagonizing the Christian world, which (as I will explain later) was a different concern from that which drove the British or the Ottomans to pursue such a policy.

21 Dumper, 174–75.

22 The label "Jew" represents both a national and religious form of identification since the categories of "secular non-Orthodox Jew" and "ultra-Orthodox Jew" are meant to differentiate the secular from the religious. See Yiftachel, "Ethnocracy," 364–90.

23 Both Dumper and Benvenisti have exhaustively documented the subject of making Jerusalem Jewish. See Benvenisti, *City of Stone,* especially chapters 4 and 5; Dumper, *The Politics of Jerusalem,* chapters 3, 4, and 5.

24 Dumper describes these events as follows: "On June 27, 1967, the Knesset passed an amendment to the 1948 law stating that the 'law, jurisdiction and administration of the state shall extend to any area of Eretz Israel *designated by the Government by order.*' The next day, the Israeli government carried out two important legislative acts. The first was to issue an order designating an area of 30,000 *dunums* of East Jerusalem and the West Bank stretching from Qalandia airport in the north to Sur Bahir in the south, and including the Old City of Jerusalem, for coverage by the amendment of the previous day. The second was to pass another amendment enabling the Israeli Municipality to West Jerusalem to extend its boundaries over exactly the same area to which the Law and Administration Ordinance was applied." (Dumper, 39; see map page 40.)

25 Benvenisti, 164.

26 Benvenisti describes this situation as follows: "Between 1967 and 1995, only 9,000 apartments were built for Arabs (as opposed to 65,000 for Jews), of which only a few hundred received government incentives. In (formerly Arab) East Jerusalem, by 1995 there were 38,000 new Jewish residential units, compared with only 21,000 Arab residences. An indication of the housing shortage among the Arabs is the fact that their average housing density is twice that of the Jews: 2.2 per room vs. 1.1. One third of the population lives in overcrowded conditions of more than three persons per room in contrast to 2.4 percent of Jews." (Benvenisti, 164–68).

27 Benvenisti, 164–65.

body suspended, and its municipal and administrative bodies turned over to the jurisdiction of West Jerusalem.[24] Shortly after, a development plan was adopted to create a Greater Jerusalem modeled after the mosaic theory—in essence, a plan to preserve the "traditional character" of Jerusalem as a segregated pluralist space made up of an assortment of homogenous but separate religious neighborhoods. This is how Teddy Kollek, the promoter and enforcer of the mosaic theory, envisioned his plan:

> This is part of the traditional character of Jerusalem and the new neighborhoods will certainly not change this. . . . The model of the Old City divided into religious and ethnic quarters—Jewish, Christian, Armenian and Muslim—is presented as a successful means for creating coexistence based on separate, undisturbed cultural and ethnic development of its constituent communities. According to the mosaic theory, the pattern of homogenous neighborhoods diminishes the tensions that arise when people of differing cultural backgrounds live side by side.[25]

Rather than attaining a peaceful pluralist Jerusalem, the mosaic plan became a pretext for launching (as Benvenisti has argued) "an aggressive intrusion into Arab areas via the construction of Jewish neighborhoods on expropriated land," leading to "extreme polarities" among the constituent communities. The designation of Jerusalem as a mosaic of self-contained "ethnic and religious communities" provided the framework for *willing* East Jerusalem to be Jewish. The plan for Greater Jerusalem, as has been openly admitted by a number of city official planners, projected the creation of physical and demographic facts—namely, appropriately located Jewish majorities—on the ground that these would "ensure Israeli rule over the unified city." One necessary measure toward that goal was to safeguard the ratio of the population at 28 percent Arabs and 72 percent Jews by effectively obstructing the growth of the Arab population and limiting its living space.[26] Palestinian needs, as one official brazenly put it, were "of no concern to the senior officials [since] they were interested in only one thing, what was it possible *not* to give the Arabs."[27] This non-benign neglect was blatantly visible in the 1992 budget of Jerusalem, which allocated less than 6 percent of its total to Palestinian neighborhoods. The Palestinian Arabs, while tolerated, were seen not as a community with legitimate equal rights "but as a *foreign element*, whose demands impinge on basic Jewish interests."[28]

My purpose, however, is not so much to chronicle how Israelis established Jewish dominance in Jerusalem as to underline how statistical representation of Jerusalem as a mosaic of religious kinds played an essential part in the reordering of the city as a national space for the Jews with the Palestinians tolerated as a "minority" of homogenous religious communities fated to live, in their own homes, a life of "non-Jewish" nonexistence. The body of statistical "facts" collected under these assumptions helped construct an authoritative image of a "Jewish Jerusalem" grounded in numerical knowledge.

The People of Jerusalem under Description

I turn now to my second central analytical concern, the assumption that statistical classification of "groups" and naming of "kinds" (e.g., Muslims, Jews, Christians) can transcend historical time. While certain classifications do remain verbally the same over time, they change in meaning. Religious, ethnic, and national identifications are socially produced, neither fixed nor predestined. The products of historical events, social and material forces, and ideologies, these identifications are not preordained by human nature or biology. Extending this line of argument to Jerusalem, I suggest that the violence over Jerusalem today, even its "ethnic" and "religious" modes of expression, is not historically given, as it has been frequently portrayed in the scholarly and nonscholarly literature.

Ian Hacking's work is again quite helpful. Hacking tells us that among philosophers it is an acknowledged "fact of logic" that "intentional human actions must be actions under a description." That is to say that if choosing an identification[29] is an *intended* act, it must have a description, because what a person does depends on "the possibilities of descriptions."[30] Thus, the opportunities for people's choices of action are dependent on the descriptions available to them. In relation to national identification, this means that there must be a particular national "identity" by which someone identifies himself and under which he choose to act before there can be a person of that national kind. As a voluntary act, therefore, identifying oneself must fall under a descriptor (i.e., Israeli Jew, Israeli Arab, etc.). In this sense, to identify oneself as an Israeli Jew depends on the availability of the relevant descriptor; a descriptor, it should be stressed, that is embedded in a particular time and social setting, for descriptions do not operate in an empty space of language but unfold within particular institutions, practices, and material interactions with other people. As Hacking points out, descriptions of human identifications are neither natural nor fixed throughout time, inasmuch as their meanings and significance change with the change in the setting. He gives the example of George Washington and the nineteenth-century descriptor "pervert." Hacking suggests that it

> would not have been possible for God to make George Washington a pervert. God could have delayed Washington's birth by over a century, but would that have been the same man? God could have moved the medical discourse back 100 years. But God could not have simply made him a pervert, the way He could have made him freckled or had him captured and hung for treachery.[31]

In light of these views, I wish to question the notion that conflict (often referred to as either "tribal" or "religious") *is* endemic to the region, that is, a feature that goes back to Biblical times. This notion is founded on the misconception that the categories of religious identification (Muslim, Christian, and Jew) are fixed and unchanging. It essentially assumes that institutions change but that people and their inherent religious conflicts remain the same. It also assumes that the difference between one historical

28 Benvenisti, 126. I use the term *tolerance* with qualification because what is tolerable and what is not, in the context of Israeli politics, is decided in terms of either tolerating Palestinians as a non-Jewish minority living in allocated and controlled places or not so tolerating them (which would imply their expulsion). The liberal administration of the Laborite Teddy Kollek, while tolerant by this standard, was interventionist and exclusionary, rather than neutral and inclusionary, as judged by the pluralist conceptualization of tolerance that John Rawls (a leading liberal theorist and philosopher) founds on the notions of "equal liberty" and "justice as fairness." See John Rawls, *A Theory of Justice* (Cambridge: Harvard University Press, 1971), especially chapter 4; John Rawls, "Justice as Fairness: Political Not Metaphysical," *Philosophy and Public Affairs*, vol. 14 (Summer 1985), 308–22.

29 I use *identification* rather than *identity*, when possible, because *identity* denotes more a fixed sense of being, thus eluding the processes involved in the social formation of the self. On the problematic of the term *identity*, see R. Brubaker and F. Cooper, "Beyond Identity," *Theory and Society*, vol. 29, (2000), 1–47.

30 Hacking, "The Making Up of People", 230–231.

31 Hacking's full argument in "The Making Up of People" is more complicated than presented above. He tries to demonstrate that categories are neither natural (read: static) nor totally invented (read: a human construct). Instead, they represent a process, a view that he calls dynamic nominalism and explains as follows: "The claim of dynamic nominalism is not that there was a kind of person who came increasingly to be recognized by bureaucrats or by students of human nature but rather that a kind of person came into being at the same time as the kind itself was being invented. In some cases, that is, our classifications and our classes conspire to emerge hand in hand, each egging the other on." Hacking, "The Making Up of People," 228.

32 J. McCarthy, *The Population of Palestine: Population History and Statistics of the Late Ottoman Period and the Mandate*, (New York: Columbia University Press, 1990), 2. Categories of taxation under the Ottomans included taxes on agricultural land, livestock, marketing, export duties, real estate. In addition, there were other taxes levied on Christians and Jews, the poll tax (levied only on male adults of sound health), and the pilgrim's fee. See K. J. Asali, "Jerusalem under the Ottomans: 1516–1831" in *Jerusalem in History*, K. J. Asali, ed. (London: Scorpion, 1986), 200–27.

33 The first demographic study of Palestine was conducted under the Ottomans following their conquest of the area in 1516. Its purpose was fiscal; the Ottomans wanted to know whom they could tax. It was only in the nineteenth century, under the Tanzimat (the reform era), that counting for the purpose of conscription was introduced. By the end of the nineteenth century, following the administrative reorganization of the empire, enumeration of the population became more exhaustive. The census of 1890, for example, collected

era and another lies merely in who is in charge of managing the conflict and how they do so.

While it is true that there have been Jews, Christians, and Muslims in Jerusalem for many centuries now, and that the city has been a site of conflict for some time, both the *meanings* of these forms of identification and the issues that have been at the heart of the conflicts involving them have changed over time. Therefore, it is senseless to speak of them as being the *same* religious identifications or the *same* religious conflicts.

More important for our purposes, the act of counting is always part of a particular, time-specific policy endeavoring to institutionalize a certain set of social meanings, categories, and identities, and therefore a certain social reality. For example, in the Ottoman Empire in the nineteenth century, enumeration of the population was primarily meant to facilitate the implementation of the empire's taxation and conscription efforts. While Muslim heads of households were registered for both taxation and "their usefulness as soldiers," the *dhimi* (the label used for Christians and Jews) were registered primarily "for their tax-paying abilities."[32] Muslims, as the only subjects "subject to conscriptions, were registered by their military status and availability for service," while non-Muslims "were registered by their economic status, the usual division being 'rich,' 'average,' and 'poor.'"[33] This explains why, for example, the figures collected on Muslims were for males between the age of sixteen and sixty and included such facts as name, place in the family, date of birth, and any physical handicaps ("blind," "crippled," etc.). It also explains why counting by religion was applied only to the city, where the majority of *dhimi* Ottomans resided, not in the rural areas, which were largely inhabited by Muslims. There, the populace was counted by households and not differentiated by religion.[34]

Furthermore, Muslims, regardless of their sect (*shi'a, sunni,' alawi, durzi,* or other), were registered under the category of "Muslim," while Christians were entered under their different denominations (Greek Orthodox—the dominant denomination— Greek Catholic, Roman Catholic, Armenian Orthodox, Protestant, etc.).[35] The explanation for this practice lies in the governing strategies emerging under later Ottoman rule. Counting Christians by denomination evolved out of an Ottoman decentralized system of rule known as the *millet* system—in essence, a system founded on maintaining the religious and political autonomy of diverse communities. Under the *millet* system, the Christian and Jewish communities (recognized as "People of the Book") were granted official status, which in practice meant that the Greek Orthodox and Armenian Orthodox patriarchs and the Grand Rabbi of the capital were recognized not only as the religious but also as the political heads of the Greek Orthodox, Armenian Orthodox, and Jewish populations of the Empire. It also meant that the hierarchical heads of each of these communities were held responsible for collecting taxes, enforcing religious law, overseeing education, and keeping order in their respective communities. Within this decentralized system, the Muslim

Ottoman Porte, as the primary caretaker of Muslim affairs, practiced a hands-off policy with regard to the affairs of the Christian and Jewish communities. But since the Christian community was made up of several different denominations that were antagonistic to one another, the Ottoman Porte, in a spirit of communal autonomy, arranged under special treaties ("capitulations") to grant European countries the power to protect their respective Christian denominations in the Empire (e.g., the French were the caretakers of Catholics, the Russians of the Orthodox, the British of the Protestants, etc.).[36] In the case of Jerusalem, this arrangement translated into giving European countries the power to administer the Christian holy places, which they exercised through their churches and denominations.

This arrangement with Christian Europe was made when the Ottoman Empire was at the height of its power, thus little concerned with any danger the Europeans might pose to Ottoman hegemony. Things did, however, change dramatically in favor of Europe. Emerging as the uncontestable world industrial power in the nineteenth century, European countries came to dictate their own terms to the "Sick Man of Europe," the European label for the Empire. Protective arrangements made earlier with the Ottomans shifted accordingly. Forced to cede more and more of its power, a weakened Ottoman Porte began to grant European consuls exclusive powers over their nationals in Jerusalem and elsewhere in the empire. One Israeli historian described conditions in Jerusalem in this period as follows:

> The consulates' power and influence grew steadily in the course of the century, with the consuls taking orders from no government except their own and their offices constituting a sort of miniature government. From their reports, it seems that the consuls thought of the Holy Land as annexed territory.[37]

Competition deepened and intensified as rival European countries reached out to co-opt the "non-Muslim"[38] communities (as Ottoman *dhimi* communities came to be known) as a way of inserting their power and asserting control over the holy sites. Even the meaning of the term "protection" went through substantial mutation, being dictated by a secularized Europe conceiving the world more in terms of political and legal "rights" and less in terms of religious belief and practice. Under the rubric of "rights," Europeans managed to extend their "protection" to groups other than Christians and beyond their own particular denominations. It enabled the British, for instance, to extend their protection to the Jewish minority, which, as the historian Alexander Schölch points out, became an effective way to foster their own influence in the region. Finding themselves undercut by fierce competition from the French (protectors of the large Catholic minority) and the Russians (protectors of the large Orthodox minority), the British had to "find or to create their own minorities to be 'protected.'" They did so by "taking the Jews under their wing" along with "a small Protestant community created by way of conversion."[39] It is important to note in this context that the British in this period sought only to protect the Ashkenazi Jewry, the new immigrants from Europe, as distinct from the local Sephardim, the Jewish com-

data on education as well as on the social and economic make up of the Empire's population. It was then that the category of religious and ethnic make up of the population became a prime identifier for the political management of the empire. This, as I explain above, was the outcome of the rising power of Europe, which formed a serious threat to Ottoman hegemony in the region. See J. McCarthy, *The Population of Palestine: Population History*, 2–5.

34 McCarthy, 15. In the case of the villages surrounding Jerusalem, many of its rural inhabitants were Christians but somehow were not registered under that category. Jerusalem and its countryside became an independent administrative province (*sanjak*) in 1886 due to the special religious and political position Jerusalem had come to occupy internationally.

35 This policy stems from the official position of the Ottomans, who, as Sunni Muslims, refused to recognize any sect other than Sunnism. All Muslims belonging to other sects were labeled simply as Muslims, meaning Sunni Muslims.

36 In fact, the first so-called capitulation was granted to France in 1535, which secured "French merchants a privileged position in the empire, guaranteed French subjects the right to religious freedom, and gave the Latin clergy the custody of the holy places in Jerusalem." Asali, "Jerusalem under the Ottomans," 206. By the seventeenth and eighteenth centuries, according to Asali, capitulations were offered to other European countries and were revised to include them as the "protectors" of their own denominations in the empire. Asali, "Jerusalem," 221.

37 Dumper, 181–82.

38 It is important to note that the category "non-Muslim" is most likely a recent creation by Europeans, since it was not a category in usage under the Ottomans. The Ottomans used the category "People of the Book" or "dhim" to refer to Christian and Jewish Ottoman subjects.

39 Alexander Schölch, "Jerusalem in the 19th Century (1831–1917)" in *Jerusalem in History* 228–48. The protection of the Jewish population by the British was arranged in the 1840s, before which point the Jews had no European backing.

40 It was also endorsed at the Versailles Treaty in 1919; the League of Nations followed suit, as did the British Mandate in Palestine.

41 The newly arrived Ashkenazi immigrants initially accepted the authority of the Sephardim but gradually broke away because of conflict over the distribution of funds raised in the diaspora. This led to the emergence of several independent Ashkenazi communities that later regrouped under one General Committee with a Chief Rabbi, rivaling the Sephardim community and their Chief Rabbi. Similar disputes lasting 30 years broke out between the Sephardim and Ma'aravim, which often turned violent and resulted in beatings and jailings. Dumper 197–99, see also Arieh, *Jerusalem in the 19th Century: The Old City*, 283–84.

munity officially recognized by the Ottomans. This favoritism polarized the Jewish local community between local and non-local elements.

In sum, then, while the classification of the population under the Ottomans was postulated on religious difference, it was tied to a governing strategy that generated different forms of action and interaction as well as different conflicts. The conflicts that dominated Ottoman Jerusalem in the seventeenth and eighteenth centuries were, for example, of intra-Christian nature—that is, between the Roman Catholic, Greek Orthodox, and Armenian Orthodox clergy and their European backers—and were focused primarily on access to and custody of Christian holy sites. Dissension was exacerbated during the second half of the nineteenth century by the arrival from the U.S. of Protestant missions from the Mormons and other Christian fundamentalist and evangelical groups. In an effort to ease tension and regain control over Jerusalem, the Ottoman Porte attempted to enforce an agreement known as "the Status Quo Legislation of the Holy Places," which essentially assigned the Greek Orthodox Patriarchy as the primary caretaker of the Christian holy sites. Although the Europeans endorsed the agreement in the Paris Peace Convention of 1856 and the Congress of Berlin in 1878, the Ottomans were still unable to regain control of or to eliminate the rivalry among the Christian factions.[40]

Moreover, European rivalry over the protection of "minorities" polarized the local communities, generating conflicts across communal lines and between local and nonlocal groups. By the end of the nineteenth century, tension between Muslims and Jews—especially Zionist settlers—was on the rise, an outcome not only of the rapid growth in Jewish immigration but of Jewish acquisition of Muslim land. Dissension between Sephardim and Ashkenazim and between Sephardim and Ma'aravim (Moroccan Jewry) became typical in this period. Disputes within the Jewish community centered on two issues: (1) Rabbinical power, or the question of who had the final authority in the community, the Ashkenazi Chief Rabbi or the local *rishon le-zion*; (2) the distribution of funds raised in the diaspora to maintain the Jewish presence in Jerusalem.[41]

Governing strategies under the British were dramatically different from those of the Ottoman era. A form of invisible colonialism, the British Mandate rule over Palestine was driven by two governing strategies: (1) protection of British imperial interest in the region; (2) the Balfour declaration, with its promise to facilitate a national homeland for the Jews in Palestine. The British, importing with them a polity organized around citizenship and rights and a concept of the nation-state grounded in a secular, centralized system of governance in which religion is reconfigured as a distinct domain, nonetheless continued to practice classification by religion, which had evolved under a *decentralized* Ottoman governance and in a context where politics and religion were never articulated as distinct domains of social action. The British justified their action as "socially necessary" because "of the complete jurisdiction enjoyed by religious communities in matters of the personal status of their members."[42] But as historian J. McCarthy argued, the first census taken by the British in 1922 "was designed for a political purpose—the enumeration of Palestine residents by religious group as the basis for proportional voting for a projected Legislative Council."[43] In other words, statistical enumeration by religion under the British was practiced to adjudicate indigenous communal claims for political representation, which in turn facilitated "normalizing the pathology of [communal] difference"[44] rather than the sharing of political hegemony or "the capacity to generate consent through the institutional space of civil society."[45]

One can surmise that enumeration by religion under the British was not a reflexive continuation of an older practice but a reflective act based on the British logic of governance. Even more important, it created new identifications favoring new forms of political practice and control. Categorization by religion within this context, while "not a figment of British imagination," to borrow Appadurai's description of the persistence of the caste system in colonial India, "reified and refracted what [was] already there—that is, an indigenous social imagination that appeared to valorize group difference in a remarkable way."[46]

In addition to the practice of classification by religion, the new conditions produced by the implementation of the Balfour declaration obliged the British census bureau to add a new category of identification founded on the "national" difference between "Jews" and "Arabs." In contrast to the 1922 census, the 1931 census included a question that allowed for the first time a "national" self-identification by residents and justified it as follows: "In the current life of Palestine . . . the further distinction between 'Arabs,' 'Jews' and 'Others,' which may be described as racial or national, has been found to be necessary."[47]

Again, my aim is not simply to narrate history but to highlight the point that the disposition and character of the people under description, as well as the conflicts arising between them, have changed between historical eras because the meanings of these descriptions and, by implication, the character of the conflicts they produce are contingent on social setting. As such, the possibilities for how Muslims, Christians, and Jews act under these descriptions has differed from one historical period to another, from one regime to another. Moreover, what it is to be a Muslim, Christian, or Jew has also changed from period to period, which raises the question of whether it makes sense to view these identities as constant over time.

For example, one can reasonably argue that "Muslim" is only one possible identification to choose from under the British. A person could also choose identify himself as an "Arab," in addition to being a Muslim, to demarcate a national difference; he could also choose to be a "secular Muslim" or a "practicing Muslim," now that religion and politics were articulated as two distinct domains of social action. These choices were available under the British but not under the Ottomans, since these descriptors (*secular, Arab*) did not even exist. The same can be said about the descriptor *Jewish*, which has changed dramatically over time. To be Jewish under the Ottomans meant to be local and Sephardic, to practice Judaism, and to speak Arabic; after 1948 to be Jewish is to choose between being Sephardic or Ashkenazi, "ultra-

42 *A Survey of Palestine: Anglo-American Commission of Inquiry*, vol. 1 (Palestine: Printed by Government Printer, 1946), 140–41.

43 McCarthy, *The Population of Palestine*, 28, 30.

44 Appadurai, 130.

45 N. Dirks, *Colonialism and Culture* (Ann Arbor: University of Michigan Press, 1992), 7.

46 Appadurai, 119.

47 *A Survey of Jerusalem*, vol.1, 142–43.

orthodox" or "secular and non-orthodox" (but not an "Arab"). In other words, in the Israeli context the meaning of the identifying category "Jewish" has changed and is constituted more in terms of national (Israeli) identity.

Similarly, the actions of a Muslim or a Christian under the Ottomans embodied meanings that are different from the ones they carry under Israeli rule. Instead of being bifurcated as a local or nonlocal Muslim or Christian, as within the Ottoman Empire, in the Israeli state to identify someone as a "Muslim" or "Christian" translates into two alternative ways of being a "non-Jew" and an "Arab" (but not a "Palestinian"). But, as Hacking points out, people do interact with their classifications and sometimes do circumvent their description.[48] This is best exemplified in the way Palestinians have been able to override their categorization as "non-Jews" and, through political, cultural, and other forms of resistance, to assert their distinct, national "Palestinian-ness" both locally and internationally.

In light of these observations, it is clear that the utilization of statistical numbers from earlier historical periods (e.g., the Ottoman period) to validate present claims (e.g., that Jews have always been the majority in Jerusalem, hence have a right to it) poses a conceptual problem. The official representation of Jerusalem as a typically segregated city (both communally and residentially) and the employment of statistics from different eras to verify its communally segregated character are also conceptually problematic.[49] They are problematic because the concepts of classification of people by type—as illustrated above—inhabit a social setting and depend on institutions, law, and practices for their actualization. And since different regimes have different governing strategies that favor different modes of political practice and forms of control, they tend to generate different possibilities for action and choice. So regardless of whether a given set of numbers is accurate or not, the more pertinent question is whether it is viable to use descriptions such as "Jewish" or "Muslim" at all as if they were timeless categories. To be Jewish in the Ottoman Empire was not the same as to be Jewish under the Israeli state. It is clear that today's religious and national identifications, whatever form they take, must be understood within the framework of today's reconstituted identifications: identifications, one might add, that have been reconstituted under the Israeli regime of power. Statistical knowledge, it should be added, is but one form of representational knowledge that has contributed to the creation of these identifications.

Conclusion

The questions of how statistics come to be informed by new descriptions; of how this affects the conceptualization of the statistics-gathering process; and of how the enumeration process, with its new categories of identity, helps inform the ways people act and conceptualize themselves are empirical questions and, as such, await further elaboration and research. Even without historical analysis of these mechanisms, the argument presented here is important insofar as it challenges the very concept of statistical knowledge as reflective of and religious conflict as inherent to Jerusalem.

48 Hacking, *The Social Construction of What?,* 31–32, 34.

49 In spite of his skepticism regarding statistics and their ideological usage, Benvenisti refers to the Ottoman statistics of 1905 to suggest that Jews were the majority in Jerusalem: He says that "out of the 7,500 family units whose permanent place of residence was Jerusalem [about half] were Jewish, some 30% were Muslim and about 20% were Christian." He then continues, claiming that Jews represented the majority in Jerusalem before the coming of the British and that they continued to grow throughout that period, reaching 55% in 1922." In his presentation, the category "Jewish" is fixed and ahistorical. "The Ottoman records," he states, "reveal the extreme degree of communal segregation characteristic of Jerusalem, including residential segregation . . . The compulsive recording of the ethnic and residential fragmentation of the city's population has not been confined to the distant past." Benvenisti, 170.

A Shared City of Peace:
Proposal for a Capital Region for Israel and Palestine
Oren Yiftachel and Haim Yacobi

None of us is completely free from struggle over geography. That struggle is complex because it is not only about soldiers and cannons but also about ideas, about forms, about images and imaginings.[1]

1 Edward Said, *Culture and Imperialism* (London: Vintage, 1993), 6.

Introduction

Peace between Israelis and Palestinians is commonly perceived as involving the establishment of a Palestinian state on most of the territories conquered by Israel in 1967, including East Jerusalem (also known as Al-Quds). But even among those who support the legitimate rights of Palestinians in the occupied territories, many have reservations about the partition of the Jerusalem/Al-Quds urban area, which is a likely result of any such settlement.

In this essay we propose a model for Jerusalem/Al-Quds that questions the need for divided sovereignty. We argue that a binational, multicultural city is a better option for the whole city (including West Jerusalem) on planning, social, economic, and political grounds. Below, we sketch current Palestinian–Israeli relations in the city and introduce key concepts and international examples that may assist the imagination of a binational, democratic Jerusalem/Al-Quds. We propose the establishment of an autonomous and decentralized Capital Region to include the Jerusalem/Al-Quds metropolitan area.

"Jewish Ethnocracy" and the Jerusalem Region

The question of Jerusalem/Al-Quds cannot be separated from the broader Zionist-Palestinian struggle over the land of Israel/Palestine. The events and processes that have unfolded in the city since 1967 vividly illustrate the existence and consequences of a regime that has been identified as a "Jewish ethnocracy." This regime stretches over the entire land of Israel/Palestine and finds striking expression in the Jerusalem/Al-Quds region.[2]

An ethnocratic regime is one established by a dominant ethnic group for the purpose of ethnicizing a contested territory. The dominant "ethnos" appropriates the state apparatus to facilitate its geographic, economic, and political expansion. Ethnicity, not citizenship, becomes the key to resource distribution. Ethnocratic regimes often use a democratic facade of open (though not universal) elections and of relatively open media to facilitate a decidedly undemocratic seizure of contested territories and polities. Such regimes existed in previous centuries in Australia and Canada and exist today in states such as Estonia, Latvia, Serbia, Sri Lanka, and Malaysia.[3]

Most ethnocratic regimes are chronically unstable. The expansionist strategies of the dominant ethnos commonly generate resistance from dispossessed and marginalized groups, liberal and left-wing domestic elements, and international bodies and organizations. These pressures can open cracks in the legitimacy and hegemony of the majority group, causing a series of transformations and dislocations, often violent.[4] Major urban areas are often the flashpoints of such events, as in Belfast, Montreal, Sarajevo, and Kuala Lumpur. These cities became focal points for both ethnocratic regimes and their challengers.[5]

The responses of ethnocratic governments to destabilizing pressures range from reinforced domination to compromise. The first involves denial of the rights of subject groups and the tightening of ethnic control (which often tends to escalate conflict in the long term). The second entails a gradual reconciliation with minority groups and the commencement of a process of democratization (which may face short-term crises but is generally more stable in the long term). The ethnocratic state of Israel is faced with a similar range of options throughout its territory, including the Jerusalem/Al-Quds region.

Despite Israeli-Zionist rhetoric representing Jerusalem as a "unified city," the Jerusalem/Al-Quds area has been an exemplar of an ethnocratic city since 1967. This approach has been pursued by both state and city authorities, which have persistently promoted a project of Judaization: that is, the expansion of Jewish political, territorial, demographic, and economic control. This attitude has even been formal and transparent within Israeli political discourse, as exemplified by the following recent media report:

---

2 O. Yiftachel, "Israeli Society and Jewish-Palestinian Reconciliation: 'Ethnocracy' and Its Territorial Contradictions," *Middle East Journal* 51.4 (1997): 505–19.

3. The concept of "ethnocracy" is developed further in some of Yiftachel's papers and by Mann. See O. Yiftachel, "Nation-Building or Social Fragmentation? Internal Frontiers and Group Identities in Israel," *Space and Polity* 1:2 (1998): 149–69; O. Yiftachel, "'Ethnocracy': The Politics of Judaizing Israel/Palestine," *Constellations* 6.3 (1999): 364–90; M. Mann, "The Dark Side of Democracy: The Modern Tradition of Ethnic and Political Cleansing," *New Left Review* 253 (June 1999): 18–45.

4 See Lustick's groundbreaking work on the rise and fall of ethnonational hegemonies: I. Lustick, *Unsettled States, Disputed Lands* (Ithaca: Cornell University Press, 1993).

5 For comparative analyses of ethnically divided urban areas, see S. Bollen, *Urban Peace-Building in Divided Societies* (Boulder, Colo.: Westview Press, 1999); S. Bollen, *On Narrow Ground: Urban Policy and Ethnic Conflict in Jerusalem and Belfast* (Albany, N.Y.: State University of New York Press, 2000).

Prime Minister Netanyahu, the Mayor of the city of Jerusalem Ehud Olmert, and the Minister of Finance, Ne'eman, will meet on Friday in order to discuss the revolutionary proposal of Olmert. According to the Mayor's proposal, the City of Jerusalem will get a special national priority, in order to struggle against the demographic decline in Jewish population in the city.[6]

As has been documented widely,[7] Israel has used its military might and economic power to relocate borders and boundaries, grant and deny rights and resources, shift populations, and reshape the city's geography for the purpose of ensuring Jewish dominance. Two central Israeli strategies have been (1) the massive construction of an outer ring of Jewish settlements ("satellite neighborhoods" in Hebrew), which now host over half the Jewish population of Jerusalem, and (2) a complementary containment of all Palestinian development, implemented through housing demolition and the prevention of immigration to the city.[8]

Israel's ethnocratic management has meant that despite the clearly binational reality of the Jerusalem/Al-Quds region, which has approximately equal proportions of Jewish and Arab inhabitants, urban governance has been totally dominated by Jews. Palestinians in the metropolitan region have been divided into two main groups: (1) residents of the enlarged Jerusalem municipality, who were placed under Israeli law[9] (in a move erroneously described by Israelis as "annexation") and given Jerusalem residency rights (but not Israeli citizenship); and (2) those residing in adjoining localities, who remained by definition in the "occupied territories," with no rights of residency or movement in the city.

Palestinians have also been excluded from the city's decision-making forums—most notably City Hall—by their refusal to accept the imposition of Israeli law and by the distorted municipal boundaries imposed on the city. This political weakness has meant that Israel has been able to quickly Judaize large parts of the Al-Quds urban area and surrounding hills with little (or ineffectual) Palestinian resistance. Judaization has taken place while Israeli decision-makers and state leaders portray the city as "reunited," "integrated," and "democratic."

Israel wishes the Palestinian residents of East Jerusalem to see Judaization as an "inevitable fact" that should be received passively. This view was expressed by the previous mayor of Jerusalem, Teddy Kollek, who governed the city for twenty-nine years and was considered dovish within Israeli-Jewish circles:

So, I do not want to give them [the Palestinians] the feeling that they are equal. I know we cannot give them a sense of equality. But I want, here and there, when it does not cost so much, and when it is just an economic effort, to give them, anyway, the feeling that they can live here. If I will not give them such a feeling we will suffer.[10]

6 *Ma'ariv* [newspaper], May 27, 1997. (Original in Hebrew; translated by the authors.)

7 For details of Israeli Judaizing policies see, among many others, Bollen, 2000; M. Dumper, *The Politics of Jerusalem Since 1967* (New York: University of Columbia Press, 1996); R. Khamaisi, "Israeli Use of the British Mandate Planning Legacy as a Tool for the Control of Palestinians in the West Bank," *Planning Perspectives* 12 (1997): 321–40; D. Klein, *Doves over Jerusalem's Sky* (Jerusalem: Jerusalem Center for Israel Studies, 1999) [in Hebrew].

8 For details and data see *Israel and the Occupied Territories: Demolition and Dispossession: The Destruction of Palestinian Homes* (London: Amnesty International, 1999); *On the Way to Annexation—Human Rights Violations Resulting from the Establishment and Expansion of the Ma'aleh Adumim Settlement* (Jerusalem: B'tselem, 1999).

9 Following the 1967 war most Palestinian residents within the Jerusalem municipal area were not offered Israeli citizenship and have refused to apply for it since this would legitimize the Israeli occupation.

10 Teddy Kollek in a protocol of the Jerusalem city council, December 17, 1987, cited in *A Policy of Discrimination—Land Expropriation, Planning and Construction in East Jerusalem* (Jerusalem: B'tselem, 1995), 7.

The city's one-sided management has also meant that economic development and services are nearly entirely geared toward the needs and aspirations of the city's Jewish population, leaving the Arab neighborhoods in a state of neglect and underdevelopment. Results include the gradual physical decline and stagnation of the city's Arab sectors, the cutting off of Arab Jerusalem from the Palestinian hinterland, and the subsequent exodus of Palestinian businesses north and south of the city. At the same time, development has occurred at a breakneck pace in the city's ever-expanding and modernizing Jewish areas.[11] However, the city's Palestinian community has continued to grow through natural increase and has struggled to continue residential construction activity despite a restrictive Jewish City Hall—indeed, often in defiance of the city's rules and regulations.

Managing Divided Cities

Our proposal is based on information from the fields of political science, urban planning, political geography, public policy, and ethnic relations, all of which can contribute to the stable and legitimate management of ethnically and nationally divided cities and other political institutions.[12] Such management is usually based on principles that tend to transform ethnocracy into democracy, that is, to introduce ethnic power sharing; broad participation in decision making; symbolic representation of all major parties in the city's landscape; and proportionality in the allocation of public resources, including land, infrastructure, public facilities, and ongoing capital flow. Most approaches to the management of ethnically and nationally mixed spaces also call for maintaining and fostering ethnic and local autonomy and stress the importance of institutionalizing local democracy.[13]

Several examples may prove useful for imagining a shared future for the Jerusalem/Al-Quds region. One is Brussels, which has been delineated as an autonomous binational province as part of Belgian constitutional changes undertaken during the last two decades. Belgium has been transformed from a unitary state into a bi-ethnic federation with large-scale autonomy granted to Dutch-speaking Flemish and French-speaking Walloons in their respective regions. Within this new state structure, Brussels has remained a joint capital city, "belonging" to both Walloons and Flemish. It has a separate constitutional status and is governed by both groups according to the principles of power sharing and accommodation. Brussels' urban affairs are administered in a decentralized fashion as if it were a "cluster of cities" where local planning, development, and education decisions are made by local communities.

11 Another aspect of the ongoing drive for (Jewish) development has been the increasingly adverse impact of international capital on the city's landscape, often without long-term planning or environmental controls, and with little participation of the city's communities.

12 For reviews of such knowledge, see Bollen, 1999; Dumper, 1996; I. Lustick, "The Fetish of Jerusalem: A Hegemonic Analysis," *Israel in Comparative Perspective*, ed. M. Barnett (Albany: State University of New York Press, 1996), 143–72; O. Yiftachel, *Planning a Mixed Region in Israel: The Political Geography of Arab-Jewish Relations in the Galilee* (Aldershot, England: Avebury Press, 1992).

13 Regarding these principles, see leading texts on public policy in multiethnic democracies: A. Lijphart, *Democracies* (New Haven: Yale University Press, 1984); W. Kymlicka, *Multicultural Citizenship: A Liberal Theory of Minority Rights* (Oxford: Clarendon Press, 1995); J. McGarry and B. O'Leary, eds., *The Politics of Ethnic Conflict Regulation* (London: Routledge, 1993).

Like Jerusalem, Brussels happens to have a prominent international status, being the administrative hub of the European Union. Although tensions between Flemish and Walloons have not disappeared under the new arrangement, and despite the excessively rigid and overregulated structure of Walloon-Flemish relations, the Brussels region appears to be functioning reasonably well. The new governing arrangements have gradually moderated the scope and level of conflicts between the two groups and institutionalized ways of resolving ethnic urban tensions.[14]

Another example is Chandigarh, India. Prime Minster Nehru promoted the building of this city during the early 1950s. It was to be the capital of the state of Punjab and was planned by Le Corbusier as a modern, open government center. But during the early 1960s ethnonational pressure by the Sikhs caused the partition of Punjab into two states, Haryana to the south and Punjab to the north. Yet the peoples of both states wished to maintain their capital in the internationally acclaimed city of Chandigarh, which was geographically close to the new border.

As a result, an autonomous region was carved out around the city, officially controlled by the Indian federal government in New Delhi but in practice self-governed by its multiethnic residents, who periodically elect representatives to City Hall. Chandigarh functions coterminously as the capital of two states, and even some of the government buildings, such as the Supreme Court and house of parliament, are shared, with different wings of these buildings designated for Punjab and Haryana use. Like Brussels, Chandigarh has a decentralized internal structure, with most urban affairs being determined on a "sector" (quarter) level. Chandigarh has many features unique to its Indian setting, yet offers a useful example of a capital city shared by two states with a history of ethnic conflict and separatism. These two states have managed to sidestep their territorial and ethnic tensions and to manage jointly a city cherished by both peoples.[15]

Both Brussels and Chandigarh illustrate the ability of two overlapping ethnic groups to share a capital city with a reasonable degree of stability and prosperity; equally important, the governing arrangements in these shared cities have assisted in stabilizing and democratizing ethnic relations far beyond their own boundaries.

The strategy presented below for the Jerusalem/Al-Quds region also draws on the many ideas, plans, and proposals already formulated by experts and activists for Jerusalem/Al-Quds. Notable among these have been the options prepared by the Jerusalem Planning Center at the Orient House, by the Jerusalem Institute for Israel Studies, and by experts such as Abu-Odeh, Benvenisti, Hasson, Khamaisi, and Khalidi.[16]

14 M. De-Ridder, "The Brussels Issue in Belgian Politics," *Western European Politics* 9 (1996): 376–92; A. Murphy, *The Regional Dynamics of Language Differentiation in Belgium: A Study in Cultural-Political Geography* (Chicago: University of Chicago, 1998).

15 G. Singh, ed., *Punjab: Past, Present and Future* (Delhi, India: Ajanta, 1994); R. Kalia, *Chandigarh: The Making of an Indian City* (New Delhi, India: Oxford India Paperback, 1999).

16 A. Abu-Odeh, "Two Capitals in an Undivided Jerusalem," *Foreign Affairs* 17 (1992): 183–88; M. Benvenisti, *City of Stone: The Hidden History of Jerusalem* (Berkeley: University of California Press, 1996); Dumper, 1997; S. Hasson, "Local Politics and Split

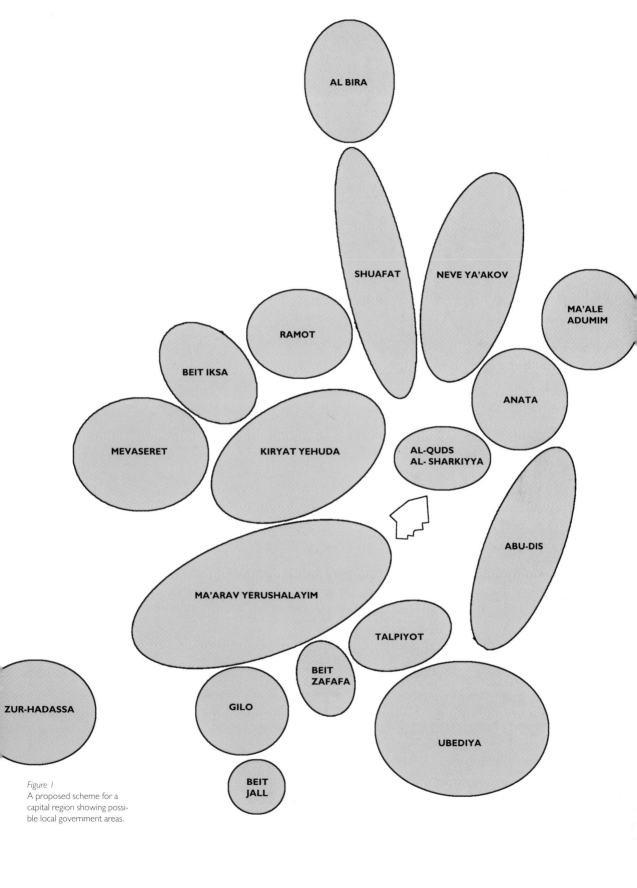

Figure 1
A proposed scheme for a capital region showing possible local government areas.

Citizenship in Jerusalem," *International Journal of Urban and Regional Research* 20 (1996), 116–33; M. Hirch and D. Housen-Curiel, *The Jerusalem Question— Proposals for Its Resolution* (Jerusalem: Jerusalem Institute for Israel Studies, 1994) [in Hebrew]; W. Khalidi, "The Future of Arab Jerusalem," *British Journal of Middle Eastern Studies* 19 (1992), 133–44; Klein, 1999.

Toward a Single Capital Region for Jerusalem/Al-Quds

Our proposal would enable the Jerusalem/Al-Quds region to function as one metropolis while reflecting the ethnonational identities of its two peoples. It is presented below in conceptual outline. We recognize that its details must be further worked out before it can be implemented.

The main components of our strategy (to be expanded below) seek to transform the city from ethnocracy to democracy by redesigning its political geography. Key steps include the following:

- Demarcation of an autonomous Capital Region under joint Israeli and Palestinian sovereignty; this region is to function both as the capital of Israel and Palestine and as a modern, democratic metropolis.

- Establishment of an umbrella entity, the "Capital Region Authority," to oversee the development and planning of the Capital Region.

- Creation of a set of new local municipalities to manage most aspects of urban life in the various quarters, towns, and villages that make up the Capital Region.

- Demarcation of a small area around the Old City to be managed by an interreligious "Holy City Council" (see Figures 1 and 2).

These steps will create a binational, multicultural city shared on equal terms by Israelis and Palestinians while allowing the many communities and localities comprising the Jerusalem/Al-Quds area to express and enhance their identity and character. The metropolitan region will be administered by a decentralized, federal-type urban regime, and governed openly and democratically.

A Worthy Move?

Why should Israelis and Palestinians prefer this option? Why should they head toward a joint urban future that may be fraught with tensions and rivalries? Why should they attempt to create a shared polity and society with a group toward whom they may feel mistrust, anger, and fear? Is the model we propose a risky recipe for endless conflicts and struggles between mutually suspicious collectivities?

We suggest that despite the unavoidable difficulties and risks associated with any period of profound transition, and despite ongoing tensions between Israelis and Palestinians (which are not likely to disappear quickly), the one-city approach is preferable to partition on several grounds. First, it appears that both states will benefit from the new arrangement. They will both have the entire Jerusalem/Al-Quds

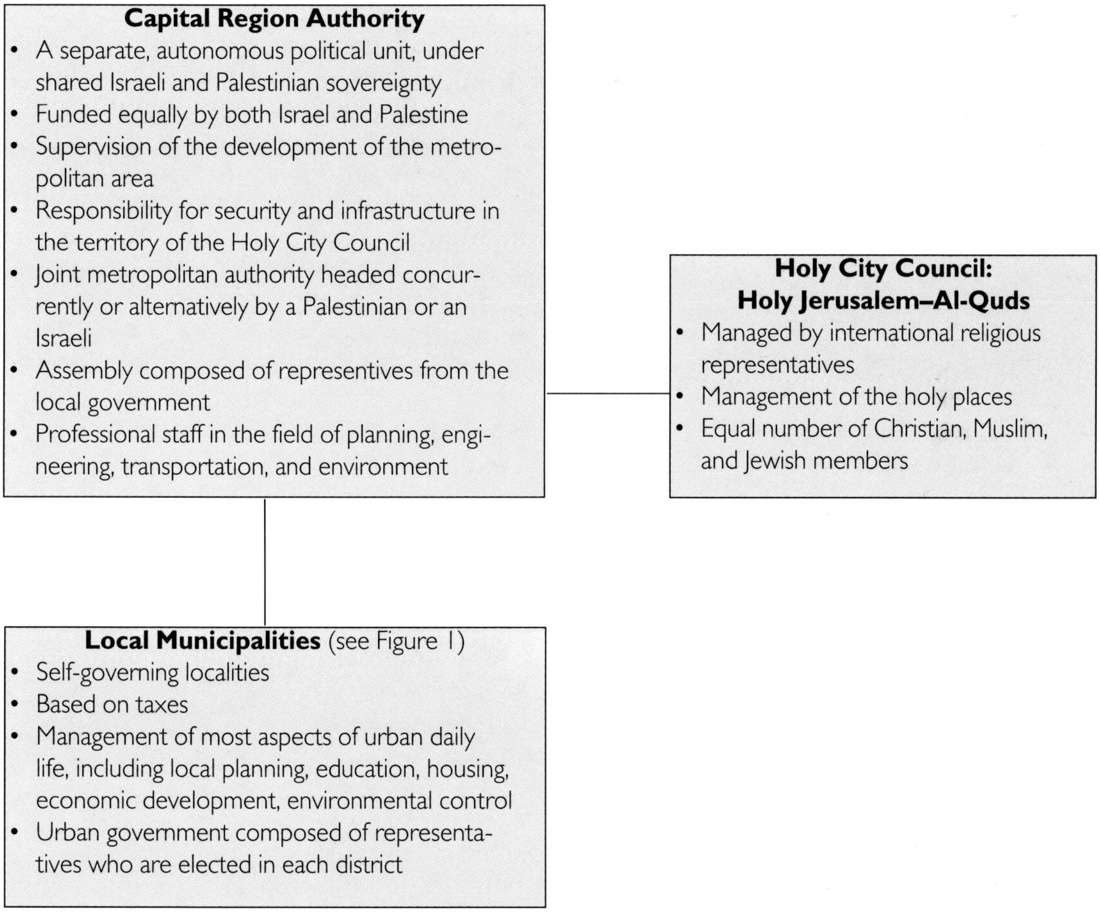

Capital Region Authority

- A separate, autonomous political unit, under shared Israeli and Palestinian sovereignty
- Funded equally by both Israel and Palestine
- Supervision of the development of the metropolitan area
- Responsibility for security and infrastructure in the territory of the Holy City Council
- Joint metropolitan authority headed concurrently or alternatively by a Palestinian or an Israeli
- Assembly composed of representives from the local government
- Professional staff in the field of planning, engineering, transportation, and environment

Holy City Council: Holy Jerusalem–Al-Quds

- Managed by international religious representatives
- Management of the holy places
- Equal number of Christian, Muslim, and Jewish members

Local Municipalities (see Figure 1)

- Self-governing localities
- Based on taxes
- Management of most aspects of urban daily life, including local planning, education, housing, economic development, environmental control
- Urban government composed of representatives who are elected in each district

Figure 2
Capital Region administrative structure

region, with its enormous symbolic and economic resources, as an official part of their sovereignty. Under this arrangement, the domestic and international status of both the Israeli and Palestinian governments will be enhanced, as the proposed approach requires each to sacrifice little in terms of geographic control while offering the gain of coexistence with the neighboring nation.

What is more, a united city will greatly enhance chances for economic development and prosperity. Given the momentum of economic globalization and the potential for a diminishing role of state borders, an integrated Jerusalem/Al-Quds metropolitan region is likely to attract international investment and become a true cosmopolis.[17] As an integrated urban region, it would receive enhanced tourist flow, a driving force of the city's economy. Partition would hamper such prospects.

Collective and personal security is also likely to be enhanced under a united arrangement. On a collective level, the mutual recognition of Palestine and Israel in the capital city of its neighboring nation will ease both Israeli-Palestinian and Middle Eastern tensions and alleviate security threats deriving from the city's contested status. Personal security will also be augmented, mainly because both states (with their well-developed security apparatuses) will have a strong interest in maintaining law and order in their political capitals.

Finally, on a broader level, achieving peace within a united Capital Region will send a message of genuine reconciliation to the rest of Israel/Palestine and beyond. Of course the injustices of the past will keep surfacing, and claims and counterclaims for the city are likely to linger for generations, accompanied by possible outbreaks of violence. Also, the legacy left by manipulation of the term "united Jerusalem" during the last three decades—a term that has only thinly veiled forceful conquest and domination—is also likely to hamper efforts to built trust in a shared city.

Yet our proposal for the city entails genuine (if "thin") unity, both geographically (by including the entire metropolitan region, in contrast to the current distortion of urban boundaries by Israeli authorities) and politically (by incorporating the city's Jewish and Palestinian collectivities equally into the political structure). This reality is likely to gradually change attitudes and increase mutual Jewish-Palestinian confidence. Such a process might transform both people's consciousness toward the "other" as well as toward their own territoriality.

Hence, it may be that instead of viewing the issue of Jerusalem's future as an obstacle to peace, as has been traditionally the case with policy makers on both sides,[18] a united Jerusalem/Al-Quds can become a catalyst for Jewish-Palestinian reconciliation. The model of a shared Jerusalem may form a reference point for groups elsewhere in Israel/Palestine, where creative frameworks for just, equal, and democratic coexistence between Israelis and Palestinians need to be invented and implemented.

17 For a wider discussion of the concept of the cosmopolis see L. Sandercock, *Toward Cosmopolis: Planning for Multicultural Cities and Regions* (London: Wiley & Sons, 1998), chapter 7.

18 Historically, most proposals that have dealt with the future of Jerusalem have emphasized division of the city. For a detailed review of these proposals see Hirch and Housen-Couriel, 1994; Klein, 1999; Hasson, 1996.

Putting Flesh on the Bones

Our proposal delineates the entire Jerusalem/Al-Quds metropolitan area—the Capital Region—as a distinct political unit under shared Israeli and Palestinian sovereignty. It will stretch between al-Birrya in the north, Ma'aleh Adumim in the east, Beit Jalla in the south, and Mevaseret Zion in the west, an area where some 750,000 people reside (about half Jews and half Palestinians). The area will be placed under joint Israeli and Palestinian sovereignty and managed by a Metropolitan Authority headed concurrently (or alternatively) by a Palestinian and an Israeli. The Capital Region Authority is envisaged as a "thin" political institution. Its Assembly will consist of representatives from the region's local governments and from the Israeli and Palestinian ministries. Its main staff will be professionals in the fields of engineering, planning, transport, and environment.

The urban region will include two capital precincts, which will host the Palestinian and Israeli government quarters. The Israeli government precinct will remain in its place (and will probably be enlarged) while the location of the Palestinian precinct will be chosen by the Palestinian people and the Al-Quds community. Some possibilities include the Sheikh Jarrakh, Wadi Joz, or Jabel Mukabber areas. The city as a whole will be mutually recognized as a state capital by both Israel and Palestine. This will guarantee the rights of both peoples in the city and slow the disastrous demographic and geographic competition between Israelis and Palestinians that has gone on since 1967.

The name we have chosen to describe the metropolitan area—the Capital Region—purposely avoids the titles "Jerusalem" and "Al-Quds." This is done in order to avoid the manipulation and distortion of spatial representation by which both sides have attached the names "Jerusalem" and "Al-Quds," with their immense symbolic powers, to areas that had never been part of the city. This approach has been particularly evident among Israeli-Jewish policy makers and shapers of the public discourse, who have imposed the name "Jerusalem" on many localities in the city's eastern, northern, and southern hinterlands.

This occurred, for instance, with the unilateral expansion of the Jerusalem municipal area in 1967 over localities such as Shua'fat, Beit Hanina, and Sur Baher, and with the building of new Jewish settlements on surrounding (often distant) hills such as Gillo and Ramot, now considered part of "Jerusalem." Such manipulation was evident in later years with the invention of new terms and entities, such as "Greater Jerusalem" or "the Jerusalem envelope," which covered even larger areas and acted as "signposts" of Israeli control over outlying areas. Given the sanctity of Jerusalem in Jewish culture, the effect of this geographical distortion has been twofold: (1) to legitimate the Judaization of Arab areas redefined as part of "Jerusalem" and (2) to freeze, silence, or marginalize any critical voices by portraying them as "supporting the division of Jerusalem."

The name "Capital Region" aims to evade the religious, historical, and political mega-importance attached to anything associated (whether historically or by means of symbolic manipulation) with "Jerusalem" (or, to a lesser extent, with "Al-Quds"). We hope to create a mainly administrative and professional entity that will govern the city's everyday affairs and future development without constant reference to heroic or tragic national narratives or to sacred religious and historical sites.

As a parallel step, our proposed plan will delineate a small area, including the Old City and its immediate vicinity, as "Holy Jerusalem/Al-Quds."[19] This area of about three square kilometers will be the only locality in the metropolis to carry the names "Jerusalem" and "Al-Quds." This will be historically credible in the eyes of many, as the area in and around the Old City truly reflects the location of the sacred and cherished Jerusalem/Al-Quds to which so many Jews, Muslims, and Christians have developed special bonds.

Therefore, unlike other proposals for the area (most notably the one associated with Abu-Mazen and Beilin), our plan aims to radically reduce the geographical extent of Jerusalem/Al-Quds. We perceive this as a long-term step in diffusing the potential of these names to invoke hard-line national narratives and to harden political positions, as has been so destructively evident during past decades. Let us contract Jerusalem/Al-Quds to its appropriate and credible proportions.

Under our proposal the small area designated "Holy Jerusalem/Al-Quds" will be declared as existing under "divine ownership" and be managed by an international, interreligious Holy City Council consisting equally of Christian, Muslim, and Jewish representation. It is expected that the area will be largely preserved and hence face relatively little redevelopment pressure. The responsibility for security and infrastructure, and the official sovereignty, will remain with the Israeli/Palestinian Capital Region Authority, but this will have little impact on the actual management of holy places, interreligious affairs, and tourism, which will be controlled by the Holy City Council. This arrangement will allow both Israeli and Palestinians symbols of sovereignty (such as flags or signs) to be hoisted over key points, such as the Haram al-Sharif or the Wailing Wall, while the actual running of the Old City will be managed by a body independent of the Israeli and Palestinian states.

Governing Urban Communities

A linchpin in our proposed model is the tier of local municipalities, where most actual urban governance will take place. This part of the urban governance structure will form the backbone of the region's communal, local, and urban planning management. Whereas the umbrella Capital Region Authority will be, as noted above, made up mainly of professional experts and the Holy City Council of religious figures, the

19 This approach has already appeared in previous proposals for reducing conflict over the future of Jerusalem; see Hirch and Housen-Couriel, 1994; Hasson, 1998. In recent debates over the city, several negotiators have used the term "holy basin" to refer to the same area.

local municipalities will perform the full range of urban governance functions, including local planning, education, housing, economic development, environmental control, and other daily procedures of urban democracy.

Accordingly, each local council will govern a population of around 30,000 to 50,000 residents. An effort will be made to arrange the metropolis into quarters and towns that will reflect the various religious, denominational, historical, local, and ethnic characters of the multitude of communities in the Capital Region.

At times, drawing the boundaries of local council regions will merely involve the recognition of long-standing or geographically distinct communities, villages, or towns as self-governing localities. Such localities may include, for example, Beit Hanina, al-Azariyya, Beit Safafa, Mevaseret Zion, Gillo, or Ramot. In other places, however, several neighborhoods of similar complexions will need to be amalgamated and new local councils created as centers of urban government. This redesign of municipal entities will attempt to create blocks of neighborhoods in such a way as to reduce the current frictions between radically different populations (such as secular and ultra-orthodox Jews) over the shaping of public spaces.

The naming of the new local councils will also be important; we suggest symbolic names that may reflect (or create) local attachments and characters. These may include titles such as Yerushalayim Hama'aravit (for secular Jewish neighborhoods), Kiryat Yehuda (for the orthodox Jewish areas), Al-Quds al-Sharkiyya (for the inner Arab neighborhoods), and Ikssa al-Foq (Upper Ikssa, for future Arab suburban neighborhoods in the city's northern parts).

What will be the nature of the Capital Region's association with the Israeli and the Palestinian states? The city's Palestinian and Israeli residents will be full members of their respective national political communities. As such, they will vote for their own parliaments and be subject, respectively, to the Palestinian and Israeli legal systems. The entire Capital Region will be open to both Israelis and Palestinian Jerusalemites for work, residency, and leisure. In case border controls are required by either of the two states, these will be placed at exit points from the city. This arrangement will ensure that the Israeli and Palestinian states are able to control movement into their sovereign areas without compromising free entry from either state into its capital city.

The special status of the Capital Region Authority will be further expressed in its autonomy in areas such as infrastructure, metropolitan transport, and environment. In order to diffuse potential tensions between the Israeli and Palestinian states and the city's municipalities, the Regional Authority will concentrate on professional matters, overseeing the smooth functioning of the region's urban systems. It will have its own set of "ministries" for environment, planning, transport, infrastructure, and the like, as well as a Capital Region police force.

The Capital Region Authority will not draw on local taxes but will be funded equally by the Israeli and Palestinian states. A special long-term fund should be established for the purpose of "affirmative development," that is, development aiming to reduce inequalities. The Jerusalem/Al-Quds area is rife with disparities, most notably between Jewish and Palestinian neighborhoods but also between the wealthy and the poor portions of each national community.

This special "affirmative development" fund, which may be drawn from international sources, is imperative for the improvement of Arab-Jewish relations. The effects of decades of neglect and discrimination that have left the city's Arab areas in a grave state of disrepair and underdevelopment must gradually be rectified. The fund will also enable the city to increase residential opportunities for its Palestinian residents, who have been highly constrained by Israeli policies. This will be achieved either by constructing new Arab neighborhoods or by compensating Arabs for property lost through unilateral confiscation or expropriation.

Concluding Questions

The institutional and geographical arrangements outlined above will create a federal-like metropolis that could be described as a "cluster of cities." This suits the current wisdom in metropolitan governance and the planning of divided cities, which emphasizes the advantages of decentralized urban management. This approach seeks to strengthen local democracy and identity while avoiding the alienation often associated with large urban areas and maintaining an overarching metropolitan identity.[20]

Are Israelis and Palestinians ready to face the challenge and risks associated with sharing Jerusalem? Are they willing to compromise the notion of absolute ethnonational sovereignty for the economic, cultural, and environmental welfare of the city's residents and visitors? Can they abandon the drive to create ethnocratic and counter-ethnocratic spaces in their national capital?

We are aware of the difficulties and hardships tied to the implementation of a shared-city strategy but believe that a transformation from ethnocracy to equal coexistence is possible. If it is to take place, it must at least be imagined by those policy makers who are likely to make major decisions about the city in the near future. We hope they will lead to the establishment of an undivided city, which would fit the description of Jerusalem in sacred texts as both City of Peace (Ir Shalom) and City of a United Whole (Ir Shalem), thereby providing a model for the rest of Israel/Palestine and beyond.

20 Barlow, 1996; P. Marcuse and M. Van Kempen, eds., *Globalising Cities: A New Spatial Order?* (London: Blackwell, 2000); Sandercock, 1998.

Epilogue

At the time of finalizing the first draft of this essay (summer 2000), intense negotiations were taking place between Israeli and Palestinian leaders over a peace agreement, including the question of Jerusalem. It appeared that redivision of the city was being considered in these talks, supported also by the Americans. In October, it became clear that the negotiations had failed. Among other issues, the future of Jerusalem/Al-Quds became one of the significant points for disagreement and a trigger for the al-Aksa Intifada. We recognize that if an Israeli-Palestinian peace depends on a divided Jerusalem, this may provide a short-term option; however, even if this occurs, our ideas for a shared city are likely to remain relevant in the long term, given the stubborn reality of common Israeli-Palestinian planning, economic, and environmental issues in Jerusalem/Al-Quds. The recent eruption of conflict and the stalemate in peace negotiations only underscore the need for a novel approach such as the one proposed here.

James Wines

Water never rests . . . If a dam is raised against it, it stops. If a way is made for it, it flows along that path. Hence it is said that water does not struggle. —Lao-tzu

You cannot step twice in the same river, for fresh waters are ever flowing in upon you. —Heraclitus

Premises

Jerusalem has been a city of religious strife and environmental abuse for more than three thousand years. While credited as one of the earliest centers of culture and venerated as a sacred site for Muslims, Jews, and Christians, the reality has been a situation of perpetual hatred, sanctioned in the name of God. Extending this climate of strife to the present, the current war between Palestine and Israel is simply one more confirmation of business as usual. The fundamental basis of contention remains the same: in a popularity contest among three self-anointed "chosen peoples," each constituency remains confident of its own favored position (to the exclusion of all others) in the eyes of the Almighty.

In researching this project, it seemed both fruitless and perilous to approach any architectural idea for this city from a political or religious perspective. While looking around for common ground to motivate a design proposal, the eternally shared Israel/Palestine water crisis seemed like a worthy focus. On further investigation, however, this proved to be just another contentious battleground. In fact, the paltry water supplies gleaned from the answered prayers of all three religions throughout history have invariably been credited as evidence of God's preference for one faith over another—a condition of favoritism that depended, naturally, on which group had the highest level of greed, the largest reservoirs, and the strongest army at any given time.

Project Description

As a result of the above observations, SITE chose to design a "Civilization Center" for the Western Wall Plaza in the Old Jewish Quarter. This decision was based on the fact that the area is presently a bleak and alienating space, desperately in need of shade, water, vegetation, and a cultural attraction (other than the Wailing Wall) for visitors' participation and enlightenment. It is also a potentially ideal environment for the installation of a nonsectarian, nonpolitical place of public assembly. Sidestepping the prevalent water-war issues in the Middle East (they always loom large in Jerusalem), this new center is intended to serve as a continuously changing environment where people can congregate to acknowledge the value of all things terrestrial. Water is the central theme of the plaza—with a focus on its universal status as the earth's most precious resource and not as an isolated regional problem with festering political implications.

The current Western Wall Plaza, built after the Six-Day War, is an inhospitable and relentlessly sun-baked slab of concrete. As an alternative, the SITE concept proposes a series of glass, stone, brick, stucco, and perforated-metal walls that produce a souk-like assembly of inside/outside corridors, rooms, and people spaces. The articulation of these various partitions—including a series of gardens, shade arbors, and water walls—is intended to maximize pedestrian enjoyment and, depending on the season, offer shelter from heat, cold, wind, and rain.

In order to stay away from religious/political associations, the Civilization Center walls are designed as transparent, punctured, fragmented, and screenlike structures. They are also intended to serve as a visual and physical alternative to the oppressive mass of the nearby Wailing Wall. The vertical surfaces and certain sections of paving are based on earth-centric (as opposed to metaphysical) symbolism, gleaned from universal sources throughout history. Most of the signs and symbols woven into the walls come from ancient Egypt, Mesopotamia, Greece, China, and various aboriginal cultures—especially those civilizations with multiple deities (as opposed to the concept of a single God, reflecting the image and behavior of man). The plaza is conceived to function as an acknowledgement of humanity's debt to sun, rain, bodies of water, greenery, and the continuity of nature's processes. The imagery is also influenced by the presence of a certain classic, nature-based symbolism in twentieth-century psychology and by the way these signs have been interpreted as a representation of stratification in social values and the potential of the psyche to embody rebirth and salvation in the collective unconscious.

Sections of the walls and spaces between them are intended for ecological exhibitions and demonstrations of the latest innovations in environmental technology.

Notes on the Sketchbook

This collection of drawings for the Civilization Center represents a work in process and the ever-changing implications of the concept itself. While perforated, vegetation-encrusted, and symbol-embracing walls are a basic ingredient, these elements are supposed to be constructed in way that invites future alterations and additions. By offering the opportunity for a continuous metamorphosis, it is hoped that this plaza will simulate the mutable and evolutionary qualities of nature and the interactive characteristics of ecology.

UNIVERSAL SYMBOLS

Sun

Water

Cypress

Olive Branch

Moon

Fire

Water/Fire

Fire

Phoenix Rising

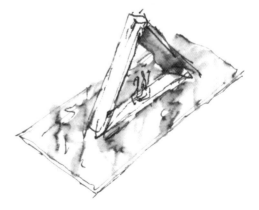

Civilization Center

Cross

Celtic Cross

Fish Trinity

Trefoil Trinity

Rosary Beads

Bread
(broken)

Chalice
(wine)

Dove and Olive Branch

Crown of Thorns

Anchor

JEWISH SYMBOLS

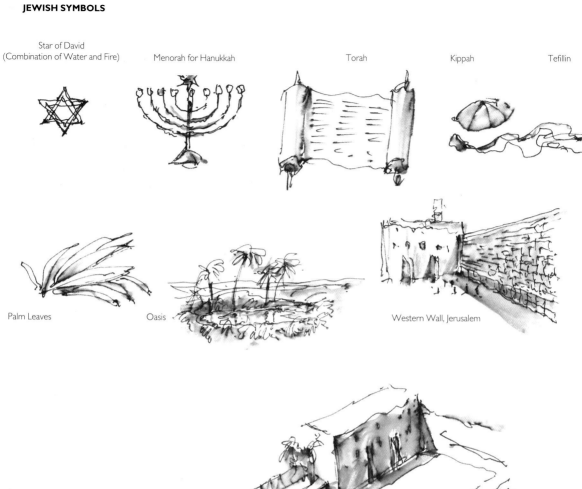

Star of David
(Combination of Water and Fire)

Menorah for Hanukkah

Torah

Kippah

Tefillin

Palm Leaves

Oasis

Western Wall, Jerusalem

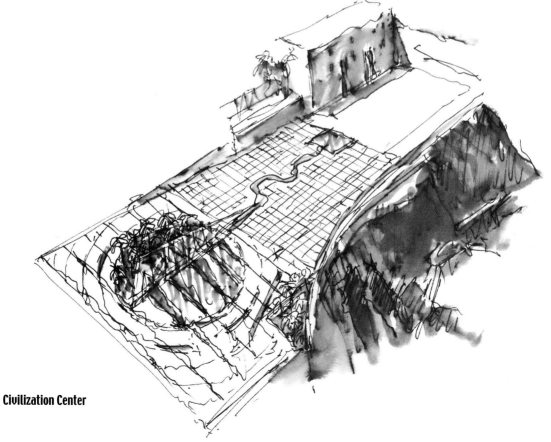

Star and Crescent   Compass   8-pointed Star   Dome of the Rock

Hand of God   Mosque Lamp   Dome and Minaret   Islamic Arches   Prayer Beads

James Wines

Spaces between the Hills

Stella Betts, David Leven, and David Snyder

Our proposal is the outcome of selective observations of the physical conditions and daily activities of the Ramallah-Jerusalem-Bethlehem region. These observations form the basis upon which our project rests, though by no means do they constitute an exhaustive study of the region's complex interplay of political, social, cultural, and religious elements. We therefore suspend any discussion of politics per se and focus instead on the urban-geographical fabric and what can be learned from the daily life of the region.

Our project begins with two investigations, one examining the natural topography of the region and how it affects urban growth, the other charting the schedule of the region's daily life—its particular temporal rhythm.

Our topographic analysis shows that the Ramallah-Jerusalem-Bethlehem region is profoundly shaped by two unique valley systems: one entering from the east and the other from the west. These extrude the region into a north-south linear urban formation. Road systems conform to the topography, neighborhoods are defined by the often precipitous nature of the landscape, and vegetation patterns are dictated by the interface between desert and highland ecological zones. These natural valleys or, more specifically, these spaces between the hills, which have functioned as the true physical borders of the region, are the sites for our proposed interventions.

As the natural conditions of the landscape determine the built environment in the region, so the confluence of the Christian, Muslim, and Jewish prayer times (the structure of the annual sacred cycle) frames the structure of daily life. Daily human activity occurs in the intervals between prayer, that is, between predetermined sacred times. Because the sacred schedules of the three major religions in the area are not synchronous and because the various religious communities share the same regional space, there are overlaps and gaps where the cycle of one

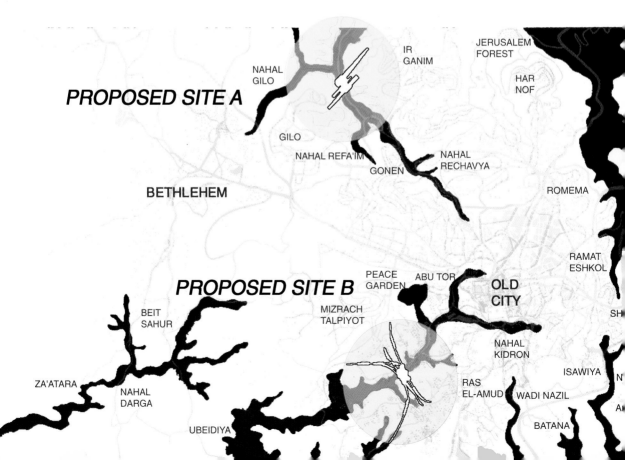

faith impacts the daily activities of the others. The temporal structure of the region is given largely by the staccato of daily, weekly, monthly, and yearly prayer times.

We propose a series of structures occupying the spaces between the hills. Following the centuries-old pattern whereby each new generation, society, political power, and religious authority has added its own layer to the urban construct of Jerusalem—sometimes incorporating earlier strata, sometimes concealing the remains of earlier ages—we, too, propose to add a new uppermost layer to the region. However, our proposal does not seek to cover over or supplant any existing elements of the built landscape; rather, it is a statement of hope, a vision of the future which takes into account existing sociopolitical and religious oppositions and redefines the space between them—literally. These unoccupied and unclaimed spaces between the hills become the next layer of the Ramallah-Jerusalem-Bethlehem region, a

region in which the coexistence of Palestinian and Israeli, of Muslim, Christian, and Jew, is openly expressed.

By choosing the spaces between the hills as the locus of our intervention and terrain for future development within the region, we hope to demonstrate the vision of the region as an integrated whole whose uppermost layer is founded not on the disputed earth but in its interstices, those which have traditionally acted as natural boundaries and defining edges separating neighborhoods and communities.

We propose three sites for occupying the spaces between the hills. Each site consists of a spanning structure which includes residential, commercial, educational, recreational, and municipal elements along with its central regional programmatic function.

Each of the three sites depicts a different architectural strategy in relation to the topographic conditions.

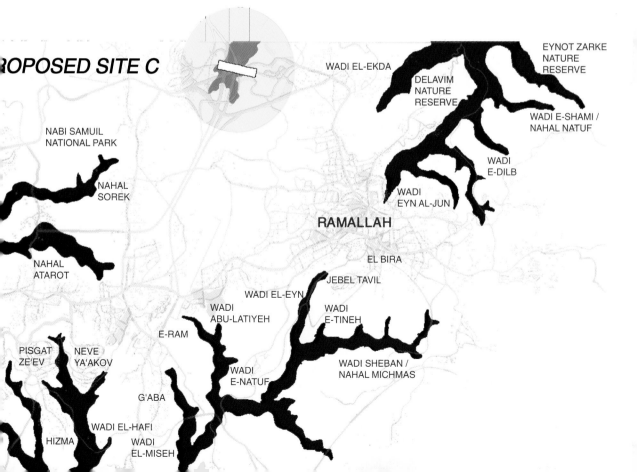

EXISTING RECREATION SYSTEMS IN
RELATION TO DAILY PRAYER CYCLES

SUNDAY   MONDAY

**ZOOLOGICAL GARDEN
TENNIS COURTS**

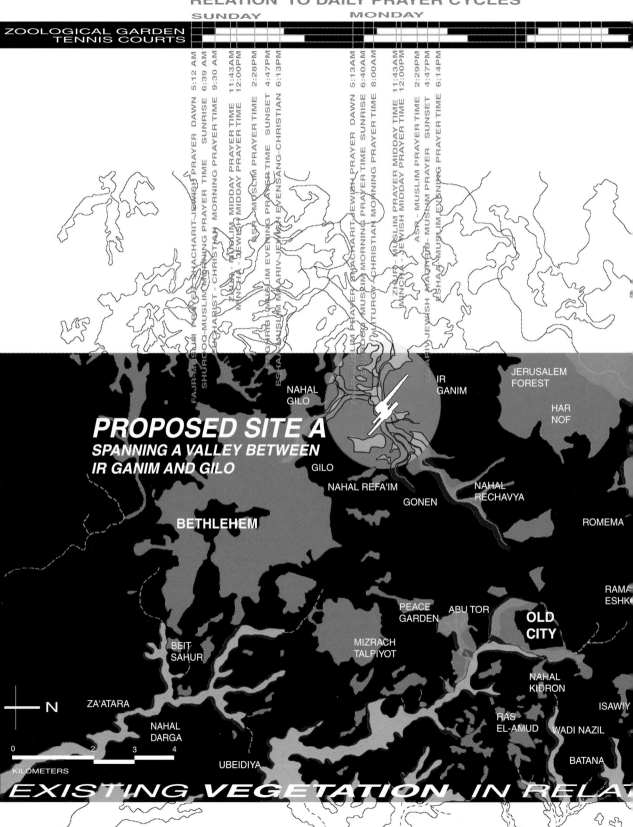

FAJR-MUSLIM PRAYER DAWN 5:12 AM
SHACHARIT-JEWISH MORNING PRAYER TIME
SHUROOQ-MUSLIM SUNRISE 6:39 AM
LITURGY-CHRISTIAN MORNING PRAYER TIME 9:30 AM
ZHUR - MUSLIM MIDDAY PRAYER TIME 11:43AM
MINCHA - JEWISH MIDDAY PRAYER TIME 12:00PM
ASR-MUSLIM PRAYER TIME 2:28PM
MAGHRIB-MUSLIM EVENING PRAYER TIME 4:47PM
EISHA-MUSLIM MAARIV-JEWISH EVENSANG-CHRISTIAN SUNSET 6:13PM

FAJR-MUSLIM PRAYER DAWN SHACHARIT-JEWISH PRAYER 5:13AM
SHUROOQ-MUSLIM MORNING PRAYER TIME SUNRISE 6:40AM
LITURGY-CHRISTIAN MORNING PRAYER TIME 8:00AM
ZHUR - MUSLIM PRAYER MIDDAY TIME 11:43AM
MINCHA - JEWISH MIDDAY PRAYER TIME 12:00PM
ASR - MUSLIM PRAYER TIME 2:29PM
MAGHRIB-JEWISH MUSLIM PRAYER SUNSET 4:47PM
EISHAQ-MUSLIM EVENING PRAYER TIME 6:14PM

NAHAL
GILO

IR
GANIM

JERUSALEM
FOREST

HAR
NOF

PROPOSED SITE A
*SPANNING A VALLEY BETWEEN
IR GANIM AND GILO*

GILO

NAHAL REFA'IM

GONEN

NAHAL
RECHAVYA

ROMEMA

BETHLEHEM

PEACE
GARDEN

ABU TOR

**OLD
CITY**

RAMA
ESHK

MIZRACH
TALPIYOT

BEIT
SAHUR

NAHAL
KIDRON

N

ZA'ATARA

RAS
EL-AMUD

WADI NAZIL

ISAWIY

NAHAL
DARGA

BATANA

0   2   3   4

KILOMETERS

UBEIDIYA

EXISTING VEGETATION IN RELAT

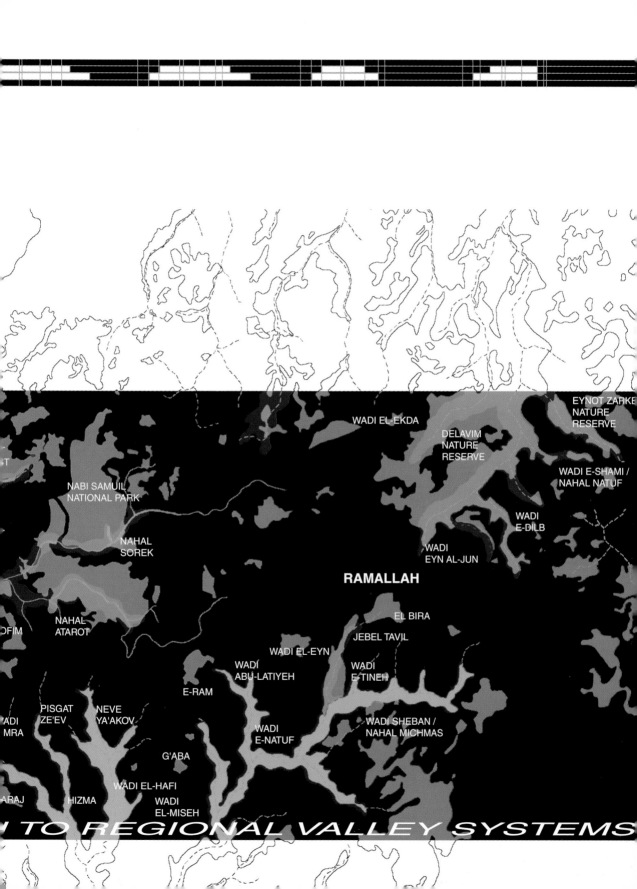

TO REGIONAL VALLEY SYSTEMS

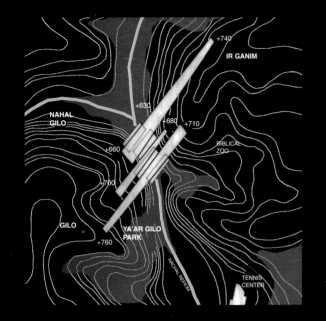

**PROPOSED SITE A
RECREATIONAL SEESAW**

A seesaw that negotiates the topography with a series of ramps. The central regional programmatic function for this site is a recreational node composed of a ramping park system that generates the primary form and function of this typology. In this space between the hills, playing fields exist and form the connection to the adjacent existing neighborhoods of Ir Ganim and Gilo, as well as the Refa'im and Nahal Gilo nature preserves.

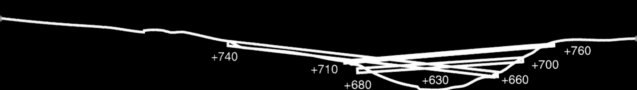

AWN FAJR - MUSLIM PRAYER / SHACHARIT - JEWISH PRAYER / S

ath, Morning joggers run along path/LITURGY-CHRISTIAN MORNING

INCHA- JEWISH MIDDAY PRAYER / Soccer practice, Little softball le

UNSET MAGHRIB-MUSLIM PRAYER / MAARIV-JEWISH PRAYER Ir

am practice Nature walk ESHA-MUSLIM EVENING PRAYER / After d

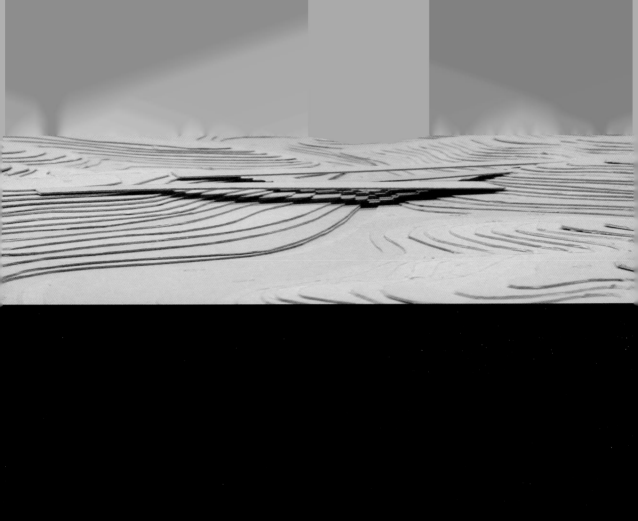

E SHUROOQ- MUSLIM MORNING PRAYER Cyclists ride along bike

R /Indoor swimming- Adult hour, Stretch Class / ZHUR - MUSLIM PRA

ennis Courts reserved for private lessons / ASR- MUSLIM PRAYER

wimming-group lesson, Pick-up Basketball, Soccor league playoffs, Tra

alk Playaround Evening Tennis Courts Indoor swimming - family hour

LIBRARY
JEWISH SHOPS
MUSLIM SHOPS
CHRISTIAN SHOPS
MUSEUMS
TRAVEL AGENT
HAIRDRESSER
GOVERNMENT
POST OFFICE
BANKS

FAJR-MUSLIM PRAYER DAWN 5:13AM
SHACHARIT-JEWISH PRAYER 6:40AM
SHUROOQ-MUSLIM MORNING PRAYER TIME SUNRISE 8:00AM
LITURGY - CHRISTIAN MORNING PRAYER TIME

ZHUR - MUSLIM MIDDAY PRAYER TIME 11:44AM
MINCHA - JEWISH MIDDAY PRAYER TIME 12:00PM

ASR - MUSLIM PRAYER TIME 2:30PM
MAGHRIB-MUSLIM PRAYER TIME SUNSET 4:48PM
MAARIB-JEWISH PRAYER
ISHA-MUSLIM EVENING PRAYER TIME 6:15PM

NAHAL
GILO

IR
GANIM

JERUSALEM
FOREST

HAR
NOF

GILO

NAHAL REFA'IM

GONEN

NAHAL
RECHAVYA

BETHLEHEM

ROMEMA

RAMAT
ESHKOL

PEACE
GARDEN

ABU TOR

OLD
CITY

MIZRACH
TALPIYOT

PROPOSED SITE B
SPANNING A VALLEY BETWEEN
ABU-DIS AND MIZRACH TALPIYOT

N

ZA'ATARA

NAHAL
KIDRON

ISAWIYA

RAS
EL-AMUD   WADI NAZIL

2   3   4

BATANA

KILOMETERS

UBEIDIYA

ABU-DIS

ZHUR - MUSLIM PRAYER MIDDAY TIME   11:44AM
MINCHA - JEWISH MIDDAY PRAYER TIME   12:00PM
ASR - MUSLIM PRAYER TIME   2:30PM
MAGHRIB - MUSLIM PRAYER   4:49PM
SUNSET   4:49PM
ESHAA - MUSLIM EVENING PRAYER TIME   6:16PM
MAARIV - JEWISH PRAYER

EYNOT ZARK
NATURE
RESERVE

WADI EL-EKDA

DELAVIM
NATURE
RESERVE

WADI E-SHAMI /
NAHAL NATUF

NABI SAMUIL
NATIONAL PARK

WADI
E-DILB

NAHAL
SOREK

WADI
EYN AL-JUN

RAMALLAH

EL BIRA

NAHAL
ATAROT

JEBEL TAVIL

...OFIM

WADI EL-EYN

WADI
E-TINEH

WADI
ABU-LATIYEH

E-RAM

PISGAT
ZE'EV

NEVE
YA'AKOV

WADI SHEBAN /
NAHAL MICHMAS

...ADI
...MRA

WADI
E-NATUF

G'ABA

WADI EL-HAFI

...RAJ   HIZMA   WADI
EL-MISEH

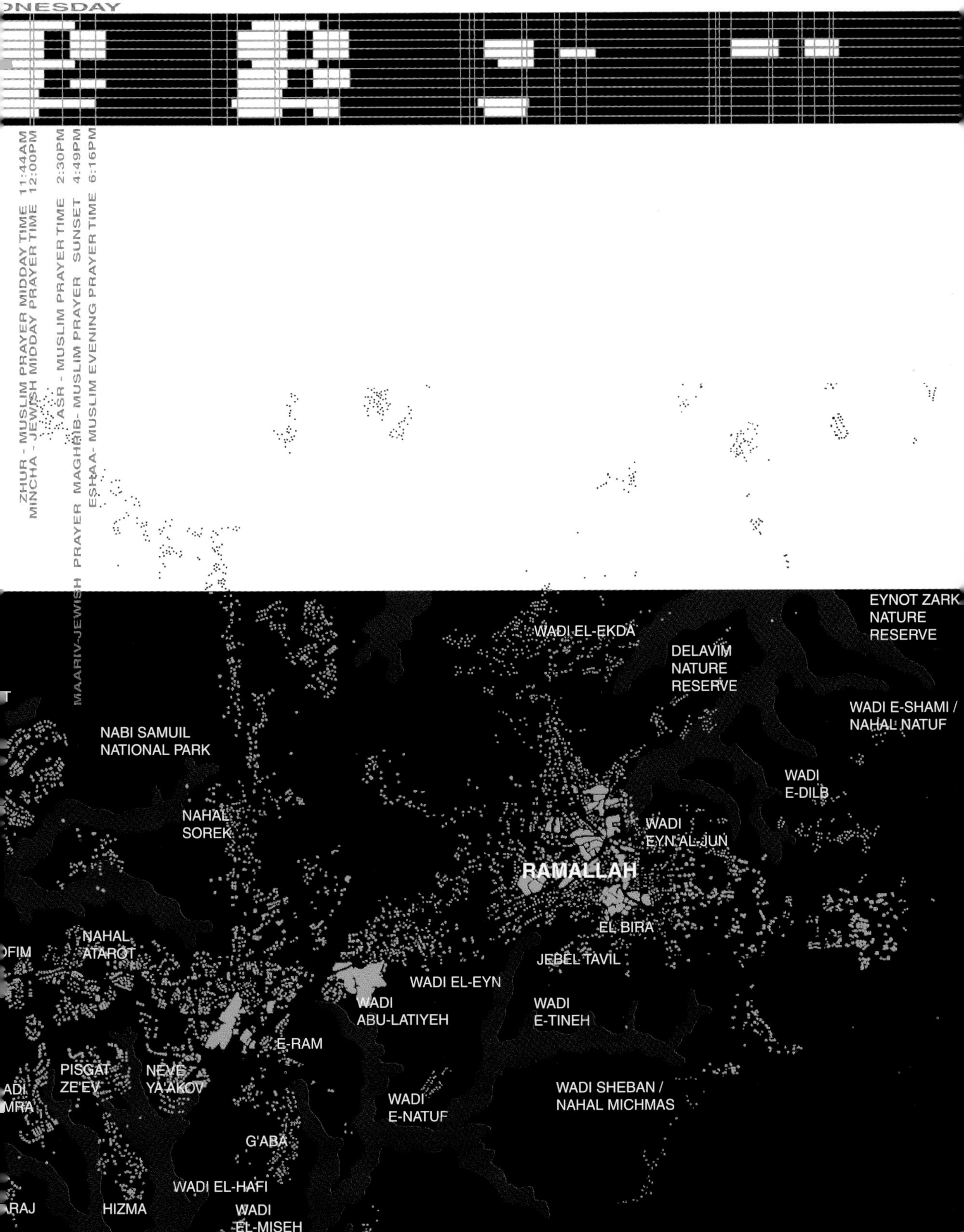

...TO REGIONAL VALLEY SYSTEMS

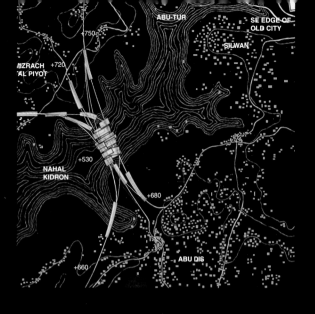

PROPOSED SITE B
MUNICIPAL NECKLACE

A necklace that stretches across the hills suspending beaded structures. The central regional programmatic function for this site is a bureaucratic/municipal center composed of series of buildings threaded along a major new east-west regional artery. In this space between the hills, city offices, and the regional government complex exist and form the connection to the adjacent existing neighborhoods of Abu-Dis and Mizrach Talpiyot; they also establish visual connection both to and from the historic core of the Old City.

DAWN FAJR-MUSLIM PRAYER / SHACHARIT-JEWISH PRAYER / MOR

PRAYER / LITURGY-CHRISTIAN MORNING PRAYER Jerusalem city o

peration, Department of Motor Vehicles opens, Department of Health be

PRAYER / MINCHA-JEWISH PRAYER Office workers take lunch at loca

oon operations at city offices SUNSET MAARIV - JEWISH PRAYER / N

ipal offices close daily operations Vendors close up carts outside of m

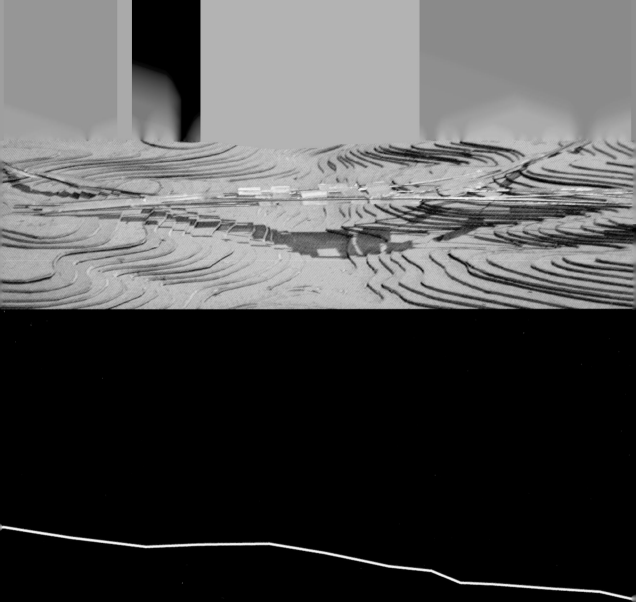

RAYER-CHRISTIAN PRAYER / SUNRISE SHUROOQ -MUSLIM
ben, Civil Court hears first cases of the day,   Central Post Office begins

brning meetings, Munipal Offices close for lunch break   ZHUR - MUSLIM
rants Performers entertain lunch crowd, ASR-MUSLIM PRAYER After-
B-MUSLIM PRAYER   Mayors office conducts press conference Muni-

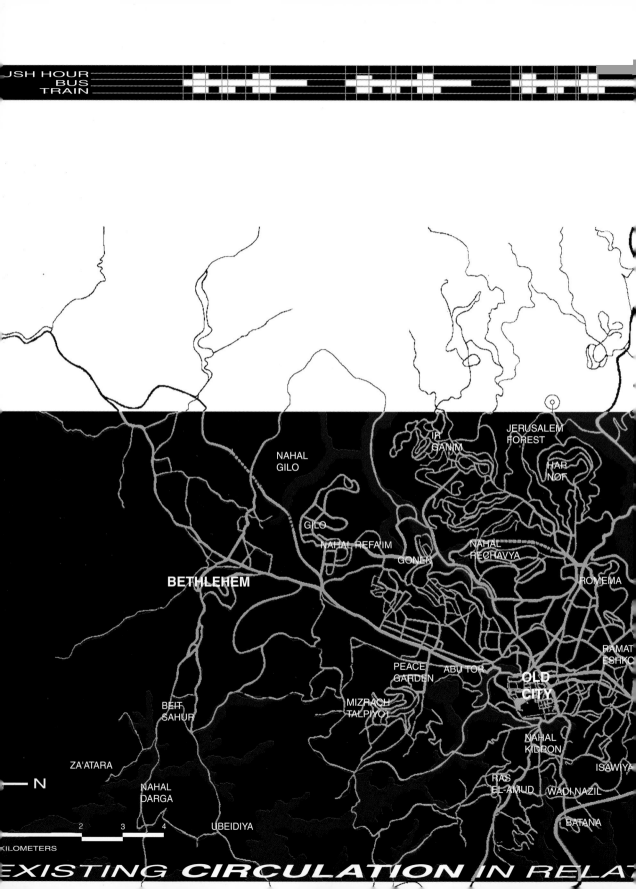

RUSH HOUR
BUS
TRAIN

JERUSALEM
FOREST

IR
GANIM

HAR
NOF

NAHAL
GILO

GILO

NAHAL REFA'IM

NAHAL
RECHAVYA

GONEN

ROMEMA

BETHLEHEM

RAMAT
ESHKO

PEACE
GARDEN

ABU TOR

**OLD
CITY**

MIZRACH
TALPIYOT

BEIT
SAHUR

NAHAL
KIDRON

ISAWIYA

ZA'ATARA

— N

RAS
EL-AMUD

WADI NAZIL

NAHAL
DARGA

UBEIDIYA

BATANA

2   3   4

KILOMETERS

EXISTING CIRCULATION IN RELA

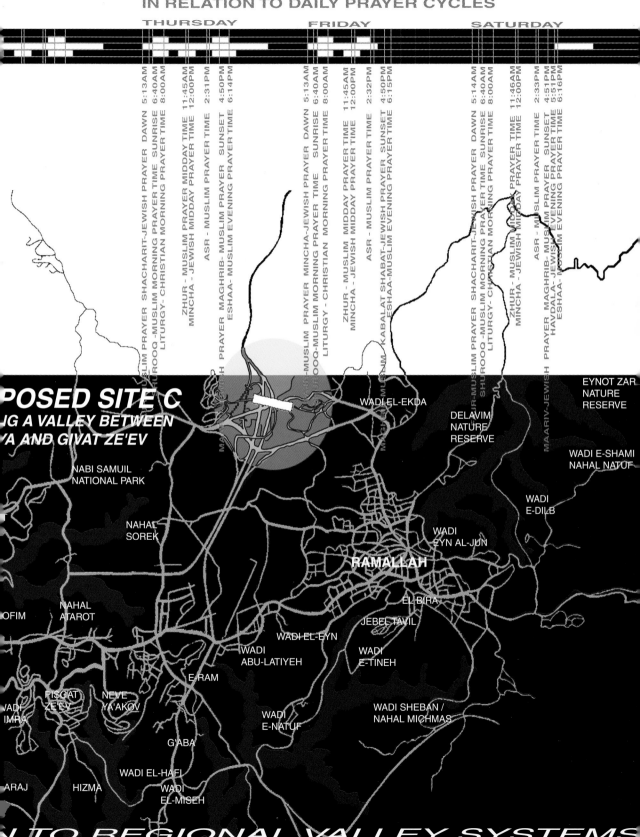

EXISTING TRANSPORTATION SYSTEMS
IN RELATION TO DAILY PRAYER CYCLES

THURSDAY   FRIDAY   SATURDAY

THURSDAY
- SLIM PRAYER SHACHARIT-JEWISH PRAYER DAWN 5:13AM
- SHUROOQ-MUSLIM MORNING PRAYER TIME SUNRISE 6:40AM
- LITURGY- CHRISTIAN MORNING PRAYER TIME 8:00AM
- ZHUR - MUSLIM PRAYER MIDDAY TIME 11:45AM
- MINCHA - JEWISH MIDDAY PRAYER TIME 12:00PM
- ASR - MUSLIM PRAYER TIME 2:31PM
- H PRAYER MAGHRIB- MUSLIM PRAYER SUNSET 4:50PM
- ESHAA- MUSLIM EVENING PRAYER TIME 6:14PM

FRIDAY
- UR-MUSLIM PRAYER MINCHA-JEWISH PRAYER DAWN 5:13AM
- SHUROOQ-MUSLIM MORNING PRAYER TIME SUNRISE 6:40AM
- LITURGY - CHRISTIAN MORNING PRAYER TIME 8:00AM
- ZHUR - MUSLIM MIDDAY PRAYER TIME 11:45AM
- MINCHA - JEWISH MIDDAY PRAYER TIME 12:00PM
- ASR - MUSLIM PRAYER TIME 2:32PM
- KABALAT SHABAT-JEWISH PRAYER SUNSET 4:50PM
- ESHAA-MUSLIM EVENING PRAYER TIME 6:15PM

SATURDAY
- AIR-MUSLIM PRAYER SHACHARIT-JEWISH PRAYER DAWN 5:14AM
- SHUROOQ-MUSLIM MORNING PRAYER TIME SUNRISE 6:40AM
- LITURGY- CHRISTIAN MORNING PRAYER TIME 8:00AM
- ZHUR - MUSLIM MIDDAY PRAYER TIME 11:46AM
- MINCHA - JEWISH MIDDAY PRAYER TIME 12:00PM
- ASR - MUSLIM PRAYER TIME 2:33PM
- PRAYER MAGHRIB- MUSLIM PRAYER SUNSET 4:51PM
- HAVDALA- JEWISH EVENING PRAYER TIME 5:51PM
- ESHAA- MUSLIM EVENING PRAYER TIME 6:16PM

POSED SITE C
IG A VALLEY BETWEEN
YA AND GIVAT ZE'EV

EYNOT ZAR NATURE RESERVE

WADI EL-EKDA

DELAVIM NATURE RESERVE

WADI E-SHAMI NAHAL NATUF

NABI SAMUIL NATIONAL PARK

WADI E-DILB

NAHAL SOREK

WADI EYN AL-JUN

RAMALLAH

EL BIRA

OFIM

NAHAL ATAROT

JEBEL TAVIL

WADI EL-EYN

WADI ABU-LATIYEH

WADI E-TINEH

E-RAM

WADI IMRA

PISGAT ZE'EV

NEVE YA'AKOV

WADI E-NATUF

WADI SHEBAN / NAHAL MICHMAS

G'ABA

WADI EL-HAFI

ARAJ   HIZMA   WADI EL-MISEH

N TO REGIONAL VALLEY SYSTEMS

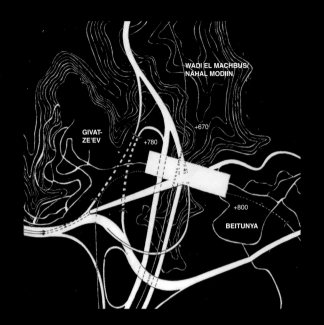

WADI EL MACHBUS/
NAHAL MODIIN

GIVAT-
ZE'EV

+670

+780

+800

BEITUNYA

PROPOSED SITE C
TRANSPORTATION STAPLE

A staple that joins the land on either side with a single bar. The central regional programmatic function of this site is a new transportation hub composed of a multilayered/function terminal for all communication systems. In this space between the hills, a central train, bus, and vehicular interchange exists and forms the connection to the adjacent existing neighborhoods of Beitunya and Givat Ze'ev as well as creating a western gateway into the newly conceived region.

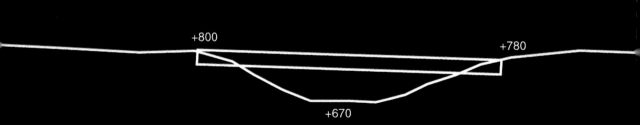

+800

+780

+670

DAWN FAJR - MUSLIM PRAYER / SHACHARIT - JEWISH PRAYER / S

PRAYER / Buses leave for Damascus Gate, East Jerusalem, Hebron, M
CHRISTIAN PRAYER /Morning Rush Hour Traffic, Trains leave for Beers

MUSLIM PRAYER / MINCHA-JEWISH PRAYER / Trains leave for Tel Av

Trains leave for Cairo. Tel Aviv, Aman/ Buses leave for Jericho, Damascu

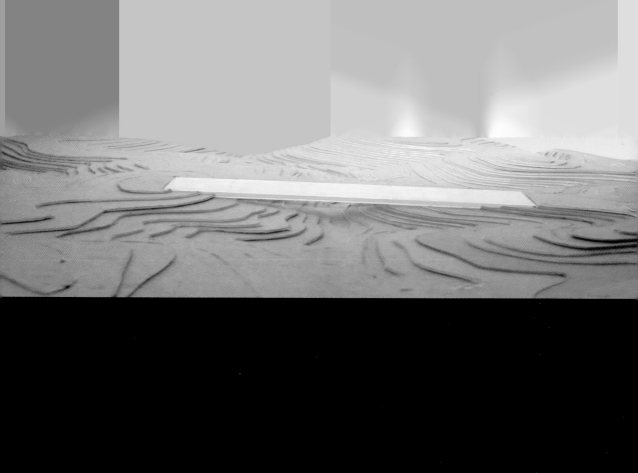

E SHUROOQ-MUSLIM PRAYER/ EUCHARIST -CHRISTIAN MORNING

ppus, Gaza /Trains leave for Haifa, Tel Aviv, Aman Express / LITURGY
-rusalem / Buses leave for Gaza,Ein Kerem, Yad VaShem, Rafiah / ZHUF

ss, Beersheva, Haifa / Mid-day Rush Hour / MAGRIB-MUSLIM PRAYER

Hebron Abu Tor ESHA-MUSLIM EVENING PRAYER / MAARIV- JEWIS

To Hell and Back: Jerusalem's Queer Center

Amir Sumaka'i Fink[1]

Hide and Seek

It is 1946, and David Balaban has recently moved from his kibbutz to Jerusalem. Balaban is studying at the Hebrew University, where he majors in biology. He is twenty-something, with penetrating eyes and a commanding voice. His hair is cut in a pompadour, he wears khakis with a wide belt, and all his shirts are starched white. He listens more than he talks, and when he does say something, he says it firmly and slowly. Balaban is beautiful, and he has captured the hearts of several of the women he knows (and my heart as well). He has just completed two years of service in one of the nationalist organizations that preceded Israeli statehood. He makes it clear that he has already done his part, as expected of a young man. He is, in fact, always careful to follow the rules—he lives by the slogan "To the farms, up in arms, and education for liberation." For two years he dealt in farms or arms—he won't say. And now he is to begin teaching in an elementary school. In the time remaining before the opening of the school year, Balaban is giving private lessons to Uri Berman, a young boy being raised by his grandfather because his parents have been sent abroad by the Zionist movement: mother with Jewish refugees in Italy and father in the U.S., as a diplomat. Uri misses his parents very much. Especially his father. Every chance he gets, he sneaks into the forbidden room, his parents' bedroom. He dozes on their bed; he tries on his father's hat in the mirror. He scolds Balaban for nearly sitting in his father's chair in the dining room.

1 Translated from the Hebrew by Jacob Press.

The Berman family lives in a spectacularly bourgeois Talbiyeh apartment that is almost too spacious. It has the comfort and grace of the Arab mansions that were built between the two World Wars: finely detailed floors, high ceilings, and wide and ornamented terraces. David Balaban lives not far away, in a modest, rented ground-floor room with a separate entrance from the backyard. As a rule, he leaves his apartment key under the mat in the foyer. It stands to reason that this is the key's place. It stands to reason that this is an invitation to a guest who is in on a secret.

Uri is a difficult child: he is late for his lessons and would rather play with his gang of friends in their pseudo-underground. Only boys. They're too young to be drafted into the Haganah, the Jewish underground, but that doesn't stop them from manufacturing explosives, hating the British and the Arabs, organizing imaginary battles, swearing to accept the rule of the group and to do everything in their power to bring the struggle for the homeland to success, or placing under surveillance everyone whose behavior seems suspicious—whether lovers in the woods or the curly-haired teacher David Balaban.

While eavesdropping on one of the Haganah briefings in their neighborhood, the boys learn that there is an informant in their neighborhood. Members of the underground are dropping like flies. When Balaban is seen on several occasions talking to an Arab young man—and even giving him documents and letters—it is clear to them that this is their man. They inform one of their older brothers, who is active in the Haganah. The answer is not long in coming: Balaban is not the informant. The collaborator will soon be punished. Balaban too.

The British agent was shot and killed by Haganah men. The same men arrive at Balaban's apartment a few days later. It is just as they expected. Balaban and his Arab partner are caught naked, in one another's arms, in bed. Their bodies speak of tenderness and mercy when the warriors burst into the room armed with sticks and clubs and beat them unconscious.

Uri watches the attack through Balaban's window. He had followed the teacher himself. He had been in Balaban's apartment, picked through his belongings, found a picture of the young Arab man and even dared to demand an explanation from Balaban when the latter caught the boy, an uninvited guest in his house. Balaban made it clear to Uri that he does not pass information to Arabs. When Uri spat out at him that he was a liar, Balaban said that he had never lied to him and that he never would lie. "But there may be some things in my life that you don't know about, Uri." Uri finally understood the nature of these things only when it was too late to forewarn the teacher of the evil now coming to pass. Uri cries out to the men of the underground that they should leave the couple be, but the matter is out of his hands, and he goes home, embittered and tearful.

Uri meets Balaban only once more, by chance. David Balaban has grown a beard, and he is walking his bicycle up a steep hill. Uri calls out his name. Balaban looks at him with penetrating eyes. A shiver. End.

"Where is Balaban today?" I ask Dan Wolman, who wrote and directed the film *Hide and Seek* in 1980, the first full-length Israeli film dealing explicitly with a homosexual theme.

"You're talking to him," he answers, but immediately regrets it. "Well, not really. In a sense, I'm both Balaban and Uri Berman, but I'm younger than both—I wasn't Uri's age until the 1950s."

Wolman filmed *Hide and Seek* in the house in Talbiyeh where he grew up. The house is on what we know today as Jabotinsky Street, but it was built on Emir Abdullah Street by Christian Arabs. Like many of the Jewish residents of Talbiyeh, which was a mixed neighborhood until 1948, Wolman's parents rented their apartment from its Arab owners. Wolman's entire film is shot in Jerusalem: in the forest near the Jerusalem Theater, in Romema, at the Zionist Youth Camp, and elsewhere. At first, he wanted to make a film based on the life and death of Ya'akov Yisrael De Haan, the homosexual writer and poet and leader of Agudat Yisrael who immigrated to Jerusalem from Holland and was assassinated by the Haganah in June 1924. But Wolman says that the project was too grandiose, and he could not raise the necessary budget. The screenplay on De Haan gave birth to a play, "Bells in Jerusalem," which was staged at the Khan Theater in Jerusalem in 1981. The screenplay for *Hide and Seek*, too, was influenced by the story of De Haan. Once Balaban comes under suspicion of being a spy, one of the boys in the gang drops a threatening letter in Balaban's mailbox in the teachers' room: "We know all about you and your Arabs. Traitor. The Day of Judgment is near. The Black Hand Gang." Wolman says that this is a verbatim citation of the letter that De Haan received shortly before his murder.

In the Jerusalem of *Hide and Seek* there are Jews—mostly Ashkenazim, but also Sephardim—Arabs, and British soldiers. Jerusalem is a small city, much of which is in decay. Residents travel by foot or bicycle. There are no clear borders, except at the beginning of the movie, when British paratroopers lay barbed wire across a temporary checkpoint. *Hide and Seek* is seen through Uri's eyes. For him, Talbiyeh is "here," and it seems that in Talbiyeh, there are no Arabs. The Arab neighborhood to which he follows Balaban when he goes to meet his Arab partner is "there." But Uri spends a considerable portion of his time "no place"—forests, clearings, and abandoned ruins. To the viewer of Wolman's movie, it appears that "no place"—no one's place—makes up a considerable portion of Jerusalem, or at least a considerable portion of the personal Jerusalem of the teenaged Uri Berman.

"No place" is where children play hide-and-seek with the reality that lies beyond. "No place" is where things happen that don't happen in the heart of the neighborhood: couples make love, gangs of boys act as a hierarchical underground, and Balaban speaks in Arabic to two Arabs—one of them, his lover. It's a bit surprising that "no place" appears to be a totally safe place. Certainly safer than "there."

Maybe even safer than "here." Wolman locates the first meeting between Balaban and his friend in "no place" and even calls the place "the city park," an actual and venerable institution for Jerusalemite gays.

"No place" is the queer place, a place where everyone can live out their fantasies so long as they don't interfere with the fulfillment of the fantasies of others. Everyone who comes to Wolman's Jerusalem "no place" does indeed arrive with the intention of fulfilling a fantasy, but Balaban's gay fantasy comes into conflict with the spy-catching fantasy of the gang of boys. Balaban and his lover pay the price. Not surprisingly, they are attacked only when they take that extra step and bring the fantasy back "here," to Balaban's house.

The important and obvious existence of "no place" in Wolman's movie would seem, on the surface, to be the director's unselfconscious regurgitation of the myth of "the land without people" that was propagated by certain Zionist ideologues. After all, the year is 1946 and in "no place" there are already abandoned buildings and overgrown clearings, seemingly up for grabs. Clearly, though, inducing anything about the Land of Israel in general from Uri Berman's private world would be a serious mistake for us as viewers.

I asked Wolman why Balaban's Arab lover has no name. Why don't we know even a single thing about him? Wolman says that he wanted to create an atmosphere of mystery, to give this secondary character power. "You could say it was a way to build sexual tension," he says. As a viewer, I wanted to know more about this attractive man, who was mortally wounded only because of his relationship with Balaban. Wolman is willing to give me only the slightest thread of fantasy: after they began shooting the film, he saw a beautiful Arab construction worker, who was working next door to the house where Wolman grew up, the location of the filming. A similar-looking man made an impression upon the director many years earlier. Wolman asked the worker if he would agree to play Balaban's lover. He agreed and the final result was an extraordinary work of art.

The days of *Hide and Seek* were not simple days for those who wished to protect their privacy, or to hold their own counsel in making independent decisions about their way of life. The one who seems, more than anyone else, to express a point of view sympathetic to David Balaban is Uri's grandfather, who says, at one point, "They just don't know how to leave you alone in this country." The grandfather works assiduously with his friend, Mrs. Rosenzweig, on the definitive Hebrew translation of Thomas Mann's *Death in Venice*. The weaving of *Death in Venice* into *Hide and Seek* foreshadows a tragic end. And as if it isn't enough that they are translating the book, an unbreakable link between the atmosphere of the book and the film is forged at a crucial moment. The grandfather is reading to Uri from his translation of Mann's description of the labyrinthine alleyways of Venice. "What city does this describe?" asks the grandfather. "Jerusalem," answers Uri.

In many medieval cathedrals there was a labyrinth positioned in the center, for instance, in Chartres. The labyrinth, of course, evoked the Greek myth of King Minus of Crete, at the center of whose labyrinth the Minoan Minotaur lay in wait. In the Christian version, it is Satan who stalks the maze, and the labyrinth is a parable of life: Satan must be overcome to achieve one's goals. Only those who can overcome temptation will reach their goals; only one path is the true one; they who walk in it will be redeemed. Leonardo da Vinci removed the labyrinth from the church and placed it in the garden, the garden of the chateau at Villandry. Thomas Mann hid it in the alleyways of Venice. It is not difficult to identify who Satan is for Mann—or rather, what Satan is. And in Jerusalem? Is there in *Hide and Seek* a homoerotic overtone in the relationship between Balaban and Uri, between the man and the boy—as in *Death in Venice*? It seemed to me that the pillow fight between the tutor and the pupil was indeed tinged with sexual excitement.

The parallels between Wolman's Jerusalem and Mann's Venice are evident not only in the tragic elements in their stories of same-sex love. When seen in the context of the early 1980s, it is also a clear political statement: Jerusalem is sinking and will continue to sink, this city is an endless collection of dead-end paths. You wanted Jewish sovereignty in the Israeli capital? You got a ghetto—in other words, Venice, the city whose Jewish quarter gave the world this universally beloved term. This is the "new foundry," *ghetto nuovo*, that was carved out for the Venetian Jews in 1516. Wolman's oeuvre is preoccupied with this evolution of Jerusalem, from his film *My Michael* through *Hide and Seek* to *The Distance*, which deals with Jerusalemites who have moved to Tel Aviv, like Balaban/Wolman.

In *Hide and Seek*, Wolman sees no future for the queer place in Jerusalem. He locates in the city one of the rare violent episodes of Israeli gay bashing. Wolman does not argue for a historical source for the tragic end of *Hide and Seek*. And if there is one thing that disturbs me in this graceful movie, it is the import of a violent episode of a kind that does not happen frequently in Jerusalem. Don't we have enough violence in Jerusalem? Do we have to invent more? This outburst gives expression to Wolman's sense of despair over the fate of his city, a total and final abdication of the queer place in Jerusalem. Onward to Tel Aviv!

My Jerusalem: 1992–1997

I was born and raised in Haifa but I lived in Jerusalem for five years, the same five years in which I grew into my queer identity. These years, 1992 to 1997, were also formative years in the history of the gay and lesbian community in Israel.

Once, there was a Turkish bath on Yehezkel Street in the Bukharan quarter and there the youths, bachelors, and young fathers of the city would meet—the rest can be left to an active imagination. Reality and fantasy intermingled there in the mists of

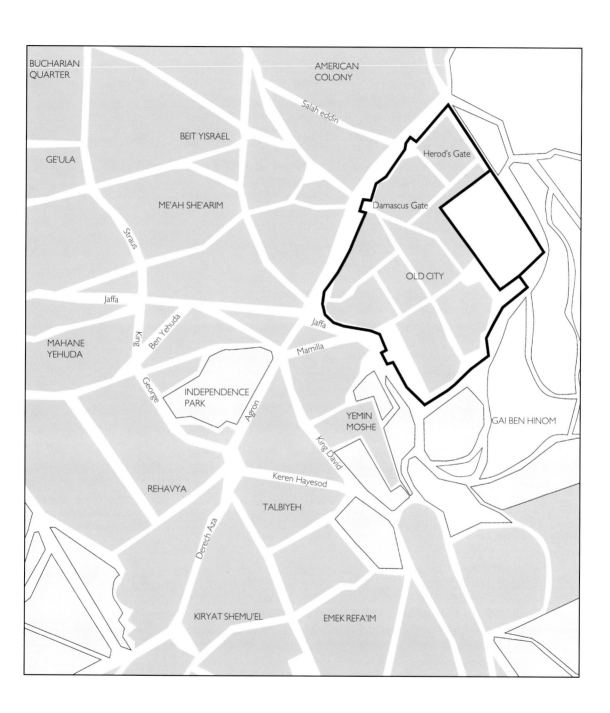

the sauna, and those who now tell its story do so only in distant retrospect, in the form of oral history. A description of the bath in the Bukharan quarter appears in the monologue of "Dan" in the book that Jacob Press and I coauthored.[2] Dan describes the place as it appeared in the 1980s, on the eve of its death: a three-story structure in a traditional neighborhood already becoming predominantly ultra-Orthodox. The place was open on alternate days for women or men only. We don't know much about the women's days, but rumors of the "men's days" continue to echo. As Jerusalemites are always reminding each other, overcompensating for a sense of inferiority, in those days you could see caravans from Tel Aviv, winding slowly up the hillsides, making a pilgrimage to the capital.[3] Dan describes the Turkish bath as a place where heterosexuals and homosexuals bathed together in harmony. Men who wanted to initiate a sexual encounter would hint of this to their desired partner, who would accede, decline—or have no idea that any attempt at communication had even taken place. Sexual relations were consummated in dark hallways, or the interested parties would leave the premises in tandem. Inside the building, everyone wore towels; on the roof, they sunbathed au naturel.

The closure of the Turkish bath, in response to the violent pressure of the ultra-Orthodox at the beginning of the 1980s, stands, in my eyes, as a microcosm for the transition of Israeli society in general—and the Jewish neighborhoods of Jerusalem in particular—from the Age of Innocence to the Age of Dana International. The Turkish bath was similar in many ways to neighborhood baths throughout the Middle East. In many of these baths sexual activity is common and does not merit specific categorization according to the modern, Western notions of "homosexual" versus "heterosexual." According to certain eyewitnesses, there are still, in the Land of Israel, certain public baths that are similar to the Turkish bath in the Bukharan quarter. These establishments are in Arab towns and the majority of those who frequent them are also Arab. The Israeli Jewish poet Rami Sa'ari recently published a Hebrew poem describing his sexual experiences in the Turkish bath in the Nablus neighborhood of Bab es-Sakha.[4] Did those who bathed in the Jerusalem Turkish bath define themselves as homosexuals? Certainly there were some who did. But for others, whose identity was not structured by Western concepts, this had no meaning or appeal.

One gay institution has survived from the proto-gay period to the gay period: Independence Park. Many of the parks in the center of Israel cities are called "Independence Park." According to *Hazman Hawarod*, the national gay Israeli periodical, many of these parks are gay meeting places, including the Independence Parks in Tel Aviv, Jerusalem, Beersheba, and Netanya. The public and the authorities are relatively tolerant of the existence of such meeting places, where encounters can include sexual relations within the park itself, in the bushes, or in a more or less private corner.

2 Amir Sumaka'i Fink and Jacob Press, *Independence Park: The Lives of Gay Men in Israel* (Palo Alto, Calif.: Stanford University Press, 1999), 182–83.

3 Amit Zvi, "Behind the Walls," *Hazman Hawarod* 43 (July 2000), 4.

4 Rami Sa'ari, "The Autumn of the Situation" (Hebrew), *Ha'aretz, Cultural and Literary Supplement* (October 27, 2000).

At least two of these parks, the one in Tel Aviv and the one in Jerusalem, contain Muslim cemeteries. Jerusalem's Independence Park was used for interment from the thirteenth century to 1927. For many, this situation is an appropriate physical manifestation of a kind of misguided emotional goulash that mixes up sex with death, homosexuality with filth. Or, in the apologetic idiom of post-Zionism: our pleasure is built upon a foundation of dead Arabs; even when we just want to be left alone to fuck in peace, the winds of politics howl among the tombstones.[5] But the truth deserves to be spoken: the planning of most Israeli cities was carried out in practice by real-estate speculators seeking to sell houses to the upwardly mobile. Why didn't they build on spaces that are now Independence Parks? Because they valued open, green spaces? There used to be many more—they're gone. No, they didn't build because they were not permitted to. Depending upon their antiquity, cemeteries are considered either archaeological sites or holy places. So to what do we owe the last remaining green spaces in our cities? The fact that some Israelis respect the heritage of others.

I don't know when Independence Park in Jerusalem first became a meeting place for gays in the city. It was not necrophilia, real or metaphorical, that brought us to the park. Nor were we drawn to Mamilla's Pool, the great reservoir of Herodian Jerusalem, located in its midst. The location of the park as the city's most central "no place" is what made it into a pilgrimage site. First of all, the location is adjacent to several of the oldest hotels in the western part of the city. Tourists have always presented an important opportunity for sexual expression in this conservative city. Tourists can also take their partners-of-the-moment back to their rooms. Secondly, the park has the necessary combination of open spaces and darkness, even after its 1996 face-lift, when much greenery was uprooted. (At the time, there were those who suspected that the park's redesign was conceived with the goal of driving the gays away. The suspicion was proven to be unfounded.)

In the arbitrary division of the city that took place on November 30, 1948, the park became part of the state of the Jews. It was quite close to the "city line," the term used for the Green Line where it crossed into the city limits of pre-1948 Jerusalem. On tourist maps, though, the park does not belong to any of the city's neighborhoods. If you ask Jerusalemites what neighborhood Independence Park is in, many will answer, with some slight hesitation: "It's downtown."

Around the park are two circles of life: the institutional circle and the residential circle—both are indispensable to the continued existence of the park as Jerusalem's queer center. In the institutional circle are structures that are active in the mornings and afternoons, such as the two schools located to the northwest of the park, and the Department of Commerce and Industry, formerly the Palace Hotel, located on the margins of the neighborhood of Mahaneh Yisrael, southeast of the park. The institutional circle also includes buildings in which many visitors reside, for instance,

5 Hagai El-Ad, "Ahuzat-Bayit: Celebrating Autumn with the Opening of a New Home for the Agudah in Tel Aviv," *Hazman Havarod* 46 (November 2000), 4.

the Sheraton Plaza Hotel southwest of the park, Beit Agron to the north, the Lazarist and St. Rosary monasteries and the Alliance Française and the American consulate on the south—to name just a few.

The residential circle is no less important. While Independence Park does not belong to any of Jerusalem's large residential neighborhoods, it is located within reasonable walking distance of a considerable portion of them. The park is a mediating space between Arabs and Jews, between the secular and the ultra-Orthodox, between the religious and the merely traditional. Maybe also between Ashkenazim and Mizrahim. North of the park, beyond the old commercial center of the city, and beyond the administrative center of the Russian compound, only ten minutes' walk from the park, are the ultra-Orthodox neighborhoods Me'ah She'arim, Beit Yisrael, Ge'ula, and others. To the west and south of Independence Park are the secular, traditional, and sometimes Orthodox neighborhoods. They are Nahla'ot, Rehavya, Kiryat Shemu'el, Talbiyeh, Yemin Moshe, and Emek Refa'im. To the east and northeast, the Arab neighborhoods of the Old City and beyond: Bab az-Zahra, Wadi al-Joz, and Sheikh Jarah. Morasha (Musrarah), to the northeast, is a mixed Jewish neighborhood, from ultra-Orthodox to secular. Everyone who comes to the park must leave his place, his neighborhood, his public and cross over to "no place." But on the way to the park, he doesn't have to pass through any of the "other" places: the Arab doesn't pass through a Jewish neighborhood, the ultra-Orthodox Jew doesn't pass through a secular or Arab neighborhood, the secular Jew doesn't pass through an Arab or ultra-Orthodox neighborhood.

Between the institutional circle and the residential circle there are several blocks of retail, restaurant, government, and private office space. This space includes almost all of Jerusalem's downtown: Jaffa, Ben Yehuda, and King George V Streets; also Nahalat Shiv'ah, mostly restaurants and businesses; also the commercial/touristic area along Hamelekh David and Hamelekh Shlomo Streets. These are not "no place." They are, in fact, the center for the minority that rules Jerusalem (at the moment): the (unwritten) secular-traditional-Orthodox Jewish alliance that was created by the Zionist movement. Maybe you could say: the Israeli minority of Jerusalem.

Most any Jerusalemite can walk the streets of downtown without eliciting special notice, and it is here that almost all the city's gay bars and clubs are found, including Shunra, Zman Amiti, and the Q. The cafes Tmol Shilshom and Zig Zag, as well as the gay and lesbian community center, the Open House, are also in this area.

In the western portion of Independence Park, there was, for a few years in the 1990s, a bar called Hand Bag.[6] It was one of the very few exclusively gay bars in Jerusalem's history. It occupied an old stone building with a low dome and it was so popular that not all of those who wished to enter were able to. For this reason, you couldn't always tell who was coming to Hand Bag and who was coming to the park. Or, to put it a different way, to come to the Hand Bag you came to Independence

6 Yossi Wolfson, "Less Plastic, More People," *Hazman Havarod* 43 (July 2000), 24.

To Hell and Back: Jerusalem's Queer Center

To Hell and Back: Jerusalem's Queer Center

Park. The location of the Hand Bag was, in my opinion, among the boldest acts in the history of the gay and lesbian community in Jerusalem. What did the creators of Hand Bag do? They went to the place that was seen by homophobes—among them many gay men—as the epitome of the underside of gayness: public sex acts, anonymous liaisons, orgies. In this place they planted a stake and declared: this is our place. Let's make it nicer and more comfortable—we'll put in a bar for ourselves. The chutzpah would be comparable to the opening of a gay cafe in one of the stalls of a cruisy bathroom in an American mall. Only the placement of the Open House on the Ben Yehudah pedestrian mall, flying the pride flag over the heads of all strollers, can compare with Hand Bag in its degree of boldness.

There are those who have made—or make—"place-y" uses of "no place." That is to say, they make "no place" into their place. For instance, in the past, until the beginning of the 1990s, the Israeli police would stop gay men in Independence Park for questioning. The police would ask those strolling in the park to present identification documents, and they recorded their identity—from here, it was a short path to the police department's database. At the time, the police department argued, in response to public protest, that they were not compiling a "Pink List"—they were simply adding an additional piece of data to the many other items appearing in their computerized profiles. Yet the police did not deny that, if necessary, it would be possible to elicit a Pink List from the computer with the stroke of a key. A list such as this was then—and is now—accessible to anyone with legal (or illegal) access to police files, whether a member of the security services or a criminal hacker or a criminal hacker from the security services. As a consequence of the fact that people from a certain place (i.e., the Israeli authorities) penetrate "no place" and interfere with the realization of the fantasies of those who are there, they make "no place" into a part of their place. This is a grievous harm to "no place," albeit a temporary and limited one. Why temporary and limited? The policemen did not interrogate every person who entered the park—they did it occasionally and irregularly. In addition, not everyone whose name found its way onto the Pink List was harmed by it, at least not immediately. We are not dealing with a place that conquers "no place"—it is "no place" that triumphs.

Invasions such as these into the heart of the queer place are not the exclusive province of the Israeli establishment alone. While gay bashing in the park meeting places is not a widespread phenomenon in Israel, certain incidents were recorded when the wave of immigration from the former Soviet Union began at the beginning of the 1990s. The perpetrators, gangs of new immigrant toughs, passed through the parks and targeted gay new immigrants from the former Soviet Union, whom they accused of giving new immigrants a bad name. The perpetrators perceived the parks as the "Israeli place" and they saw victims as representing "Russians" in a distorted and perverted way to Israeli society. Incidents of this kind have decreased over time, maybe because of police activities; maybe because of gay organization for self-defense; maybe because the perpetrators, too, began to understand that the parks, especially the one in Jerusalem, are not the "Israeli place," but rather the queer place, "no place."

Telephone dating services and computer chat rooms have recently made the park considerably less popular as a meeting place for gays in Jerusalem. Virtual meeting places are more comfortable, safer, theoretically more anonymous and, most important, more convenient for users. But the virtual gay place is still not accessible to everyone, like Independence Park is, and there are not a few people who have cause to regret this change. As if this was not enough, then came the Al Aqsa Intifada, beginning in September 2000, which drove even more cruisers away from the park (just as the previous intifada did). Both Jews and Arabs are now more fearful than in the recent past—Jews are concerned about Arab violence; Arabs are concerned about threats to them from the authorities, both Palestinian and Israeli. Against their will, but as a result of this fear, many gays are returning to the place from which they came to "no place." In this place, there is only a closet waiting for them.

The existence of this queer place was always in my consciousness, as something protecting me from my bourgeois lifestyle and that of others. The park—every time I passed through it or around its outskirts—reminded me that I still have fantasies that have yet to be realized, that I may never realize. What's more, Independence Park in Jerusalem played a central part in my coming-out process, even though I lived in Tel Aviv and in Haifa at the time and I had never been there in my life. How was this so? In 1990, the wonderful short film "After" was screened for the first time. The director, Eitan Fuchs, located the central dramatic events of the film in the park: a combat soldier in basic training, whose feet lead him into the midst of the park, discovers that his tough-as-nails commanding officer is also gay. All in the course of one short afternoon's leave in Jerusalem. I, too, was a soldier at the time, and I felt that I recognized, as if it were my very own, every step that the protagonist took. Later, the park became a kind of symbolic island of stability for me: it had always been there, no one had ever tried to close it down, and because of the cemetery and Mamilla's Pool it would always be there. The park made me feel secure. If—perish the thought—one day all the political, legal, and social achievements of the lesbians and gay men of Israel were wiped off the face of the earth, we could always go back to the park. It was there for us when the State of Israel was one big closet, which you could come out of only by going somewhere else: across the sea.

My Jerusalem flowed along different axes of movement: Herzl, Eshkol, Jaffa; the express lanes where the buses gallop, where more than one burst into cruel, terror-stoked flames. We lived then, Yossi and I, in Yefe Nof, a neighborhood that is an offshoot of Beit Hakerem. In Beit Hakerem and Yefe Nof, throughout the mid-

Jerry Levinson's proposed route for the Jerusalem gay pride parade.

1990s, we knew six or seven male couples and a few more single gays. Others lived and still live in Emek Refa'im, Hamoshava Hagermanit, Hamoshava Hayevanit, and Bak'a. Also in Rehavya, Nahlaot, downtown, and other secular or mixed neighborhoods. We were studying at the Mt. Scopus campus of the Hebrew University, where there was also the Other 10 Percent—the first gay and lesbian student group in Israel. I worked downtown. Was there something gay about these places? Only our quiet, barely noticed presence. Nothing else.

Lately, there has been talk of having a gay pride march in Jerusalem similar to the one that has taken place annually in Tel Aviv since June 1998. In the Tel Aviv gay pride parade, the entire community marches from point A to point B, where a demonstration is held, featuring politicians and entertainers. Along the route stand local residents, the curious, and those who are themselves not yet quite ready to march.

The idea of having a pride march in Jerusalem was first raised by a non-gay city council member, Ornan Yekutieli, at a meeting that took place in July 2000. Yekutieli delivered a rousing speech in support of the idea, concluding with the words: "And may we speedily in our days merit to see a pride march passing through Jaffa Road and King George and Ben Yehuda Street. Next year in Gay Jerusalem." Yekutieli worked into this pronouncement references to prayers that are well known to almost all Jews, adapting them to the context of the subject at hand. He also suggested a precise route for the Jerusalem pride march. It looks as if he intended for the march to start at the city hall plaza on Jaffa Road, go up Jaffa Road to the intersection with King George, and from there, after a short march on King George, to the Talita Kumi landmark, then down the Ben Yehuda pedestrian mall, where the Open House is located, to Zion Square. Here, certainly, would be the traditional demonstration. This route, as noted above, is Jerusalem's retail and commercial center, also known as "the triangle," a center that took shape during the days of the British Mandate. Yekutieli's route covers the heart of Israeli Jerusalem. It doesn't pass through an ultra-Orthodox or an Arab neighborhood, and it forges a direct connection between Israeli and homosexual identity. Did Yekutieli think there were no gay Arabs or ultra-Orthodox lesbians? Yekutieli was aware of their existence, but, by the same token, he was aware of the magnitude of the taboo on the Arab and ultra-Orthodox streets.

The reaction of Jerusalem's mayor, Ehud Olmert, surprised and moved many. Olmert was quoted as saying that he had no objection to having a pride march in the city, but the gay and lesbian community had not requested a permit from city hall to hold such a parade.[7] In Olmert's words, "The gay and lesbian community is a respected community, just like any other one." Even if Olmert doesn't redeem this particular IOU, it was of great worth as a statement of policy, a public declaration by someone who is, in the opinion of many, the future leader of the Israeli right.

Yekutieli's suggestion and the mayor's reaction also stirred responses from the gay and lesbian community. Many believed that the residents of Jerusalem, as well as the members of the community, were not yet ready for a pride march in their city. Meanwhile, Jerry Levinson, Chair of the Board of the Open House, suggested an alternative route for the pride march: "Starting from Ge'ula, through Independence Park approaching Gai Ben Hinom, and from there to the eastern part of the city."[8] The Hebrew name of the neighborhood of Ge'ula means "redemption," a word associated in Jewish literature with the coming of the messiah and the end of days, but appropriated by the Zionist movement to be used in a nationalist context—and now, perhaps, by the gay and lesbian community. Ge'ula is located on the central north-south axis of Jerusalem. The marchers in this future—or futuristic—march would go up and then down Strauss Street, continue on King George until Avida

7 Eyal Hareuveni, "Pride and Prejudice," *Kol Hair* (July 28, 2000).

8 Pagi Sidur, Hanan Amior, and Amotz Toktali, "Haim Miller, It's Behind You" (Hebrew), *Kol Hazman* (August 4, 2000), 26–7.

To Hell and Back: Jerusalem's Queer Center

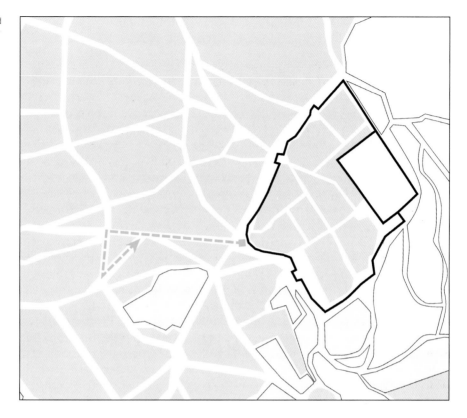

Oman Yekutieli's proposed route for the Jerusalem gay pride parade.

Street and from there proceed to Independence Park. The march would cross the park from west to east, to Hamekhes Square, and continue to the eastern part of the city by way of Ha'emek Road, which separates Mamilla from a new neighborhood, David's Village. And from here, they would march down the valley that is parallel to the walls of the Old City's Armenian quarter and toward the wadi adjacent to the western margins of Mt. Zion, Gai Ben Hinom, which continues to the east and passes south of Mt. Zion.

Thus Levinson's itinerary takes the marchers through neighborhoods belonging to the three major populations of the city: the ultra-Orthodox, the Israelis, and the Palestinians. In addition, it passes not only through Independence Park, but also through another notable queer Jerusalem landmark: Gai Ben Hinom. This valley is notable not only because the Hebrew word "gai" is pronounced very similarly to the word "gay" in English, but also because it is the very valley that gave us the English words "Gehenom" or "Gehenna": Hell. Many, especially in Christian cultures, promise gays damnation as our certain fate: "Turn or burn!" they cry. But we can take the terms that they use against us and make them into our public symbols in such a way that they can't do us any harm: so, for example, we have done with the term *queer* in English and *mitromem* in Hebrew. So it may also be someday with Sodom, when this sleepy Israeli desert resort becomes an international gay attraction. So, also, with Gehenom. In the pride march, we can enter the gates of Gai Ben Hinom and pass through them safely.

What then? Up to this point, Levinson has given us precise instructions. From here forward the instructions are hazy: the eastern part of the city. To Silwan? David's City? Ras El Amud? The Western Wall? The Temple Mount? The Mount of Olives? Anything is possible.

Queer Jihad, Queer Intifada: 2001

There are gay Arabs in Jerusalem. Not a single one of them can live openly in the Arab neighborhoods. Coming out of the closet means becoming an outcast under the best of circumstances, or a dead man under the worst. Gay Arabs come to Independence Park and sometimes to other meeting places, but rarely to formal communal activities, whether social or political. Many of them are fearful of coming out to other gay Arabs. To come out is to open yourself to risks, particularly within Arab society. But there is also cause to be concerned about attempts at blackmail by Israeli security services: "Collaborate with us, or else…" In spite of these concerns, there is a core group of a few dozen gays, most of whom know each other. The most well-off among them spend several weeks a year in Europe. There, the masks come off and their true desires are revealed. Straight at home, gay on vacation.

In East Jerusalem, there is no institutionalized meeting place for gays, no bar, club, or community center. At times, the walls of the Old City, with winding paths and gardens, serve as a place where you can meet a partner for an hour, but I am unaware of any particular part that is a known meeting place. In Ramallah, there were recently two gay-friendly cafes. Of course they didn't advertise themselves as such, but word got around. It took wing. A similar club that was active in Amman, the capital of Jordan, was recently closed by order of the government, and its owner left the kingdom. The man was not sufficiently discreet and was thus hounded into exile.

The Al Aqsa Intifada did not improve the situation of the gays of the Palestinian Authority. Mubarac Dahir's recent article for Gay.com has a very misleading headline: "Renewed Fighting with Israel Forces Palestinian Gays into Closet."[9] The reader might reasonably conclude that there were in the Palestinian Authority gays who were "out of the closet" and who have now been forced back in. As Dahir tell it, there was almost no homosexual activity among Palestinians before the Oslo Accords: everyone took part in the nationalist struggle, sacrificing for its sake the sat-

9 Mubarac Dahir, "Renewed Fighting with Israel Forces Palestinian Gays into Closet."

To Hell and Back: Jerusalem's Queer Center

isfaction of their spiritual and sexual needs. Dahir describes the changes that have taken place in the lives of gay Palestinians since the Palestinian Authority was established as a "respite," and "an opportunity to start seeking and finding one another—even if the opening was little more than a hairline crack." Dahir's descriptions are based upon his conversations with two pseudonymous gay Palestinian-Americans who recently visited the Palestinian Authority. In Dahir's description, this Golden Age is equated with the situation of gays in the United States during the 1950s: meeting places are not exclusively for gays, and so there is the need to check with a code question if your conversational partner is gay or just a friendly straight. The question currently asked is, "Are you part of the clique?" This question is compared by Dahir with the famous American query, "Are you a friend of Dorothy?"

The central weakness in Dahir's description is in his summary of the days that preceded Oslo Accords. He assumes that when the cannons roar, the passions are silenced. But before the days of Oslo and for most of the days of the intifada, almost every Palestinian who so desired could enter the territory of the State of Israel, whether with permission or without. Many Palestinians lived double lives: gays while they lived (for reasons of work) in Israel, conventional family men while at home. Since the creation of the Palestinian Authority and the increase in the number of terror attacks in the territory of the State of Israel, the ability of gay Palestinians from the Palestinian Authority to gain access to the queer centers of Israel has been limited, though it has not been entirely eliminated. Since the outbreak of the conflict known as the Al Aqsa Intifada, they have suffered at the hands of both sides, as Mubarac Dahir describes. In my opinion, these facts form the background for the rise in the number of those who define themselves as gay in the Palestinian Authority and the creation, maybe for the first time, of homosexual relationships among Palestinians in Palestinian society. I'm not saying that this is the first time that Palestinian society is seeing male-male sexual relations, but not every instance of such relations is "gay," or is performed between two gay men. Homosexuality—closeted as well as open—is a way of life dependent upon culture.

The number of same-sex Jewish-Arab couples in Israel is miniscule. Jerusalem is the mixed Israeli city with the largest Arab population—both in numbers and in proportion—but there are only one or two mixed couples living together in the western part of the city, and none at all in the east. (There are, notwithstanding, numerous short-term sexual relationships between Jewish and Arab Jerusalemites.) Tel Aviv has very few mixed partnerships, though still more than Jerusalem. One such couple made headlines during the mid-1990s, but their names were never made public. This anonymous Jewish resident of Tel Aviv and his life-partner, an Arab resident of Gaza, were separated by political circumstances, when not only was it forbidden for Palestinians from the Territories to reside for any period of time inside the State of Israel, but this rule was also enforced. The Israeli partner appealed to then-Prime

Minister and Defense Minister Yitzhak Rabin, asking that his Arab partner be permitted to live with him in Israel permanently. Rabin looked favorably upon the request and appealed to the chairman of the Palestinian Authority, Yasser Arafat, asking that this family be unified. Arafat located the Gazan, and he was permitted to move to Tel Aviv. A perfect Hollywood ending.

The Open House of Jerusalem is trying to help Palestinian gays to organize socially. This is being done with careful thought. On the one hand, no one wants to appear patronizing; on the other hand, it is clear that only in one society from among the three that make up Jerusalem can a gay live outside the closet: the Israeli society. The Open House is located in the center of the "Israeli place" in the city, and it is from here that its people are trying to help queers in other sectors to help themselves. Hagai El-Ad, executive director of the Open House, explains this in a letter to the editors of Gay.com: "Unlike in Israel, where the rights of lesbians and gays are protected by law, in the Palestinian Authority the situation is quite different—hence the importance of gay centers open and inviting to Palestinians in accessible locations. In this sense, Jerusalem has the greatest promise, and the Open House is the greatest hope."

El-Ad also adds that "among Palestinian Israelis being gay is still very much a social taboo." Activists of the left and those who deal in Jewish-Arab "coexistence" have a hard time swallowing this bitter truth: the vast majority of their Arab fellow travelers, in the democratic State of Israel, in the Territories, and in the Palestinian Authority are virulently homophobic. The knowledge that their allies oppose the granting of any rights whatsoever to members of the gay and lesbian community is almost certainly unpleasant to many of the community's activists. The fact that these homophobes are a majority among the elected officials of the Arab public in Israel, representing parties to which gays and lesbians have traditionally been sympathetic, merits discussion in the media and within the community. This is a debate that not a single person has dared to initiate until now.

Joining the homophobes are also some radical academics. In their eyes, the international effort to express concern over the trampling of the rights of gays and lesbians in Arab countries is nothing but sexual colonialism. In the opinion of such theorists, the sexual colonialists—who divide the world into heterosexuals, homosexuals, bisexuals, and transgendered people—impose this worldview upon those cultures that are supposedly primitive in their approaches to sexuality and gender. Must every person in the four corners of the earth accommodate himself and become a member of one of these four groups? Joseph Massad of Columbia University argues, for instance, that what he calls the "Gay International" (not to be confused with Dana International) is a classic example of sexual colonialism: the Western gaze that defines every man who sleeps with a man as a homosexual or bisexual. In his paper "Reorienting Desire: The Gay International and the Arab

10 Joseph Massad, "Reorienting Desire: The Gay International and the Arab World," *Public Culture* (forthcoming: Spring 2002).

11 Irshad Abdal Haqq, "Homosexuality and Islam in America: A Brief Overview," *The Journal of Islamic Law and Culture* 5/1 (2000): 78–96.

World," Massad focuses especially on the new phenomenon of gay Muslim organizations.[10] These organizations, among them Al-Fatiha and Queer Jihad, have also come under fire from fundamentalist Muslims in the West.[11]

One cannot argue with fundamentalists. There is no reason to suppose that they will ever retreat from the prohibitions that are in the writings. Let us only pray for the day when a pious Muslim will see homosexuality in the same way my Jewish Orthodox friends see it. The latter equate homosexuality with the desecration of the Sabbath, for which the Torah prescribes an identical punishment: death by stoning. My Orthodox friends are certainly sorry to see the public desecration of the Sabbath—a ritual I perform religiously every week—but the desecration of the Sabbath according to Orthodox religious law does not stand between us. The fact that I have had anal sex with a man becomes in a similar way simply one more sin among many that I have on my head. These sins will continue to accumulate all the days of my life. But do we not all sin?

Unlike the makers of Islamic religious law, who are tied to traditions, it appears that those who oppose sexual colonialism are simply avoiding a single important point: sexual colonialists have been around for more than a century, and they have achieved enormous success. The meaning of this success is that there are gay Muslims, human beings who define themselves as homosexuals and whose religion is Islam, and they have rights that must be respected. Jewish-Israeli culture and Palestinian-Israeli culture have been cross-pollinating for more than fifty years. Jerusalem has been a united city for more than thirty years. Even though each of the city's three populations has its own center, to those who are attracted to their own sex there was always only one—Independence Park. I assume that not all of the Palestinians who have sex with men see themselves as gay. But I know that there are Palestinians who define themselves as gay and they have the right to live full lives— open, safe, and equal. The battle of the opponents of sexual colonialism against the Muslim gay organizations only aids and abets the ongoing persecution of gays in Arab countries. Just as no one is razing all colonial-era buildings in the Arab countries, or forbidding the speaking of French in Syria or Lebanon, so also one must behave with extreme care when confronting the legacy of cultural colonialism. All the more so where the subject is of mortal consequence.

Mortal consequences also stand at the center of the most painful point of contact between gay Arabs and gay Jews: murder. Since 1980, thirty-five gays have been murdered in Israel, several of them in Jerusalem, by their sexual partners. This, according to the film director, Ran Kotzer, who is currently working on a documentary film on the subject. There were many additional, unsuccessful attempts at murder. A large majority of the victims, if not all, were Jews. Most of the murderers were caught. Almost all were Arab.

Alon Hager, Kotzer's collaborator in this project, has published an article in which he cites additional facts[12]: most of the victims met their murderers in public meeting places, then brought them back to their homes, where they were killed. In most cases, sexual relations preceded the murder. Most of the murderers were "tops" and most of the victims were "bottoms." Most of the victims were of a much higher socioeconomic level than their murderers. Most of the murderers had a petty criminal history, mostly breaking and entering. Many of the murderers continued to inflict wounds upon their victim even after death ("overkill"). In a large portion of the cases, the murderer stole items of no apparent value from the victim's home. Most of the victims were many years older than their murderers. In many cases, the murderer had also had sex with the murdered before the day of the murder. Sometimes the sexual relations were accompanied by the passing of some form of material compensation from the victim to the murderer.

Hager's analysis focuses on the psychology of the murderer, who sees himself as a straight man willing to play the active role with a man in return for compensation. When he becomes aware that he is enjoying himself, that he is experiencing sexual pleasure with another man, his internal homophobia intensifies. In order to quiet it, he demands greater and greater rewards. When the victim refuses to give more than he has already given, this internal homophobia cannot be quieted unless the gay man—that which is outside of him and that which is inside him—is murdered with excessive violence.

If we are to accept Hager's analysis, we must assume that the murderer has thoroughly internalized the conception that every man who has sex with a man, active or passive, is understood as gay or bisexual. It is a fact that most of the murderers were Arabs—Palestinians from Israel or from the Territories or from the Palestinian Authority. There is more than a touch of sexual colonialism in the general assumption that all of the murderers are, basically, homophobic homosexuals. As I have already pointed out, there were, and still are, quite a few influences from the Western understanding of sexuality on Palestinian society—influences, but certainly not wholesale adoption. The fact that a large majority of the murderers were tops in sexual relations must make you wonder. In Arab society as a whole, and in the Palestinian society in particular, there is clear division between the insertive and receptive roles in sexual relations between men. They are not considered to be secondary categories of a single phenomenon, homosexuality, but as two different sexual categories. Another variable worthy of investigation is how many of the murderers were married (to a woman) when they committed their crime. A married man who has sex with his wife and at the same time is a top in sex with a submissive man is rarely considered sexually deviant in traditional Arab societies.[13]

Ran Kotzer argues that the large socioeconomic gap between the murderer and the murdered is the most important parameter in the attempt to understand the

12 Alon Hager, "They Are Killing the Gayness in Themselves" (Hebrew), *Hazman Havarod* 43 (July 2000), 21.

13 Bruce Dunne, "Power and Sexuality in the Middle East," *Middle East Report* 206 (1998), 8–11.

To Hell and Back: Jerusalem's Queer Center

motive for murder. In his opinion, "the nationalist motive" is insignificant. Sometimes it is simply an excuse and an afterthought that is manufactured in order to become eligible for family help and social support: it's better to be an Arab who murders Jews than a gay man who murders gays.

I don't completely rule out the possibility that some of the Arab murderers have internalized Israeli-Western conceptions of sexuality and homophobia, but the assumption that this was true of all of them is pure and simple sexual colonialism. Hager and Kotzer's attempt to deny the nationalist element is symptomatic of the illusion that queer society is supernational. Homosexuality is understood in many Arab societies as a Western illness, a disgusting weakness. It should be assumed that many of the murderers don't see their (insertive) part in the sexual act as equal in worth or similar to the (receptive) part of the murdered, and therefore they are not humiliated because they find sexual relations to be pleasurable. Instead, it seems more likely to me that the murder is a logical extension, for them, of the act of sexual penetration they have already executed. Sex is only a warm-up exercise for murder. It is not incidental that sexual terms pepper the daily discourse of Israeli-Palestinian conflict. In Israel, we often hear, "We're gonna fuck the Arabs," the meaning of which is, without a doubt, "we'll kill the Arabs." The link between the insertive role in sex and victory in the national struggle, like the link between the receptive role and loss in this battle, is as old as time itself. Sometimes murderers have testified that they killed their victims as part of an initiation into one of the terrorist organizations, or as a first step in becoming "born-again" Muslims. The murdered were, above all, easy prey. Available, vulnerable, and Jewish.

If Jerusalem is Torn Apart

If Jerusalem is torn apart, its queer place, Independence Park, will move from the center of the city to its margins. If the new "city line" becomes a closed border, as it was between 1948 and 1967, Arab gays will be cut off from the Jewish ones. The Arab gays who have Jewish partners will ask to come to live in Israel. The rest of the Palestinian gays will make every effort to emigrate to Europe or to the United States. Gays will not be able to live openly in the Palestinian state for many more years. But if the new "city line" is an open border, Jerusalem will shut down completely during hours of darkness—or during all the hours of the day—because of continuing Palestinian terrorism. In a situation such as this, the Israeli population will surely uproot itself, and only the ultra-Orthodox will remain. That is to say, most of those who are openly gay will leave the city, and the lives of those who remain will be more complicated than ever. Only if Jerusalem is not torn apart, we may see, against all odds, the blossoming of a unique queer community.

Comments on United Development Corporation's Proposal for the "Economic Modernization of Jerusalem"

Thom Mayne, Rose Mendez, and Caroline Barat

Globalization has reduced the size of the world. Borders have disappeared both physically and culturally; we live by the laws of commerce. One taste, one language, one mind, one entertainment dominate. United Development Corporation's proposal for the economic modernization of Jerusalem calls for a creative and collaborative development initiative that participates in larger global movements and defines a new income base for the city of Jerusalem, one that would mobilize private, local, and global investors as well as public, local, and global constituencies. Its focus on tourism is strategic; its aim is to feed what seems to be an insatiable appetite for entertainment and a growing demand for the experience of synthetic history.[1] "Jerusalem: City as Seamless Theme Park" would build in Jerusalem a replica of that city's ancient self in recognition that human societies change and that adaptation is a normal part of human development, even within a milieu deeply dedicated to the preservation of continuity—albeit the continuity of three thousand years of irresolvable conflict.

The centerpiece of the plan is clearly inspired by the work of Baptist minister Marvin Rosenthal, head of the organization Zion's Hope, who has made history in Florida with his Orlando theme park Holy Land Experience™. Holy Land Experience lets Disney-jaded tourists experience a pilgrimage for the price of a $17 ticket. (A Bethlehem Silver 7-Day Pass can be had for $31 and a Jerusalem Gold Annual Pass for $59.) ITEC Productions, a division of ITEC Entertainment Corporation, developed a solution for Rosenthal by "compressing literally thousands of years of biblical history down to an entertaining and inspiring three- to-four-hour guest experience."[2] ITEC's designers "carefully selected personalities, places, and events that best represent key biblical ideas identified by the client"(Rosenthal), seeking "to make the [guest] experience engaging and compelling while preserving the integrity of the core message." ITEC brought to its work a "commitment to accuracy" that "translates into a fully immersive environment where every element—from the architecture and costumes to the lighting and background music—is carefully designed to support the theme."

Although utilizing the ITEC design as a prototype, United Development Corporation greatly expanded the concept in both scope and scale, visualizing the

[1] Numerous studies have shown that in our increasingly digitized virtual world, people seek the real: real experiences, real events, real interaction with products and services, the sense of "being there" (not to be confused with the book by Jerzy Kosinski). Perhaps Jeff Bezos, founder of Amazon.com, said it best: "I like seeing other people, I like seeing what they're buying. I like touching things. I like smelling things. The physical world is still the best medium ever invented."

[2] By "experience," I believe that ITEC refers to the Kierkegaardian view that there is an alienated dichotomy between the world of values and that of lived "experience." All quotations in this paragraph are from www.itec.com/pr/zion/holyland.htm and www.itec.com/pdf_files/solution/holyland.pdf. Ticket information for Holy Land Experience may be found at www.theotherorlando.com/updates/holyprice.html.

to Atarot Airport

to Ben-Gurion Airport

0   5 km

| Main Traffic Routes | Primary Streets | Municipal Boundary (1967) | Armistice Line (1949-67) |

| Arab Neighborhoods | Jewish Neighborhoods within the Armistice Line | Jewish Neighborhoods beyond the Armistice Line | Old City |

Arab and Jewish Neighborhoods, 1991

total transformation of the Holy City itself. The masterplan for "Jerusalem: City as Seamless Theme Park" integrates three major components to provide the synergy and economics needed to fuel the project:

1 "The Holy Lands"—the historic re-creation district proper.
2 A Disney World–like theme park parallel in scale to the real thing in Orlando, but emphasizing action-laden simulations of recent local history—with an emphasis on pyrotechnics.
3 Three themed hotel/gambling/convention/shopping center complexes loosely modeled, respectively, after the Venetian, the New York New York, and the Bellagio, thus piggybacking on three highly marketable brand identities.

The Holy Lands complex has been designed to encompass the standard religious triad and will be positioned at the northern boundary of the Old City on a site of approximately one square kilometer.[3] The action-park site is on the largest property of the three—11,080 hectares (27,379 acres). The hotel sites require a total of 18 hectares (45 acres) and are located at the northwest of the Old City, between the Holy Lands and the theme park. The total complex straddles the 1994 armistice line, equalizing development between Israelis and Palestinians—who now perceive the Oslo Accords' boundary as the line of opportunity, accommodation, and coexistence, and begin to recognize limits to the idea of sovereignty.

The benefits of this proposal are numerous. Providing an enormous boost to the local economy, the total development represents an investment of $9.3 billion and would produce an annual projected income of $775 million ($1,200 per capita). The project would employ over 10,000 people while attracting approximately 18 million tourists per year, over three times the present population of Israel.

With the influx of such a great number of tourists from the broader, international community—persons immune to the recent past and more interested in immediate fulfillment—one could anticipate an easing of tensions between Israelis and Palestinians. Given the magnitude of the development and its accompanying status, Jerusalem would acquire legitimacy and authority to renew its identity and image. Over time, the success of the aggregate development could be expected to deplete the economy of Old City itself, which would be the most logical site for future expansion of the project.

Given the urgency of the current political situation, this proposal should be strongly and swiftly supported by all organizations connected to the Arab/Israeli conflict. There is no other solution but to share the Holy Lands, a view expressed by then President Bill Clinton at the Camp David summit meetings of 2000. Clinton said that Jerusalem "must be an open and undivided city, and it must encompass the internally recognized capitals of two states, Israel and Palestine." A beautiful dream: two states sharing a capital—and capital.

3 Jerusalem's Old City, a total area of one square kilometer, houses some of the holiest sites of the world's three major monotheistic religions.

Comments on United Development Corporation's Proposal

1 The New York- New York

2 The Bellagio 3 The Venetian

4 The Holy Land Experience 5 Walt Disney World

To Atarot Airport

ﾠrion Airport

4

1
2

3

The Old City

5

0   2.5 km

| - - - - | Armistice Line | | Main Traffic Routes | | Primary Streets | | Secondary Streets | | The Old City |

| Green Areas | | Buildings | | The Holy Lands | | Theme Park Zone | | 20-Acre Hotels |

Jerusalem City Map and Proposed Zones

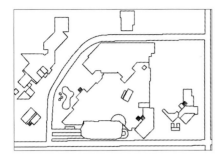

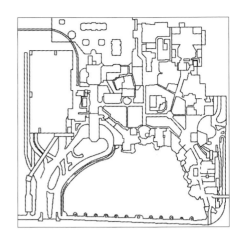

**1   New York, New York Hotel and Casino
Las Vegas, 1997**

Scale   20 acres

Hotel   2,035 rooms at 300/500 sf each

Casino   Recreates the ambience and excitement
of the Big Apple. 84,000 sf; 80 gaming tables;
more than 2,200 slot machines

Pool   2,500 sf of water heated to 82°; 8,000 sf deck;
three small spas;
health club

Restaurants   11 private venues

Attendance   unknown

Cost   Free entry
Rooms range from $59 to $309
$485 million construction

FEATURES

Skyline   Features 12 of New York's most popular towers at third
the actual size; 300-foot-long replica of the Brooklyn
Bridge; 47-story replica of the Empire State Building; 150 ft
replica of Statue of Liberty

Entertainment   Includes the hit show "Michael Flatley's Lord of the Dance"
and The Empire Bar and Lounge

Retail Shops   12 private venues;
convention rooms;
business center

1,000-seat theater
Coney Island Emporium (Arcade)
Manhattan Express Rollercoaster®:
Simulates a barrel-roll in a jet fighter; rolls 180°, hangs 86 ft
in the air; max speed – 67 mph; highest drop – 144 ft

**2   Bellagio Hotel
Las Vegas, 1998**

Scale   25 acres

Hotel   3,025 rooms

Casino   116,000 sf

Pool   6 distinctive pool courtyard settings
Spa Bellagio, beauty salon

Restaurants   13 distinctive restaurants
10 bars and cafes

Attendance   Tens of thousands of people visit the resort every day

Cost   Free entry
Rooms range from $159 to $499
Resort: $1.9 billion
Art collection: $300 million
Fountains: $40 million

FEATURES

Gallery   Bellagio Gallery of Fine Art: collection of works by Monet,
Renoir, Cezanne, Van Gogh, Gaughin, Matisse, Picasso,
and others

Fountain   Located in a 12-acre, 27-million-gallon lake in front of the
Show   hotel; features 900-foot-long series of 1,200 fountains and
laser lights accompanied by music. Can shoot up to
17,000 gallons of water more than 250 feet in the air at
any one time

Monorail   Connects Bellagio to Monte Carlo

Convention   45,000 sf Grand Ballroom, 23,000 sf Bellagio Ballroom,
Hall   and 14 meeting rooms ranging in size from
1,000 to 10,000 sf business center

Gardens   The Bellagio Conservatory and Botanical Garden:
home to exotic plants and flowers such as orchids, lilies,
and hyacinths

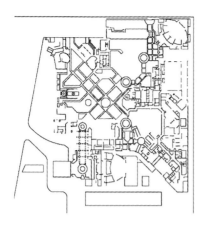

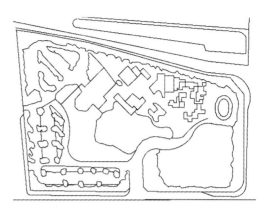

**3   Venetian Resort-Hotel-Casino
    Las Vegas, 1999**

Scale	17 acres
Hotel	3,036 rooms, approx. 700 sf each
Casino	120,000 sf Venetian Palace 2,500 slot machines 118 gaming tables
Pool	5 swimming pools 11 acres of pool deck Canyon Ranch SpaClu, 65,000 sf
Restaurants	11 specialty restaurants
Attendance	Total occupancy through March 17, 2001, was 99.4%
Cost	Free entry Rooms range from $109 to $399 Construction: $1.5 billion

FEATURES

Shopping	The Grand Canal Shoppes: 500,000 sf retail space; more than 50 shops; quarter-mile Venetian streetscape and Grand Canal with gondola rides
Entertainment	4 lounges with live music 1,400-seat entertainment venue The Theatres of Sensation
Convention Space	Wedding Chapel Sands Expo Convention Center: 1.7 mil. sf Venetian Congress Center: 500,000 sf meeting space includes the 85,000 sf column-free Venetian ballroom
Gallery	Hermitage-Guggenheim Museum: joint venture with the Guggenheim Foundation: 7,660 sf structure designed by Rem Koolhaas; set to open in 2001

**4   Holy Land Experience
    Orlando, 2001**

Scale   15 acres

FEATURES*

In addition to the Qumran caves and the Temple facade, features include authentic-looking Jerusalem streetscape and marketplace, a recreation of the famous Garden Tomb, and a display of rare priceless Bibles and related ancient manuscripts. In the courtyard of the wilderness Tabernacle, guests will witness an ancient and moving ceremony centered on the sacred Ark of the Covenant. Familiar biblical figures will relate their stories inside a Bedouin tent while, nearby, key moments from the Old and New Testament will come alive in a sweeping motion picture presentation accented by dramatic in-theater special effects.

· Bible exhibit
· Tabernacle
· Theater
· Restaurant & outdoor dining
· Oasis palms cafe
· Performance area
· Biblical garden area
· Golgotha
· Bedouin tent
· Garden tomb
· Oasis/waterfall feature
· Burning bush feature
· Noah's Ark children's play space
· Ye Olde Bazaar
· Old Scroll Shop

Entry: Adult $17; Child $12

*Based on text found at
 www.itec.com/pr/zion/holyland.htm

5 Walt Disney World
Orlando, 1971

Scale 27,400 acres, but only a small portion of this is the built-up area of the Magic Kingdom

FEATURES

The Magic Kingdom opened with 35 major attractions, and new ones have been added at a rate of more than one a year.

The Flagship Magic Kingdom, Adventureland, Frontierland, Liberty Square, Fantasyland, Tomorrowland, and Main Street USA

EPCOT Center with its Future World and World Showcase
The Disney-MGM Studios
River Country
Discovery Island
Typhoon Lagoon
Pleasure Island

Cost Entry: Adult $48; Child $38

Attendance These venues, along with Disney resort hotels, are visited by over 30 mil. people a year. Its first-year attendance of over 10 million people put Walt Disney World ahead of the UK, Austria, and West Germany as a vacation attraction. In the first decade, more than 126 million people passed through the gates of WDW, surpassing the Eiffel Tower, Taj Majal, Tower of London, and Egyptian pyramids. In 1980, with 13 to 14 million visitors annually, WDW received 1.4 million or 10% of the foreign visitors to the United States.

Revenue · 2000 revenues grew to $25.4 billion
· 27% of the Walt Disney World Company's fiscal 2000 revenues was generated by their Parks and Resorts Unit 27% of $25.4 billion = $6.9 billion
· During the park's first two years, WDW brought into the area $110 million in payroll salaries, $28 mil. in state taxes, and over $100 million in local purchases
· By early 1972 around 20,000 new hotel and motel units were under construction, resulting in 6,000 construction jobs

---

OPERATIONAL STRATEGIES FOR FUTURES PLANNING

FORECASTING follows a time series. Quantitative data is collected that covers a period of time and is analyzed in search of recognizable patterns. The data may then be smoothed to eliminate the most significant variations and to identify underlying trends. Moving averages and exponential smoothing are two methods of reducing the extremes in data by creating a flatter line. In a third method, linear regression, a straight line is produced that statistically fits the data with a minimum of divergence between the line and the actual readings. This works well where there is a clear linear trend and the data increases or decreases by a constant amount for each unit of time.

SCENARIOS explore alternative futures and their likely consequences. They are intended to provoke thought about the consequences of different courses of actions, rather than to attempt to build accurate forecasts. Thought experiment uses human reasoning and experience, even intuition, to evaluate the likely path of change.

RETAIL "Think of the store as everywhere..." A new retailing term—multi-channeling—sums up the concept best: "The store is no longer at the mall, on the Web, or in a catalogue – it's wherever the customer is when he chooses to shop, browse, and buy. Consumers move seamlessly from one channel to another when shopping. For you to be where they are, you need to be everywhere."

TRENDS are measured in terms of percentage growth and decline. Exponential trends in either direction are unlikely to continue forever and tend to follow what is known as the growth or S-curve. They show a pattern of growth that is initially very slow, and beyond a certain point it explodes before decreasing and trailing off toward its limit. A series of S-curves is known as an envelope curve. This describes, for example, the way in which successive developments have extended the capacity of a particular technology. For example, the vacuum tube, the transistor, and the chip have successfully extended the capability of electronics. Expressed as a forecast, the envelope curve assumes that further technological developments will continue the process.

SPECULATION is intended to be thought provoking and to highlight potential opportunities and risks. It is often trend-based but it can also be innovative and challenge established wisdom. Speculation, by its very nature, embodies questions about what we, or society, really want.

OPERATIVE CONCEPTS Modulation of various temporal scales: Zooming in—zooming out (macro history/micro history). Modulation of various physical scales: Zooming in—zooming out (global/local spheres of influence).

Comments on United Development Corporation's Proposal

MAGIC KINGDOM

Osprey Ridge
Golf Course

Disney's Bonnet Creek
Golf Club

RIVER
COUNTRY

Cypress
Golf Club

Magnolia
Golf Course

Eagle Pines
Golf Course

Lake Buena Vista
Golf Club

DOWNTOWN
DISNEY MARKETPLACE

FANTASIA
GARDENS

DISNEY'S
BOARDWALK

EPCOT

DISNEY'S
TYPHOON
LAGOON

NEY'S ANIMAL KINGDOM

DISNEY'S
MGM
STUDIOS

0   500   1000   2000

Jerusalem: United City, Two Sovereignties

Moshe Safdie

Introduction

In the past century, Jerusalem has grown from a one-square-kilometer walled city of 20,000 to a sprawling metropolis of 1,000,000 that stretches from Ramallah in the north to Bethlehem in the south, from Ma'ale Adumim in the east to Mevaseret Zion in the west. As the sacred city of three religions and home to numerous ethnic groups, it has always been an interpenetrating puzzle of peoples and cultures. Divided for centuries into quarters—Christian, Muslim, Armenian, and Jewish—its communities met in the north-south and east-west central markets, remnants of the Roman Cardo and Decomanus. The city expanded beyond its walls at the beginning of the twentieth century, forming neighborhoods of religious and secular Jews, Jews of Eastern and European origins, Christian and Muslim Palestinians, Germans, Ethiopians, Russians, and Anglicans—enclaves of diverse identities, languages, living habits, and economic means.

In the first half of the twentieth century Jerusalem expanded under one unified administration or another. First came that of the Ottomans, then (from 1918 to 1948) the British Mandate. During this whole period Jerusalem's expansion issues were similar to those faced by other cities of similar scale: accommodation of growing population, of the automobile, and so forth. Jerusalem's complex topography of steep slopes, valleys, plateaus, and mountain ridges, along with the desire to protect its historic architectural heritage, led to a number of strategies resolutely enforced by the activist British administration. The "stone law," for example, decreed that the exterior walls of all buildings in the city must be constructed of Jerusalem limestone. The romantic notion that newly expanded neighborhoods and public buildings must stylistically echo the historic architecture led to such monuments as the Government House, the YMCA, and the Rockefeller Museum. These were followed by the somewhat less romantic yet highly contextual buildings of the European Jewish immigrants. International Style inspired the Hebrew University campus, garden towns such as Rechavia and Talbiah, and Hadassah Hospital on Mount Scopus (by Eric Mendelsohn). There was also great expansion of Arab neighborhoods, mostly in the style of the Mediterranean urban vernacular.

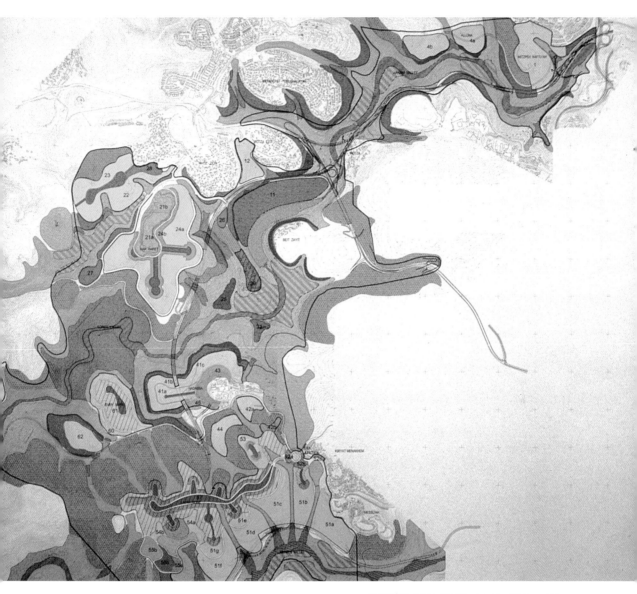

Plan for West Jerusalem. The plan, covering an area of 2,650 hectares, has been developed to guide the growth of Jerusalem into the expanded city limits toward the west. The plan calls for the preservation of all valleys as open spaces and defines sites for development. The arterial road system proposed earlier has been reconceived and realigned.

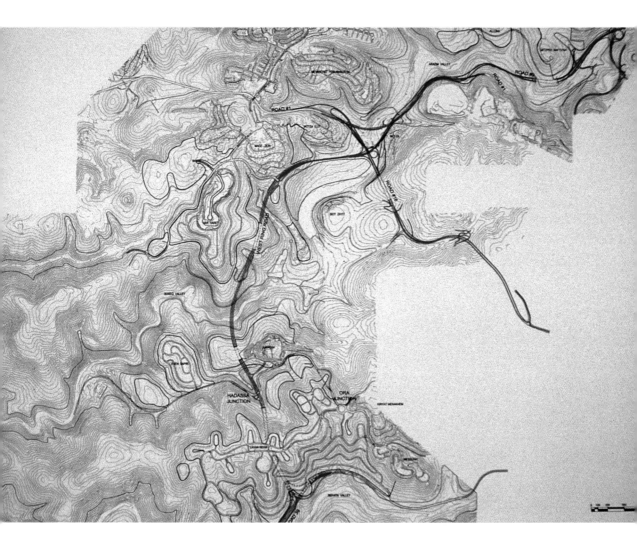

West Jerusalem masterplan. The proposed arterial road
system. Utilizing models of the region with the scale of
1:2,500 and 1:1,000, the arterial road system was recon-
sidered so as to preserve the integrity of the valleys and
to better serve the proposed new neighborhoods. A
series of tunnels and bridges minimizes the impact on the
natural landscape. The proposed western Ring Road—
the newly designed entry to the city—and Highway 39,
which connects Beit Shemesh to Jerusalem, are integrated into a single limited-access system.

With the number of cars in this poor city being relatively small, the scale of streets and alleys remained intimate. The open spaces around the Old City—the Kidron and Hinom valleys—were zoned as open space to protect the identity of the Old City.

The British period's charming, romantic, and picturesque city already harbored major internal political, religious, and social conflicts. The emerging conflict between Palestine's Jewish and Arab populations first erupted into violence in 1928. Somewhat more subtle were the growing conflicts between secular Zionists and the Orthodox Jewish clans, divisions that became physically manifest as the Orthodox isolated themselves in ghettolike neighborhoods.

From an urban-development perspective, however, these enclaves were interwoven and connected by a single business district and a unified system of roads and a public transportation. Under the Mandate's auspices, well-administered municipal services generally provided a fair distribution of resources and infrastructure to all parts of the city. Moreover, explosive growth, rising automobile ownership, and the collapse of the traditional urban structures had not yet occurred by 1948, when the British Mandate ended.

The 1948 War of Independence led to the division of the city into two separately administered, hermetically sealed urban entities. We are familiar with the distorted patterns of urban development that occurred as a result of this division. By 1967, when the city was reunited under Israeli administration as a result of the Six-Day War, the two cities had grown extensively. Most growth had occurred on the Israeli side. Immigrants had poured into the city, necessitating the construction of many new neighborhoods. Somewhat slower growth had occurred in the sleepy Jordanian-administered side, where tourist and pilgrim traffic was relatively limited. Jerusalem remained a cul-de-sac both for the inhabitants of the Jordanian-administered West Bank and for Israelites, whose economic and cultural life centered in the expanding coastal plain around Tel Aviv.

To fully understand the impact of these nineteen years of division, one must consider how the city might have evolved had division not occurred. Population growth during that period would have undoubtedly been accommodated by the construction of new neighborhoods in the direction of existing infrastructure and the most convenient topography. A combination of factors—north-south historic roots, land ownership, and convenience—would have undoubtedly led to the growth of a linear city along the north-south axis of the mountain plateau toward Ramallah and (to a lesser extent) Bethlehem. To the east the forbidding Judean desert would have discouraged development, while to the west, difficult topography and forestation would have been equally discouraging.

The plateau would have offered itself as a convenient, eligible, and easily organized site for expansion of the city. The resulting city would have been served by a number of north-south and east-west routes. The latter would have crossed the city both south of the Old City and north of it (along the historic Ayalon Valley, which extends eastward to Jericho and Amman). A single business district would have expanded north from the British central business district (CBD), that is, from Jaffa and the Damascus Gate toward the Atarot airport. Neighborhoods would have clustered east and west of this center. Given the number of Arab villages and expanding Jewish neighborhoods along this axis, the outcome would have been a reasonably random interweaving of Jewish and Arab populations.

Post–World War II expansion would have been influenced by the destructive urban development patterns of the 1950s and 1960s. These affected most European cites and were visible in other cities in the region such as Haifa and Tel Aviv, which grew from four-story Garden Cities to full-fledged, automobile-dominated metropolises. A brave new world of wide boulevards, parking lots, and widely spaced buildings began to emerge; the urban syntax was changing everywhere, and it certainly changed in Jerusalem, even under the conditions of division. New medium-rise apartment blocks built on the Israeli side of Jerusalem during the years of division, defying topography and history like loyal soldiers, present a powerful contrast to the land-hugging historical vernacular.

The united post-1948 city described above was not to be. The armistice between Jordan and Israel drew a complex and artificial line through the city that defied all urban logic. It placed the walled city under Jordanian control and cut a border through the former British Mandate's business district north along the plateau, with the eastern neighborhoods going to Jordan and the western to Israel. Part of the CBD was affected by its proximity to a belligerent border of walls and barbed wire, snipers and danger. Each community proceeded with urban development cognizant of this division. In time the border proved almost impassable—only United Nations personnel and a few international travelers were able to cross it. A whole generation of Israelis and Palestinians grew up without experiencing the physical presence of the other half, which became abstract, a forbidding mystery. For example, Teddy Kollek, mayor of Jerusalem since a year before unification, was asked after 1967 why building permits had been given for certain towers, including a twenty-story tower on King George Street. He responded, "We had no idea how ugly they looked from the Mount of Olives"—from the principal vantage point of East Jerusalem. This underlines the extent to which urban policies were made in isolation at that time, owing to the artificial division.

The years of division forced Israelis to expand their business district westward and to build a government complex at some distance from that district, far from the border, near the western entrance to the city. New neighborhoods with affinities to the Tel Aviv–Jerusalem highway—the lifeline of the city—were also built to the west. The orientation of the Israeli city was thus westward.

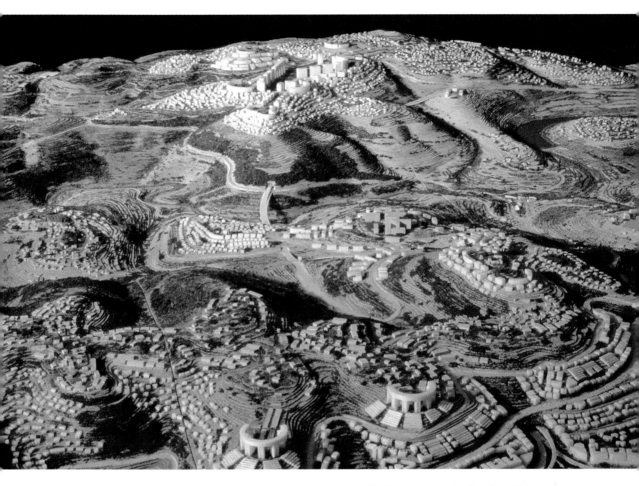

West Jerusalem masterplan. Overall model of the region
on a scale of 1:2,500. This model was used as the design
instrument for developing the plan. The arterial and local
road systems, along with the proposed buildings, were
placed on the model as the design evolved to ensure the
perfect fit between the complex topography, major landscape features, and proposed development.

West Jerusalem masterplan. Model of the Reches Lavan Ridge, the southern section of the region. This model, at 1:2,500 scale, was utilized to determine general road systems and development areas.

The Jordanian city, growing more slowly, evolved a small business district in the Salah eddin area outside the Damascus Gate. Much development on the Jordanian side consisted of sporadic, dispersed construction at the perimeters of villages and strip development on the road to Ramallah, where the well-to-do built their villas. By and large, Jordanian construction was small in scale and more compatible with the city's historic fabric. High-rise, skyline-disrupting construction arrived on the Israeli side by the late 1960s with the Clal Center, the Hilton and Plaza hotels, and Migdal Ha'ir.

United yet Divided

Though the city was officially united under a single administration in 1967, this was perceived by the Palestinian population as an occupation, not a unification. Patterns of development since then have, therefore, been anything but normal. Once again it is important to consider what Jerusalem's development over the past thirty years might have been, absent the Israeli-Palestinian conflict. Urban development would (as before) probably have seized on the northern plateau for its convenience. Existing strip development toward Ramallah would have laid the foundation for growth in that direction. The western Israeli neighborhoods would, logically, have expanded on adjacent land—Katamon toward Bethlehem, Romema toward Nebi Samuel. Most important, a single business district would have emerged, connecting the Israeli and Palestinian centers of the divided years into a single development area bridging the Damascus Gate area and the Israeli downtown and expanding north-ward. This would have offered a convenient framework for public transportation, a single network for all the city's residents.

Most of this did not occur because of the dynamics of the conflict. For the Israelis, who controlled development, the underlying strategic goal was to prevent the physical redivision of the city in the event of a negotiated settlement with the Palestinians. Since, during the nineteen years of division, two cohesive urban districts had emerged along either side of the Green Line (the post-1948 border), Israel's strategy was to expropriate land and build new Jewish neighborhoods on the eastern side of the line in a dispersed pattern that would create a checkerboard of Jewish and Palestinian neighborhoods. This would in turn render a new border physically impossible. From an urban-development point of view, this strategy presented extraordinary challenges and paradoxes. The new neighborhoods were isolated by design from older Jewish neighborhoods and unrelated to any existing infrastructure and services. Thus, the neighborhoods of Gilo, East Talpiot, French Hill, Ramot, and (later) Pisgat Ze'ev were dispersed north, south, and east, adjacent to Arab villages and towns such as Beit Jalla, Sur Bacher, the American Colony area, and so on. New commercial and social services had to be constructed to make these "satellite

Jerusalem: United City, Two Sovereignties

towns," as they were called, relatively self-sufficient. As a result, the CBD was weakened and ceased to be "central" at all. Roads were hastily constructed to connect the satellite towns to the city, traversing virgin land.

On the Palestinian side, growth was more contiguous with existing development but did grow rapidly as business and employment opportunities expanded after reunification. Palestinians poured into Jerusalem, giving rise to a new political consideration that to this day strongly affects Israeli urban policy and national economic strategy: the demographic balance.

A Jewish majority in Jerusalem first occurred in 1856, during the Ottoman administration. This majority was maintained as the city grew, and at the time of unification in 1967 the ratio of Jews to Palestinians stood at about 2:1. During the years of division there was little concern on the Israeli side over the population balance between Jews and Arabs. Once the city united, however, relative numbers became a primary strategic issue affecting control over the city's future. Israeli administrations were concerned that if the Palestinian population was to expand relative to the Jewish population as a result of faster natural growth and employment-driven immigration, Israel would be at a disadvantage in terms of its claim to the city. Thus, in addition to its policy of dispersing neighborhoods to prevent redivision and of seizing territories in every part of the metropolitan area, the Israeli government evolved policies, including economic incentives, to promote growth of the Jewish population. Ironically, however, some of these policies had the opposite effect. For example, the encouragement of tourism by the subsidized construction of hotels provided jobs that were mostly filled by Palestinians, thus encouraging the expansion of the Palestinian population. Providing high-tech and other jobs more likely to attract secular Israelis proved more difficult. However, relief came (perhaps unexpectedly) as a result of the Orthodox Jews' high immigration and birth rates.

In order to maximize the city's Jewish population, new city limits were established shortly after 1967, annexing areas that were beyond the Green Line. A cursory examination of this border reveals a strangely undulating line that defies logic or topography. Conceived primarily by Moshe Dayan, the border was devised so as to keep certain Arab neighborhoods out of the city while maximizing the number of Jews in it.

Thus, although Jerusalem has been under a single administration for over thirty years, many aspects of its development have been urbanistically illogical. It is essential to consider these irrational aspects of the city as one considers its future. For example, while infrastructure (including the power grid, water supply, and sewer system) has been integrated, the quality of municipal services is not equitable. Jewish neighborhoods have benefited from a higher level of physical and social services. With the exception of Road 1, a boulevard extending from the Damascus Gate and effectively linking the Palestinian population in Ramallah to Jerusalem, most highway construction

Mamilla District. Montage of the Mamilla model, showing its integration into the city. Note the connection to Jaffa Gate leading to the downtown. The Mamilla District is a 150,000 sq ft, mixed-use complex including residential and hotel facilities, a pedestrian shopping street, and parking services for the district and the Old City. It was conceived as a bridge between the old and new cities, and a connection between the Israeli and Palestinian parts of the city.

has been in response to the needs of the Jewish population (and the expansionist strategies of the Israeli government). Moreover, most expansion of hotels and tourist and commercial activity has occurred west of the old CBD. Since "reunification" the city has continued to exist as two adjacent but separate cities, causing the Palestinian and Israeli business districts not only to fail to connect but to each expand separately (toward the east and the west, respectively). Separate development also was encouraged by the existence of two totally separate public-transportation systems.

In spite of these structural divisions, in times of relative calm—that is, before the intifada of 1986 and during subsequent periods between violent eruptions—the Arabs and Israelis crossed the invisible border in large numbers. Arabs shopped on the Israeli side and Israelis converged on the Old City and the eastern city, frequenting restaurants and businesses. Pilgrims and tourists used facilities on both sides. These crossings have been rudely interrupted every time the political climate has changed, as it did, for example, in October 2000, when the Al Aqsa Intifada broke out. Within one week of the commencement of hostilities the Old City was transformed from a congested marketplace surrounded by thousands of parked vehicles and tourist buses into a desolate place with few people in sight.

Mamilla District. Model of Mamilla showing the district under construction in 1998, as well as its relationship to the surroundings.

The Near Future: Pitfalls and Opportunities

The government of Israel and the Palestinian National Authority are now negotiating their future relationship, which will presumably include some agreement about Jerusalem. As architects and urban planners, we must consider the implications of the probable outcome of these negotiations for the life of the city's residents, both Palestinian and Israeli and for urban development strategy.

The development and character of Jerusalem have always been affected by changes in its political circumstances. Under the Turks, Jerusalem was a sleepy Mediterranean town made unique by its sacred history and diverse population; under the British, a romantic multicultural colonial city with opportunities and unresolved conflicts side by side; during the years of division, two sleepy cities constrained by their cul-de-sac status within their respective economies. As a united city under Israeli administration, Jerusalem saw a period of enormous expansion for all its member communities, this growth facilitated by unified administration yet conditioned by deep conflicts associated with occupation and the Palestinians' desire for self-determination.

The ongoing negotiations present new problems and opportunities. Although the Camp David II discussions were not conclusive, it was evident that both Palestinians and Israelis have modified their traditional positions. The Palestinians, who in the past demanded sovereignty over all parts of the city which had been under Jordanian control prior to 1967, including the Old City, are prepared to accept the presence, under Israeli administration, of the Jewish neighborhoods built beyond the Green Line, and to accept some form of division of the Old City and holy places. The Temple Mount, the Haram al-Sharif, remains a complex issue of enormous emotional impact.

The Israeli position to date has been that the entire city must remain under Israeli sovereignty. Yet at Camp David it became clear that Israel is now considering accepting Palestinian sovereignty in those areas of the city primarily populated by Palestinians. For the Israelis, too, control over the holy places remains a contentious and complex problem.

We can assume for the moment that some clever formula can be devised to satisfy both Israeli and Palestinian aspirations within the Old City and holy places, and move on to the urban-development implications of such an agreement. If Palestinian sovereignty over Palestinian-populated areas had occurred in 1967, right after the Six-Day War, the natural result would have been Palestinian development of a contiguous geographic area clearly separated from the Israeli area. However, the policies implemented during the past three decades have created an entirely different situation.

Today the city is an interlocking puzzle of Israeli and Palestinian islands; it is impossible to form contiguous Palestinian or Israeli zones. It is also impossible for any

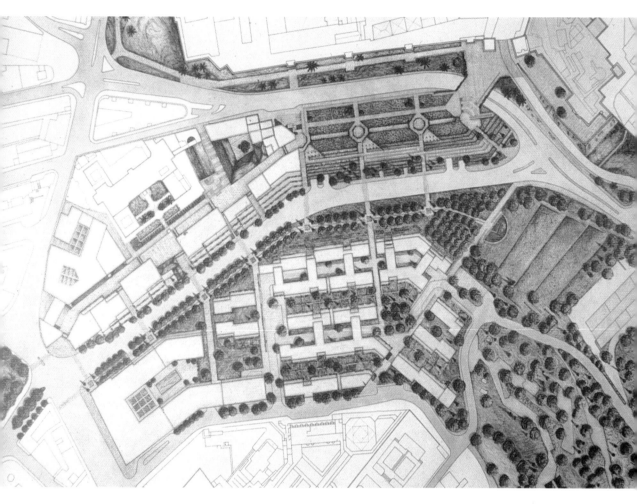

Masterplan of Mamilla, showing the mixed-use plan and the open-space system. Jaffa Gate and the city walls are at the upper right corner.

future Palestinian and Israeli entities to be served by separate transportation systems, since the routes connecting Jewish and Arab neighborhoods overlap profusely. Moreover, the Palestinians must have access to a continuous corridor between the two parts of the West Bank, that is, Hebron and Bethlehem in the south and Ramallah and Nablus in the north. Such a corridor can only be created by cutting through areas now populated by Israelis. Conversely, on the Israeli side, the town of Maaleh Adumin requires connection to Jerusalem, crossing Palestinian routes. Duplication of infrastructure and transportation routes is also infeasible given that Jerusalem remains a relatively poor city.

We must be realistic about these and other political facts that are bound to make the development of a coordinated and cohesive plan difficult. The Palestinians, after many years of Israeli administration, will undoubtedly demand full planning control in any territories over which they gain sovereignty. It is unlikely that they will consider kindly any suggestion that land-use, transportation, and infrastructure planning should be coordinated with Israel. It is also possible that after the city is redivided—albeit this time with open borders —new competitive forces shall be

Mamilla District. Mamilla Street, converted to pedestrian use. The existing preserved buildings are to the left, new construction is to the right. This street extends from Jaffa Gate into the downtown.

unleashed. The Israelis will probably continue to be obsessed with maintaining a majority in the city and will seek to do so by promoting dense development in the areas they control. There is already an Israeli move to encourage the construction of high-rise buildings in the CBD, motivated more by nationalism than by economic considerations. This obsession with tall buildings is clearly a nationalistic-symbolic affair, since there is little evidence of economic pressures to build high-rises in the city. Similarly, after agreement is reached it is likely that intensive development will occur in the Palestinian parts of Jerusalem, as we have seen recently in Ramallah and Gaza, with many expatriate Palestinians wishing to own (as Jews have long owned) a *pied à terre* in the holy city.

These complementary forces—Israeli aggrandizement and Palestinian catch-up development—could overwhelm preservation successes of recent years and compromise Jerusalem's historic character.

These issues should be considered in the current debate in Israeli planning institutions over high-rise buildings. The champions of tall buildings state that a limited number of "jewel-like" structures constructed on specially selected sites would be beneficial, and insist that high-rises are an economic necessity for a revitalized downtown. But experience shows that spot zoning does not work. Once you accept high-rises, they will sprout everywhere—on both sides of the city. As for "jewel-like" buildings, most towers end up being designed and built by quite average architects and developers. Nor is the argument of economic necessity convincing. Washington, D.C., and many European cities have demonstrated that vitality need not equal high-rise development. Israeli planners might do well to take the moral high ground and forbid all high-rise towers (i.e., those exceeding ten stories), setting a standard that can then be proposed for all parts of the city in the future.

Mamilla District. Night photograph of the project. This model shows the pedestrian Mamilla Street extending from the downtown central business district toward the markets of the Old City. The valley of Henon is restored as an open-space park system as it extends toward Independence Park.

The Israeli-Palestinian response to the new situation is already resulting in policies that could lead to ecological and environmental disasters. Creative counterpolicies are thus needed. On the Israeli side, for example, acceptance of the fact that much of East Jerusalem could become inaccessible to Israeli development has led to the initiation of the "West Jerusalem Plan," which is being undertaken by my office. Our planning mandate has been to consider the areas recently annexed to the west of Jerusalem, lands on the Israeli side of the Green Line—in particular, those areas heretofore zoned for agriculture, forestation, and open space. This is a topographically complex region of discontinuous mountain ridges and deeply sloping valleys of extraordinary natural beauty. A number of expressways (including Route 39, connecting Jerusalem to Beit Shemesh; the Jerusalem Ring Road, running from Ramot to Malcha; and the proposed Highways 9 and 16) have been planned for this area. The Israeli government had demanded that this area, comprising 2,650 hectares, should be designed so as to accommodate 100,000 families (approximately 300,000 people).

In accepting this commission, we stipulated several conditions:

- The alignment of the expressways, though already designed by road engineers, would undergo a total redesign subject to considerations of topography and preservation of open space.

- We would not undertake the accommodation of a predetermined number of housing units in the new development. We would determine an appropriate number of units after defining those areas available for development and those to be preserved as open space—for example, historic terraced valleys and forests.

- In designing the character of the new development, quality-of-life issues would be taken into account and housing densities would be based on the optimal housing types likely to attract families currently leaving the city.

Three years later, through a planning effort involving the construction of large models (1:2,500 and 1:1,000 scale), the expressway system has been totally redesigned. It is now adapted optimally to the topography, thus minimizing damage. Approximately 30,000 housing units have been proposed in three development areas interconnected by roads and a public transportation system. All the valleys in the planning areas are to be preserved as open spaces for public recreation and conservation.

Yet on the regional scale there is something artificial about our plan. The topography is difficult, the whole development expensive. In a unified city free of territorial considerations, development could have been more readily undertaken on the plateau areas on the Jerusalem-Ramallah axis. Yet given the probable outcome of Israeli-Palestinian negotiations, the land considered in the West Jerusalem Plan is probably the only land available for the expansion of the Israeli population. The Palestinians will find themselves in a similar predicament, seeking opportunities for

View of the Damascus Gate area showing the triangle currently used for trucking, parking, and other secondary uses.

Model of the Damascus Gate plan, showing the sunken piazzas, the oval green overlooking the Old City, and the conversion of the Street of the Prophets into a pedestrian street leading toward the Damascus Gate.

densification on their own side. The West Jerusalem Plan thus demonstrates dramatically the need for a complementary East Jerusalem Plan to define infrastructure and roads and development areas and to preserve open space in the eastern half of the metropolitan area. Here lies the crux of the urban development paradox involved in the current negotiations. Simplistic logic would suggest that the Palestinian National Authority, on its own, is the appropriate generator of an eastern development plan. Yet while West Jerusalem remains entirely under Israeli control in any possible negotiated scenario, the eastern half of the city is not so certain to be under absolute Palestinian national control. One must consider, for example, the major Jewish neighborhoods (Pisgat Ze'ev, French Hill, the Hebrew University campus, and Maale Adumim), which will remain under Israeli control, and the fact that the eastern half of any ring road connecting Ramallah and Nablus with Bethlehem and Hebron must traverse Israeli as well as Palestinian territory. Current Israeli proposals for the eastern portion of the ring road are amateurish, not having been subject to the rigors of three-dimensional modeling. Nor have they been generated with attentiveness to Palestinian expansion and development needs. A study of the scale and scope of that undertaken by us for West Jerusalem is urgently needed and should address the following issues:

- Definition of areas of possible Palestinian expansion, i.e., both existing villages and towns and land for new development.

- The character, scale, and density of such developments.

- Institutional and commercial requirements, such as secondary centers, government buildings, and other institutions that the Palestinian population currently lacks.

- A road system and public transportation system would serve these developments, as well as comparable Israeli developments.

- Slating of areas for conservation and open space.

Such a plan could only be the result of cooperation between Palestinian and Israeli planners, urban designers, and engineers. Without Israeli input, Palestinians would be frustrated; without Palestinian input and initiative, no plan has any chance of being embraced. Whether any such collaborative effort is possible in the current atmosphere of recrimination is an open question. On the Palestinian side there is bound to be suspicion of domination by Israeli interests. On the Israeli side, while there may be willingness to collaborate, there is also a habit of planning in an atmosphere of total control. The Israeli mind-set will require some reorientation, particularly at the administrative level, before it can consider a planning process in which Palestinian interests and needs are primary considerations.

Divided yet United

There remains the question of what kind of life a united city of separate sovereignties would offer its residents. In the past century, shifts of political power have deeply affected the residents' life experiences. Under Ottoman rule and the British Mandate, all segments of the population met and interacted in Jerusalem's business districts, first the markets of the Old City and then the CBD. In the nineteen years of division there was a rigorous separation much like that experienced by Berlin: two cities, side by side, living separate lives. In the past thirty-odd years, under the slogan "Jerusalem—A United City" (i.e., under Israeli control), the city has gone through several phases, being relatively open and free during times of quiet and de facto separated during the intifadas.

The prospect of a united city with divided sovereignty thus raises the question of how urban development polices will impact the kind of interaction that will occur between the two populations. If we are to learn from historic models, the experience of a united city is established primarily in those places where diverse populations come together for business, commerce, entertainment, recreation, and social services. What can be done to encourage this type of space-sharing in the years to come? Jerusalem's two business districts are physically divided today by Road 1 and the open area bounded by the Russian Compound, Damascus Gate, and the Salalia-Dia area. This last area is currently the transportation hub of the Palestinian population and the site of a station along Jerusalem's new light-rail line (currently nearing construction). It is potentially a hub for the entire city and is also the crossroads of the tourist and pilgrim traffic en route to the holy places in and around the Old City. With tourism, pilgrim traffic, and transportation passing through one pivotal point between the Arab and Jewish CBDs, there is an opportunity to weave them together into a single center of greater impact and diversity.

The Mamilla Development, near completion, has been presumed to be one element in such a strategy, anchoring the Israeli CBD at Jaffa Gate and pulling activity closer to the Old City and the Palestinian CBD. The Russian Compound, the Damascus Gate area, the development currently under construction along Road 1, and the still-undeveloped Wadi Joz area are all potential sites for this integrated, sovereignties-bridging center, which could give Jerusalem the kind of core it requires. Moreover, a unified center would make possible a more efficient transportation system. There is no experience more integrating than sharing a bus or light-rail system. (There is also less chance for terrorist attacks on integrated buses.)

The object of merging the centers demands a strategic plan for the square kilometer north of the Old City. In the past decade there have been a number of official Israeli initiatives in this area and also many academic studies (such as the five-year Harvard-Jerusalem study). The problem is that neither Israeli nor Palestinian planning entities can develop an effective plan independently. This presents an opportunity—

Damascus Gate. Two per-
spective renderings showing
the two levels of the plan.
The sequence of markets on
the upper level is evident.

nay, a crying need—for immediate collaboration. To date, all transportation planning has been under Israeli auspices. It is essential that the Palestinian voice be added to this process, even as light-rail and road systems are moving toward construction. It is also essential that broad decisions on land use and infrastructure planning be developed jointly. It is very likely that, following successful negotiation of a treaty, there will be an investment onslaught on both sides of the city; it would be a tragedy if this occurred before a plan was in place to harness this energy wisely.

Finally, we must consider that, given the historic heritage of the city, a united city of two sovereignties could be the setting for destructive competitive forces. Consider, for example, how nationalistic voices on the Israeli side are currently overwhelming preservationist voices, arguing for the building of a series of high-rise towers within the visual basin of the Old City. Architect Ram Karmi currently proposes a sixty-story tower on King George Street. This ill-considered proposal—which has been rationalized in the most esoteric terms—could, if allowed, easily provoke a counterreaction from the Palestinians, who might want to build higher on their side. One sees how easy it would be to embark on a "war of the towers." I believe that the historic conservation of Jerusalem must, therefore, be placed at the negotiating table as one of the principal points to be agreed upon, an issue of importance not only to the Israeli and Palestinian communities but to the world at large. Given that Jerusalem, apart from its role as the capital of Israel and of the Palestinian state, is also a center for Christianity, Islam, and Judaism worldwide, its historic heritage is a matter for international concern. Though it will be difficult to convince Israelis and Palestinians to forego full authority over planning in the parts they control, they should appreciate the need to consider the international community. A planning-review agency under international auspices might be established, though, unfortunately, such a proposal might provoke instant distrust among Israelis. Any suggestion, for example, that UNESCO might have a role in setting conservation standards is likely to be rejected on the ground that past United Nations interventions have mostly been hostile. This suggests that we need to invent an overseeing authority not based within the UN, one that might be trusted by both parties.

One may hope that a united Jerusalem of shared sovereignty shall go forward, one way or another, as a model of sensitive planning, building upon the great beauty and unique qualities of the Sacred City.

Jerusalem: Toward a City of Equals Capital of Two States

Omar Youssef

Lexicon for a Planned Ethnocracy

Any attempt to write about the future of Jerusalem or to create visions for its development is a difficult process, similar to schizophrenia. It is a journey in a huge void, a void that separates the dream of a balanced city from the reality of Jerusalem's division.

In Jerusalem, the problems of planning are sharpened and complicated artificially by the political situation, by propaganda, and by the claims of the Israeli authorities to sole dominance over both sides of the city (West Jerusalem and East Jerusalem). Masterplans are usually prepared according to the ethnic policy of the Ministry of the Interior. As a result, restrictive regulations hinder the natural flow of life needed for the city's healthy and balanced development. Oren Yiftachel has said: "Israel as a Jewish state has been building an ethnocracy. . . . Here we can observe that the legal and political foundations of the Jewish state have created a distorted structure which ensured a continuing uni-ethic seizure of a bi-ethnic state."

Driven by the Zionist mythology of "a land without people for a people without land," Israeli settlement policy has worked to marginalize the Palestinians, both Christian and Muslim. It has hampered their development by employing sophisticated institutional devices that facilitate the continuing immigration of Jews (and only Jews) to the region. This has been accomplished partly by the transfer of land from Palestinian to Jewish hands. The same macro policy applied to Israel or Palestine is used in the micro arena of Jerusalem; such a policy can easily be detected in East Jerusalem by scanning the socio-urban situation on the ground, where we can read a long story of ethnic bias toward and marginalization of the Palestinian community.

Jerusalem with the monuments of the three major monotheistic religions: Wailing Wall (Jewish), left; Dome of the Rock (Islamic), middle; churches on Mount of Olives (Christian), right.

Omar Youssef

In order to understand the realities of Jerusalem and its developments, let's look at a brief Dictionary of East Jerusalem:

Historic City

Jerusalem is a city that is rooted too deeply in the factual and cultural history of this world. It has survived many reigns and regimes that have left their prints on its walls and its typologies, producing a rich mixture that gives it cultural uniqueness—and fuels its conflicts.

Divided City (1948–1967)

In 1948 Jerusalem was divided into two parts which developed separately and autonomously into two different cites—different, that is, in levels and patterns of development: West Jerusalem and East Jerusalem (see next two terms).

West Jerusalem

The more urbanized and developed western side, with its relatively flatter topography, became West Jerusalem. Urban development in West Jerusalem continued to be influenced by the masterplans of the British Mandate. Mandate plans for the western side were more elaborate because the first Palestinian attempts to expand out of the walls of the Old City headed west. The Western planning and building mentality produced a more dense and ordered urban tissue in this part of Jerusalem.

East Jerusalem

East Jerusalem developed gradually in the hilly and less urbanized eastern part of the city. Following topography and existing patterns of land ownership, villages developed into city neighborhoods around the Old City. This produced a loose network of communities on the surrounding hilly topography.

The Old City

The Old City remained in between, belonging to East Jerusalem but flanked by both sides. Still without a masterplan of its own after thirty-five years of occupation, the Old City is becoming dilapidated. The exceptions are the Jewish quarter, the new settlements in the Muslim and Christian quarters, and some lucky institutions.

RAMALLAH

EAST
JERUSALEM

Armistice Line 1949

WEST JERUSALEM

Municipal Boundary 1993

BETHLEHEM

RAMALLAH

Armistice Line 1949

EAST
JERUSALEM

Municipal Boundary 1993

WEST JERUSALEM

BETHLEHEM

Palestinian Settlements

Jerusalem: Toward a City of Equals

Expropriation and the Settlement Belt

Following "unification" a confiscation and expropriation campaign was launched against Palestinian-owned land, tearing apart the city network of East Jerusalem. One third of East Jerusalem was expropriated and designated for the sole use of Jerusalem's Jewish population. This land was used for building the "dense residential" settlements of Ramat-Eshkol, French Hill, Neve Yacov, Gillo, East Talpiot, Ramot, Reches Shoafat, and (recently) Jabal Abu Gneim (Har-Homa), now in its final stages.

These settlements spread across the Green Line through East Jerusalem, creating a network of Jewish neighborhoods advancing toward the Jordan Valley. These neighborhoods are themselves well-connected urban grids but are isolated from the surrounding Palestinian communities, which are restricted from developing and forced to remain at semi-urban or rural densities.

This fragmented urban grid intersects with the north-south axis of the city of Jerusalem, creating a congestion point in the French Hill area. It also produces fragmented neighborhoods in the city of Jerusalem, diminishing the life and the vitality of East Jerusalem and its social and economical coherence.

Occupation and Unification

As the result of the 1967 war Israel occupied the West Bank and East Jerusalem. Shortly afterward, Israel declared Jerusalem *unified*. International law and the U.N. Security Council do not, however, recognize this act. Shortly after 1967 the Israeli authorities annexed seventy square kilometers of occupied Palestinian land, including East Jerusalem's municipal area of six square kilometers.

Israel, euphoric over *unification*, did not regard East Jerusalem as a neighboring city but as a reconquered landscape with some Palestinian inhabitants that had to be tolerated. According to the ethnic policy of the Israeli authorities, Palestinians must not exceed 25 percent of the population of Jerusalem. Thus the planning vision for East Jerusalem was that it be transformed into a fragmented island isolated by the urban grid of West Jerusalem and by Jewish settlements beyond the Green Line. *Unification* meant turning East Jerusalem into the underdeveloped rural backyard of the *unifier*.

Captive City

Checkpoints and their architecture are encountered daily in the landscape of East Jerusalem.

Exclusion by Selective Municipal Borders

The annexed area forming East Jerusalem was chosen according to expansive military interests, not urban considerations. The municipal borderline cut through the landscape, aiming to include as much land and as few Palestinian inhabitants as possible. In effect, surrounding villages were excluded from connecting with their urban mother, the city of East Jerusalem. This situation was aggravated after imposition of closure and placement of military checkpoints on the eastern municipal border, denying these communities the right of access altogether. This diminished the vitality of East Jerusalem and deprived it of a large part of its essential commercial and social base.

These effects can be clearly detected by studying the agglomerations of commercial and public activities forming around the checkpoints and the municipal borders. The closure pushed the energy from the center to the periphery, where many businesses found it more convenient to move in order to reach customers from both inside and outside of Jerusalem. This phenomena is manifest in areas like Al-Ram (on the northern border), Al-Aizerieh (on the eastern border), and Bethlehem (to the south).

Green Is Dangerous!

In order to limit Palestinians' growth and development and in order to isolate and "protect" Israeli settlements, wide belts of open space and exaggerated "green areas" (i.e., zones in which no building is permitted) have been imposed on East Jerusalem. These zones are colored green on the official maps. Such zones create allergies in Palestinians who want to build a home but find out that most of their hopes have been painted green on the mayor's table.

What's more, when the map shows green around a Palestinian area it means zoned for open space, i.e., no future expansion, while around the Jewish settlements green means unplanned, i.e., available for any future proposals. So, even their green is different from ours.

Experience has shown that the green areas are used as a reserve to serve the expanding interests of West Jerusalem and its Jewish population, while the Palestinian neighborhoods remain congested by restrictive building limits. This situation has encouraged illegal building by Palestinians in spite of the brutal threat of demolition.

All this has affected East Jerusalem and its inhabitants and forced them to shift toward its outer boundaries. Many Jerusalemites who could not find a space in East Jerusalem have had to look for housing outside the municipal line, as in the Al-Ram area and in Al-Aizerieh, in the shadow of Jerusalem.

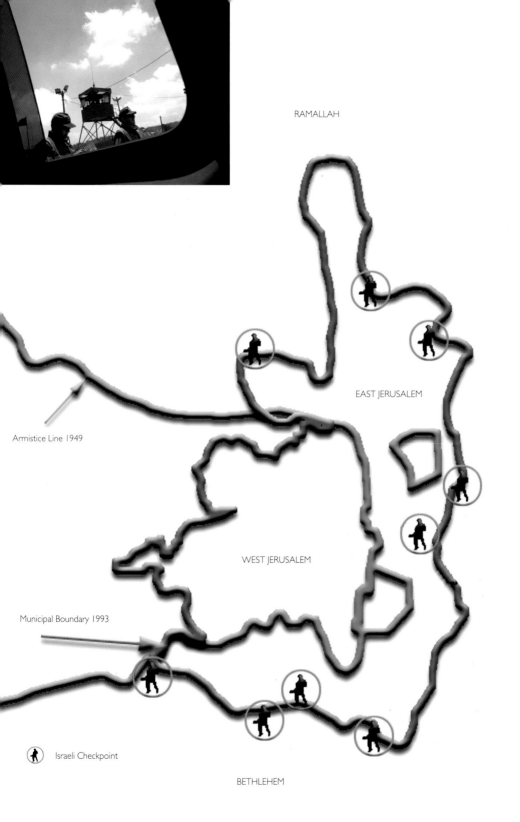

RAMALLAH

EAST JERUSALEM

Armistice Line 1949

WEST JERUSALEM

Municipal Boundary 1993

Israeli Checkpoint

BETHLEHEM

Omar Youssef

The settlement of Maale Adumim sits like a fortification on top of the hill. Shipping containers were given to Bedouin families to compensate them for the lands they had to evacuate for the sake of settlement.

What To Do

Jerusalem cannot be a viable city based on the zero-sum game of the planning regime. There must be a more equitable mix of national interests, and such a mix can only be obtained by empowerment of the national Palestinian community in East Jerusalem.

This mix can be achieved by political negotiations between the two sides on the basis of U.N. Resolutions 242 and 338 (land for peace) and by accepting Palestinian sovereignty in East Jerusalem. Thus we will recognize the realities of two sovereign cities that for a long time have been bypassing each other instead of weaving together. East and West Jerusalem have been two different worlds, the world of the occupier and the world of the occupied.

Emphasis should be given to maximal planning autonomy for Palestine with little intervention from the Israeli side, except on the level of coordination and in those areas where there are shared or conflicting national interests.

It is time to end the occupation and to recognize the Palestinians and their right of sovereignty in East Jerusalem. This will help both Jerusalems begin to interact as equals on the basis of mutual interests, autonomous decisions, and constructive coordination.

This brings us to a Twin City vision in which Jerusalem shall be
- capital of two states, Palestine and Israel;
- two municipalities under a coordinating council;
- equally open to all religions;
- a world center for multicultural activities and a model for conflict resolution;
- open both to the world and to its regional context;
- well connected to Cairo, Amman, Damascus, Beirut, and Tel Aviv.

This Jerusalem will be an open city accessible to all visitors and pilgrims from the Western world as well as the Eastern and Islamic worlds. To realize this vision will require more than just a political agreement; it will require a serious engagement for peace and the goodwill of both peoples.

I propose a Free Zone of Jerusalem County to incorporate both East and West Jerusalem, enjoying special autonomy to manage the life of the Twin City in pursuit of peace and coexistence. This would also save Jerusalem from being a propaganda instrument of any side. You can see both parts as Siamese twins who cannot be divided yet have independent, different minds. Such a Jerusalem would move toward an open city of equals.

Five Packages

Pursuant to this dream, some interventions are necessary. These can be grouped into five packages of projects, all priorities in developing East and West Jerusalem as equal partners.

Package 1. *Access and Upgrade: Healing East Jerusalem*
Socioeconomic and environmental assessment and rehabilitation of the Palestinian neighborhoods in East Jerusalem are necessary to satisfy their needs for growth and development. The following projects should be undertaken:

- encourage Arab businesses and Palestinian-managed institutions to partici-pate in the Jerusalem mosaic.
- develop Palestinian-managed industrial zones.
- raise the density of the existing Palestinian neighborhoods in East Jerusalem while preserving their mixed commercial-residential character.
- upgrade the level of services in East Jerusalem.
- add new levels of urban functions suitable to the status of an open, world city.
- develop public transportation systems connecting East Jerusalem neighbor-hoods to each other and to West Jerusalem.
- locate areas for potential future growth and development.

Package 2. *Heritage: The Old City and Its Basin*
A masterplan for the Old City and its environment should be prepared, with an eye to having it declared a UNESCO (United Nations Educational, Scientific, and Cultural Organization) World Heritage Site and looking for a balance between the needs of such a site and those of a living city.

Special attention should be given to the city's surroundings, especially to the high-rise tower policy adopted recently by the municipality of West Jerusalem. The discourse about this policy must, of course, include the Palestinians.

Package 3. *Sewing the Cities Together*
With its existing rich mixture of touristic, diplomatic, international, institutional, and educational facilities, optimally placed to serve as a connecting bridge between the north-south and east-west axes, the forum in East Jerusalem at Sheikh Jarrah could become the pulsing heart of the city. A more commercial- and services-oriented area in the Wadi Al-Joz "industrial zone" would be an appropriate complement. This arrangement would blend well with the educational and institutional nature of the Mount Scopus area, which contains Hebrew University and Hadassah Hospital.

A peculiar coincidence standing as a metaphor of how culture and heritage values suffer under occupation. This is a mamluk-style madrasa (old Islamic school), transformed to be a border police station.

Package 4. *Coexistence and the French Hill Bottleneck*

Aiming for a coherent, viable city means viewing the most decisive bottle-neck connecting both the Palestinian and Israeli built-up corridors as a useful urban junction for East and West Jerusalem. Binational occupational and resi-dential patterns in the French Hill area are to be encouraged.

This means a pilot project for change-of-use and a new masterplan aimed at developing the residential area of French Hill into a work-plus-living environment. This development should take place with an eye to integration with the East Jerusalem Forum and the campus of Hebrew University.

French Hill's position on the main axes of East Jerusalem and West Jerusalem offers good chances for its success as a multicultural mixing pot. Palestinian students at Hebrew University who are living in the French Hill could be the first grass roots of such a project.

Package 5. *A Bilingual City: Opening the Settlements*

After settling the questionable status of the Jewish settlements in East Jerusalem, the following steps should be taken:

- Settlements should become "normal" neighborhoods open to the housing market for all city residents, Palestinians and Jews, without discrimination.
- Gradual interaction between the settlements and surrounding neigh-borhoods should be encouraged.
- Rigid, repelling "edge zones" are to be softened to create areas of common interest offering common services and commercial, cultural, and youth activities.
- Bilingual schooling should be encouraged, preparing the new genera-tion for a future of peace and coexistence.

Final Thought

An old slogan of the sixties said it well. Let us be realistic—let us look for the impossible.

"Imagine." —John Lennon

Omar Youssef

A Plan for East Jerusalem

Michael Sorkin and Andrei Vovk[1]

1 With Jonathan Solomon, Victoria Marshall, Yukiko Yokoo, and Jacob Kain.

The mark of modern urbanity is heterogeneity: every city is shared. Jerusalem is both the eternal prime example and exceptional case. Perhaps more than any other city, Jerusalem's *genius loci* is founded in geographies of difference: an enormous panoply of religions, sects, ethnicities, classes, nationalities, and lifestyles commingle here, all expressed in complex—and often conflicting—sets of spatial and social practices.

This proposal makes no attempt to alter or redeploy Jerusalem's incredible assortment of styles of inhabiting space; it is devoted to more general urban values and distinctions. Jerusalem is rapidly moving toward becoming the capital city of two states: Israel and Palestine. Whatever else may be true of these two nations and their labyrinthine histories of development and conflict, their capitals will find a measure of their expression in the "normal" infrastructure of any capital city—ministries and embassies, bureaucracies and businesses, symbolic and honorific sites, a city hall and a parliament—all the installations that make a capital city functional.

Both Palestine and Israel embody ancient cultures in new states. Israel, of course, has had a fifty-year head start in "nation-building." Israeli Jerusalem is already replete with impressive government buildings, its Knesset, its national museum, concert halls, convention hotels, a football stadium, various monuments to the triumphs and tragedies of the Israeli and Jewish people—with all the deepening patina of permanence that the accumulation of such institutions implies. As peace negotiations progress, finding appropriate spatial vessels to contain Palestine's national ambitions, too, must begin. Inescapably, this infrastructure will coexist with its Israeli equivalent, and this doubleness will itself become a distinctive element of the city's character.

Palestine—though rich in historic architectures and spaces—is poor in the institutional architectures and urban structures of nationhood. There is no parliament building, ministries are housed in improvised quarters in several cities, and face-to-face encounter—so critical to democratic governance—is made difficult both by the daily difficulties of occupation and by the lack of suitable physical facilities and circumstances. Forced for years to be subsidiary to Israeli convenience, Palestinian Jerusalem—Al-Quds—lacks a logical physical armature by which to distribute the means and symbols of its own autonomy.

This plan is a schematic proposal for putting into place the first elements of such an armature. It is based on limited physical investigations of the city and on research in printed materials. Such conventional analysis—however meticulous—can only go

The renaturalized Kidron Valley provides a seam to join the city.

so far. As architects and urbanists, we pride ourselves on the capacity to read cities phenomenologically, to get the sniff of their formal desires. We are not prejudiced against the kinds of demographic, economic, and statistical analyses that propel orthodox planning methodologies; rather, we feel that after all the polling, inventory-ing, focus-grouping, and programming are done, there remains a space of indecision that can only be filled by artistic conviction, by the act of architecture.

Cities are synergistic organisms, complex and interactive; changes anywhere in the city have an effect everywhere, an urban chaos-effect. Whatever the particulars of sovereignty at the political level, Jerusalem is about to rethink its style of division, and the physical city must inflect itself in the direction of this difference. New centers of attention will re-weight the city and reinvent its connections. Politics may pre-scribe a simply twinned city, a city with a double center, but the facts on the ground will be far more complex—though perhaps, at the same time, more tractable con-ceptually.

Jerusalem has—and will always have—its physical and symbolic center in the Old City. Other sites can only be subsidiary, both imaginatively and morphologically. The Old City's aura is a key to the deployment of both the Palestinian and Israeli ideas of nationality and it is also a key to the arrangement of the city's other centers and places, all of which, in one way or another, orbit around and reflect it. This aura is transmitted by visual and physical access, by the influence of the Old City's materi-ality and forms on its surroundings, and by the practices necessary to maintain the Old City in its condition of relative autonomy. These adjustments are delicate and must be continuously recalibrated. Nevertheless, it is clear that the preservation of the Old City—whether from internal alteration or from disappearance in a sea of sprawl—is the leading item on the formal agenda.

Al-Quds will, for reasons both symbolic and practical, occupy the eastern por-tion of the city; the elements of its formal infrastructure will be sited there. East Jerusalem has a preexisting double center. The central business district (CBD), adja-cent to the Old City, has excellent scale and offers a substantial spatial reserve for further development. The adjoining Old City is Al-Quds' symbolic generator for growth and heritage; a gigantic financial machine; the most important component of its economy; a metonym for Jerusalem.

Although development of the East Jerusalem CBD is very much a phenomenon of the nineteenth and twentieth centuries, the district shares much of the architec-tural and urban character of the Old City, a character that forms a logical basis for growth. Both have complex circulation and subtle but rich geometry. Both give pri-macy to pedestrian movement in the movement hierarchy. Both are very mixed in use, not only site-wide but within individual structures. Both employ a low-rise, stone-clad architectural vernacular. Both are strongly inflected by the city's hilly topography. And both control the sun through narrow streets, small openings, abundant recesses, covered streets and spaces, and a favored interiority of courts and other enclosed volumes.

Because of a complex interaction of political, natural, demographic, and economic factors, contemporary East Jerusalem's logical axes of potential growth extend to the east and north of the existing CBD. In this proposal, Wadi el Joz and its extension into Sheikh Jarrah are seen as the critical sites for urban elaboration, tremendously favorable locations in terms of access, character, and development potential. An added advantage is their current under-utilization, which will allow development to proceed with minimum displacement of existing residences. It is here that we propose that the primary administrative district for the new capital be located.

The form and extent of the district derive from several primary qualities of the site. As a general project for the vitalization of East Jerusalem, the revival and renaturalization of the Kidron River valley is indispensable. Forming a continuous swath of green space, circulation, and visual relief from surrounding densities, this valley has the potential to become, in effect, the Central Park of East Jerusalem, a space defining extraordinary value at its edges by offering superb views and access. Moreover, this green seam flowing through the larger city can provide a space and poetry of healing: instead of the Green Line—a signifier of division—this newly revived linear space might function as a suture stitching the physical city together, a common space and shared amenity.

Symbolic prominence, preservation of views, respect for existing patterns, and considerations of convenience have led us to suggest a crescent of official construction on the south side of Wadi el Joz. Behind this collection of buildings we propose a major park and civic space to serve both as a focus for public gatherings and as a space of mediation between official uses to the south and a smaller-scaled, private texture to the north, where we suggest that the pattern revert to the more intimate and familiar texture of adjoining areas: small-scale construction, mixed (including residential) use, and a labyrinthine, aggregated character. Wadi el Joz is also commended by its gentle, enclosed feel. Instead of the hilltop machismo that has characterized so much Israeli planning for the city, this new development would be more at one with the land, less domineering.

The location of the parliament, the most important civil symbol of nationhood, might also be here. A more interesting and dramatic choice, however, would be the site of the Augusta Victoria hospital or the eastern hillside just beyond it. Overlooking incomparable views of the desert's sweep, saturated by sunrise, this is a place of amazing gravity and beauty, suited to the ceremonial weight of the key institution of autonomy and self-government. To reinforce the logic of this location while tying the major components of East Jerusalem together (Old City, CBD, new administrative district, park, and parliament) and promoting connections between

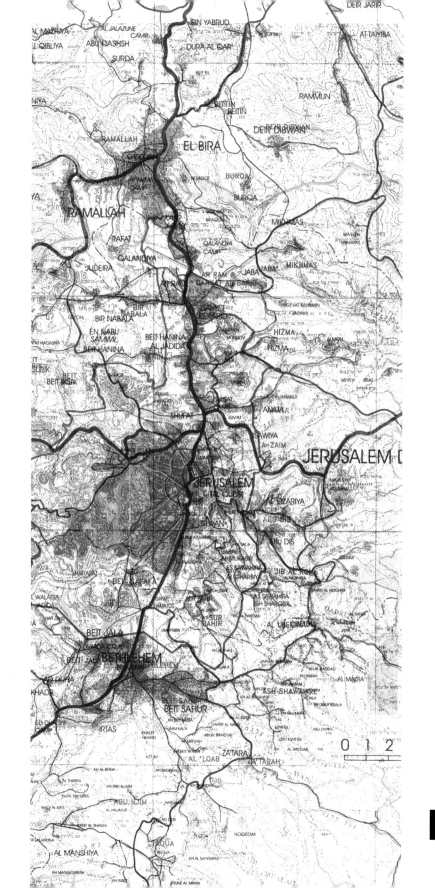

0 1 2

East and West Jerusalem, we also propose to upgrade the existing Sultan Suleiman/Derekh E-Tur/Sheikh Anbar axis to the quality of a grand boulevard, the Champs-Elysées of Palestine.

As suggested in the introduction to this book, the future of Jerusalem is linked to the development of a set of knowledge-based activities. These include the burgeoning high-tech developments in West Jerusalem but also (and most critically) the panoply of educational facilities in and around the city. These include not only the countless religious schools and institutions that contribute so much to the city's singular character but also a network of colleges and universities, including Hebrew University, Bezalel Academy, Bir Zeit University in Ramallah, and Al-Quds University. Hebrew University is a great intellectual ornament to Israeli Jerusalem (if less of an architectural one) and, given the prominence of its site, its activities, and its population, one of the physical centers of the city's life.

It seems appropriate that Palestinian Jerusalem develop a comparable center of higher education as a symbol of national pride, as an economic driver, and as a site of cooperation between the two nations sharing the city. Relocation of the existing Al-Quds University could form the logical nucleus for this endeavor, and several locations suggest themselves as possibilities for a new campus. One of these is Abu Dis, on the eastern edge of the city, where both space and infrastructure are available. A more interesting site, however, is the area of Sheikh Jarrah. This location is more central, would enjoy continuity with the proposed administrative district in Wadi el Joz, and would allow for synergistic interaction with Hebrew University on Mount Scopus.

A look at the larger picture of East Jerusalem reveals a crescent structure of neighborhoods girdling the Old City. The development of these neighborhoods from an original village structure suggests a larger concept of growth. The first component of this strategy is to strengthen the autonomous character of each neighborhood both by reinforcing boundaries and by adding additional infrastructure to focus and link them. This plan suggests a chain of neighborhood parks to reinforce the sense of locality and pride. These green spaces might function as attractors for civic development, and as locations for new mosques, schools, clinics, and so on.

We have also suggested additional circulation infrastructure to link these neighborhoods to each other and to urban centers at the next scale up. Perhaps most important of these circulatory structures is a sinewy north-south boulevard that would demarcate the long, green Kidron River valley and limit westward growth of adjacent neighborhoods. Sites along this boulevard would command some of the most charismatic views on the planet: sunsets over the Old City and the glowing Dome of the Rock. It is perhaps not inappropriate to observe that this boulevard would invent some of the most valuable building sites in Palestine—a potential magnet for investment.

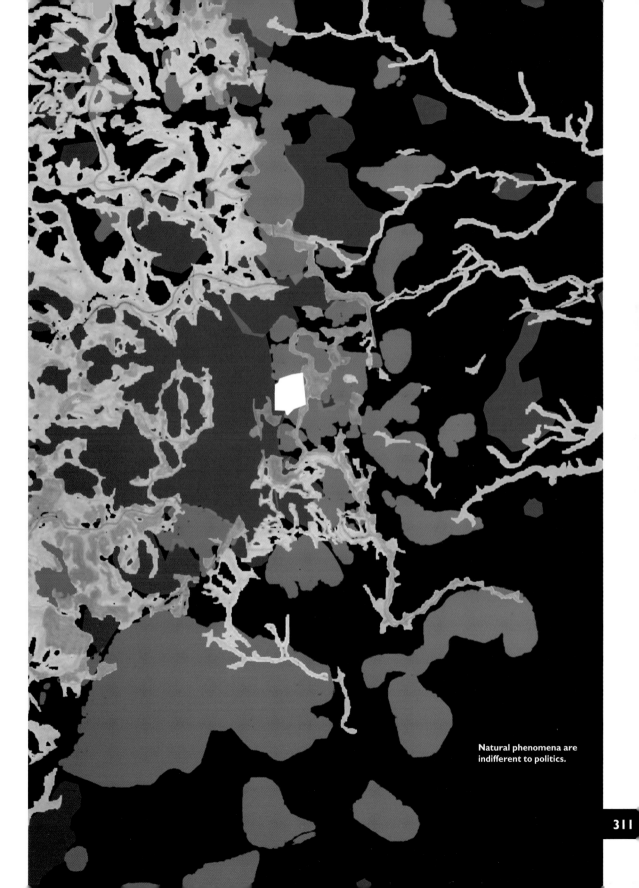

Natural phenomena are
indifferent to politics.

Although one might think of the character of Jerusalem as artificial, the site of infinite manipulation, the city's topography, climate, and vegetation predicate its destiny. Essential to the urbanization of Jerusalem and its region is the ridge of hills that runs north-south through the city, creating a linear conurbation that stretches from Ramallah to Bethlehem and extends (less densely) to Nablus and Hebron. This continuous urban fabric—a classic linear city—is a source both of character and of difficulties for the urban system.

On the plus side of this arrangement is the stunning environmental singularity of the long border between the Mediterranean ecology that sweeps in from the sea, and the desert, which begins precipitously at the ridge line. This ecological double-ness forms a visual and conceptual armature for future growth. Also, the linearity of the system is most accommodating to efficient movement. It seems self-evident that existing roadways should be augmented by a regional rail system that might extend as far as Nazareth in the north and Hebron in the south.

The danger is sprawl. The growth of a continuous urban fabric risks functional and environmental inefficiencies, the degradation of a fragile landscape, and the submergence of the identities of individual towns and villages in a single urban entity. Jerusalem has suffered two types of sprawl, and future growth must adjust to both. The first is the familiar pattern of contiguous growth of the urban periphery due to population, economic, and life-style pressures. This is visible in the steady march of new construction to the west, threatening an uninterrupted conurbation to the sea, and in the unplanned growth of Ramallah to the north, among other Palestinian localities in the Al-Quds ambit.

The second form of sprawl—one unique to Palestine—is colonial sprawl, the new Israeli developments on occupied territory. A kind of sinister suburbanism, these fortress-like "gated communities" reproduce the worst aspects of American urban growth, raised to the flashpoint. Though different in origin, both forms are destructive of the urban fabric, extending its reach beyond any morphological logic, taxing its environment, distorting its systems of movement, and creating a poisonous social environment. This project treats both forms of sprawl impartially, for despite their different origins and the different arguments advanced for their necessity, both must be restrained by rational limits to the city's growth.

Our proposal is quite simple and is based on the fact that the area of Jerusalem's urbanization is already vast, especially when compared to cities and towns in the north-south corridor. For reasons of both ecology and character, we suggest that additional development in Jerusalem take the form of increased density within existing areas of settlement rather than of aggrandizement of additional territory. Only by adhering to such limits can this city, so dear to so many, hope to preserve the character that distinguishes it from every other city in the world.

An urban growth boundary both protects open space and the environment and suggests development, density, and refinement.

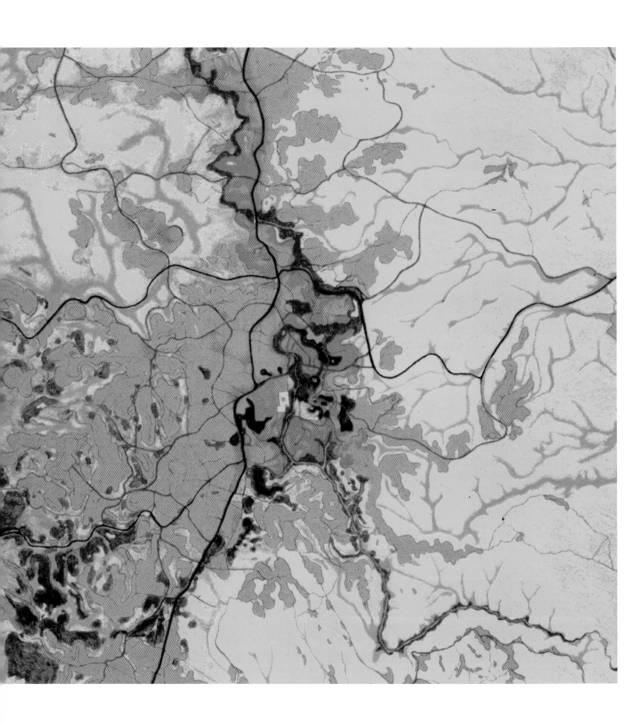

A Plan for East Jerusalem

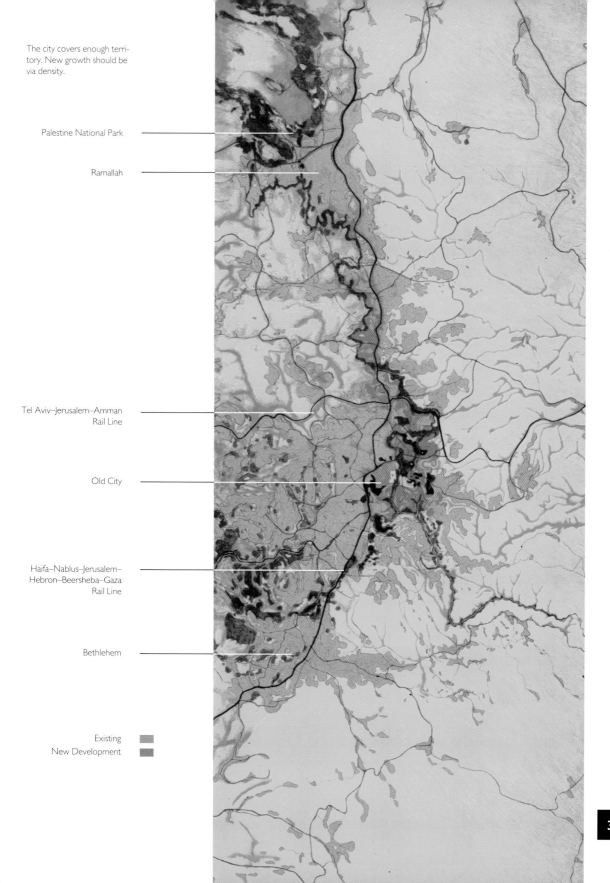

The city covers enough territory. New growth should be via density.

Palestine National Park

Ramallah

Tel Aviv–Jerusalem–Amman
Rail Line

Old City

Haifa–Nablus–Jerusalem–
Hebron–Beersheba–Gaza
Rail Line

Bethlehem

Existing
New Development

315

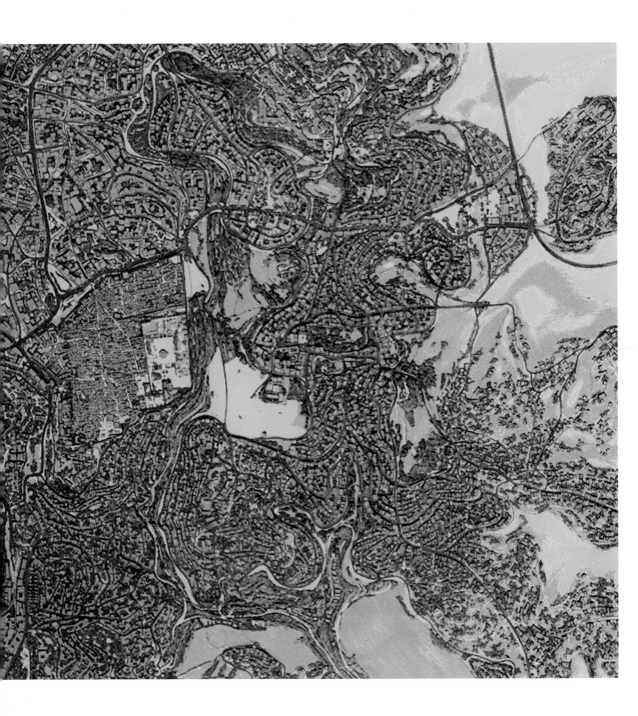

A Plan for East Jerusalem

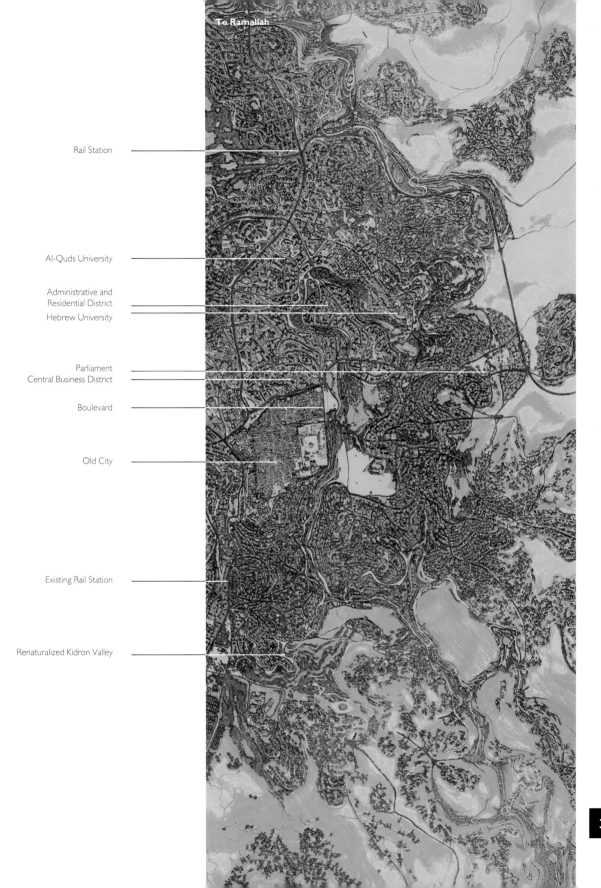

To Ramallah

Rail Station

Al-Quds University

Administrative and
Residential District

Hebrew University

Parliament
Central Business District

Boulevard

Old City

Existing Rail Station

Renaturalized Kidron Valley

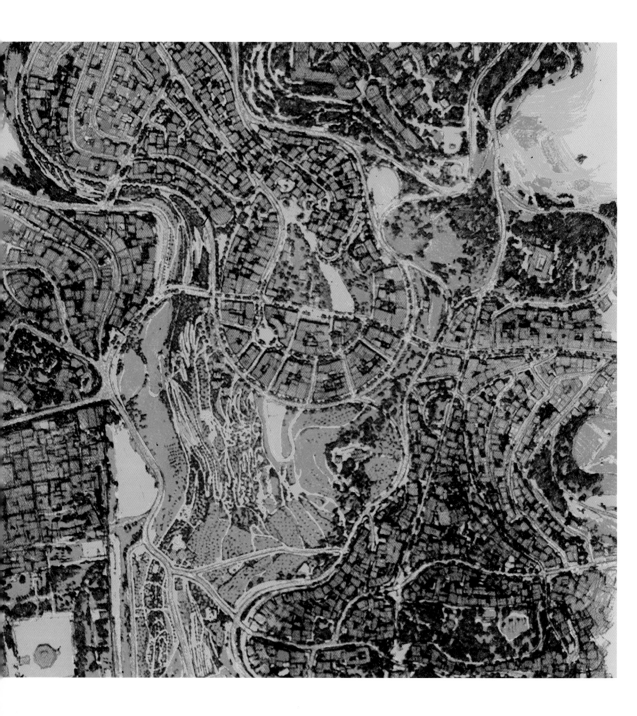

A Plan for East Jerusalem

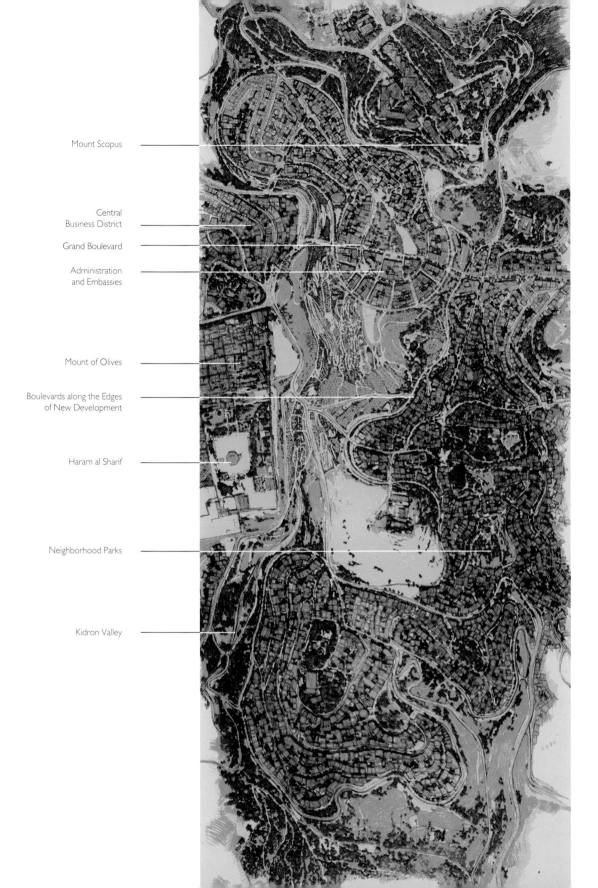

Mount Scopus

Central
Business District

Grand Boulevard

Administration
and Embassies

Mount of Olives

Boulevards along the Edges
of New Development

Haram al Sharif

Neighborhood Parks

Kidron Valley

The Spectre of Jerusalem

Ariella Azoulay

A few days after the signing of the Oslo Accords in Washington, D.C., secret talks began between the Israelis and the Palestinians on the future of Jerusalem. On behalf of Israel the talks were conducted by Deputy Foreign Minister Yossi Beilin and on behalf of the Palestinians by Abu Mazen. The deliberations continued for a relatively long time, a year and a half, ending on November 1, 1995. They took place unbeknown to either Prime Minister Yitzhak Rabin or Foreign Minister Shimon Peres.

On November 4, 1995, three days after the conclusion of these talks, Yitzhak Rabin was shot dead in Tel Aviv's municipal square. A few days after the assassination, a draft of the agreement—the Beilin–Abu Mazen Accord—was presented to the new prime minister, Shimon Peres. Peres rejected the agreement, contending that the time was not right to deal with it.

Some would say that Peres was afraid of losing the forthcoming elections if the agreement were to become public. He preferred to suppress the topic of Jerusalem, just as he chose to leave Rabin's assassination out of his party's election campaign. In contrast, Likud leader Benjamin Netanyahu wanted to bring these matters to the surface. He conducted an aggressive election campaign under the slogan "Peres will divide Jerusalem." Underlying this slogan is the assumption that Jerusalem is united, and that if and when the city should be divided this would be due to the deliberate action of a leader such as Peres, willfully disrupting both the city's unity and a people united in solidarity around the idea of the city's unity. One should remember that the "unified city" of Jerusalem is composed of: Jerusalem the sacred and Jerusalem the profane, heavenly Jerusalem and worldly Jerusalem, the Jerusalem of maps and the Jerusalem of neighborhoods, the Old City of Jerusalem and Jerusalem that has burst its own boundaries in a construction boom, Jerusalem without running water or sanitation and Jerusalem of exclusive housing compounds, Jerusalem of refugee camps and Jerusalem of expropriated lands, Jerusalem of fantasy and Jerusalem of harsh and sometimes bloody reality,

Jerusalem of the secular and Jerusalem of the ultra-Orthodox, Jerusalem of the Jewish settlers and Jerusalem of the Palestinians, Jerusalem of history and Jerusalem of the future, Jerusalem of the '48 settlers and Jerusalem of the '67 settlers, Jerusalem of its citizens and Jerusalem of its inhabitants whose right to live in the city is being denied them. On election day in May 1996, Netanyahu's proved to be the winning campaign; Netanyahu was voted into power, while Peres and his party joined the parliamentary opposition.

During his campaign, Peres suppressed the issue of Jerusalem. He acknowledged that the reality of the city exceeds the unifying signifier *Jerusalem* and was afraid that any discussion of the topic would make it evident that Peres himself recognizes this excessiveness, and for him these conflicts that pervade Jerusalem constitute a point of departure for negotiations and cannot be seen as the basis for a unifying image of the city. Peres knew what everyone knows: Jerusalem is not one. It is not homogeneous and exists in the conflict-ridden present rather than in the eternal history of the Jewish nation. Netanyahu, on the other hand, who conducted a campaign of "virtual reality," was unafraid of this excessiveness or its ability to influence the signifier *Jerusalem*, so he invoked the signifier freely during the course of his campaign.

Both Peres and Netanyahu understood the power of the signifier Jerusalem. The former wanted to get rid of it and deny its existence. The latter, perhaps to some extent because of the other's behavior, wanted to call attention to it.

Following Netanyahu's 1996 ascent to power, the existence of the Beilin-Abu-Mazen Accord became public knowledge. It was written up in the press and its principles were presented at various forums, although the agreement itself—the actual document—was never made public. The agreement remained an unknown, a secret, something that people could talk about but not see. For the document contains a terrible secret. It doesn't divide Jerusalem but accords recognized symbolic status to whoever rules whichever part of the city. In other words, the Beilin–Abu Mazen Accord exposes the most terrible secret of all: that Jerusalem can't be divided because it isn't united in the first place. (I will return below to the contents of the accord.) In May 1999, Netanyahu once again focused his election campaign on Jerusalem. This time the signifier *Jerusalem* aroused no echo; Ehud Barak, leader of the labor party, won the election.

Talmon
Efrat Shvily

During the 1999 election campaign Ehud Barak made use of televised footage in which Ehud Olmert—rightist, Likud member, and mayor of Jerusalem—declared his confidence that neither Barak nor any other leader would divide Jerusalem. On another occasion Olmert even apologized to Shimon Peres and retracted his statement (made during the 1996 elections) that Peres would divide Jerusalem. Should we conclude that Olmert handed power to Barak on a silver platter? Did his assurance that Jerusalem would not be divided decide the elections? Did Olmert's remarks carry more weight with the public than Netanyahu's, who declared that Jerusalem would be divided under Barak's rule? Could it be that although Barak won the election, the voice for which people really voted was Olmert's? All these questions can be subsumed under a single, larger one: what is the connection between the city of Jerusalem, which adorns the State of Israel like a crown, and the leader who serves as the country's head of government?

On the day Yigal Amir assassinated the prime minister, this connection was impalpable or at least didn't appear significant. The false background against which the assassination was frequently understood was the struggle between the Right and the Left, between the religious and secular segments of the population, which was portrayed by almost everyone as a struggle between the forces of light and the forces of darkness—one way or the other. In this essay, I would particularly like to emphasize the connection between the city of Jerusalem and the assassination of the head of state.

On the evening of November 4, 1995, a young man arrived in Tel Aviv's municipal square with a gun in his pocket. He took off his skullcap, thus concealing his religious identity, and awaited Yitzhak Rabin's departure at the conclusion of the peace rally which was taking place in the square at the time. In a confession delivered the day after the assassination, Amir described Peres as the man who had led Rabin astray, that is, as the one truly responsible for the deteriorating situation. Yet, he emphasized, he preferred to wait for Rabin. Peres had given to Rabin his power of peace-making speech, but Amir preferred to ignore the "owner" of the ideas and wait for the "owner" of the voice, for the authority, for the one whose speech assumes symbolic status when it leaves his throat: the prime minister himself. Amir's choice of Rabin over Peres thus expressed a romantic rejection of the verbal, a preference for the ceremonial, for the owner of the authentic voice—even as literal target—over the contents of speech. Expressly because Rabin had undergone a transformation (from deliverer of Jerusalem in 1967 to the one chosen by Peres to give up Jerusalem in the 1990s), Amir saw him as the more dangerous, the one who could muster the people behind him. From Amir's viewpoint, to put it crudely, Peres wasn't worth the bullet. Amir ascribed symbolic value to his own action by setting it in a scene he conceived of as lying beneath the gaze of divine providence, a scene in

Ashdod
Efrat Shvily

Jerusalem
Efrat Shvily

The Spectre of Jerusalem

which he came to the rescue of the people of Israel, who had lost sight of where their leader was taking them. Amir planted himself opposite Yitzhak Rabin on the stage of history: true prophet versus false prophet.

The Oslo Accords (signed August 20, 1993) marked a turning point in Israeli politics. The old regime of representation was challenged by a new one. In the framework of the old regime, exchange relations were regularized according to transcendent and religious values which themselves are exempt from exchange; in the framework of the new, each value can in principle be exchanged or substituted. These two regimes of representation express themselves in two regimes of subjectivity. In the first, the subject is constituted in relation to an inner secret, a nucleus of truth hidden inside him, which shapes all his actions and speech and which all his actions and speech express. In the second, the subject is constituted as a result of the mimetic relations between himself and his surroundings. In the single figure of Rabin both these contradictory forms of subjectivity were contained; Rabin symbolized, in the flesh, the possibility of a reconciliation between these two elements. Rabin—from whose throat had issued a voice of transcendent truth, the historic truth of the Jewish people—had become someone who borrowed his voice from other mortals. Amir wanted to save Israel from Rabin, Rabin from Peres, and Rabin from himself—all on behalf of the people of Israel.

Amir was thus concerned for the fate of the Land of Israel, but he was no less concerned about the danger posed by the mimetic subject. The subject that imitates others, the subject that has no inner truth, that does not truly belong to history, community, nation, tradition, or religion; the subject that imitates an Other, follows it, is seduced by its suggestions; the subject that has no boundaries and reflects everything it encounters. Amir wanted to extirpate this subject and did so, paradoxically, while manifesting that he was just such a subject. For, as already mentioned, an hour before assassinating Rabin, Amir took the skullcap off his head. That is, he got rid of the symbol differentiating him from the secular population and identifying him as the Other. The removal of the skullcap can be interpreted a simple camouflage action, but it is difficult not to regard it as expressing a desire to be assimilated, to resemble the others to enter into mimetic relations with the Other. After Amir removed his skullcap he gripped the gun in his pocket and waited in a military-style ambush for his target. Like a devoted soldier in the Israeli army, he stood on guard and rose to defend his nation. He had done so previously as a soldier fighting against the Arab enemy, and now he did so as a soldier fighting against the Jewish enemy.

When the secret of the Oslo talks was disclosed, a political and psychological barrier that had constrained Israeli politics since the 1967 war was broken and a radical change ensued in the structure of the political discourse. Since the mid-1970s, the Israeli Left had developed the practice of simulating peace talks with the Palestinian leadership. Alongside the talks of this nature conducted by the Left, which was then in the opposition, secret talks were also apparently conducted by Mossad agents and other official representatives; there were certainly rumors to that effect. In other words, the opposition openly simulated negotiations while the authorities secretly simulated negotiations (apparently). In the beginning, the secret Oslo talks were a combination of these two practices: the group dynamics of the Left's open simulation, and the secrecy of the government's simulation prior to Oslo. These earlier talks were never the real thing, nor were they a substitute for it. They were just a presentation of what could or should be. In Oslo the simulation became the substitute, and then it became the real thing. It was only when the Israeli government publicly acknowledged the talks that the change occurred—that the talks, which had been a simulation of negotiations, turned into real negotiations.

What is the mark of "real" negotiations? Like anything real, they have a visible part and an invisible part, neither of which can be entirely canceled out, whereas a simulation, being two-dimensional and lacking depth, is either entirely open or entirely secret, and it dissipates when the other side of the show—open or secret, it makes no difference—is exposed. The secret talks conducted by the government, if such there were, dissipated the moment rumor of them leaked out, for the State was strictly prohibited from talking with the P.L.O. The open talks conducted by the Left dissipated the moment it appeared that an official element was involved in them behind the scenes, for the Left couldn't possibly represent the State.

The greatest transformation wrought by the Oslo Accords since they became public has, as already mentioned above, been primarily—both in principle and from a chronological viewpoint—a change in the regime of representation dominating the political discourse in Israel, first of all with respect to the main ideal that has informed Israeli political rhetoric, namely, "peace." For decades peace had been whispered and shouted by people as a signifier for which the proper referent would be supplied by everyone when the time came. Everyone knew, too, that simply saying *peace* didn't make peace happen. But now that the infinite distance was suddenly slashed, peace seemed within reach, just behind the door: palpable and threatening to those who had always known that peace could be real only if it was false, palpable and inviting to those who had always believed in the possibility of its realization or had come to believe in it now. The relation between signifier and referent became mysterious, and on both sides an urgent need to ascertain its character emerged. Everyone belabored the signifier to disclose its true, hidden referent. The signifier turned into a punching bag that everyone struck, but in vain, for it remained a ball of rags, hot air, a piece of paper, which could not divulge the true referent. This all happened, so it seems, because of the nature of the interim agreement.

Maale Adumim
Efrat Shvily

Jerusalem
Efrat Shvily

The Spectre of Jerusalem

In Oslo a transition was proclaimed from occupation as a de facto *permanent* situation to occupation as a de facto *temporary* situation, as well as an intent to transition from de jure occupation to de facto Palestinian independence and perhaps (the optimists hoped) even de jure independence. It was a transition to transitional conditions. From the moment the Oslo talks came out of the closet, "the peace process" became a simulation of the end of the occupation and of the continuing occupation as well. For you'll never be able to know that the occupation has ended; the state of transition is a state of occupation as much as a state of occupation coming to its end. Israel has to look like a conqueror, though it is no longer (at least not in Zone A under the rule of the Palestinian Authority) a conqueror in effect, but a peace agreement has not yet been negotiated. The Palestinians have to look like freedom fighters in the locations with respect to the issues that have yet to be agreed upon, because the state of occupation continues. The Orient House, for example, is a symbol of the Palestinians' continuing struggle over Jerusalem. But for a long time the Palestinians abandoned the entire eastern part of the city to Israeli encroachment at the price of simulating sovereignty over a single building. Har Homah (a new settlement in the suburbs of Jerusalem), to take another example, is a symbol of the Israeli government's determination to retain control of greater Jerusalem and prevent its division, but for a long time now all construction activity at the site has been frozen. The external signs of the end of the occupation, "the tokens of Palestinian sovereignty," are the only evidence that the occupation is about to end or that peace is about to arrive. The simulation of the peace process and of the end of the occupation continues under the new regime, and it will continue even if Palestinian independence is eventually declared. The declaration itself (which will eventually take place one day) has a clear simulative character. The discourse, which explicitly recognizes the declaration of independence as a simulation of independence and talk about the anticipated declaration as a simulation of the declaration, actually constitutes Israeli-Palestinian recognition of the independence of the simulation. The Israelis have actually extended such recognition for some time, after having summarily dismissed the Palestinian people for years and raised them from the dust by virtue of this dismissal itself. Now they are summarily uniting Jerusalem and actually dividing it by virtue of these very declarations, which testify time and again that they're the main adhesive holding the "reunited" city together.

Israeli recognition of the simulation and its independence begins in Jerusalem, which has become the distinct site of the simulation, its locus. Since the Israeli conquest in 1967, Israel's takeover of Jerusalem has come to resemble the stance of a Narcissus at the edge of a swamp, generating itself with an excessive regard for its own reflection in the water. Every time a reflection other than what Narcissus wants to see has appeared, he has employed one of the three mechanisms at his disposal for turning it into the desired reflection:

1 Cartography

The Israeli sovereign draws the city maps, and so uses cartography as a means of maintaining its demographic "balance." The annexation of East Jerusalem and its sur-roundings incorporated as much land as possible for future Jewish development and as few Arab suburbs as possible. Later changes in the rather flexible municipal boundaries served to bring more Jewish neighborhoods into the city. Today there are 411,000 Jews and 166,000 Palestinians living within the jurisdiction of the city of Jerusalem. But a different map, which would have taken into account the dynamics of Palestinian life in and around the city and geographical reality in the Palestinian sec-tions of the city, would yield a very different demographic ratio.

2 The Legal Apparatus

The conditional residency granted to Palestinians enables the Israeli authorities to control the demographic composition of the city on an almost daily basis.

3 Planning and Housing

The ratio of new housing for Palestinians to new housing for Israelis is 1:8. Palestinians are denied permission to build much more often than are Israelis. Between 1967 and 1995, 64,000 apartments were built in Jewish neighborhoods (half of them on confiscated land that had mostly belonged to the Jordanian govern-ment) and only 8,000 for Palestinians.

The Israeli occupation and administration of the city are based on ambivalence with respect to both representations (maps, statistical tables) and the represented objects (urban space, population). On the one hand, the occupation regime uses tidy, objec-tive language, a scientific language that distinguishes between representations and their objects. On the other hand, the same regime plays a very active role in manu-facturing both the represented objects and their representations, as if there's no distinction between them. When data gathered "in the field" fail to reflect the desired map of Jerusalem, the map is changed; when a reading of the map reeks a bit too much of apartheid, the data are altered. In this way even Jerusalem, the most metaphysical of cities, also participates in the loss of the sovereign distinction between the original and the simulacrum, territory and map, the thing in itself as opposed to its representation.

In any event, this state of affairs has not resulted from the fragmentation of the field of vision and action, nor from the decentralization of the forces active in Jerusalem. On the contrary, it has come about due to Israeli over-control of these fields of vision and action. What seems at first sight to be a Postmodernist practice of representation—a free and open market of identities, territories, maps, and narratives, a wild fairground of simulations—at second glance turns out to be the outcome of the manipulation of data, maps, and territory, of control over various markets, of a massive intervention in exchange relations. Israel manages the actual city to conform to the desired map of the city, and draws up maps to reflect the desired city. The adaptation of the city to the map and of the map to the city has distorted matters to such an extent that 70,000 out of 170,000 identity card–bearing Palestinian inhabitants of Jerusalem have been forced to live outside the city over the years since 1967. Most of these persons (over 70 percent) reside in suburbs near the city. These Palestinians are in the process of losing their resident cards, which means they can't live in the city where they were born.

It is a two-faced practice. On one hand, Jerusalem can be acted upon; it can be fortified, built, expanded, or contracted, all in the framework of an economy of demographic and political interests. On the other hand, Jerusalem can be preserved outside any economy, and its transcendental standing preserved. But due to the need to manufacture more and more Jerusalem in order to maintain the demographic balance, the city's transcendental status has been pressed into service as a resource that can be used to baptize more areas in the name of Jerusalem. Immediately after the conquest of Jerusalem in 1967, Israel turned the city's transcendental status into a resource and the city itself into the land that supplies this resource and testifies to its existence. Israel alone exercised control over the allocation of this resource and its distribution over adjacent areas—that is, the determination of the city's actual boundaries—and, in consequence, over the right of its residents to become its inhabitants.

Over several decades Israel portrayed the Palestinians as a group entity with which one could not enter into negotiations, and Jerusalem as a city over which there could be no negotiations. Once the barrier against direct negotiations with the Palestinians broke down, it was clear that in one way or another Jerusalem, too, would become part of the negotiations. In the Oslo Accords it was agreed that Jerusalem would come up for discussion in the framework of the permanent status talks. Thus both the Israelis and the Palestinians could be proud of their achievement—the Israelis for signing an agreement without agreeing to the division of Jerusalem, the Palestinians for having established Jerusalem as a subject to be negotiated. Actually, in order to sign the Oslo Accords the Israelis had to share the secrets of the simulation—in other words, control of the simulations administration—with the Palestinians. As long as the simulation was managed by Israel alone, Jerusalem's transcendental status was ensured. When the barriers came down and the Palestinians became partners to negotiations, Jerusalem lost its unequivocal status and became a polysemic sign at the center of a plethora of conflicting interpretations. Since the Oslo Accords, the simulation has become the constitutive rule of political reality. The simulation hasn't canceled out the meanings but multiplied them in conflicting directions. Double meanings multiply and propagate at an amazing rate, and no suspicion of pretense can any longer be proved. The "real intentions" of any party cannot be exposed, and not just because intentions are revealed through additional signs such as gestures, sayings, and actions, but because the "state of transition" itself endows any such signs with a double meaning. And the more simulations accumulate and the more possibilities of interpretation multiply, the greater becomes the desire for clarity. Highly motivated individuals, those with a strong messianic bent, can't tolerate the simulative character of the historic situation. Yigal Amir expressed the reaction of one who pines for an unequivocal, true, and final interpretation of political reality. He assumed that he was in possession of such an interpretation and was convinced that it was exactly opposed to the illusion in which everyone else was caught up. The assassination in Tel Aviv's municipal square on the evening of November 4, 1995, took place in the glare of the spotlights; it expressed an intent to bring out into the light this sole interpretation and impose it on an immeasurably more ambivalent reality. Yitzhak Rabin's assassination was thus an ultimate attempt to burst through the tissue of simulations in order to allow reality, the "naked truth," to appear.

With three shots of his gun, Yigal Amir demanded that the simulations be abandoned once and for all; he demanded a release from the immanent simulative quality imposed by the conditions of historical reality and a return to unequivocal distinction between war and peace, liberation and subjugation, the real and the virtual, the true and the false. Yigal Amir's action in the municipal square expressed a desire for a return to the real, and his action, like other violent actions that demand the appearance of the real, ignored the power of the dialectical relations between police and terrorism, unemployment and production, an event and its media images. He, and others like him, also failed to see these three levels as global, viral networks, which repeatedly eradicate any boundary that local elements may try to erect between nations, national territories, or social spheres, and which impose simulation as the only regime of representation. When simulation is the regime of representation, one can act upon reality only by means of simulation. Any attempt to impose upon reality a violent event—an act that will tear away once and for all the layers of images piled one on top of another—is met immediately by a response on the part of the various networks, which try to restore the simulative dimension of the event and endow it with conflicting meanings, all of which are consistent with the existing order and none of which is capable of really undermining the prevalent conditions: hybrid areas, transitional periods, a blurring of unequivocal distinctions. Any attempt to impose

Jerusalem
Efrat Shvily

Jerusalem
Efrat Shvily

The Spectre of Jerusalem

upon reality a symbolic representation that has an unequivocal interpretation, which can once and for all separate the real from the virtual, encounters such a response, and instead of exposing the truth about the reality subject to interpretation, the attempt conceals the simulative conditions of both the reality and the interpretative activity itself.

Yitzhak Rabin was assassinated but the truth wasn't divulged. He was mourned by all, the grief knowing no boundaries between Right and Left. Those few who dared to say something concerning the assassination that didn't confirm the consensus arrived at only hours after the crime, or who didn't open their remarks with "I condemn," became immediately suspect and in some cases were taken in for questioning by the police. Those in Yitzhak Rabin's party, under the direction of Shimon Peres, joined with the atmosphere of mourning that descended upon the country and with depoliticizing the assassination, which meant removing it from the exchange economy of the elections. Benjamin Netanyahu, by contrast, didn't pass up the opportunity to divulge the truth that Yigal Amir had failed to expose in the municipal square. He continued Amir's work and proclaimed the truth that had been denied— "Peres will divide Jerusalem." As opposed to the Labor party, which attempted, after the signing of the Oslo Accords, to play the simulation game and let the Palestinians in on it, Netanyahu stated an unequivocal formula from which any obscurity was removed: Peres would divide Jerusalem. Thus Netanyahu played the simulation game masterfully. Having expropriated "peace" from the Labor movement under the slogan "Peace with security," he understood that in order to win in a regime of simulations he must create the simulation of an unequivocal truth, as well as a simulation of sole possession of the simulation.

During the three years he was in power, Netanyahu simulated a continuation of the peace process. What he failed to understand is that such a simulation isn't a one-man act but a new regime of representation that operates in reality, within which everyone is contained and negotiates. In May 1999, when Netanyahu once again tried to play the Jerusalem card, he was roundly defeated. It turned out that the division of Jerusalem, in itself, wasn't such a threatening issue. In 1996 the signifier *Jerusalem* had functioned like a sharp knife slicing through the obscurities, but in 1999 the same signifier appeared illusory and irrelevant, a ghost that Netanyahu had raised from the grave. He turned the Orient House into a symbol of the all-out war over Jerusalem, but the Orient House, the object of the struggle, didn't appear to be more than it is—a symbol. The voters for Barak apparently preferred to support a policy of dividing the city's symbols without dividing the city itself, leaving the city "in our hands" and giving it to the Palestinians too at the same time.

The most fundamental point in the Beilin–Abu Mazen Accord is an agreement on the flexibility of Jerusalem's boundaries. This actually means that the Palestinians

Mizpe Jericho
Efrat Shvily

The Spectre of Jerusalem

won't condemn Israel for having flexed Jerusalem's boundaries for years, while Israel will give up its sole proprietorship of the flexing process. Instead of one side denying its actions while the other side condemns them and demands the return of what has been stolen, both sides in effect agree to place Jerusalem on the operating table, to renounce its status as a missing object in the discourse and turn it into an object that is present to view and to intervention, and into speech that is guided by an observant view and regularized, systematic intervention. In effect, the two sides have agreed to be partners in creating the simulation of the city. Nothing betokens this agreement so much as the complex that houses the Palestinians' national institutions, which are set to rise 2.3 kilometers east of the Al Aqsa mosque, exactly the same distance at which Israel's Knesset is located west of the Al Aqsa mosque.

By assassinating Rabin in the municipal square, Yigal Amir sought to divulge the truth about Jerusalem, which had been suppressed during the negotiations with the Palestinians. Immediately after the assassination, Benjamin Netanyahu gave this truth a voice when he warned that Peres would divide Jerusalem. Peres thought that if he suppressed Jerusalem and Rabin's assassination, he would win the people's trust. Today, after Netanyahu's removal from office and the election of Ehud Barak, it seems that Yigal Amir's wish to divulge the truth about Jerusalem is about to be expressed in the most literal way. The Beilin–Abu Mazen Accord puts Jerusalem on display and shows that many of the city's characteristics are not latent in the object Jerusalem itself, but stem from its place in the symbolic order. Abu-Dis (according to the Beilin–Abu Mazen Accords, Abu-Dis is the future location for the Palestinian parliament), located at a distance of 2.3 kilometers from the Al Aqsa mosque, can turn into Jerusalem just as Ma'ale Ha-Edumim (an Israeli settlement in the suburb of East Jerusalem) has turned into Jerusalem in the past.

Author's note. The demographic data in this essay are taken from publications of B'tselem Reports, an Israeli organization for human rights in the occupied territories (B'tselem 1995; 1997), and from the daily press.

Throughout the years development plans for Jerusalem have been prepared with preference to political over urban considerations, from the construction along the Green Line immediately after the conclusion of the Six-Day War (the purpose of which was to obscure the border), through Israel's policy of expropriating and annexing areas in both the eastern and western parts of Jerusalem and its discriminatory policy regarding construction permits, which restricts Palestinian construction and the expansion of Palestinian neighborhoods with the express purpose (in part fulfilled) of driving Palestinians from the city by the pressure of a housing shortage.

This article was presented at the Bellagio conference in 1999 and is part of my book *Death's Showcase* (MIT Press, 2001).

Ariella Azoulay

Sour Justice, or: Liberalist Envy

Joan Copjec

Laura **and Envy**

Grant me, for the moment, the assumption that film noir is (among other things) a compendium of base human emotions, and you will be less surprised by my beginning this discussion of the religious and ethnic tensions that perturb cities such as Jerusalem with a scene from one of the classics of the noir genre. I have in mind the 1944 film *Laura*, particularly that scene in which the narrator, Waldo Lydecker, discovers that Laura, the woman whom he has calculatedly transformed into his most admiring devotee, has begun spending her evenings with another man. As he peers up from the street at the drawn shade of her second-story window, Lydecker catches a glimpse of two silhouettes—not the single one he would have preferred to see. From this moment on he will not rest until he has utterly demolished the career of the man who casts the second silhouette, a painter named Jacoby.

The question is: Why does Lydecker set himself on this path of destruction, which will lead him to annihilate not only Jacoby, but also Laura, whom he will later shoot in the face with a shotgun at close range (or so he thinks)? The readiest answer is that he longs for that sexual involvement with Laura which Jacoby apparently enjoys. Nothing, however, could be further from the truth, for Lydecker feels only disgust for such sexual liaisons. This is unmistakable both from his own comportment toward Laura and from his frequent contemptuous remarks about the

earthiness and obvious corporeality of her other suitors. We must take these expressions of disgust at face value, for Lydecker is definitely not jealous of Jacoby—he is envious of him. What's the difference? Crabb's *English Synonyms* (1816) offers this answer: "Jealousy fears to lose what it has; envy is pained at seeing another have that which it wants for itself."[1] This distinction isn't bad; in opposing *has* to *wants*, it accurately conveys that jealousy is grounded in the possession of a certain pleasure, while envy stems from a lack of it. Yet one would be wrong to assume that envy's lack can be filled by the possession of that pleasure it is pained to see another enjoying. As Crabb goes on to remark, "All endeavors . . . to satisfy an envious man are fruitless." Why? Because what he wants and what he perceives as the other's enjoyment are not at all the same thing. And since the envious man does not want for himself what the other has, the attainment of that other, altogether foreign pleasure will never appease his desire.

It is no coincidence that the "two silhouettes on a shade," the object of Lydecker's perception, is a cliché. You will miss its meaning, however, if you ascribe this cliché to the film rather than to the character who beholds it; that is to say, it is Lydecker himself who is responsible for the hackneyed form his discovery takes. If his perception is neither immediate nor fresh, but filtered through a stock image, this is because his envious look is not inspired by desire. The pleasure he observes taking

1 Cited in Melanie Klein, "Envy and Gratitude," *The Writings of Melanie Klein*, ed. Roger Money-Kyrle (London: Hogarth Press and the Institute of Psycho-Analysis, 1975), 182.

place at a distance remains alien to him, turned in on itself. The look with which he beholds this (to him) complete and absolute yet incomprehensible pleasure has thus a malevolent potency; it is bitter.

As has been documented, "virtually all languages, ancient and modern," have a term for the "evil eye" that accompanies envy, with its apparent intent to poison or pollute.[2] While every other "mean and hungry look"—of anger, greed, or jealousy—focuses on harm, is concentrated on robbing the other of some coveted object, only the evil eye of envy seeks to steal enjoyment itself. In seeking to leave the other bereft of that which brings him pleasure, those other malicious looks nevertheless would leave the other's capacity for pleasure intact. Not so envy, which wants nothing so much as to spoil the very capacity for enjoyment. As Crabb observes, "The envious man sickens at the sight of enjoyment. He is easy only in the misery of others."[3]

In the famous judgment of Solomon, it is his discernment of the presence of an evil eye that allows the wise leader to unmask the false mother. Having just lost her own precious, irreplaceable child, she is still far too bereaved to desire another. What she wants, then, as Solomon sees, is decidedly not the real mother's bundle of joy (that this foul-smelling, puking little package could be the source of someone else's joy must, in actual fact, seem unfathomable to her), but the extinction of the other's maternal satisfaction. For this reason, splitting the child in two is not so much a compromise she is willing to accept as a ruination for which she longs.

It is generally acknowledged that pleasure is a private matter: "To each his own," we say. But the incomprehensibility with which we encounter another's pleasure is not in itself a cause of hostility. What must be added for envy to arise is an obstacle that prevents the envious person from relishing his own pleasure. Some deficit must be felt which spoils the pleasure that remains, makes it distasteful. When this happens, the deficit can never be made good, never be filled by anything in this world, and the envious person thus begins to regard with malevolence the idiotic passions of others. I have noted that it is the irremediable loss of her child that initiates the bereaved mother's envy; turning again to the film *Laura*, we find at its heart a loss that is similarly abysmal. According to the ordinary view, the film depicts a struggle between Lydecker, whose contentments are said to be purely intellectual, and MacPherson (one of Jacoby's successors), whose passions are more corporeal. But if the film were merely about a battle between two positive passions, Laura would not have been the direct object of a shotgun blast. It is therefore necessary to suppose that while Lydecker does derive his only pleasure from intellectual pursuits, this pleasure is never felt by him to be adequate to fill the loss that deracinates all his endeavors. This supposition is confirmed by the film itself, especially the final sequence.

At the outset I identified Lydecker as the narrator of the film. A question related to this role hangs suspended throughout the film: From where—from what point in

2 Peter Shabad, "The Evil Eye of Envy: Parental Possessiveness and the Rivalry for a New Beginning," in *Gender and Envy*, ed. Nancy Burke (New York and London: Routledge, 1998), 255.

3 Klein, 182.

Sour Justice, or: Liberalist Envy

the narrative—does he narrate the story that unfolds? The final sequence, in which the location of the point of enunciation becomes a question with narrative consequences, gives the answer. As Laura in her bedroom listens to Lydecker's weekly radio address, she assumes he is in the radio studio and that she is thus at least temporarily safe from him. We, the audience, can already see, however, what she will soon learn: through prerecording, Lydecker's voice has been separated from his body. While his voice is being transmitted from the studio, he is in the next room preparing to murder her. This revelation cues our attention to the critical separation of voice and body that will conclude the film. Shot by the police, Lydecker falls to the floor and with his dying breath utters a simple, "Good-bye, Laura." These are his last living words, but they are not his last words in the film. As the camera lingers on a sprung clock, we once again hear his voice (this time off-screen) speak the film's final line: "Good-bye, my love."

From where do these words come? Not, clearly, from Lydecker as he lies dying on the floor. While his final living words clearly issued from the diegetic space of Laura's apartment and from his visibly wounded body, these words emerge from elsewhere. The difference between the two spaces is audible in the lack of room tone in the second "good-bye." This lack suggests that the final line was, like Lydecker's radio address, recorded in a sound studio, not on the film set and thus not in the diegetic space of the film. In narrative terms, we might locate the place of their enunciation on the other side of death, somewhere beyond the grave. In other words, the film does not close in the dream that is to us life on earth (recalling Lydecker's words on the radio—"They are not long, the days of wine and roses. Out of a misty dream our path emerges for a while, then closes in a dream")—but on the far side of that dream.

Laura is no ghost story and it would be unwise to try to make it into one by mistaking the import of its ultimate positioning of Lydecker's voice-over narration outside time (vide the sprung clock), outside the narrative space, beyond earthly life. By locating his enunciation beyond the grave, the film gives us insight not into the ontological character of its world but into the psychology of Lydecker. It is he who places himself—or that which is most precious to him, what he most deeply wants— beyond earthly life and all the pleasures it can offer. He speaks and perceives the world as one who is dissatisfied with it, precisely because, by definition, it lacks and therefore cannot give him what he desires. Life for him is as insubstantial as a dream; what he wants is something more profound.

What about Laura? Does he want her? The answer is a complex "no." She is, for him, an idealization. That is to say, she represents not so much what he wants as the unavailability of what he wants. She is a stand-in for what is missing from the world, what he cannot touch; she embodies not a positive good, not a particular pleasure, but the distance that separates every good in reach from that absent good he longs to possess. This is manifest in the opening line of the film, spoken by Lydecker: "I'll never forget the day Laura died." As the film reveals, however, Laura did not die on the day he so vividly recalls for us as the day of her death. This premature expression of mourning betrays Lydecker's melancholy attitude toward Laura, as toward life in general. The melancholic mourns the structurally lost object by allowing it to cast a shadow on the living, which suffers therefore an untimely death. Here we touch on the structural truth of envy: it is always closely tied to the idealizations which it both feeds on and feeds. For envy's unhappiness is the very stuff from which idealizations are contrived.

We might even venture to say that the baffling opening sequence (which offers an image of MacPherson examining objects on display in Lydecker's apartment, while Lydecker, unseen, sits writing in his bathtub, his voice-over narrating the film) demonstrates that MacPherson himself, along with the suitors before him, are the literary creation of Lydecker, who invents a series of robust, athletic-looking enemies from the feeling of his own emaciated impotence. That is, Lydecker not only destroys his enemies with his pen, but invents them in order to destroy them.

Earlier, I justified my reference to *Laura* by suggesting that film noir trades in base emotions. I might have added that it does so as part of a broader speculation on the dark entanglements of urban relations. Noir films are about the city and the myriad ways in which life in it turns toxic. During the historical period of the genre's development, racial and ethnic tensions were just barely perceptible through the smog. The hard-boiled detective (the protagonist of many noir films) might, for example, have to venture into a black neighborhood or jazz club, areas generally skirted by whites, in order to track down some lead. But these parts of town were usually in deep background; in the foreground, typically the detective's office, the denizens of discounted, unimaginable neighborhoods would stream through one by one: quirky, deformed, but never clearly racialized. It was as if they had been required, by some artistic rule, to doff such telltale traits at the detective's door as the price of entering. That this is exactly what was going on is also the surmise of later films of the period and of more recent revivals—think, for example, of *Kiss Me Deadly* or *Bladerunner*—in which the formerly doffed traits are returned to these characters. The gallery of rogues is exposed as a gallery of racial types.

Envy and Justice: Rawls and Freud

But if noir adumbrated envy as the fathomless and bitter source of social rivalry, social and political theorists did not pick up on the clue; they have given no serious consideration to this vice and its injurious contributions to social relations. The exception is John Rawls, whose benchmark *A Theory of Justice* does indeed pause to examine the place of envy in social life.[4] Because the aim of Rawls' book is to pro-

4 John Rawls, *A Theory of Justice* (Cambridge: Harvard University Press, 1971). Future references to this book appear in the body of the text.

Sour Justice, or: Liberalist Envy

pose (as the title indicates) a theory of the possibility of justice, envy—which stands in justice's way—is set aside at the beginning. For as a neo-Kantian, Rawls wants to locate the possibility of justice in reason, and thus brackets those motives of self-interest—such as envy—that cause reason to swerve from its proper destiny, which is by definition disinterested, not selfish. But he can avoid the topic of envy only so long, since he cannot pretend to be unaware of a significant challenge to his assumption that envy is a mere obstacle to justice—an obstacle to be overcome. According to this challenge, articulated most forcefully by Freud, envy is not simply an impediment to justice, but the very condition of our notion of justice.

Freud argues in *Group Psychology and the Analysis of the Ego* that the intensity of envy's hostility is so noxious that it threatens to harm even the one who envies, who thus calls for a truce in the form of a demand for justice and equality for all. That is, envy defends itself against its own invidiousness by transforming itself into group feeling. The *esprit de corps* cementing group relations is guaranteed by the following pledge: "No one must want to put himself forward, everyone must be the same and have the same."[5] From this Freud draws the following radical conclusion: "Social justice means that we deny ourselves many things so that others may have to do without them as well, or, what is the same thing, may not be able to ask for them. This demand for equality is the root of social conscience and the sense of duty."[6]

Freud's conclusion blasts the foundations of the theory of justice that Rawls lays out; Rawls must, therefore, deal with it head-on. First, he argues that the notion of equality Freud targets is different from the one he, Rawls, proposes. An equality that is "bound in the end to make everyone including the less advantaged worse off" (538) may be one kind of equality—the one implied by strict egalitarianism's insistence that all goods be equally distributed—but it cannot be accepted as a definition of equality, as such. Rawls believes he is protected from the charge that his theory of justice aspires to equality in Freud's sense because his theory respects "the plurality of distinct persons with separate systems of ends" (29); that is, he rejects utilitarianism's false notion that we all desire the same things and argues instead that individuals have—and have a right to have—different desires. As we will see presently, however, Rawls does finally allow one common desire to sneak back into his theory, and even to assume a primary place there.

Rawls begins by focusing, as Freud did, on the emergence of envy among siblings in the nursery. He speculates that Freud may have inaccurately described what goes on in this ur-scene of envy; rather than the amoral feeling of envy, sibling rivalries may actually exemplify legitimate moral resentment about being unfairly denied one's due share of parental attention and affection. The siblings may vie with each other, not out of a feeling of impotence or a lack of self-confidence—the roots of envy, in Rawls' view—but out of a confident conviction that their claims to their parents' affection are equally valid, that is, out of feelings of fairness and self-worth. By

5 Sigmund Freud, Group Psychology and the Analysis of the Ego, in *The Standard Edition of the Complete Psychological Works of Sigmund Freud*, ed. James Strachey (London: The Hogarth Press and the Institute of Psycho-Analysis, 1953–1974), XVIII, 20–121.

6 Ibid.

redescribing the nursery scenario in this way, Rawls seeks to distinguish Freud's notion of equality from the one at stake in his theory of justice and thus to reclaim the scenario for his theory. His redescription implies that the siblings do not have the *same* desire, but instead want their *different* desires to be recognized by their parents. Rawls thus avoids strict egalitarianism's demand that equal shares of goods (or the good) be distributed to all in favor of a demand for equality of opportunity and recognition. His belief is that this demand is a demand for justice and that this sort of justice is immune to Freud's accusation that it springs from an illegitimate feeling of envy. But all Rawls has done is simply inverted Freud's argument: a now legitimate or "benign" feeling of envy is argued to derive from a now primordial notion of justice.

Rawls' first mistake is to assume that Freud's notion of envy implies a desire for the object of another's desire. Yet, just as Lydecker is envious without wanting what Laura's other suitors want, so, too, according to Freud's theory, may siblings in a nursery want different things and be envious still. In fact, in order to be sure one understands what envy is, one would do well to perform a little thought experiment by adjusting slightly that nursery scene which is the locus classicus of the evil eye: the beginning of *The Confessions*, where Saint Augustine notes the look of bitterness on one brother's face as he beholds his sibling nursing at their mother's breast. You mustn't imagine that the envious brother fears the enviable other is sucking at a source that may run dry, thus leaving him, the next in line, thirsty. Augustine makes it clear that this source is a "richly abundant fountain of milk" and able, presumably, to accommodate both.[7] But you will understand the point better if you imagine the envious brother to be a bit older than the nursling and therefore greedy not for breast milk, but for something more suitable to his age—something cold, from the fridge: a Coke, perhaps. As he regards his younger brother, he is nevertheless overcome by an envy that eats him up inside. Why? Because no matter how much pleasure he gets from a refreshing glass of cold Coke, he worries that his brother may get more from that trickle of warm milk, for which he, the elder, has long ago lost his taste. It's not the object—the milk—that he begrudges his brother, it's the satisfaction.

That, in its most compressed form, is the point: envy envies satisfaction. This odd fact is the source of the excess cruelty with which envy is invested. For if one simply envied an object, one could devise strategies—even vicious ones—to steal it away from another. But no strategy can ever obtain the pleasure of which we feel we are robbed if the source of that pleasure (which another possesses) is unappealing to us. No strategy but one: destroy the other's ability to take pleasure, to enjoy. This can be done either by annihilating the other, in which case we begin a battle whose fatal consequences we cannot be sure of controlling, or by demanding equality, in which case we submit ourselves to the same proscription on enjoyment to which we submit the other.

7 Saint Augustine, *The Confessions*, trans. Maria Boulding, O.S.B. (New York: Random House, 1997), Book I. Jacques Lacan, in *The Four Fundamental Concepts of Psycho-Analysis* ed. Jacques-Alain Miller, trans. Alan Sheridan (London: Hogarth Press and Institute of Psycho-Analysis, 1977), 116, makes the suggestion that one of the siblings might be older than the other and thus uninterested in mother's milk, but St. Augustine hints at this possibility himself when he writes, "What then was my sin at that age? Was it perhaps that I cried so greedily for those breasts? Certainly if I behaved like that now, *greedy not for breast, of course, but for food more suitable to my age*, I would provoke derision." (9, emphasis added).

Since the psychoanalytic picture of envy does not depend, as Rawls assumes, on denying the uniqueness of individual pleasure, he cannot claim to have corrected Freud's view by insisting on this uniqueness. He thus fails to provide himself with a basis for simply inverting the priority of envy and justice. His argument about the *difference* of desire is just so much stage business to distract us, if we are not attentive, from what is really going on, that is, from Rawls' attempt to pose equality as the cause of envy, rather than the reverse. But this faulty premise cannot slip under the radar of Freud's corrosive critique. On the contrary, it places itself, along with the whole theory of justice as fairness, squarely in the latter's path and betrays the theory's own envy-tainted origins. How so? In his reinterpretation of the nursery example, Rawls contends that the siblings' supposedly envious demands are in fact demands for "the attention and affection of their parents, to which . . . they justly have an equal claim"; in other words, they are bids for recognition from a parental other (540). But such bids are precisely what Freud's theory of the envious origins of the demand for equality have prepared us to expect. The transformation of hostile feelings of envy into social feelings of equality and community can only take place, Freud says, through the mediation of an other who is not a member of the group; the "necessary precondition" for the formation of a sense of community "is that all [its] members should be loved in the same way by one person, the leader." He later adds, "The demand for equality in a group applies only to its members, not to the leader."[8] In Rawls' scenario, universal desire—which he denies, in one form at least, to utilitarians—has resurfaced as a common desire for recognition, from the same parental figure.

8 Freud,. 121.

In his otherwise astute essay "The Strange Destiny of Envy," John Forrester takes Rawls to task simply for refusing to cede Freud's point that a base passion such as envy could be the source of such lofty and rational ideals as equality and justice.[9] This limited charge miscalculates the extent of the damage done by Freud's argument. Rather than gold from ore, as Forrester assumes, the proposal that envy is transformed into a demand for justice extracts vinegar from sour grapes. Instead of simply supplying the demands for equality and justice with an ignominious, but still triumphant history, Freud thoroughly discredits them. Any political program structured according to their demands will thus be subject to his reproach.

9 John Forrester, "Psychoanalysis and the History of the Passions: The Strange Destiny of Envy," in *Freud and the Passions*, ed. John O'Neil (University Park: Penn. State University Press, 1996).

Two questions: first, what is Forrester's error and, second, what is Rawls'? Forrester goes wrong because he fails to question the relation between the superego and ethical action, assuming implicitly that the function of the first is to rally the second. What the superego rallies, rather, is a pinched and nasty moralism, such as is described in Freud's myth of the overthrow of the primal horde by a fraternal society. According to this myth, evidence of the repressed murder of the single exception to the fraternal order—the priapic patriarch—returns in the brotherly taboo against the slightest trace of exceptionalism. Differences are from this point on denounced and abhorred, as is every form of *jouissance* (enjoyment) that cannot be conscripted into the antiexceptionalism of the fraternal cause. Again, the rule is: "Everyone must be the same and have the same." This is a superegoic injunction; it must not be confused with an ethical command.

Rawls' error is failing to see that his image of brothers demanding validation of their unique desires is nothing but a bad-faith version of Freud's myth. The desperate fiction of incommensurable desires submitting themselves to a common measure scarcely disguises its own absurdity. As psychoanalysis teaches, one has to limit the Other's knowledge to make room for *jouissance*, which flourishes only where it is not validated by the Other. Turning this around, one could say that out of a number of unique desires it is impossible to construct any big tent, any subsuming whole, that would not quash the differences themselves or increase hostility toward them. This is the poison pellet in Freud's theory of group formation to which Lacan drew our attention in various ways, but never so vividly as in his characterization of the utilitarian project as the misguided attempt to cut enough holes in a piece of cloth for a number (the greatest number!) of people to stick their arms and heads through it.[10] Any social theory that includes a reference to *jouissance*, as it must, will find that no single cloth will be sufficient to cover all desires. In the words of Willie Stark in Robert Penn Warren's *All the King's Men*, every piece of cloth will be as inadequate as "a single-bed blanket on a double bed and three folks in the bed and a cold night. There ain't ever enough blanket to cover the case."[11]

Opposing utilitarianism, Rawls raises what he takes to be a fatal objection to it, in effect protesting: "But, Mr. Bentham, my good is not the same as another's . . . and your principle of the greatest good for the greatest number [thus] comes up against the demands of my egoism."[12] In other words: I want what I want, not what my neighbor wants. But my egoism is quite compatible with a certain altruism: I am content to allow the Other what he wants. The problem with this bad-faith version of the egoistic demand for equality is that it always runs afoul of the Other, who is always suspected of not being as altruistic as the one who formulates the demand. That is, the problem always stems from our uncertainty about the Other and thus our fear that he will not do what is right and allow me my desire. In raising his egoistic/altruistic objection, I would argue, Rawls does not avoid utilitarianism but articulates a more clever version of it. What corrals his theory within an expanded utilitarianism is his commitment to normative judgment, to a measure or standard of pleasure, which is the inevitable consequence of his insistence on "parental" recognition. Ignorant of the structure of pleasure—which, as Freud taught, is only ever partial, never complete—and believing naively that complete satisfaction is attainable by anyone who, unimpeded by bad fortune, sets about realizing a rational plan (409), Rawls is not well positioned to see that the supposed need for a recognition of one's pleasure turns structural incompleteness into the occasion of envy.

10 Jacques Lacan, *The Ethics of Psychoanalysis*, Book VII, ed. Jacques-Alain Miller, trans. Dennis Porter (New York and London: Routledge, 1992), 228.

11 Robert Penn Warren, *All the King's Men* (New York: Harcourt Brace, 1996), 73.

12 Lacan, 187.

Sour Justice, or: Liberalist Envy

As a Kantian, however, Rawls does admit that a consideration of pleasure is crucial to a theory of ethics. Though we have seen how his image of siblings seeking affectionate recognition of their differences is disqualified under Freud's concepts, we may want to know how it fares under Kant's. Now, despite his reputation as a cold rationalist, Kant knew well that a purely abstract moral law had no chance of receiving a hearing from an embodied subject. This is why he wrote the third *Critique*: to heal the gap that had erupted between reason (as he had so far theorized it) and pleasure, to show the indispensable role aesthetic pleasure, specifically, played in the practical use of reason, that is, in an ethical, or free, act. The difficulty is in understanding just what this role is. What does it mean to say, as Kant does, that aesthetic pleasure is prompted by beholding a beautiful object, which object symbolizes our morality?[13]

13 Immanuel Kant, *Critique of Judgment*, trans. Werner S. Pluhar (Indianapolis: Hackett Publishing, 1987), para. 59.

The first answer to come to mind is that the beautiful object represents the end that the ethical act strives to attain. This teleological answer is, of course, wrong in Kant's terms. For if an ethical act is free, it cannot be guided by anything but itself. It cannot, then, be guided by an external goal, since this goal would become the basis of morality, that on behalf of which the act was undertaken. Such an act would not be free, but would be bound by the idealized vision it served to realize. External to will, an independent goal cannot claim any basis in moral law. Nothing guarantees, therefore, that the goal is freely chosen and is not concocted out of self-interest. It is this antiteleological argument that is at the root of the "postmodern" condemnation of master strategies, masquerading as benevolent, which would solve urban problems by imposing "just" and "proportionate" schemes over vast territories, in order to create "ideal cities." Such strategies, which start with a whole that they then proceed to carve up, are doomed to fail; naively taking the whole for granted rather than questioning its possibility, they soon run into the single-bed blanket problem: it is always too short and too tight for a growing humankind.

Envy, Beauty, and Will

Once this visionary answer to the question of the role of the beautiful is rejected, an alternative is ready to step forward. According to this answer, the beautiful object does not represent a goal to be sought, but is, rather, that which incites us to abandon our selfish goals. An example of this argument can be found in the recently published (and beautifully written) *On Beauty and Being Just*, by Elaine Scarry. Beauty, Scarry maintains, is always a call for distribution; it exerts on us a pressure to surrender our imaginary position at the center of the world and to extend our regard laterally, to others. Beauty gives us an "opiated" sense of "adjacency" and thus prepares our sense of justice. Beautiful things, she opines, "act like small tears in the surface of the world that pull us through to some vaster space; . . . so that when we land we find we are standing in a different relation to the world."[14] Concurring with the belief that it is "fraternity" that "underwrites liberal theories of justice" (95) and equality, Scarry embraces what she refers to as Rawls' "widely accepted definition . . . [of] fairness" as the "symmetry of everyone's relation to each other" (93). Similar in many respects to the first definition of the role of beauty, this one, articulated by Scarry, is nevertheless distinct. For while the first presented the beautiful as a goal to be achieved, the second presents it as a salutary fiction that boosts the spirit of ethical will and persuades us to believe in the possibility of justice and in the reality of moral law. Before accepting Rawls' revamped nursery scenario as just such a compelling fiction, however, one must note that it stands condemned on the same grounds as the first: it implies that the unbridgeable gap between subjective happiness and the public good of the community can be healed through public recognition.

But if both definitions of the role of beauty have a certain staying power, even among some who attempt to think in the Kantian mode, this is because each answers to some fundamental argument of Kant's theory. The first attaches to an understandable reluctance to surrender the notion of purpose altogether, for, as Kant insists, "in the absence of all reference to an end, no determination of the will can take place in man. . . . [H]ow the question, 'What is to result from this right conduct of ours' is to be answered . . . cannot possibly be a matter of indifference to reason."[15] A will that envisions to itself no definite goal is incapable of achieving satisfaction, Kant remarks. The second definition of the role of beauty, on the other hand, thrives on Kant's insistence that the pleasure one takes in beauty depends on a sense of harmony, of fitness and balance, which is occasioned by beholding the beautiful object. These attributes describe, Kant argues, not the object itself so much as the faculties of the beholder, which are on this occasion in accord. Scarry's argument revolves around this aspect of balanced symmetry, which she promotes as the essential attribute of beauty, and she finds confirmation of her view that this attribute is the sine qua non of the beautiful in, for example, Aristotle's depiction of justice as a perfect cube, equidistant in all its parts; in the spectacle of trireme ships, which she claims nourished Athenian democracy; in public parades, in which a plurality of classes and "genders" move in concert and on an equal footing. But if all these beautiful things function not as ends to be achieved, images of ideal societies to be realized, neither do they serve merely as inert analogies for political fairness. One is heartened to observe Scarry begin to take her distance from others who argue from analogy, who see in the symmetry of beautiful things a merely formal similarity to the symmetry of relations of moral fairness. Her bolder claim is that aesthetic symmetry encourages and helps to bring about the actual symmetry of just relations. Insofar as it conceives the beautiful image as something that actively impels us to act, to create something anew, this position is clearly more attractive, but it is ultimately inade-

14 Elaine Scarry, *On Beauty and Being Just* (Princeton: Princeton University Press, 1999), 112. Further references to this book will appear in the body of the text.

15 Immanuel Kant, *Religion within the Limits of Reason Alone*, trans. Theodore Greene and Hoyt Hudson (New York: Harper and Row, 1960), 4.

Sour Justice, or: Liberalist Envy

quate. By insisting that the beautiful object compels us to bring into being the second term of an analogy—the justice that would be analogous to a beautiful, symmetrical image—Scarry invents something akin to the notion of the half-said, by which Lacan interpreted Kant's categorical imperative. The imperative is only half "said" because it requires an act to complete it. There is no fully stated law followed by an obedient and actualizing act; rather, the act retroactively constitutes the half-stated law. But because Scarry makes no such provision for retroaction in her scenario, the beautiful image still acts on the will, externally, rather than in it. There is then no act of creation here, only mimicry.

And this is to say nothing of the fact that the privileging of balance and symmetry betrays a disappointingly conservative notion of the aesthetic object! Noting that the current denigration of the beautiful is the result of an unfavorable comparison with the sublime—a comparison Kant initiated with his division of the aesthetic into these two categories, the first "feminine" and small, the second "masculine" and great, or powerful—Scarry reminds us that this division is neither long-standing nor uncontested. This useful reminder prepares us for a full-scale redefinition of the beautiful, one that would include the forceful and perturbing aspects of the sublime, but in the end Scarry declines to deliver on her implied promise. Her definition of the beautiful remains explicitly "pacific"(107). Opportunity lost. And yet, despite these criticisms, Scarry's moving book will be admired for its sustained attempt to take seriously Kant's enigmatic formulation: beauty symbolizes morality.

It is this *symbolizes* which has got everyone stumped, or did, until Freud came along to distinguish a "pure" or "empty" signifier (*Vorstellungrepresentanz*) that did not represent anything and was therefore unlike other signifiers. The *Vorstellung-representanz*, which is the "representative" of the drive, the only form in which the drive appears to us, holds representation itself in place; it is, as it were, the strut, the support, of representation. Now, if beauty could be shown to concern this pure signifier, the problem we posed of free will's mimetic relation to it would disappear, for beauty would not represent anything. Nothing represented, nothing mimed. But, if not a representation, what then might beauty be? In the vocabulary of Lacan, beauty would be a semblant, an apparent nothing or that which makes nothing appear. This raises a further question: why would nothing incite an autonomous or ethical will to action?

Kant has often been accused of formulating the notion of an issueless desire, of a hopeless will, about which we cannot even be certain that it has ever succeeded in acting freely. In truth, Kant was himself sensitive to this problem. A practical use of reason has still to be reasonable, that is, it has to have some cause to believe in the chances of its own success, despite the fact that moral, disinterested acts seem as a rule less likely to be rewarded than conniving or calculated ones. While Kant's notion of reason disallowed any guarantee of heavenly reward, market and social forces were increasingly valorizing acts of cunning; ethical will thus stood, at the time Kant wrote, in sore need of motivation. What reason could Kant give to practical reason to believe it had any place in the modern world, to believe that this world did not itself conspire against it? In Dieter Henrich's thesis, Kant's solution was to argue that along with moral will there arises spontaneously a "moral image of the world," that is, an image of the world as not indifferent or opposed to acts that are ethically motivated.[16] This moral image—which is the cause of ethical action, which makes it reasonable to act unselfishly—is not to be confused with a belief in the existence of God. It is rather an image of the world in which moral will is a genuine—that is to say, an integral and constitutive—part. Not a world against which the autonomous subject stands, ready to do battle with it, but in which the subject finds a place for himself, though one that can only be described as supernumerary, since the subject does not fit into the purely natural scheme of things.

16 Dieter Henrich, *Aesthetic Judgment and the Moral Image of the World* (Palo Alto: Stanford University Press, 1992).

If the subject is able to envision for itself this admittedly supernumerary place in the world, this is because she locates in the world an empty place, one occupied by precisely nothing. The surplus of the subject requires this deficit of the world, which, by this very incompleteness, is revealed to be incapable of realizing itself on its own. We have in Kant not a structure of opposition in which subject and world face off against each other, but an envelope or topological structure in which the subject appears twice, first as subtracted from the world and second as added to it. The role of the beautiful in this structure is to represent the nothing in which Will will be able to trace its own reflection. Thus, the quality of "fitness" that Kant emphasizes and Scarry makes so much of is it to be found not in the beautiful object, but in this relation between the subject and its world in which the subject is simultaneously at home and out of joint.

Unlike the beautiful, symmetrical image of which Scarry writes, the beautiful semblant is not external to will; it is rather that in which will represents and satisfies itself. Will, like the Freudian drive, has no end, no goal other than its own satisfaction. Like the drive, in other words, it is goal-inhibited; it is defined by its indifference to purposes other than its own, it is autonomous. The semblant does not, then, incite will to create symmetries among people or insist on their equality; it incites us to create, purely and simply. What's wrong with the rigidly formal definition of justice as fairness is that it ignores, as I have argued after Freud, the concrete reality of pleasure, which not only actively resists symmetrization, but turns lethal under its constraint. This is not to imply that ethics comes down to either fencing in pleasure so it won't wander into the neighbor's space, or liberating pleasure so that it can roam where it will. Such spatio-economic proposals for the ethical partitioning of pleasure are based in a still too naturalistic conception of pleasure, as something closer to need.

It has often been remarked that liberal theories of ethics seek merely to provide equality of circumstances and opportunity to all and to protect all subjects from natural harm. Ethics is thus reduced to a guarantee that everyone will have the basics of life. Rawls, aware of the limitations of such a project, attempts to go beyond it by advocating the recognition of individual pleasures. But he does so while adhering to a notion of pleasure that scarcely distinguishes it from a material good. He thus fails to understand adequately that once pleasure is denaturalized and shown to be constituted by a detour through the field of the Other, its equitable distribution is no longer an appropriate or feasible goal. The problem should not be posed as one of distribution, but of deprivation. That is to say, the problem is not to ensure that everyone has an adequate portion of the pleasure she wants, but to ensure that she wants it in the first place. Arising in the field of the Other, pleasure arises alongside our uncertain relation to the Other. What does he expect of me? Who does he think I am? Since the surest way of guaranteeing that the Other recognizes us for ourselves, or that he acknowledges our desire, is to make our desires his, we end up depriving ourselves of our own pleasure, choosing for the sake of a more pacific relation to the Other, to invest our pleasure in his (lost) cause. The problem with pleasure is the countless reasons we invent to forsake it. What we find most difficult is hanging on to and enjoying the pleasure we have. It is the dissatisfaction we impose on ourselves that leads us to demand the same dissatisfaction of others.

Jerusalem and the "Axiom of Equality"

If the psychoanalytic critique forbids a single Jerusalem solution, so too does it forbid talk of a shared Jerusalem that would partition its people and their pasts "fairly," through a beautiful, symmetrical scheme. There is no whole, no all-of-Jerusalem to be shared, because there is no big Other to recognize and bestow affection equally on all its citizens. This is to say, there is no external norm that can be imposed on the territory. For this reason, equality, as a program, has to be scrapped. At the end of his essay "Philosophie et politique," however, Alain Badiou makes an intriguing distinction between a "program of equality" and an "axiom of equality." The latter, he says, disengages equality from its "economist connotations" and restores it to its "subjective trenchance."[17] By "economist connotations" he seems to have in mind those considerations of "fair distribution" that form the staple of liberal theories of equality, up to and including Rawls' and Scarry's. A program of equality is as clearly destined for defeat, as is the goal of reaching infinity starting from a finite point. As we know, infinity will never be reached—no matter how much time passes—within a finite space formed by the subtraction of infinity from it. A program of equality is similarly absurd insofar as it attempts to secure recognition for pleasure while pleas-

17 Alain Badiou, "Philosophie et politique," *Conditions* (Paris: Seuil, 1992), 247.

ure essentially depends on the subtraction of the Other's recognition—or has historically depended on this subtraction since the beginning of the modern period, when happiness acquired a subjective status and the accord between individual happiness and the common good, which Aristotle had taken for granted, was no longer assured, when indeed subjective happiness and the public weal came, by definition, into conflict. In the modern period, the paradox of pleasure—its demand for recognition coupled with the impossibility of receiving that recognition—could be said to have been added to the list of Zeno's paradoxes. As Zeno demonstrated, the only way out of such paradoxes is via the axiom. One must, for example, begin axiomatically by asserting the possibility of movement, since the attempt to produce movement through an exhaustive description of the static points through which it passes merely causes it to disappear and is thus demonstrably doomed to failure. One must start from the notion of infinity because it is impossible to produce it via the finite. And one must begin with an axiom of equality rather than foolishly trying to bring it into being through some Other who would recognize and validate individual pleasures.

Lacan referred several times to the "prisoner's dilemma," a logical puzzle out of which he assayed to compose a kind of "Group Psychology Beyond the Ego."[18] In this puzzle, each of three prisoners has either a black or a while circle attached to his back. Operating with the knowledge that the prison warden had five circles, three white and two black, to distribute—knowing, that is, that two circles have been withdrawn from play—each prisoner must determine from the evidence of the two circles he can see whether the one he himself bears is black or white. The prisoner who figures this out first will be freed. Had there been five prisoners and five circles, or had the two of the prisoners been given black circles, this fateful game would have presented little problem. One prisoner could have discerned at a glance from the evidence of the others his own identity. These prisoners, however, have all been given white circles. By putting some circles out of play, and precisely those that would have allowed a simple opposition to enter into the calculations, this game approximates the differential situation of social signifiers, which never constitutes a totality. That is to say, it is never possible to define myself completely solely on the basis of my relations to others. The signifier of my own unique identity is always missing from the set.

It would seem, then, that Lacan's prisoners could remain permanently stalled, with none able to win the game since there will never be a moment when certain knowledge of any individual's own status emerges. Realizing, however, that his differential relations with his fellows are insufficient to determine his true identity, and that while he waits passively for this information to be reflected back to him, the others have time to act and thus precipitate an alteration of the situation, each prisoner

18 Jacques Lacan, "Logical Time and the Assertion of Anticipated Certitude," *Newsletter of the Freudian Field*, vol. 2 (1988).

feels compelled to act "prematurely"—in the absence of any cognitive certainty—and to determine by his act his own truth. At the end of the apologue, each of the three prisoners is freed, because each verifies, not simply on the basis of what he learns, but also through his own act of passing through the door, that he is "white." Each, in other words, produces his "whiteness," which is to say, his anonymity, by refusing to allow himself to be defined by others and by acting to block this possibility.

One could well imagine a different outcome. The prisoners, each unsure of his own identity and fearful of what the others might do to alter the situation, might enter into an unconscious, pleasure-denying pact to maintain the hell of the status quo. According to this pact, the current wary habits of the prisoners would have been routinized and prolonged to form the hardened, time-tested shell of an imaginary identity. It would be as if some transcendent point had simultaneously been added to the game—as if some prison warden had been given just enough circles to identify each of the prisoners with his own separate badge—from which point onward the prisoners' actions were overseen and were expected to continue unaltered. No one would exit this game, which would be played indefinitely.

Jerusalem is a city too full of sacred places, too full of ancestral dead, to make living there easy. Life is continuously sacrificed to the past and to the ancestral others by whose dreams the living judge and validate themselves. If the city is to become livable again, it will have to learn not how to divide itself up, but how to make nothing appear. Jerusalem's fiercest battle is not between religious and ethnic groups, but between the sacred and the semblant. So far, unfortunately, the sacred seems to be winning.

Meditations on a New Jerusalem

Lebbeus Woods

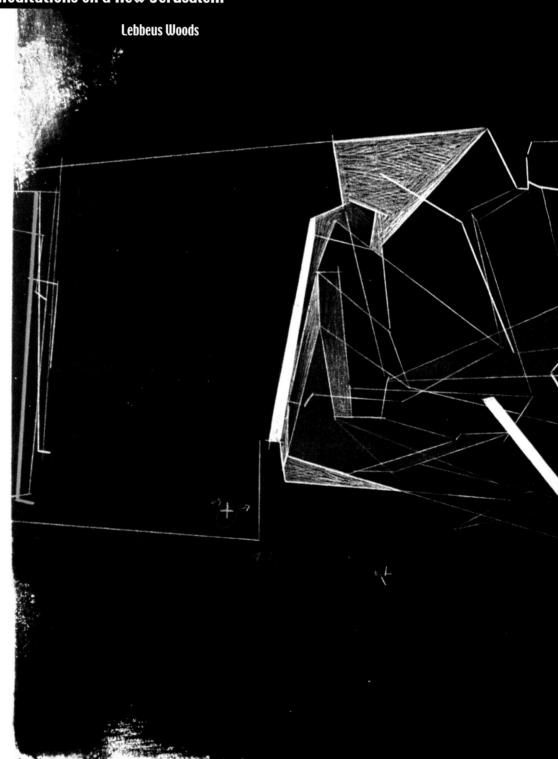

Design from an Institute for Recognitive Studies:
Question Site 1

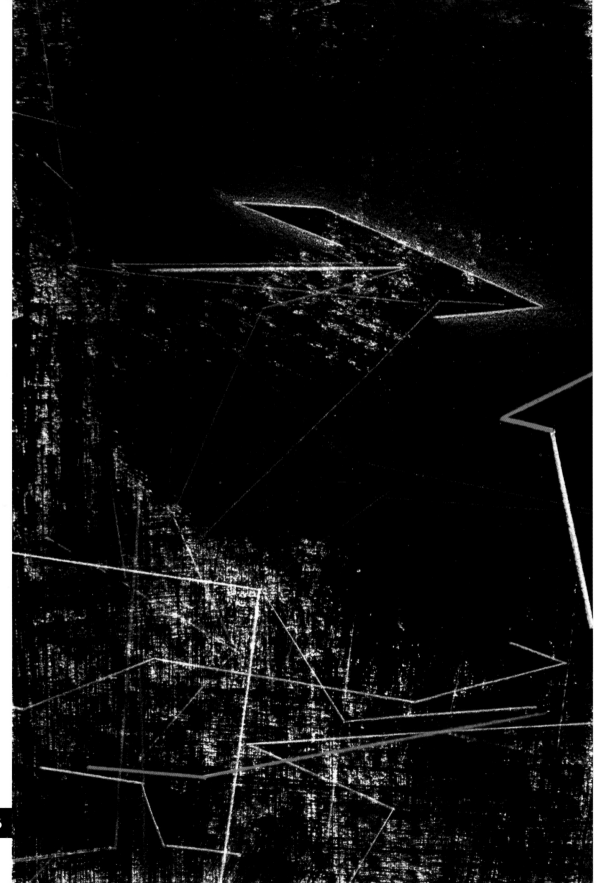

The emptiness of space
increases the more fanati-
cally it is filled.

The importance of two
things is the distinction, not
the distance, between them.

Lebbeus Woods

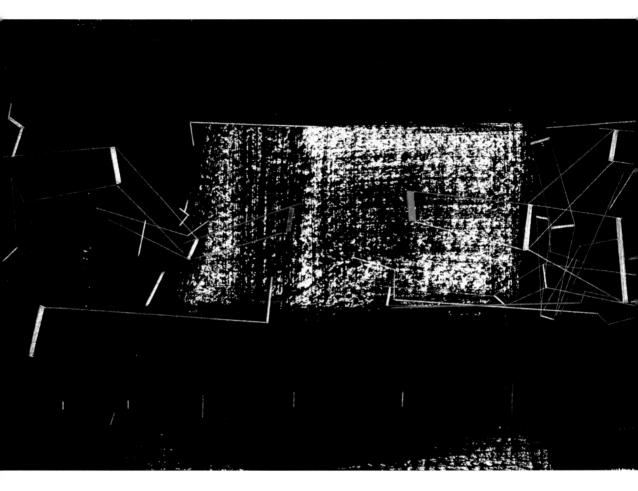

A city may be drawn anew
in language that has always
been used, but not yet
understood.

First come the forms of
what has been most desired,
then of what has been most
feared.

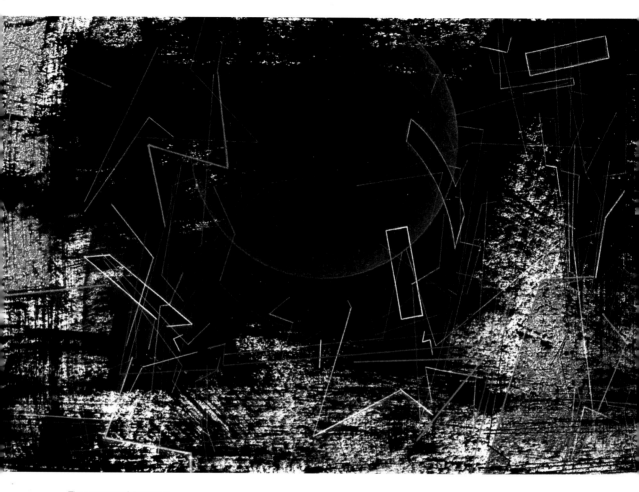

The geometry of division is a
mathematics of denial.

Conflict clarifies distinctions,
but violence effaces them.

There is a line of constant
energy connecting the obvious with the obscure.

Meditations on a New Jerusalem

Despair assumes the language of problems that desire no solution.

Architecture is a political act.

All things do not exist in the
same present.

Lebbeus Woods

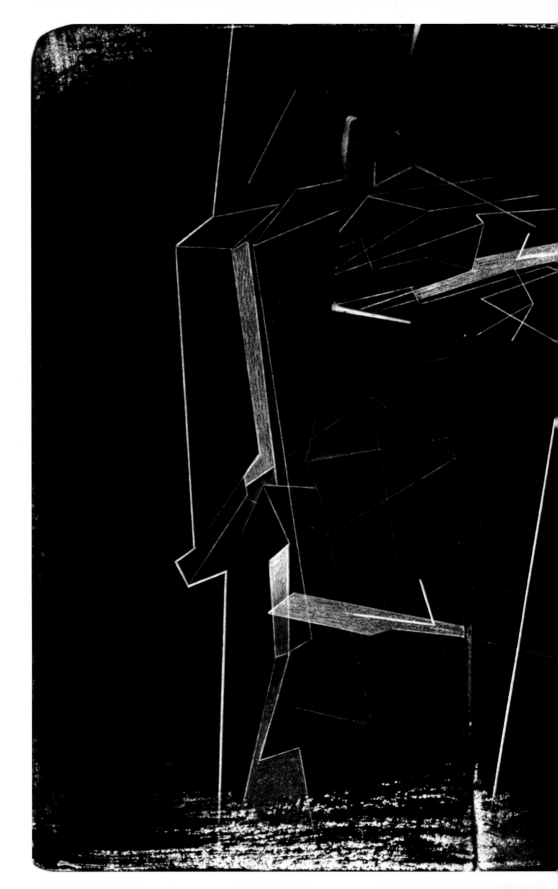

Jerusalem Portfolio

Rasem Badran

Our understanding of the nature of a particular place begins with research and analysis. We then seek familiarity with the place itself, and conclude by forming a narrative of the events that have occurred in that place and which continue to occur there. Being a narrative—a product of the coexistence of people and place over time—this understanding is constantly changing.

Below we look briefly at the nature of place, time, and man, considered from an architectural point of view; at the approach to urban design that results from these ideas; and at three design proposals for Jerusalem informed by this approach, two for housing and the other for an orphanage.

Ingredients of Narrative
Place. The usual view of architectural space is geometric, that is, mechanical and repetitive; as Muslims, our understanding of architectural space is organic and vital. By this we mean that we see the human presence in a space as bringing forth material, intellectual and spiritual meanings in that space, multiplying it (in effect) by multiplying meanings in it. This bringing-forth of unprogrammed, many-meaninged events in a space creates what we call "the social urban fabric."

Time. No culture is timeless, but a thing unfolding in time. Architecture—whether seen as static (given) or as dynamic (in process)—can help reveal what is otherwise hidden about a culture: its characteristic way of changing through time, of relating to time. And since time and space are mutually dependent, a culture's relationship to one necessarily involves its relationship to the other.

Man. Man both creates and receives culture. As in cultural creation there is never pure novelty, so in reception there is never pure passivity, but rather a creative process that produces new meanings, triggers new events. This creative process will condition, and be conditioned by, man's relationship to his place and to the way in which man experiences the passing of time. The result is a multiplicity of vital and intimate creative zones embedded in the urban fabric.

Approach to Design

Symbiosis

The coexistence in a space of apparently opposite or incompatible phenomena, or the alternate appearance of such phenomena in a space at different times, enriches human experience. A "space of probability," that is, of vital uncertainty, is created by the symbiotic relationship of opposites or unlikes in a space. This space of probability is key to the continuity of human-built spaces over time, for without change, without uncertainty, continuity becomes mere continuance, which is death.

Suggestive Narrative

The process of making sense of a given place by contriving an appropriate narrative begins, for us, with a comprehensive analysis of what is known about a place's components. Yet the narrative we seek as the goal of this activity is not linear or Euclidean. Rather, we see it as a "suggestive" narrative that moves freely in the place's space of probability, that is open to a multiplicity of readings, and that provokes human curiosity and participation. We seek a poetics of harmonious, non-homogenous diversity within a repetitive overall framework.

Intuition

The designer's intuition can be enriched by exposure to a place's hidden qualities, that is, in the spiritual and psychological content of the culture of a specific place. One seeks to understand (a) the immaterial character that both distinguishes the culture of this place from and connects it to the larger cultural mosaic, (b) the behavioral patterns formed by the permanent environmental, climatic, and geographic factors at play, and (c) the dialogue between the tangible and the intangible, between reality and fantasy, always undertaken by human creativity while shaping any space.

The Purpose of Architecture

Looking back at what has been achieved in the past fifty years of city-building, it is sad to discover that we are living in empty cities built to serve consumerism at the expense of human coexistence, moral values, and memories. Time, place, and human creativity alike are denied and annulled by such an urbanism. We claim that habitable spaces should result from the interaction of cultural, environmental, and social factors on the micro scale (with its tight dependence on detail and individualized spirituality) in symbiosis with the macro scale (climate, geography, and so forth). This is what the Islamic civilization has, at its best, always sought: a knowledge of the whole that does not deny the particular.

   In presenting the following three projects, we seek such a balance between the spiritual, the intellectual, and the material, between the micro and the macro.

① Housing in East Jerusalem
② Orphanage in Jerusalem
③ Wadi Saleh Housing

Project 1: Housing for East Jerusalem, 1972

This project is located on land owned by the Al Alami family near the Palestinian Museum. It seeks to take into account the Old City's morphology, a special urban fabric that spreads until it attaches the city's walls, which then become an integral part of the city. Our design emphasizes perceptual relations in both the horizontal and vertical directions, making public spaces social and informative in a way calculated to enhance social patterns already prevalent in Arab Islamic societies. These public spaces include streets, pathways, and vertical connection elements (staircases and elevations). Our design does not neglect the relation of this residential zone to the daily commercial facilities (al souq) embedded in Jerusalem's urban fabric. Moreover, this design seeks to accommodate the basic social cell (extended family) and its pattern of growth in the capability of these residential units to expand horizontally and vertically (especially at roof level).

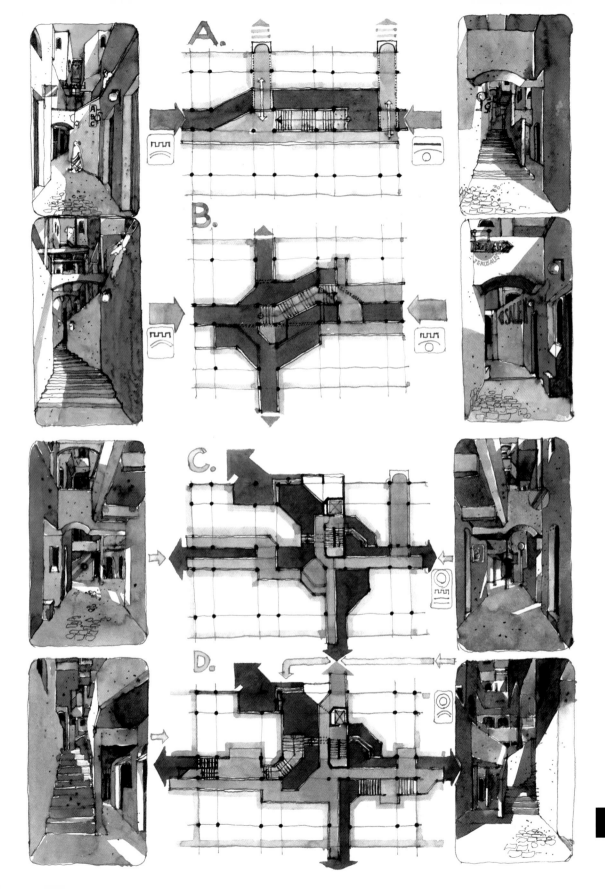

Project 2 : Orphanage in Jerusalem, 1972

This project is an attempt to create a micro urban fabric for orphans by means of functional diversity and morphological interaction with the topography of the site, which is located in the city's eastern suburbs. The ecological and natural features interact with the surroundings to create a rural environment for children in this morphological fabric, which also contains places of worship for Muslims and Christians.

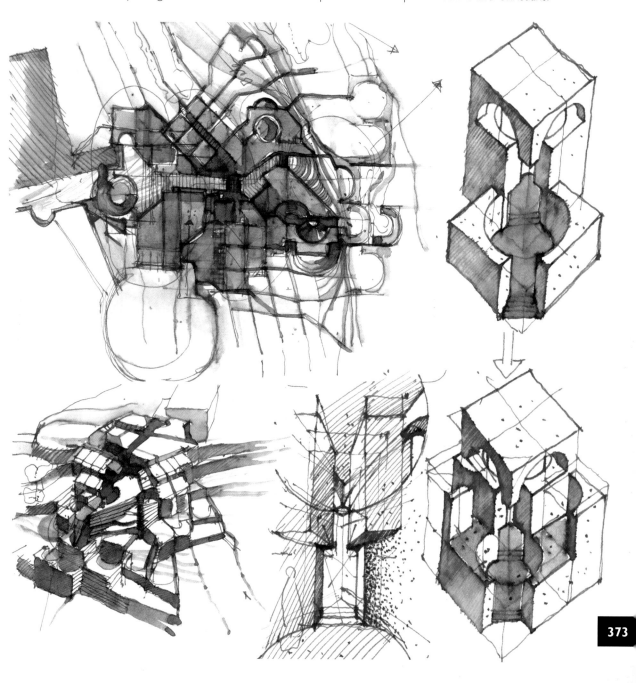

Project 3 : Wadi Saleh Housing Development, 1996

This is a proposal for a neighborhood facing Jerusalem, opposite the Abu Ghnaim Colony. The land is owned by a private group of Palestinian-Americans who were willing to start phase 1, which is the subject of this study.

   The study went through a succession of design steps: in phase 1, micro-scale development was considered within the overall context of future growth at the macro scale. The idea started from the micro-family structure, which created a sense of communal fabric that responded to the social and cultural patterns inherited from the traditional way of living.

   This can be recognized morphologically through the fractal boundaries that shape the nature of such neighborhoods, responding to the geophysical and ecological constraints of the hilly site.

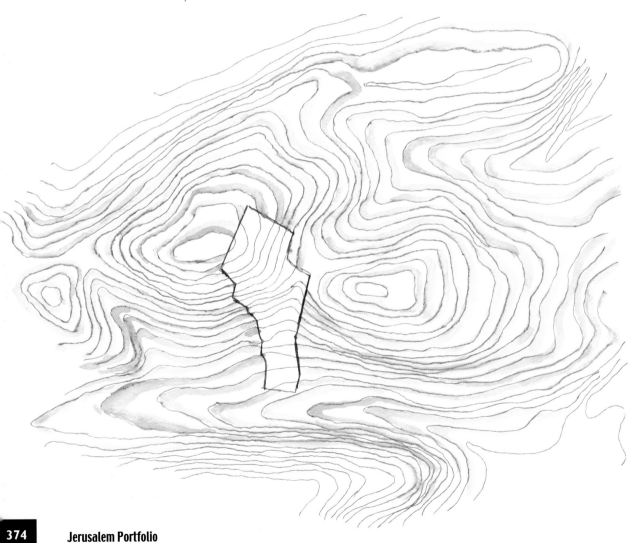

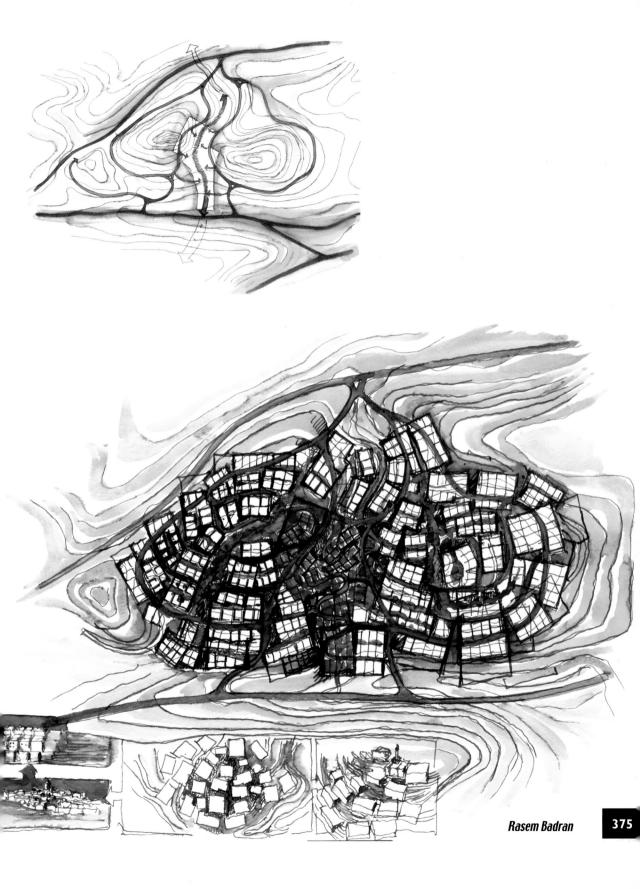

Rasem Badran

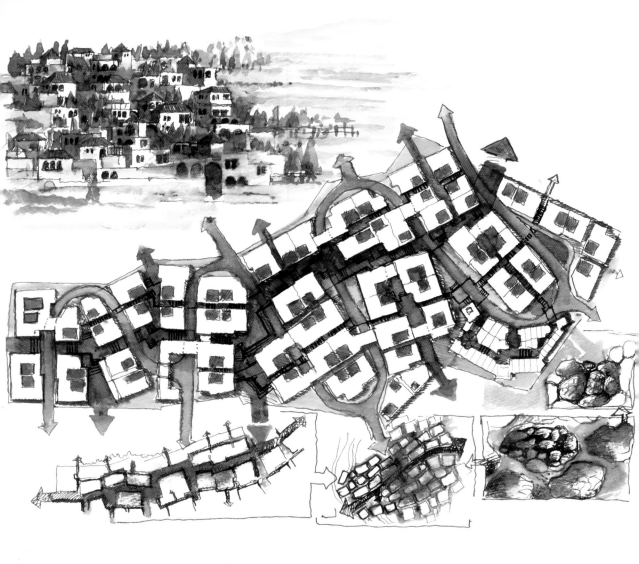

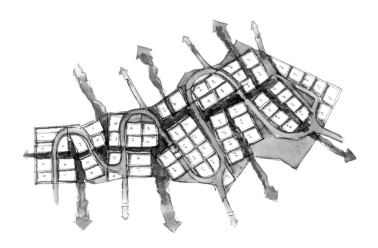

Memories of Contention: The Sacred Stones of Jerusalem

M. Christine Boyer

Introduction

Jerusalem has been called the City of Peace, although it has suffered at least thirty-seven wars and been rebuilt as many times. It is a uniquely *holy* city, a center of religious cosmology for millions of Christians, Muslims, and Jews. Long ago, stones were erected in this place to mark areas sacred to Christianity, Islam, and Judaism, and these holy stones have been the cause of centuries of dispute.[1]

For Christians, Jerusalem is the site of the Passion, Crucifixion, and burial of Jesus, although they were reluctant to locate these holy happenings at specific sites until A.D. 327, when Saint Helena, mother of the Roman emperor Constantine, believed that she discovered the cross on which Christ was crucified. The traditional narrative states that her find moved Constantine to erect a great basilica on the spot of the discovery; it is more likely that Constantine, intent on consolidating his empire in both East and West, sought the support of the sizable Christian population in the East by undertaking a massive building campaign in Jerusalem and throughout the Eastern Empire. The Christian structures of Jerusalem (and elsewhere) served Constantine as symbols of visible power to parallel his political commitments. Christianity would dominate Jerusalem from the time of Constantine to the early seventh century, and again, for a time, following the Crusades in the twelfth century. Its mark on the topography of the city is still in evidence today.

For Muslims, Jerusalem is the place of the Holy Abode where the prophet Muhammad (founder of Islam) ascended into heaven atop his winged horse Al Buraq. Around A.D. 692 the empty area where the Jewish Temple had once stood became the platform of Haram al Sharif, where the Dome of the Rock and El Aqsa Mosque were erected. For most of the time from the seventh century until the early twentieth century Muslims were in control of Jerusalem, and they too implanted visual symbols of devotion still visible today.[2]

1 Avener Falk, "The Meaning of Jerusalem: A Psychohistorical Viewpoint," *Maps Form the Mind*, ed. Howard T. Stein and William G. Niederland (Norman: Oklahoma University Press, 1987), 161–78; R. A. Markus, "How on Earth Could Places Become Holy? Origins of the Christian Idea of Holy Places," *Journal of Early Christian Studies* 2, 4 (1994), 257–71.

2 Oleg Grabar, *The Shape of the Holy: Early Islamic Jerusalem* (Princeton, N.J.: Princeton University Press, 1996).

For Jews, Jerusalem is the site of the temple of Yahweh, the Lord, and their eternal capital. The name *Jerusalem* means "founded by Salem," a Canaanite god whose name meant "perfect." Appropriately, Jerusalem became for Jews the symbol of an idealized mother who gave solace and comfort to her children if they returned from exile. Yet post-Temple Judaism did not require a monumental presence in the city until the nineteenth century.[3]

Disputing the Meanings of Stones

This paper explores how the city of Jerusalem, shared by three religions coexisting in the same space over many centuries, eventually found that its religious sites were literally petrified—defined by holy stones. What religious ideology lies behind each of Jerusalem's competing narratives of sacredness and turns its sacred places into sites of contention? Where does it come from, this desire to make the imaginary real, to turn the spiritual map of the city into a legible terrain? Can a city's topological forms and architectural expressions be a shared ground for open-ended reverie and inventive thinking, or are they inevitably reduced to static containers that freeze thought and erect barriers to common understanding? Frances Yates, in *The Art of Memory*, describes the practice of *memory work* as a mental stroll through the rooms of a house or the sites of a city, using the icons stored in this imaginary container as prompts to uncover associated ideas. This facilitates the repetition of previously stored material in an essentially static manner that, Yates argues, imprisons thought. While it cultivates the making of mental images for the mind to work on, it dwells on images stored in the past and focuses on recollection as *the* mental task.[4] In *The Craft of Thought*, however, Mary Carruthers disagrees with this static model and argues that the aim of any art of memory is not the mere recitation or reiteration of stored items but rather the aim is to provide a thinker with the means to invent new material on the spot. In other words, the art of memory is (for Carruthers) a device for discovering something new.[5] She agrees with Yates that architecture provides the major metaphor for memory locations, but insists that architecture is also a trope for invention, composition, and fabrication, not just for storage of material in a static container. She notes that the Latin word *inventio* provides the root for both *inventory* and *invention*. Having an inventory of stored images arranged in some order is essential for any inventive thinking; but these images may be associated with specific ideas in an open-ended way through analogy, transference, and metaphor, thus allowing for creative invention.[6]

Can we look at one city, Jerusalem, and examine how memory devices for inventive thinking have been constructed in this special site? All humans make patterns in order to know; they locate knowledge within and in relation to other things. The form of these patterns or networks is important, for they act as maps or

3 Oleg Grabar, "Space and Holiness in Medieval Jerusalem," *Jerusalem: Its Sanctity and Centrality to Judaism, Christianity and Islam*, ed. Lee I. Levine (New York: Continuum Books, 1999), 275–85.

4 Frances Yates, *The Art of Memory* (Chicago: Chicago University Press, 1966).

5 Mary Carruthers, *The Craft of Thought: Meditation, Rhetoric and The Making of Images* (Cambridge: Cambridge University Press, 1998).

6 Carruthers, 11.

diagrams that reveal how things are linked together. Thus a map (mental or other) becomes a machine for thinking, for storytelling—especially in first-millennial Jerusalem. The Christian pilgrim nun known as Egeria, who visited Jerusalem circa A.D. 381–384, described a mobile system of worship circulating through a network of holy sites that could vary in precise location even while marking the life, death, and resurrection of Jesus. Led by the bishop and displayed in public, this system expressed the idea that the Christian faith was a pilgrimage and a process and allowed Christians to worship for the first time in a truly public fashion. Taking the whole city into account, this form of worship defined an urban syntax and language to be expressed at different sites and at different times of the year. The city itself thus became a sacred space, its walls enclosing not only an inhabited area but an idea—Christianity.[7]

Yet the early Christians were wary of holy places. These were sites that pagans and Jews had adorned with special meaning, and Christians were cautious about worshiping at specific shrines made by man. From the beginning, Christianity was set in contention with Judaism, and this attitude reflected a polemical confrontation embedded in the city itself. If Moses had promised a Holy Land to the Jews, then Christ promised a holy "land" not of this earth but in a spiritual world. If Jerusalem was the religious and political center of Judaism, then the holy city of Christianity was the *heavenly* Jerusalem, an invisible place signifying redemption. If the visible Jerusalem lay in ruins, this was to Christians a proof that God had rejected the Jews. Belief in an immaterial heavenly city thus resisted the notion of holy places, and it was not until the fourth century, after the emperor Constantine created a Christian holy land and associated specific sites with the temporal process of storytelling, that sacred places emerged within Christianity. His great memorial churches soon generated a set of rituals associated with particular passages of the Bible. Story, text, liturgical practice, and site were woven together so that each site became a point of clarification intensified by rituals and linked to specific times of the liturgical calendar. Thus it was in Jerusalem that storytelling, ritual, and place were unified, giving rise to a new, place-bound piety. The history of the Passion and the remembrance of Christian martyrs became linked to a temporal calendar of feast days and a spatial map of sites. These in turn became part of a huge pilgrimage network.[8]

This place-bound piety was all the more amazing since the Jerusalem that Jesus knew had been obliterated by A.D. 135, when Roman troops under Hadrian quelled the last major Jewish revolt and left the city, including the site of the Second Temple in the northeast quadrant, in ruins (see Figure 1). Under Herod the Great (37–34 B.C.) Jerusalem had been one of the great showplaces of the Near East and the cosmopolitan center of the Jews. At its center was the Temple Mount, dominated by Herod's great Temple (built 19–18 B.C.), a quadrilateral platform with nine entrance gates. (It is no longer clear exactly where this and many other buildings were

7 John F. Baldovin, S.J., *The Urban Character of Christian Worship* (Rome: Pont. Institutum Studiorum Orientalium, 1987). Also Carruthers, 40–44.

8 Markus, 266

Figure 1
Hadrian's Jerusalem
and site of Temple Mount

located.) The Temple Mount became a site of Jewish pilgrimage, which had been an act of religious and social solidarity since Jews began living in Syria, Greece, Italy, Iraq, and Egypt in the late fourth century B.C. The rabbis said of the Temple: "He who has not seen the Temple of Herod has never seen a beautiful building."[9] Herod's Temple was looted and the city destroyed during the first Jewish revolt against Rome in A.D. 66–73. After the second Jewish revolt, in A.D. 132 and 135, the emperor Hadrian evacuated the Old City and its sacred center. Jews were henceforth forbidden to enter Jerusalem, and the gates of the city were closed to them for approximately five hundred years. As a punishment, the Temple was to lie in ruins, never to be rebuilt.[10]

What, then, was the significance of Jerusalem for Jews living in exile? Were Jews all citizens of Jerusalem, since it was the capital of Judea and the political and religious center of Judaism, and did they long to return to it from exile? Was the city the place where the Hebrew God was most present on earth, as compared, say, to Antioch or Alexandria? But if God had no need of a house to be built for him, what significance could the city of Jerusalem have?[11] Various texts give different answers. For example, the Bible and other ancient Jewish texts have always given precedence to the first Temple built by Solomon rather than to the City. The Temple is the place God chose for his name to dwell in and the place where the most central and most

9 F. E. Peters, *Jerusalem and Mecca: The Typology of the Holy City in the Near East* (New York: New York University Press, 1986), 34.

10 The Romans first captured Jerusalem in 63 B.C. and left nearly seven hundred years later, in A.D. 638. In 63 B.C. Jerusalem was the capital of a Jewish state with a population about two-thirds Jewish. Under Herod the Great (37–34 B.C.), Jerusalem was a showplace of the Near East.

11 Daniel R. Schwartz, "Temple or City: What Did Hellenistic Jews See in Jerusalem?" *The Centrality of Jerusalem*, ed. Marcel Poorthuis and Charra Safrai (Kampen, Netherlands: Kok Pharos Publishing House, 1996), 114–42.

M. Christine Boyer

legitimate cult can be performed. Jerusalem is simply the place where the Temple happens to be located; the city grew up around it. But Jews living in exile could not be limited to the idea that God only resided in a specific place and that his rites could only be performed in that specific site. Indeed, the prophet Isaiah had declared that God needs no Temple, for the heavens are his throne and the earth his footstool (Isaiah 66:1). It thus made no sense to attach sacredness to a specific memorial site. The temple or City of God is spiritual, not built of wood or stone.

But nonreligious Jewish literature locates Jerusalem as the central Jewish polis and the Temple as the city's cultic institution. While the preference may have been for a God that lived in the heavens, who was everywhere accessible and not just located in a building in a particular place, still Jews considered Jerusalem to be their mother city. The history of Jerusalem was the history of the Jews: of Adam, Abraham, Isaac, Jacob, Joseph, and David. Consequently, all Jews were, in a sense, citizens of Jerusalem. But with the Roman domination of the East, beginning with Judea in 63 B.C., Jews who identified themselves first as Jerusalemites and only secondarily as Roman citizens, regardless of where they lived, would inevitably meet with trouble. When Jews continued to revolt, the Romans destroyed their Jerusalem. As Jewish scripture reflects (III Maccabees), Jewish suffering was the price of the city's Jewishness; Jews in Jerusalem suffered on account of the Temple's presence.

But where and what was this revered Temple of Jerusalem? What little knowledge exists concerns only the Second Temple period brought to an end around A.D. 70 and is based on archaeological and textual evidence that is highly ambiguous and difficult to interpret. Rabbinic texts refer to a citadel, or *birah*, but what kind of place or building was it? There is a difference of opinion: some scholars refer to the *birah* as Solomon's Temple, while others claim that it is the citadel of the Temple Mount and includes the temple sanctuary and its fortifications.[12] To add to the confusion, it was long believed that the *birah* built by Nehemiah (Nehemiah 2:8, 7:2) was located to the north of the Temple Mount, at a site where Herod later located the fortress known as the Antonia. But this has been rejected by the archaeologist Benjamin Mazar, who claims the *birah* was built by Nehemiah on the Temple Mount itself and included in its fortifications the preexisting Second Temple complex (I Chronicles 28, 29).[13] In this view, the *birah* thus included both fortifications and the Temple complex. It was laid out in the form of a square, and traces of it can be observed in the present-day platform of the Temple Mount. Since Herod radically transformed the southern section of the Temple Mount in the course of building his royal basilica, whatever remains of the *birah* may exist probably lie in its northern section.

The Emperor Julian, reigning A.D. 361–363—forty years after Constantine—attempted to stop the rise of Christianity by proposing to rebuild the Temple in Jerusalem and return the city to the Jews. Julian hoped to accomplish three things by

12 Joshua Schwartz, "The Temple in Jerusalem," *The Centrality of Jerusalem*, 29–49.

13 The main evidence for the location of the Temple of Jerusalem comes from archaeological sources and literary texts, particularly excavations led by Mazar from 1968 to 1978 adjacent to the south retaining wall of the Temple Mount and in the enclosed area of the Haram al Sharif.

this act. First, he wanted to falsify Christ's prophecy that "there shall not be left one stone upon another, that will not be thrown down" (Mark 13:2). To rebuild the Temple would do this. Second, by legitimizing Judaism, Julian hoped to show that Christianity was illegitimate. Third, he wanted to restore sacrificial worship throughout the Roman empire and hoped to enlist the support of Jews in this reform. Jews had been banished from Jerusalem since A.D. 132 and only one synagogue still operated in the city during the fourth century. Yet Jews still considered Jerusalem to be their sacred city, and still came to mourn as a visible witness to the fall of the Temple and to anoint the "pierced stone" on the Temple Mount as a memory trace of where the Temple supposedly had stood.[14]

14 Martin Parmentier, "No Stone Upon Another? Reactions of Church Fathers Against the Emperor Julian's Attempt to Rebuild the Temple," *The Centrality of Jerusalem*, 143–59.

15 Yoram Tsafrir, "Byzantine Jerusalem: The Configuration of a Christian City," *Jerusalem: Its Sanctity and Centrality to Judaism*, Levine, 133–50.

16 Grabar, 275–85.

It was the Christians who first imposed a sacred map on the topography of Jerusalem, and they did this in contest with both the Roman and Jewish traditions. In A.D. 135, after the destruction of Jerusalem and the loss of Jewish dominance in the city, Hadrian built a typical military colony slightly to the west of the old town and renamed the city Aelia Capitolina.[15] Jerusalem became a more or less square walled city with fixed gates and a new *cardo maximus* (north-south alignment) and *decumanus* (east-west alignment), providing the axes of a conventional Roman grid of streets. Outside the town, on the supposed site of Christ's crucifixion and burial, the Romans placed a temple of Venus. On the site of the ruined Temple were placed two statues of Hadrian, leaving the pierced stone on the Temple Mount as the only sacred relic where Jews could worship, which they did once a year. The Romans erected a number of monuments to pagan gods and imperial victories, but there were no monuments to honor anything that had been holy in Jerusalem up to that time. The memory of sacred sites associated with Biblical figures such as Adam, Abraham, Moses, or Jesus was obliterated entirely.[16]

Beyond the southwest corner of the Roman colony was a spot the Christians called Zion, a name once given to the original Temple area. This may have been the only Christian center of worship in a house church at Jerusalem before Constantine began his work of transforming the Roman colony into a Christian city early in the fourth century. After his mother visited Jerusalem in 326 a.d., Constantine ordered the basilicas for worship and the shrines associated with the death, burial, and resurrection of Christ to be built as part of a conscious work of redesign. How were these sites selected and what did they mean?

Christian memory centers on the life of Jesus, especially his last days in Jerusalem, and thus the city was to remain a magnet for pilgrims throughout its centuries of travail. The oldest surviving account of a Christian pilgrimage to Jerusalem records a journey that took place in A.D. 333, shortly after Constantine had begun to transform Aelia Capitolina into a magnificent Christian city. The Bordeaux pilgrim was shown sites associated with events described in the Gospels, such as the newly discovered Sepulchre and the hill of Golgotha. For although the Gospels vary regarding the details of Jesus' life and death, they associate their stories with specific sites. The early Christians were unperturbed by the improbability that the sites and objects associated with particular sacred events were authentic; the importance of those sites and objects seems to have lain in the memory work they enhanced.[17] They were used both to evoke stories known to pilgrims from the Bible and as prompts to meditation on the meaning of these events. Sacred sites were embedded in communal processions outlining a structural network linking site to site and were accompanied by appropriate readings and correlated with specific times. They constructed a mental or spiritual map of Jerusalem. The processional path was a way for the pilgrim to move through the narratives of the Bible, a process in which physical activity mirrored the communal project of remembering.

More militant observations were also made about the purpose of these sacred stones. For example, Eusebius, biographer of Constantine, remarked in A.D. 340 that the new Jerusalem built on the site of the Holy Sepulchre towered over the ancient city and was directly opposed to the polluted city where Christ had been slain. On the very site of Christ's suffering and death, Eusebius noted, the emperor erected a symbolic trophy that gave witness to the Savior's victory over death and offered visible proof that Christianity had triumphed over Judaism.[18]

When events are fresh in one's mind, there is no need to create an image of them. Only with the passage of time would the events of Jesus' traumatic last days in Jerusalem, the Passion, become the central focus of the Christian tradition. In the enlarged Christian community, which could not have known Jesus directly, devotees began to retell the story of his earthly life as a preparatory series of events culminating in his crucifixion. As Christians were dispersed and Jerusalem destroyed and left in ruins from A.D. 70 to 132, later to be reconstructed as a pagan city by Emperor Hadrian, these events were located in physical space. Gethsemane, the Holy Sepulchre, the Mount of Olives, the Cenacle of the Last Supper, and the site of the Transfiguration, among other locations, became the physical markers of Christian faith, located in space and time in the Roman city of Aelia. These were thought to be the places where Jesus had been tried, crucified, buried, and resurrected, and where he had appeared to his disciples. Did contact with these places refresh and revitalize memories heretofore passed down orally but now needing markers of stone that would act as prompts to recollection? Was it because early Christians were attacked and persecuted, being marginal to both Jewish and Roman society, that they strove to locate where their faith had its earliest beginnings? Unverifiable in a factual sense, these sacred places nevertheless gave emergent Christianity a world of images or icons around which to structure its system of belief. This did not go unnoticed by the emperors between Hadrian and Constantine—a period of roughly 180 years—who tried repeatedly to erase these sites of memory. But they could not eradicate all the sacred stones nor erase the names associated with the places. These remained the

17 The following account of the collective memory of Jerusalem is taken from Maurice Halbwachs, "The Legendary Topography of the Gospels in the Holy Land," *On Collective Memory*, ed. Lewis Coser (Chicago: University of Chicago Press, 1992), 103–235. As for the Bordeaux pilgrim, she or he was shown the Temple Mount, the altar before which the priest Zacharias was murdered (Matthew 23:35), the sycamore tree from which Zacchaeus watched Jesus (Luke 19:4), and the palms whose branches were strewn before Jesus (Matthew 21:8); Carruthers, 42.

18 Eusebius of Caesarea, quoted in Joshua Prawer, "Christian Attitudes towards Jerusalem in the Early Middle Ages," *The History of Jerusalem, Early Muslim Period: 638–1099*, ed. Joshua Prawer and Haggai Ben Shammai (New York: New York University Press, 1996), 311–47.

material frame, the topography of places, that anchored Christian interests and rituals.

It was Constantine who built atop these memory markers and erected a place-bound piety on top of the old city of Jerusalem, interacting with the Roman city Aelia in an interesting manner. The Council of Nicea met under Constantine's protection in 325 and formulated the famous creed:

> I believe in one God . . . and in one Lord Jesus Christ . . . Who for us men and for our salvation came down from heaven, And was incarnate by the Holy Ghost of the Virgin Mary, and was made man. . . . He suffered death and was buried: And on the third day he rose again . . . And he shall come again, with glory, to judge both the quick and the dead.[19]

19 Quoted in Halbwachs, 228–29.

This creed selected the Passion (and, implicitly, its location in Jerusalem) as the central focus of all Christianity. But the sites of the events in the sacred story were unknown or buried under rubble; they needed to be dug up and reinvented. For example, the Tomb of Christ had to be located at a specific site and then transformed into a magnet for pilgrims. Makarios, the bishop of Jerusalem, who was present at the Council of Nicea, sought permission from the emperor to destroy Hadrian's Temple of Venus in the northeast corner of the city in order to search for the location of such a tomb. As legend has it, in 325–326 he discovered a Jewish tomb dating from the Second Temple period, hollowed out of a rock or cave, and was absolutely certain that this was the site of Jesus' burial. Even though the Gospels implied that the Crucifixion and burial took place outside the city walls of Jerusalem, and Jewish law explicitly forbade a Jew to be buried within the city walls, it was commonly assumed that these events had taken place in the middle of the city, on a wide road just like the cardo maximus, or in the middle of some other open space, like the forum of Aelia Capitolina. Although there was no proof that Makarios had discovered the tomb of Christ and in spite of the fact that even Constantine (as reported by his biographer Eusebius) acknowledged that the sites and relics of Christ's Passion had remained unknown for many years, Constantine selected Hadrian's forum as the major building site for his New Jerusalem.[20] Since authenticity was not an issue, and because he was bent on imposing a new sacred structure or meaning on the map of Jerusalem, he erected an Edicule ("little house") to enclose Makarios' rock and around this now-sacred site built the Basilica of Constantine, today called the Church of the Holy Sepulchre. Modern scholarship, however, states that Constantine's decision to center his ambitious building program on Hadrian's forum actually predated the discovery of a tomb on that spot, and that the tomb was discovered during the leveling of the site. This site in the center of Jerusalem became the focal point for all Christianity. By building on the location of Hadrian's forum and, even more important, the Temple of Venus (after the ground had been subjected to elaborate rituals

20 Annabel Jane Wharton, *Refiguring the Post Classical City* (Cambridge: Cambridge University Press, 1994), 91; Martin Biddle, "The Tomb of Christ: Sources, Methods and a New Approach," *Churches Built in Ancient Times: Recent Studies in Early Christian Archaeology*, ed. Kenneth Painter (London: Society of Antiquaries of London/Accordia Research Center, University of London, 1994), 73–148.

of purification), Constantine not only expressed the triumph of Christianity over paganism but affirmed a Roman rather than Jewish foundation of Jerusalem—and his own imperial authority over it.[21] Twenty-five years later the complex reached its full extension, including a chapel on the spot identified as Golgotha and a great rotunda dedicated to the Resurrection. By the end of the fourth century this complex had become the greatest of all martyria and the center of Christian pilgrimage. It shifted attention away from the original sacred center of Christianity, Mount Zion. By the seventh and eighth centuries, the middle of the cross atrium of Golgotha was considered to be the omphalos (navel) of the earth—the center of the world.

21 Biddle, 95–96.

Constantine selected other sites, such as the Zion complex, to commemorate the life of Christ, but left the Temple Mount in ruins even though it was supposed to have been the site of significant events in the life of Christ such as the location of one of the temptations (Matthew 4:5; Luke 4:9). At the place called Zion, Constantine built a large rectangular basilica to replace an earlier house church. From the fifth century on, this area was thought to have been the site of the Last Supper and was thus connected to the institution of the Eucharist. The Mount of Olives was thought to be the place from which Jesus prophesied the fall of Jerusalem, where he was betrayed by Judas Iscariot in the Garden of Gethsemane, and from which he ascended into heaven. Constantine erected another basilica called *Eleona* (olives) here and set a huge cross atop the mountain's summit. At the traditional location of the garden of Gethsemane, near the foot of the mountain, another large church was built to enshrine the rock of Jesus' agony.

However, all of this building activity marking Jerusalem as a Christian city came to an abrupt end in 614, when the city was destroyed by a Persian invasion. Other blows were struck when the city fell to the Arabs in 638 and was rocked by an earthquake in 746.[22] Before Constantine solidified the sacred sites in stone, holy places in Jerusalem often changed their positions (see Figure 2). For example, the Cenacle of the Last Supper had several sites: it was located on the Mount of Olives but simultaneously took place at Gethsemane or at the Grotto of Jesus' teachings. It was later moved to the upper part of the city, on the Christian hill of Zion. When new city walls were built they enclosed the supposed site of Golgotha (in the northwest of the Old City, where the Crucifixion took place and where the Holy Sepulchre would be located), while the southern quarter, where the Cenacle finally was located, remained outside the walls. This may explain why the district of the Holy Sepulchre, previously outside the city, became the center of Constantine's reconstructed Jerusalem. These constant changes may have challenged the faith of Christians living in Jerusalem, but for Christians residing outside of Jerusalem the symbolic framework became ever stronger as the actual sites were reduced to rubble and even disappeared without trace (see Figure 3, the Madaba Map).

22 Baldovin, 45–55.

Figure 2
Sites of Constantine's
monuments.

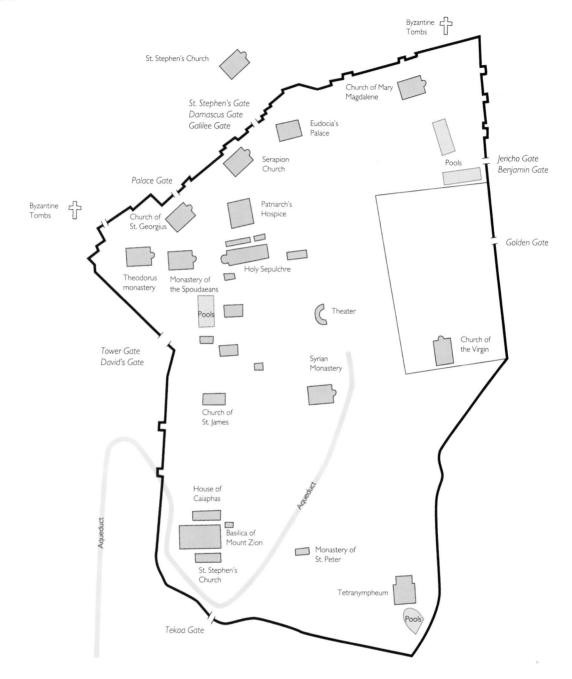

Byzantine
Tombs

St. Stephen's Church

Church of Mary
Magdalene

St. Stephen's Gate
Damascus Gate
Galilee Gate

Eudocia's
Palace

Jericho Gate
Benjamin Gate

Palace Gate

Serapion
Church

Pools

Byzantine
Tombs

Church of
St. Georgius

Patriarch's
Hospice

Golden Gate

Theodorus
monastery

Monastery of
the Spoudaeans

Holy Sepulchre

Pools

Theater

Church of
the Virgin

Tower Gate
David's Gate

Syrian
Monastery

Church of
St. James

Aqueduct

House of
Caiaphas

Aqueduct

Basilica of
Mount Zion

Monastery of
St. Peter

St. Stephen's
Church

Tetranympheum

Pools

Tekoa Gate

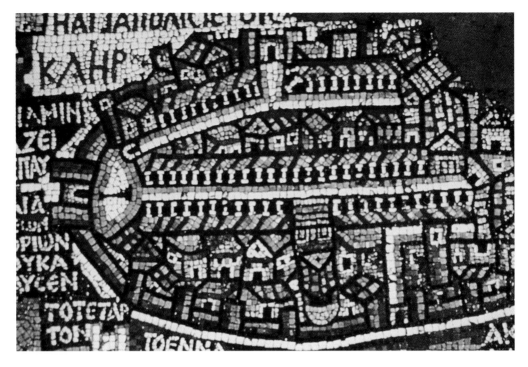

Figure 3
Madaba Mosaic of Jerusalem depicts the city surrounded by walls in an oval shape. It is a bird's-eye view seen from outside the city and looking from west to east. It shows the remains of the cardo; the two buildings connected to it are the Holy Sepulchre and the Nea. Justinian extended the cardo to the southern end of the city, enabling processions to take place along the long passage between the two churches. The Holy Sepulchre lies in the exact center of the oval city. This mosaic of Jerusalem is part of a larger map of the Holy Land uncovered in a small Byzantine church in the city of Madaba east of the Jordan River in 1884. On this extended map, Jerusalem lies in the exact center. The mosaic reiterates that the omphalos of Christianity lies in the Holy Sepulchre, not the Temple Mount. The latter is in fact absent from this depiction of Jerusalem.

As long as there were multiple Christian subgroups—including recently converted Jews, Gentiles, Greeks, and Latins—to whom various sacred sites were relevant, all locations were retained. Collective memory is not concerned with the mere factuality of history. Instead, sites of memory are linked to rites of commemoration and adoration, to feasts and processions. Since Jerusalem's sacred sites were clustered together intentionally, during the processions of Holy Week believers came together as a group unified in a single act of adoration. Each processional event supplied a narrative unfolding, a linear sequence of sites to be visited, a set of stories to be retold. And all these stories or memories held a logical place in the Christian dogma, which rose above them and drew them together into a system of beliefs. To enumerate the stories, to travel the road from site to site, was an act of faith, of remembrance.

The city of Jerusalem that provided the spatial framework for the arrest, judgment, crucifixion, and resurrection of Christ was already filled with places of memory associated with Jewish history as told in what Christians call the Old Testament. Maurice Halbwachs, in his work on collective memory, believes there was an attempt to make Christian stories more believable by associating them with consecrated places in Jewish history. In grafting the new onto the old, Christian ideology gained more structure and strength; now the events of the New Testament appeared to have been prefigured in the Old. At the same time, Christians had to find sites that would underline Christianity's differences from Judaism. This was accomplished by looking to symbols and rites that contemporary Jews had neglected, thus using the history of Judaism for support yet suggesting that Christians were guardians of memories that had been lost; Christians were renewing these neglected traditions, relocating them, even rewriting them. Thus parallels were drawn, but additions, transpositions, new combinations, and unexpected oppositions were also evolved so that Christianity could be both the same as and different from Judaism. For example, the Gospels recount that on the Mount of Olives, during the days before the Passion, Jesus, isolated and alone, looked down upon the Temple where once he had debated with his teachers. In time the Mount of Olives would be covered with Christian sanctuaries, a site that held no Jewish traditions yet was clearly linked with sites that did.[23]

Over time, more shrines, churches, and monasteries would dot the topography of Jerusalem, marking the locations of holy places. But eventually war and destruction would erase this set of memory containers. Jerusalem was destroyed by the Persians in 614 and taken by the Muslims in 638. The Romans surrendered the city, and the Christians began to lead a precarious life, many even evacuating it. Shortly afterward, the Muslims, as will be discussed below in greater detail, built upon the Temple Mount or Haram al Sharif as their holy site. In 1009, Al Hakim ordered that the Church of the Holy Sepulchre be leveled and the Christians persecuted. Within five years, however, these orders were modified and aid was given to help the Christians rebuild their church, which was completed and redecorated by 1047. Nine years later, however, the church was once again looted and closed to worship. It is during this period that the first pious settlements, or *waqfs,* were located near the walls of the Aqsa Mosque on the Temple Mount for the use of Muslims coming to Jerusalem to worship. Finally, in 1063, in a gesture of tolerance, the Christian quarter or Quarter of the Patriarch was created, a quadrilateral standing between the Tower of David (at the northwestern corner) and the eastern gate of St. Stephen (see Figure 4). A treaty allowed Christians the right to live in this quarter on condition that they maintain a section of the ramparts of the city. In this square, from which all Muslims were excluded, stood all the most holy places of Christianity, and here the Christians enclosed themselves within a bounded terrain where all their sacred memories were sheltered.[24]

23 There are many stories told of Jesus, isolated and alone, looking down from the Mount of Olives upon the Temple, where he had discussed with teachers, participated in Jewish festivals, and expelled those who sullied its sanctuary. He was thus both attached to Jewish traditions yet distinct, cut off from its community. And here was where he would offer instruction to his disciplines. Theodosius said of Calvary, "There Abraham offered his son as a sacrifice; he built a stone altar at the foot of the mountain, which is itself made of stone, where Christ was crucified (this was also attested by Anthony and Adamnanus)." Mariti recalls that a chapel near Calvary was dedicated to Adam. Peter the Deacon locates the center of the world, the *medietas orbis,* behind the Church of the Resurrection, citing the prophet who proclaimed: "The Lord has said: I have placed Jerusalem in the middle of the nations." (Ezekiel 5:5) Halbwachs, 216–17.

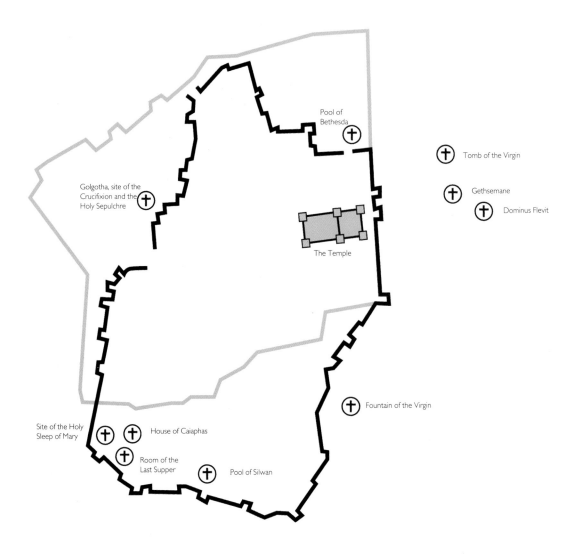

Pool of
Bethesda

Tomb of the Virgin

Golgotha, site of the
Crucifixion and the
Holy Sepulchre

Gethsemane

Dominus Flevit

The Temple

Fountain of the Virgin

Site of the Holy
Sleep of Mary

House of Caiaphas

Room of the
Last Supper

Pool of Silwan

Figure 4
Sites of the Christian
quarter circa eleventh
century.

24 Yvonne Friedman, "The City of the King of Kings: Jerusalem in the Crusader Period," *The Centrality of Jerusalem*, 190–216; Mustafa A. Hiyari, "Crusader Jerusalem 1099–1187 A.D.," *Jerusalem in History 3,000 B.C. to the Present* Day, ed. Kamil J. Asali (London: Keagan Paul International, 1989), 130–76.

25 Friedman, 191–92.

26 Joshua Prawer, "Christian Attitudes towards Jerusalem in the Early Middle Ages," *The History of Jerusalem*, ed. Joshua Prawer and Haggai Ben Shammai (New York: New York University Press, 1989), 311–47.

27 A number of these new churches lay in the area of the Jewish Quarter: St. Mary of the Germans, the Church of St. Thomas Alemannorum, and the Armenian Church of St. Stephen. Remains of these churches have been found recently. Dan Bahat, "Recently Discovered Crusader Churches in Jerusalem," *Ancient Churches Revealed*, ed. Yoram Tsafrir (Jerusalem: Israel Exploration Society, 1993), 123–27.

Jerusalem was the holy city for Christians and a site of pilgrimage, yet the physical city could not be compared to the eternal city of New Jerusalem. Not, that is, until a new concept of Jerusalem began to emerge during the armed expeditions or pilgrimages to Jerusalem called the Crusades, a concept blending into one the heavenly and earthly city. Jerusalem was the Crusaders' goal, for if Muslims held the earthly city in captivity, this signified spiritual captivity as well. Jerusalem must therefore be reconquered.[25] Following the reported call of Pope Urban II in 1095 to fight for "the cross, the blood, and the Sepulchre," Crusaders believed that earthly Jerusalem must be liberated from the yoke of the infidel and returned to the Christians, its rightful owners. Jerusalem, as the earthly home of the Lord, was the inheritance of all Christians and must be redeemed.

The ideology of the Crusades gave rise to a new holy geography of Jerusalem. The Temple Mount gained importance, offering a new symbol for the Crusaders, who believed they were purifying the temple of the Lord. Now the Old Testament became a prefiguration of the New and the Temple Mount, ignored by early Christians but held holy by the Muslims, became a new focal point as the site of the sacrifice of Isaac and the location of Jacob's dream. This citadel had been the administrative and military center of the Old Testament kings of Jerusalem—or so it was ardently believed—and it was from here that the Crusaders would rule in the name of Christianity. The Tower of David was a prize to be fought over, called by Godfrey of Bouillon "the citadel of David, the head of the entire Jewish kingdom" (see Figure 5).[26]

Jerusalem was taken by the Crusaders on July 15, 1099, after forty days of siege. The Frankish conquerors entered Jerusalem triumphant, with trumpets blaring, and massacred an estimated 60,000–70,000 Muslims, including 10,000 who took shelter on the Temple Mount, or Haram al Sharif, hoping to be spared (as was the custom). All around the Crusaders Jerusalem lay in ruins, but with the entire power of Christendom behind them they did not hesitate to reconstruct the holy places. Since Jerusalem was emptied of all its inhabitants, the Franks took over its houses by right of possession. There was thus no need to build housing, but rebuilding churches was of prime importance, even if their sites were of doubtful significance.[27] The Franks were secure in their belief that they were reawakening traditions that the local Christians had not known or had forgotten.

Some of the churches the Crusaders erected were enlargements of half-ruined structures or were reconstructions. Others were erected in new locations based on apocryphal writings and on legends that had circulated in Christian lands. A new system of holy sites thus arose based on an image of Jerusalem kept alive for centuries by Christian belief throughout far-flung areas. Totally new forms of sacred site were invented, such as the Via Dolorosa, which was based on the idea of the stations of the cross, and the *imitatio Christi*, which involved a walk in the footsteps of Christ in which the pilgrim vicariously experienced Christ's torture and death. Mystery plays from the Middle Ages, mystical meditations on the cross, and the religious iconography of cathedrals were some of the stories and symbols that pilgrims now wanted to locate in Jerusalem.

The Muslims regained control over the city after eighty-eight years of Frankish rule, and Christians were once again strangers in the city. Pilgrimage to Jerusalem acquired a new, penitential focus and attention slowly shifted back to the Holy Sepulchre. Jerusalem became for Christians a city of pardons and indulgences.[28]

Consequently, there are two periods of reconstruction during which the collective memory of Christianity sought to locate the traces of spatial sites where the icons of its religious dogma were stored: that of Constantine and that of the Crusaders. At both moments, the local topography was marked not only on the basis of local memory traces but by new sites that came from a broader notion of the holy sites of Christianity as supported by writings, descriptions, and legends originating outside of Jerusalem. These sources, though nonlocal, nevertheless gained authority from being shared by many groups over a wide terrain. Over time, with war, invasions, and occupations, the structure of the resulting memory system was damaged; gaps and confusions arose. By the end of the thirteenth century, the Christian presence in the Holy Land was greatly diminished and only a few Franciscan monks, a few Arabs converted as Orthodox Christians, and a predominately Greek clergy resided in Jerusalem.[29] Under Muslim occupation many of the rites and customs that held the Christian memory system in place had to be abandoned. Both periods of reconstruction witnessed inventive attempts to locate former holy sites and mark them with stones, giving contemporaneous belief systems a new structure; neither seemed particularly concerned with the issue of authenticity.

Jerusalem is a site of pilgrimage for Muslims as well, for it contains a *haram* (holy ground or noble sanctuary) important to Islam. Pilgrimage, or *hajj*, long precedes Islam and was incorporated into the Muslim religion. The *hajj* is an act of worship, a ritual obligation, involving a visit to a grave site. This impulse includes the architectural embellishment of that site, usually a small chapel with a dome.[30]

The prophet Muhammad, who founded Islam, was aware of the sacred status of Jerusalem for Jews and Christians, and is said to have turned toward it to pray until he was instructed by God to turn toward Mecca. Jerusalem was thus holy for Muslims, who, following the Koran, associated the Temple Mount with the nocturnal journey of Muhammad from the Holy Mosque in Mecca to the mosque in Jerusalem. On his journey to Jerusalem Muhammad was escorted by the angel Jibril on the back of the celestial steed al Buraq, which he tethered to a spot on the western wall of the Temple Mount. It was here that the al Buraq Mosque was built after 638, first activating the sacred aura of the Temple Mount or Haram al Sharif. From a rock, over which the shining golden Dome of the Rock would later rise, the Prophet was

28 Jerusalem was sacked again in 1187, yet Christians remained and pilgrims returned after the armistice of 1192. The final defeat of the Crusaders took place in 1244, and Muslim rule returned to Jerusalem. After 1517, under the rule of the Ottoman Turks, a new period of building began which lasted until the end of the sixteenth century. The walls were rebuilt using many stones from the ruins of ancient Christian churches. Following existing outlines, the new walls left the Cenacle outside. Legend says that Sulaiman had the architect executed for neglecting to include Mount Zion within the walls.

29 Grabar, 3.

30 F. E. Peters, *Jerusalem and Mecca: The Typology of the Holy City in the Near East* (New York: New York University Press, 1986).

Memories of Contention

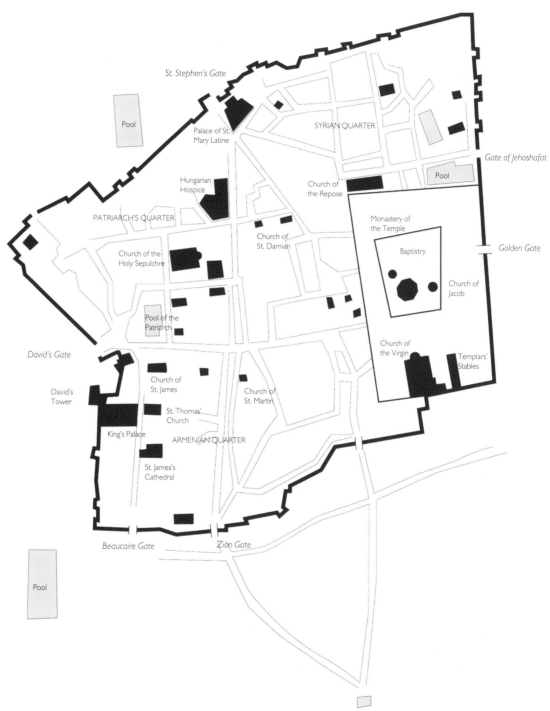

Figure 5
Crusaders' map of
Jerusalem marking their
important sites (map of
Cambri).

St. Stephen's Gate

Pool

SYRIAN QUARTER

Palace of St.
Mary Latine

Gate of Jehoshafat

Hungarian
Hospice

Pool

Church of
the Repose

PATRIARCH'S QUARTER

Monastery of
the Temple

Baptistry

Church of
St. Damian

Church of the
Holy Sepulchre

Golden Gate

Church of
Jacob

Pool of the
Patriarch

Church of
the Virgin

David's Gate

Templars'
Stables

David's
Tower

Church of
St. James

Church of
St. Martin

St. Thomas'
Church

King's Palace

ARMENIAN QUARTER

St. James's
Cathedral

Beaucaire Gate

Zion Gate

Pool

believed to have ascended to Heaven by means of a celestial ladder. Two other symbolic spots mark Muhammad's nocturnal journey: the entrance or gate to the Haram, which became known as Bab Muhammad or Bab al Buraq, and the route that Muhammad traced to the holy enclosure. Themes of mystical resurrection and eternal life were already associated with sites in Jerusalem, but now they took on Muslim connotations.

In Jerusalem, Muslim religious, charitable, and educational foundations known as *waqfs* gathered around the sites associated with the nocturnal journey of Muhammad.[31] The Arabic term *waqf* refers to a pious foundation and means literally "prevention" or "restraint." Since Islamic law protects all property belonging to a pious foundation from being alienated, it safeguards in perpetuity the use of such a site for purposes pleasing to God. Such purposes would be the building of mosques, schools, and hospitals; or the maintenance of scholars; and assistance to the poor. Thus these benefits are permanent and irrevocable for all time.[32]

The Moroccan quarter, where two charitable foundations were located in the mid-fourteenth century to the west of the wall where Muhammad tethered his horse, would become a space debated by Jews and Arabs. A small section of this wall is also associated by Jewish tradition with the last temple. The six lowest courses of drafted stones of the western wall of the Haram are believed to be remnants of Herod's Temple, destroyed by the Romans five centuries before the Arab conquest. Above this are three courses of undrafted stone, probably Roman work, and on top of this an upper stratum of stones that date from Sultan Sulaiman the Magnificent, who repaired and rebuilt the city walls in 1539–1541 (see Figure 6).[33]

The Muslims defeated the rulers of Palestine in 636, took control of Jerusalem by A.D. 638 (A.H. or *anno Hegirae* 17), and remained in the city for five hundred years, until the Crusaders' invasion in 1099. An agreement in the form of a long letter to the inhabitants of Jerusalem was made between the Muslim conqueror, Umar, and Sophronius, the Orthodox Patriarch of Jerusalem, granting all Christian inhabitants of Iliya (one of the Arabs' names for Jerusalem) not only safety for their lives, possessions, churches, and crosses but religious tolerance, allowance to practice their religion and other activities without being molested or restrained in any way. Jews, however, were forbidden to live in Iliya, and as an incentive for Christians to move as well they were offered safe conduct for their persons and property until reaching their new destinations. It is said that Sophronius took Umar on a tour of the city, showing him the ecclesiastical beauties of the Holy Sepulchre and hoping to convince him to accept Christianity. As legend has it, when the hour of prayer arrived Umar refused to pray at this Christian holy site but instead moved outside its gates to the east. This act allowed the Holy Sepulchre to remain under Christian control, for on the supposed site of Umar's prayer the Mosque of Umar was built in 935.

31 Tibawi, *The Islamic Pious Foundations in Jerusalem* (London: The Islamic Cultural Centre, 1978).

32 Tibawi, 11.

33 Tibawi, 19–20.

Figure 6
Map of important holy
sites in Jerusalem during
reign of Sulaiman.

Gate of the Flowers
Herod's Gate

Gate of the Column
Damascus Gate

MUSLIM QUARTER

Church of the
Flagellation

Gate of the Tribe
Lion's Gate

Church of
St. Saviour

CHRISTIAN QUARTER

Coptic Khan

Palace of St.
May Latine

Mituab Daoud Gate
Jaffa Gate

JEWISH QUARTER

The Hurva Synagogue

ARMENIAN QUARTER

Four Jewish
Synagogues

Gates of the Moors Quarter
Dung Gate

E-Tiah Gate
Zion Gate

Figure 7
The Wailing Place of the Jews. Photo by James Robertson and Felix Beato, 1857.

Thus, in an atmosphere of tolerance, Christian and Muslim areas became distinct. The Christians retained their churches and were relieved that Jews were prohibited from restoring the site of the Temple, while Muslims took over the huge area of the Temple Mount, which they felt legitimated their rule over Jerusalem, eventually transforming the platform into Haram al Sharif, the "noble sanctuary" of Muslim belief. In its center was the Dome of the Rock and to the south the al Aqsa Mosque, originally built by Walid in 705. Its site is believed to be the destination of Muhammad's nocturnal journey and is endowed with special sanctity. Furthermore, beneath the mosque lies the Gate of the Prophet, the route by which Muhammad entered the Temple Mount. This too is a sacred place.[34] Except for 150 years of Crusader presence, Jerusalem remained under the control of Muslims until 1917 and the treaties that ended World War I.

Although it is difficult to determine what changes were made to Jerusalem during the Muslims' rule, since most evidence comes from Christian pilgrims and is highly biased, it is certain that the Muslims did begin to transform the city into a masterpiece of medieval Islamic urbanism.[35] Their first effort was to resanctify the area of the Herodian Temple. Umar is said to have constructed a modest mosque on the Temple Mount. Arculf, a Gallic bishop who visited the Holy Land around 697, described it as a primitive, poorly built, square-shaped wooden structure erected atop the remnants of previous buildings. This modest form reflected early Muslim belief that the day of final judgment was fast approaching, hence there was no need for extravagant structures that would soon be destroyed. According to Muslim tradition, Umar was advised to locate the mosque to the north of the rock that was so important to the Jews, thus enabling Muslims facing south to Mecca in prayer to overlook the rock as well, uniting Moses' and Muhammad's directions of prayer. Umar rejected the advice, but a few years later (in 688) the elaborate Dome of the Rock was erected on the Temple Mount by Abd al Malik. Here the essential Muslim memories of Muhammad's nocturnal journey and ascension were petrified or set in stone. Some scholars think the motive for building this elaborate structure was to diminish the importance of Mecca as a holy city and to create a religious center closer to Damascus. Others believe that the Dome of the Rock was built to rival the splendor of the Christian churches of Jerusalem. The records are not precise as to its purpose, although it is clearly a unique work of art, enhanced by a shiny golden dome and exterior mosaics and extraordinary interior decorative marble and mosaics. Yet it has been said that "from the moment that a Muslim mosque was erected in Jerusalem opposite to and in open competition with the Church of the Holy Sepulchre, it became evident that both rivals considered themselves to be branches of the very same tree whose roots, it was now difficult to deny, were firmly rooted [in Jerusalem]."[36]

When Saladin recovered Jerusalem in 1187 he found that the Crusaders had wiped out both the Muslim population and the small remaining number of Jewish

34 Dan Bahat, "The Physical Infrastructure," *The History of Jerusalem, Early Muslim Period*, 8–100; Myriam Rosen Ayalon, "Three Perspectives on Jerusalem: Jewish, Christian and Muslim Pilgrims in the Twelfth Century," *Jerusalem: Its Sanctity and Centrality to Judaism*, 326–45.

35 Grabar, 10–11.

36 S.D. Goitein, " On Jerusalem's Arabic Names," *Offering unto Judah*, ed. S. Assaf, Yu Even-Shmuel, and Rabbi Binyamin (Jerusalem, 1950), 82. Quoted by Moshe Gil, "The Political History of Jerusalem During the Early Muslim Period," *The History of Jerusalem: Early Muslim Period*, 6.

inhabitants. He soon repopulated the city with Muslims and Christian Arabs, welcomed returning Jews, and restored the Greek Orthodox Patriarchate (which the Crusaders had replaced with a Latin Patriarchate). Under Islamic tolerance, the Jewish practice of lamenting at the sacred stones of the western wall of the Haram, now known as the Wailing Wall, was allowed. At the entrance to the third holiest place in Islam, on the spot where the Prophet Muhammad tethered his horse, Jews were allowed to pray at a length of wall about thirty yards long and on a pavement about eleven feet wide—a site less than 120 yards square. Since this small site was cut off from the south and west by houses belonging to Moroccans under the protection of a holy *waqf*, the site was accessible only from the north through a narrow lane. This would eventually become a point of contention (see Figure 7).

In 1840 the Jews asked for more than allowance to pray at the wall. Although the number of Jews residing in Jerusalem at this time is not known, for they refused to be counted, it was believed that most were Sephardic Jews from Spain who had learned Arabic and become Ottoman subjects. Only a minority were Ashkenazi Jews, recent immigrants from Russia, Poland, and Austria who retained their foreign nationalities. It is this latter group who tried to exploit privileges afforded foreigners. They tried to circumvent the Muslim law of the land and acquire vested interest in the Wailing Place. A foreign Jew proposed to repave the area in front of the Wailing Place. At this time foreigners were barred from owning real estate anywhere in the Ottoman Empire, so the request, which might appear as a right of ownership, was rejected. In addition it was noted that Jews had never before repaired anything in this place and it was proclaimed, as a result of the inquiry, that the Jews at the Wailing Wall must lower their voices and visit according to the old custom which forbade them to profess their religious doctrines in public.

Most pious Jews who traveled to Jerusalem came to pray and to end their days, not to foment opposition. They lived in abject poverty, in crowded and unhygienic conditions, and were content with the customs that pertained to the Wailing Place. They knew the site was on Islamic property and part of Islam's pious foundation and that the requested pavement was part of the alley leading to the Moroccans' homes.

In 1911 another attempt was made to change the status quo of the Wailing Place. With the rise of Zionism, this site took on a more overtly political role. Stools, benches, and other articles were brought to the place (without the approval of authorities), and the custom of standing at the wall was extended to include a form of prayer that used the place as if it were a synagogue. These practices restricted entry to the Moroccans' district. The authorities feared that if these practices were allowed to continue, they might become the basis of more radical claims of ownership. Thus an official proclamation stated that Jews could not place anything suggestive of ownership on the ground or against the wall. The old customs must be preserved, and thus standing on the pavement was all that was allowed.

When General Sir Edmund Allenby entered Jerusalem as part of the British occupation of Palestine on December 11, 1917, he proclaimed:

I make known to you that every sacred building, monument, pious bequest, or customary place of prayer, of whatsoever form, of the three religions will be maintained and protected according to existing customs and beliefs of those to whose faith they are sacred.[37]

37 General Sir Edmund Allenby, Dec.ember 11, 1917. Quoted by Tibawi, 23.

Yet one week earlier, the Balfour declaration had assured a national home for the Jewish people, even while acknowledging that Palestine had already for centuries been the national home of Arab inhabitants. As a result of this decision, a new Zionist plan was unfurled to secure the Wailing Place (or Wall) for Jews. Chaim Weizmann, the commander of two Jewish battalions in the British army, demanded from Balfour the handing over of the Wailing Wall as "the only one [holy place] which is . . . left to us . . . our most sacred monument, in our most sacred city, [which] is in the hands of some Moghreb [sic] religious community."[38] Weizmann offered to buy the land in dispute but this was rejected by the Moroccan community. The Muslim community was alarmed and formed an organization for the protection of El Aqsa mosque. Although public demonstrations were not allowed, strong written protests from Muslims were registered requesting the enforcement of Allenby's status quo policy at all holy places. Chief Rabbi Kuk asked the British government to entrust the wall to the care and control of the representatives of Jewry, arguing that "the Wailing Wall was a possession of the Jews throughout the world."[39] This request was rejected and the claim upheld that the wall and adjacent land was on unalienable Islamic *waqf* property and that Jews had only the right of access for devotional exercise.

38 Chaim Weizmann. Quoted by Tibawi, 24.

39 Chief Rabbi Kuk. Quoted by Tibawi, 24.

Protests continued. Herbert Samuel, a Zionist, was appointed on July 1, 1920, to set up a civil government in Jerusalem. As Tibawi states:

The writing was plainly on the wall: a tiny Jewish minority of about eight per cent of the population was claiming, in the name of "the Jewish people" of the Balfour declaration and with the protection of British bayonets, not only political predominance over the Arab majority but possession of a part of the third holiest mosque in Islam.[40]

40 This quote and the following account are taken from Tibawi, 25, 28, 35.

The government in London tried to mediate these disputes. In September 1925 Jews were forbidden to bring seats, benches, or other obstacles to the Wailing Wall. Despite that ruling, by September 1928 they had erected a screen. After a British officer removed it, worldwide protests erupted, claiming that England was interfering with Jewish forms of worship.

Eventually there was bloodshed at the site. Once again the British Mandate proclaimed that the status quo concerning all religious sites must be maintained. An international commission led by Eliel Löfgren reached the following verdict in 1930: Muslims were the sole owners of the Western Wall, it being an integral part of the

Haram al Sharif area. Furthermore, the pavement in front of the wall and the adjacent Moroccan district belonged to the Muslims. Even though Jews were guaranteed access to the wall for purpose of religious devotion, they were subject to restraint.

While Jews made no further claims of ownership of the area, they proposed that properties occupied by the Moroccans be vacated and their homes rebuilt somewhere else, even though all the documents, title deeds, and legal briefs reiterated that this was forever-inalienable *waqf* land.

With the United Nations resolution of 1947 partitioning Palestine, Jerusalem was set aside as a demilitarized and neutralized city under an international regime, with a governor appointed by the UN—a corpus separatum. Once again there were provisions for guarding "existing rights" in holy places, including religious buildings and sacred sites. Yet a Jewish state of Israel was simultaneously declared and the Arab population displaced by violent means from the greater part of Palestine. The city of Jerusalem became a battleground between Arabs and Jews. After a ceasefire and truce were established, the Wailing Wall lay beyond reach of the Jews, under Arab control. After the war of 1967, however, Israel occupied the west bank of the River Jordan, the Sinai peninsula, the Golan Heights, and all of the Arab sector of Jerusalem, including the Old City. The minister of defense could then declare, at the very site of the Wailing Wall, that Jerusalem had been "liberated" and that Jews had returned to the Wailing Wall "never to part from it again." Israel began to erase the Arab and Islamic presence, demolishing the Moroccan quarter to the west of the walls of al Aqsa Mosque. Its 650 inhabitants, 135 dwellings, and two mosques were removed, making a sizable plaza to the west of the wall. This was the very property that the international commission in 1930 had confirmed as the inalienable property of Islamic pious foundations, protected by law. Unable either to buy this land or secure unrestricted access to these holy stones, the Zionists took them by force.

Locating the East on the Map of the West

Having located a number of sacred stones on the map of Jerusalem, we need to ask when the passion for authenticity emerged. When did these sites become literal markers of the exact spot where something actually happened? The question needs to be asked because, as we shall see, the cult of authenticity adds immensely to the belief that these sites are indeed sacred. As Adorno noted, the language of authenticity molds thought, hiding behind an authority assumed to be absolute. It is reminiscent of the decline of aura, that is, of words that are deemed sacred but no longer have sacred content.[41] New mechanisms of visualization would aid in extinguishing the aura of place and would lock place into a new constellation of meaning.

41 Theodor Adorno, *The Culture of Authenticity*, trans. Knut Tarnowski and Frederic Will (Evanston: Northwestern University Press, 1973), 5–10.

42 Naomi Shepherd, *The Zealous Intruders: The Western Rediscovery of Palestine* (San Francisco: Harper & Row, 1987).

43 Victor Hugo, *Les Orientales* (1829). Quoted by Nissan Perez, *Focus East: Early Photography in the Near East 1839–1899* (New York: Abrams, 1988), 17.

In the late eighteenth century the East, or Orient, took on a new importance on the map drawn by the West. When Napoleon led his troops to Acre in the spring of 1799, it was the first European campaign in the Holy Land since the Crusades. Little had been heard from the Holy Land in the interval, until it became for the West an almost unknown terrain with few reliable maps or guidebooks.[42]

Although Napoleon's campaign was disastrous, systematically destroying all that he surveyed, it did remind the West of the obscure and neglected East. When Victor Hugo wrote *Les Orientales* two decades later he noted in his introduction, "The whole continent is leaning toward the East."[43] And so it was, as Western travelers, photographers, the military, merchants, archaeologists, philologists, diplomats, and geographers focused intensely on the Orient throughout the nineteenth century. By the 1880s Europeans were concerned with the "Eastern question," a term applied to chaotic conditions within the Ottoman Empire and involving a large territory from the Sea of Marmora and the Dardanelles to the Holy Land and (after the opening of the Suez Canal in 1867) the sea routes to the Indian Ocean.

44 W. J. T. Mitchell, "The Panic of the Visual: A Conversation with Edward W. Said," *Boundary* 25.2 (1998), 11–33.

Edward Said has argued in *Orientalism* (1978) that "the Orient" is a construct of the European imagination, yet both geography and the visual arts are excluded from his account. Said excuses this omission by claiming that it is fundamental to Islamic culture and to his own childhood experience: there were no museums in Jerusalem or Cairo when he was a boy, thus his exposure to imagery was more architectural, abstract, and calligraphic than pictorial or representative.[44] Yet this deficit needs to be addressed in any account that envisions the East.

East and west have been directional locators since the beginning of time. This is natural, for the sun rises in the east and sets in the west. Yet the east-west distinction has been used to bifurcate the globe. While the West developed a core concept of own its geography, its concept of the East has shifted constantly. Western geographers appear to have followed the advice of one of the founding fathers of geopolitics, Halford Mackinder, who said in 1908 that one should take facts from the map of the world and "play with them":

> When you have got your myriad facts, registered by the labour of all the generations which have gradually built up the map of the world in its infinite detail, you have then got to play with them. You have to acquire such facility in this respect that you are able to see with the mind's eye, not the mere map of Italy with the boot at the end of it, but the blue sky, and the blue sea, and the brilliant sun. . . . You must be able to see this image, and then to prolong it by an effort of imagination beyond the horizon. Thus to be able to visualize is of the very essence of geographical power.[45]

45 H. Mackinder, *Geographical Philosophy* (1908). Quoted by Chris GoGwilt, "The Geographical Image: Imperialism, Anarchism, and the Hypothesis of Culture," *The Formation of Geopolitics, Modernism/Modernity* 5 (September 1998), 56.

To visualize, to prolong the image beyond the horizon, was a universalizing sense-making procedure that allowed Western thought to gaze upon the world from on high, to carve it up with borders, zones, and territories. As Mackinder noted:

Our aim must be to make our whole people think Imperially—think, that is to say, in spaces that are worldwide—and to this end our geographical teaching should be addressed. This is geographical capacity—the mind which flits easily over the globe, which thinks in terms of the map, which quickly clothes the map in meaning, which correctly and intuitively places the commercial, historical, or political drama on its stage.[46]

To cast the world as an exhibition to be clothed by imperial eyes inscribes geography as a mode of seeing. To see beyond the horizon and to think in images becomes a cartographic art, filling in the blank spaces of the world, enabling the West to play with those spaces as pieces on the gameboard of politics.

First, Europeans created a central, stable West from which all other places would be distanced. Look at maps of the world created before the fifteenth century and consider how the position of the West has shifted since then. The known world lay in the northern hemisphere, and most maps focused on the Mediterranean as the ancient center of the West. It was the accepted practice to orient maps toward the east, not the north. One depiction common in medieval times was the so-called O-T map, which divided the circular earth into three parts as they were repopulated after the Deluge by descendants of Noah's three sons, Shem, Ham, and Japheth (see Figure 8). Each of the three known continents was assigned to one of the sons: Europe lower left, Africa lower right, and Asia top. Jerusalem or Palestine was located at the center of the map, at the juncture where the Mediterranean and the Nile formed a T. (Hence O-T map: "O" for the map's overall shape, "T" for the mark at its center.) As Mackinder has explained, however, Columbus' discovery of America triggered a rearrangement of the globe: not only did the Age of Discovery call for more accurately measured maps and add a new continent to the globe, it shifted the focal point of the West from lands of antiquity to lands of the present on both sides of the northern Atlantic. This became the new vision of the West, with England its central focus.[47]

As for the East, or Orient, in ancient Greece this was confined to a region comprising the northwest corner of modern Turkey and extending eastward and southward to include the Levant. In the Middle Ages, "the East" would come to be identified with the Orthodox lands of the Byzantine and Russian churches, in contrast to Latin Christendom. Yet the Mediterranean still remained the focal point of the Western world and Jerusalem its cosmological center. Not until the Age of Discovery, when the new Atlantic-centered West arose, did the East begin its move to India and beyond to China. The former Orient became a buffer zone between the Far East and the core West. In Hegel's *Philosophy of History* (1820s) we already see the creation of this new liminal zone, not quite West yet not entirely East. Hegel called China and India the "far East" and Persia and Egypt the "hither East." He wrote:

46 Mackinder, *On the Necessity of Thorough Teaching in General Geography* (1890). Quoted by Gearoid, Tuathail, *Critical Geopolitics: The Politics of Writing Global Space* (Minneapolis: University of Minnesota Press, 1996), 87, 89.

47 The fascinating problem of our time, Mackinder points out, is "to see whether, utilizing our modern resources of communication, printing, traveling, telegraphy, and the rest of them, we cannot imbue our whole people with the new idea of the British Empire." Mackinder, *On Thinking Imperially* (1907). Quoted by Tuathail, 88.

Figure 8
The Three Sons of Noah.
From Jean Mansel's fifteenth-
century manuscript *La Fleur
des Histoires.*

The European who goes from Persia to India [will observe] a prodigious contrast. Whereas in the former country he finds himself still somewhat at home, and meets with European dispositions, human virtues and human passions, as soon as he crosses the Indus [river] . . . he encounters the most repellent characteristics, pervading every single feature of society.

With the Persian Empire we first enter on continuous History . . . while China and India remained stationary, and perpetuate a natural vegetative existence even to the present time.[48]

The term "Near East" emerged in the late nineteenth century to designate the lands of the Ottoman Empire, and excised from Europe any lands infected with "orientalism" or the Orthodox Church such as in Greece or the Balkans. However, the demise of the Ottoman Empire brought into common currency a new term, "Middle East," coined in 1902 by the military theorist Alfred Thayer Mahan in reference to the area surrounding the Persian Gulf, and it drew a strategic distinction between the Near East lands bordering the Mediterranean and the Far East that stretched all the way from India to Japan. Thus for a while the term "Near East" represented the "Orient" and was used by philologists, historians, and antiquarians, perhaps for no other reason than these disciplines considered the Near East to be the origin of the West before it had been corrupted by "orientalism."[49]

Having been under the rule of the Ottoman Empire since 1517, Palestine was a neglected province of Syria by the start of the nineteenth century and extremely poor. Ransacked by robbers, thwarted by exorbitant taxation, the local population and economy were depleted. By 1800, when London's population had reached one million and Tokyo's a million and a half, Jerusalem's was a mere 9,000. Even in the mid-nineteenth century, Jerusalem remained a small medieval city, closing its gates at sundown and opening them at sunrise. The population inside the city walls was estimated at 13,000 in 1840, including 5,000 Jews, 4,000 Muslims, and 2,750 Christians.[50] Moreover, the city resembled a necropolis: its walls were surrounded by cemeteries and its chief monuments were tombs. Jerusalem was no longer the city of associative memories that it once had been. In his popular 1843 travel account *Walks about the City and Environs of Jerusalem*, W. H. Bartlett noted:

> *If the traveler can forget that he is treading on the grave of a people from whom his religion has sprung, on the dust of her kings, prophets, and holy men, there is certainly no city in the world that he will sooner wish to leave than Jerusalem. Nothing can be more void of interest than her gloomy, half ruinous streets and poverty stricken bazaars.*[51]

To the eyes of the Christian West, however, Palestine was the exalted land of the Bible even if it did exist only as an idea or mental construct. Imaginary views of the

48 Hegel, *The Philosophy of History*, 173. Quoted by Martin W. Lewis and Kren E. Wigen, *The Myth of Continents: A Critique of Metageography* (Berkeley: University of California Press, 1997).

49 Once again, in 1932, there was a major reconceptualization when the Royal Air Force consolidated two separate commands, the Middle Eastern (headquartered in Iraq) and the Near Eastern (headquartered in Egypt), into the Middle Eastern Command. By the end of World War II, the Middle East extended from Libya to Afghanistan—lands that lie conceptually not close to the West but in the middle of the East, a non-European Other.

50 Kathleen Stewart Howe, *Revealing the Holy Land: The Photographic Exploration of Palestine* (Santa Barbara: Santa Barbara Museum of Art, 1997), 11.

51 W. H. Bartlett, *Walks about the City and Environs of Jerusalem* (1843). Quoted by Howe, 16, 18.

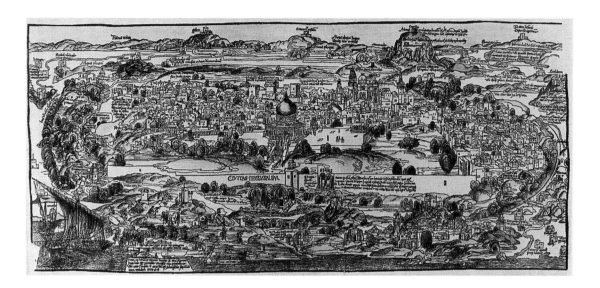

walled city of Jerusalem had appeared in the earliest illustrated books, such as the *Nuremberg Chronicle* (1493) and *Peregrinationes in Terram Sanctuam* (1486); illustrated maps would continue to be drawn and bird's-eye views imagined until contact with the city was reestablished in the eighteenth century. Since Jerusalem was under Ottoman Turkish rule from the sixteenth to the eighteenth centuries, few Christians actually visited it; yet this did not deter them from mapping the city. Some 250 to 300 maps of Jerusalem have survived from the mapmaking period following the advent of the printing press (ca.1450); there were religious maps that imagined Jerusalem at the time of Christ, and more realistic maps based on pilgrims' and travelers' accounts. These maps were often drawn as if looking down upon Jerusalem from the Mount of Olives and hence were oriented westward. The Church of the Holy Sepulchre, located in the center of the city, was depicted with its facade facing the viewer even though it actually was oriented to the south and could not be seen from the east. At the same time, the city itself was located in the Holy Land looking at it from the west. These three different orientations could be mapped simultaneously without any conflicts erupting over accurate geographical depiction or the authority of Biblical accounts (see Figure 9).[52]

Photography would bring new views and new problems, including a troubling stress on authentic and truthful depiction where before there had been mostly

Figure 9
Fifteenth-century depiction of Jerusalem seen from different perspectives. These maps often look down upon Jerusalem from the Mount of Olives and hence were oriented toward the west. The Church of the Holy Sepulchre, located in the center of the city, was depicted with its facade facing the viewer even though it actually was oriented to the south and could not be seen from the east. The city itself was located in the Holy Land as seen from the west. Apparently these three different orientations could be mapped simultaneously without any conflicts erupting over accurate geographical depiction or the authority of Biblical accounts.

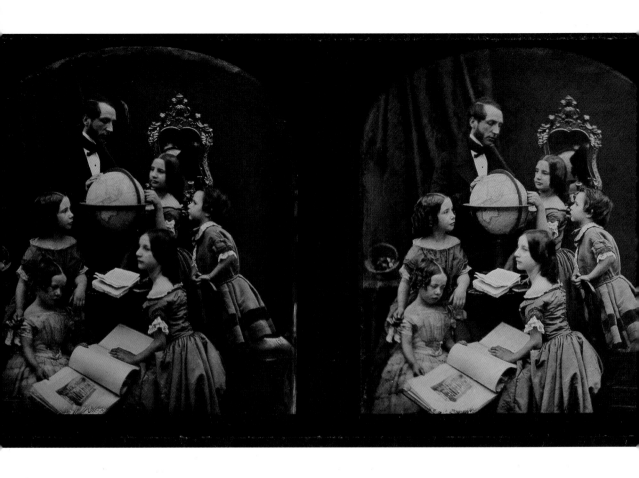

Figure 10
The Geography Lesson, a stereoscopic image taken by Antoine Françoise Jean Claudet in 1851. The book under examination was *Excursions Daguerriennes: Vues et Monuments les Plus Remarquables du Globe* (1841–42), the first book to be illustrated with daguerreotypes. It was published by the famous Parisian optician N. M. P. Lerebours.

invention and imagination. This stress would increase as Biblical scholars struggled against the Darwinian theory of evolution, which challenged certain Biblical narratives. Clergymen-scholars now assumed that by studying the monuments of the Holy Land they could authenticate the stories of the Bible; formerly, those monuments had inspired, rather than ratified, Christian memory. Such scholars also believed that by making a pilgrimage to see the sites in situ, they subsequently would be able to project images of these sites onto the imaginations of their parishioners. Thus it is not surprising that many early photographers of the Holy Land were clergymen. The Bible as their travel guide became a catalog of sites to be photographed.[53] But there were few ruins in Jerusalem considered at that time to be authentic remains from ancient times. What remains there were stemmed from the times of the Romans, Muslims, Byzantines, and Crusaders. One exception was the Wailing Wall, traditionally thought to have been part of Solomon's Temple. It became a major site to photograph. The contemporary cityscape of Jerusalem was another point of focus. In

52 Rehav Rubin, "Ideology and Landscape in Early Printed Maps of Jerusalem," *Ideology and Landscape in Historical Perspectives*, ed. Alan R. H. Baker and Gideon Bigger (Cambridge: Cambridge University Press, 1992), 15–30; Robin A. Butler, "Ideological Contexts and the Reconstruction of Biblical Landscapes in the Seventeenth and Early Eighteenth Centuries: Dr. Edward Wells and the Historical Geography of the Holy Land," 31–62.

53 James Turner Barclay, who photographed Jerusalem in the 1850s, was probably the first American to do so. He was assisted by the English photographer James Graham, who was employed by the London Jews' Society (LJS). This missionary group was supposed to focus on the plight of local Jewish populations, but by the 1890s the LJS had created one of the first (albeit nonprofessional) photojournalistic agencies. The largest American album of Holy Land photographs was published in 1863, entitled *Earthly Footsteps of the Man of Galilee and the Journeys of His Apostles*. Yeshayahu Nir, *The Bible and the Image: The History of Photography in the Holy Land 1839–1899* (Philadelphia: University of Pennsylvania Press, 1985).

54 Joan M. Schwartz, "The Geography Lesson: Photographs and the Construction of Imaginative Geographies," *Journal of Historical Geography* 22.1 (1996), 16–45.

55 Antoine Claudet (1860). Quoted by Thomas L. Hankins and Robert J. Silverman, *Instruments and the Imagination* (Princeton, N.J.: Princeton University Press, 1995), 175.

56 "Stereoscopic Journeys", *London Literary Journal* (1857). Quoted by Hankins and Silverman, 175.

general, photographers captured the major sites of sacred Jerusalem: the Church of the Holy Sepulchre, the Via Dolorosa, the Mount of Olives, the Tomb of the Kings, the Valley of Jehoshaphat.

The mania for photographing the Holy Land began as soon as the daguerreotype was invented in 1839. This period of early excitement was captured by the London photographer Antoine Françoise Jean Claudet in an 1851 stereoscopic image called *The Geography Lesson* (see Figure 10). The photograph depicts a gentleman and children gathered round a globe and looking at a volume of engravings. The actual book under examination was *Excursions Daguerriennes: Vues et Monuments les Plus Remarquables du Globe* (1841–42). This was the first book to be illustrated with daguerreotypes and was published by the famous Parisian optician N. M. P. Lerebours.[54] Claudet and Lerebours had something in common, for as Claudet explained, we Westerners might examine views of the world

> by our fireside, without being exposed to the fatigue, privation, and risks of the daring and enterprising artists who, for our gratification and instruction, have traversed land and seas, crossed rivers and valleys, ascended rocks and mountains with their heavy and cumbrous photographic baggage.[55]

Photography had domesticated the world and enhanced the West's visual education. In studying geography, as one enthusiast put it, a student would no longer identify a particular country as "a mere diagram upon the map, picked out with blue or yellow, with thin hairy lines marking out the rivers, something like a section of a caterpillar for a chain of mountains, a rough imitation of a wart for a volcano, and a quantity of names in microscopic letters to signify cities, towns, and villages."[56] Instead, thanks to the educative tool of photography, children would now learn to recognize the landscapes, architecture, clothing, and people of foreign lands.

Louis de Cormenin commented on these early photographic excursions in 1852, noting that the camera could make a tour of the world and bring back the universe in its portfolio. It made the reader travel himself, rendering things and places both ocular and palpable. The more direct the retelling of a voyage, the more it placed things under the eye, the more it gained in truth and clarity. Thus it was fortunate that a photographic excursion could be made to little-known places of the world, where information was lacking. The photographic view gave body to the Koran and to the Bible; it placed history in its natural decor and offered a new tool to those who would focus on the East. Here was an unknown land exposed to the reader in encyclopedic form: the brute facts of monuments, landscapes, animals, plants, all rendered in the quick with the power of naked truth standing behind them.[57]

Inevitably, however, the photograph's depiction of the East was ambiguous. Was it a precise and truthful guide that provided brute facts, that did not lie, or was it the handmaiden of an imaginary geography reinforcing idealistic conceptions of exoticism and romance—or both?

It was Lerebours who initiated this project of armchair geography. As soon as Daguerre's photographic process was sponsored by the state in 1839, Lerebours equipped several travelers with this apparatus in exchange for their images upon return. He collected some 1,200 views, 112 of which were reproduced in *Excursions Daguerriennes*. This volume was intended to bring to the public architectural and landscape views of a precision hitherto unknown. As Lerebours explained in the introduction:

> These extraordinary feats cannot fail to interest lovers of art, for they are indisputably extensions of the engraving . . . making it possible to become acquainted with monuments and with unique and rare works of art presently hidden away in the studies of collections and connoisseurs. . . . As a result of the newly found precision of the daguerreotype, sites will no longer be reproduced from drawings of the artist, whose taste and imagination invariably modified reality.[58]

All but one of the images in his collection—that of Niagara Falls—focused on the glorious sites of European civilization and their "origins in the lands of Antiquity." Intended as a geography book for children, *Excursions Daguerriennes* actually fired the imagination of armchair travelers and became a guide for those who embarked on voyages.[59] Jerusalem was a requisite photographic site in this imaginary geography, though it could not escape the geopolitical tensions that covered the Holy Land.

In 1833, for example, the English architect and explorer Frederic Catherwood arrived in Jerusalem. He was the first traveler to visit the Holy Land with a camera lucida and he was interested in making accurate sketches of the Islamic shrines on the Temple Mount. As a non-Muslim, however, he was forbidden access to this celebrated site. Nevertheless, under a double disguise—dressed as an Egyptian officer and claiming to be an emissary of the Egyptian governor—he gained admission. Suddenly surrounded by a mob who sensed something was not right, he was rescued by an official who calmed the mob by explaining that Catherwood had been sent to make necessary repairs on the dilapidated mosque. It would not be long, however, before the Egyptian governor paid a visit to Jerusalem and Catherwood was forced to flee.[60] This story is interesting not just because it recounts the first attempt to make precise drawings of the monuments in Jerusalem, but because it recounts a mapping made by a duplicitous foreign explorer that met with local opposition.

Back in London, Catherwood's images caught the eye of the impresario Robert Burford, who used them to develop the *Panorama of Jerusalem* displayed in 1836 at Leicester Square Pavilion with Catherwood as commentator. A few years later, in 1839, the first photographers arrived in the East. They, too, would be viewed as intrusive invaders who used unknown instruments to capture images of a closed society.[61]

57 André Rouillé, *La Photographie en France* (Paris: Maccula, 1989), 124–25.

58 Lerebours. Quoted by Nir, 34.

59 Schwartz, *The Geography Lesson*; André Rouillé, *La Photographie en France* (Paris: Maccula, 1989), 52–54.

60 Nir, 4–5; Kathleen S. Howe, *The Photographic Discovery of Ancient Egypt* (Santa Barbara: Santa Barbara Museum of Art, 1993), 11–46; Shepherd, 75–76.

61 In 1838 England opened the first European consulate in Jerusalem. The next year the Anglican Mission began to offer medical services, and the son of a pharmacist became one of the country's first local photographers.

Also in 1839 the Jewish phi-
lanthropist Sir Moses
Montefiore visited the country and sparked a social and
economic revival within the
Jewish community. By 1843,
the French had opened a
consulate, followed in 1846
by Prussian, Austrian,
Roman, and American diplomats. In 1846 the Roman
Catholic patriarch returned
to Jerusalem and in 1849 the
first Protestant church was
opened in the city. Nir,
29–44.

62 Herman Melville (1856).
Quoted by Nir, 14.

63 Melville (1856). Quoted
by Nir, 14. Nir claims that
until the 1890s there were
no Muslim photographers to
record Arabic Filastin, nor
were there Jewish photographers to portray Eretz Israel.

64 Viscount de Vogu.
Quoted by Nir, 19.

Religious ardor mixed with the desire for exotic views; in the latter category Jerusalem had to compete with Constantinople, Athens, and Rome, and many found her famous sites disappointing. In 1856 Herman Melville noted in his diary:

> No country will more quickly dissipate romantic expectations than Palestine, particularly Jerusalem. To some the disappointment is heart sickening. . . . Is the desolation of the land the result of the fatal embrace of the Deity! Hapless are the favorites of heaven. In the emptiness of the lifeless antiquity of Jerusalem the emigrant Jews are like flies that have taken up their abode in a skull.[62]

At the entrance to the Church of the Holy Sepulchre he noticed "a divan for Turkish policemen, where they sat cross-legged & smoking, scornfully observing the continuous troops of pilgrims."[63] Here were all the tropes that divided East from West: the former a land of lazy men, stagnant in development, immersed in clouds of obscurantist ideals. Yet posing the East as different from and in opposition to the West allowed it to be aestheticized into a collection of sites bathed in exotic luminosity. A retrospective view could capture this past, located in another time, and project it into the present. In his 1887 book *Syrie, Palestine, Mont Athos, Voyage aux Pays du passé* the Viscount de Vegu never mentioned the Bible, Holy Land, or Christianity. For him the "immutable Orient" represented the "immobile present" where "the historian can always find in the retarded races the living types of disappeared societies."[64]

An Array of Photographic Reporters

Less than four months after Daguerre's invention of photography had been publicly announced in Paris, two painters, Horace Vernet and Frédéric Goupil-Fesquet, arrived in Jerusalem. They were part of the large group of daguerreotypists dispatched by Lerebours to capture interesting views. Lerebours' *Excursions Daguerriennes* contained the first photographic view of Jerusalem ever published; this was probably taken by Goupil-Fesquet. This view of Jerusalem's domes, walls, and towers as seen from the Mount of Olives offered an excellent panoramic sweep of the city. In 1844 one of the first British daguerreotypists arrived, the medical doctor George Keith. His daguerreotypes were used to illustrate his father's book *Evidence of the Truth of the Christian Religion Derived from the Literal Fulfillment of Prophecy Particularly as Illustrated by the History of the Jews and the Discoveries of Modern Travelers*. The elder Keith appreciated the daguerreotype for authenticating his texts; writing in his introduction he claimed:

> Having recently visited the land of Judea, the writer may confidently affirm that it sets before the eyes of every beholder, who knows the Bible and can exercise his reason, a threefold illustration of the truth of Scripture, in respect to its past, present and yet destitute state. . . . It exhibits even among the barren but terraced mountains of Israel such proofs of ancient cultivation as show to a demonstration that the ancient fertility and glory

of the land were not inferior to what Scripture represents. Looking on it as it is, the whole land now bears the burden of the word of the Lord. And yet it shows as clearly, whenever the burden shall be removed and the Lord shall in mercy remember the land, that it yet retains the capability, as if it had never been laid waste, of blowing forth anew in all its beauty.[65]

65 George Keith, Sr., Nir, 34–35.

Also in 1844 Joseph Philibert Girault de Prangey, a Frenchman, arrived with several cameras and lenses. He had an interest in Islamic architecture, having already traveled to Seville and Granada in Spain. De Prangey's collection of views includes some one hundred daguerreotypes from the Holy Land. He took twenty-one views of the Temple Mount, focusing on the venerated Dome of the Rock. His second interest was Christian sites. He took twenty-seven views in this category, including ten of the Holy Sepulchre. Another dozen views were of tombs and villages outside the city walls. Few of these images were ever published, although the collection survives.

Two Englishmen, the Reverend George Bridges and C. M. Wheelhouse, were the first to bring the paper negative calotype technique to Jerusalem, photographing the city and its surroundings in 1849 and early 1850. Bridges' set of photographic albums, *Palestine as It Is: In a Series of Photographic Views*, presented illustrations of the Bible. He noted that many an artist had tried to interpret the views of the Holy Land

> *but heretofore no one has thought of presenting to the student of Sacred History facsimiles of these scenes, satisfying at once the requirements of truth, and the delight connected with a display of the beauties of Nature. Irrespective of all controversy upon the identity of these places . . . it is hoped that . . . they may tend rather as an additional inducement to search into the pages of the very best of all Guides to Palestine—the Book which cannot err.*[66]

66 Bridges. Quoted by Nir, 48.

Bridges was also interested in contemporary scenes, photographing the newly consecrated Protestant church. He was also aware that everywhere the eye looked it was met with ruins and rubble. One could scarcely see a monument above the confusion of broken walls and mountainous heaps.

Wheelhouse's album contained calotypes of a journey from Spain to Jerusalem taken in early 1850. He preferred landscapes over buildings, photographing the Garden of Gethsemane from a distance with trees in the foreground and the Mount of Olives in the background (see Figure 11).

Maxime Du Camp, traveling with Gustave Flaubert, arrived in 1850. He also used the calotype. Published in an album as *Egypte, Nubie, Palestine et Syrie*, Du Camp's work featured the same subjects as Wheelhouse's but at close range, emphasizing their architectural monumentality (see Figure 12). Du Camp's companion Flaubert was not very taken with Jerusalem, noting in his diary, "Jerusalem stands as a fortress; here the old religions silently rot away. One treads on dung; ruins sur-

Figure 11
General view from Mount of
Olives. Photo by Francis
Bedford, 1862.

Figure 12
Mosque of Omar. Photo
by Maxime Du Camp,
1850.

67 Flaubert. Quoted by Nir, 52.

round you wherever your eyes wander, a very sad and sorry picture."[67] In a letter to a friend a few days later he wrote:

> Jerusalem is a house of bones surrounded by walls. Everything is rotting there—in the streets dead dogs, in the churches the religions. There are many ruins. The Polish Jew in his fur cap steals silently by the decrepit walls, whilst in its shadows a Turkish soldier sleepily fingers his beads and puffs on his pipe. The Armenians curse the Greeks, who in turn despise the Latins, who excommunicated the Copts! The situation is more sad than grotesque, or possibly is it more grotesque than sad? . . . Firstly, we noticed that the slaughterhouse was in the street—an open area amid some houses where you see blood, intestines and urine in a pit, a mass of warm shades which painters could well use. The stench was deadly. . . . The animals were killed and offered for sale on this spot. The young Du Camp was on the verge of fainting.[68]

68 Flaubert. Quoted by Nir, 52.

Four years later, in 1854, Auguste Salzmann produced a large album entitled *Jerusalem* and consisting of 180 calotypes, the first major photographic work dedicated to the Holy City. This was the earliest attempt to use photographs of Jerusalem in a systematic manner and as an adjunct to archaeological work. Sponsored by the French Ministry of Public Instruction, Salzmann's journey was intended to answer a controversy over the accurate dating of ancient remains in the Holy Land. Nothing was thought to remain from the ancient kingdom of Solomon, and it was generally assumed that the ruins of Jerusalem and its environs dated from Roman and Greek times. But Salzmann's friend Félicien Caignart de Saulcy returned from the Holy Land with a fragment from the area known as the Tomb of the Kings and declared that it dated from the time of King David. This, of course, caused an uproar among archaeologists, so Salzmann set out to settle the debate by photographing details, inscriptions, and fragments from archaeological sites in Jerusalem (see Figure 13). If maps and drawings were doubted, then photography should be substituted, for the photograph did not lie. Here the photographic image entered into a new debate, not just verifying Biblical stories but supplying the accurate date of archaeological fragments. Utilizing close-up formats, Salzmann offered his photographs as "conclusive brute facts."[69] In the introduction to *Jerusalem* he wrote:

69 André Rouillé, *La Photographie en France* (Paris: Maccula, 1989), 136–43.

> De Saulcy in his knowledgeable article wreaked havoc with quite a number of commonly held opinions. It had been generally believed that not a single trace of Judaic architecture remained in Jerusalem. With Bible and history book in hand, de Saulcy was trying to prove that monuments previously thought to belong to the Greek or Roman decline were of Judaic origin. In light of these circumstances, I decided that I would be performing a true service to Science by studying and especially photographing the monuments of Jerusalem, especially those whose origins had been questioned.[70]

70 Auguste Salzmann. Quoted by Howe, 27.

The last photographer to utilize the calotype, Louis de Clercq, arrived in Jerusalem in 1859 as a member of Guillaume Rey's archaeological expedition. After returning to Paris he published four albums of calotypes entitled *Voyage en Orient*. The last two focused on Jerusalem. He photographed all the well-known sites and also included a large panorama of the Holy City from the Mount of Olives and views of the Convent of St. Anne, an Austrian hospice for pilgrims, the Huva synagogue, and other contemporary structures. The last volume featured each of the traditional stations of the cross along the Via Dolorosa. Most of the stations were houses built of stone, not noteworthy in themselves but typical of Jerusalem. Here too was a new use of the photograph: to narrate the stations of the cross. This sequence of photographs was not to be repeated until the 1890s (see Figure 14).

Francis Frith was perhaps the most celebrated photographer of Jerusalem in the nineteenth century. He visited the Holy Land in 1858, seeking to create a documentary or factual account rather than to glorify Jerusalem (see Figure 15). Introducing an album of photographs entitled *Egypt and Palestine*, he declared:

> I have chosen as the beginning of my labours, the two most interesting lands of the globe, Egypt and Palestine. Were but the character of the Pen for severe truthfulness, as unimpeachable as that of the Camera, what graphic pictures might they together paint! But we scarcely expect from a traveler "the truth, the whole truth, and nothing but the truth." I am all too deeply enamored of the gorgeous, sunny East, to feign that my insipid, colorless pictures are by any means just to her spiritual charms. But, indeed, I hold it to be impossible, by any means, fully and truthfully to inform the mind of scenes which are wholly foreign to the eye. There is no effectual substitute for actual travel; but it is my ambition to provide for those to whom circumstances forbid that luxury, faithful representations of the scenes I have witnessed and I shall endeavor to make the simple truthfulness of the Camera a guide for my Pen![71]

71 Frith. Quoted by Nir, 61.

Frith's image of the Church of the Holy Sepulchre is taken from the rear, since this was the only possible vantage point. Concerning this image, he wrote:

> The ruined state of Modern Jerusalem is strikingly brought before us by this view. The Church of the Holy Sepulchre has outside the aspect of a place long deserted, so that we could not imagine, did we not know, that it is still the object of pilgrimage and in the hands of rich Christian communities. The great square tower is seen to have partly fallen, the smaller, but loftier, towers to be decayed, and the chief dome to have lost half its outer covering. The street to the left, with its pavement sloping to the middle and the ragged awnings of the shops, is harmonious in its wretchedness. Everything looks as though the city had been sacked and was almost or entirely uninhabited.[72]

72 Frith. Quoted by Nir, 72.

James Robertson and Felice A. Beato arrived in Jerusalem after a photographic assignment in the Crimean War (1853–56). They published an album entitled *Jerusalem*, whose images were probably taken by Beato in 1857 as he passed through the city on his way to India. They focused on the most important holy places in and near Jerusalem. As works of glorification, their photos avoided the city's ruins.

Francis Bedford visited the Holy Land in 1862 as the official photographer in the entourage of the Prince of Wales. He was thus afforded access to places forbidden

Figure 13
Mosque of Omar, West
Section of Interior of the
Enclosure. Photo by
Auguste Salzmann, 1854.

M. Christine Boyer

Figure 14
Eighth Station of the Cross.
Photo by Louis de Clercq,
1859.

to other Europeans and was among the first to take a series of photographs on the Temple Mount. He too avoided unflattering scenes and stressed the picturesque landscape in his panoramic views (see Figure 16).

Not only were early photographers from the West trying to satisfy the insatiable appetite of their commercial audiences, which were calling for ever more images of the East; they but also arrived on the flanks of invading armies and as adjuncts to the military's project of mapping the land.[73] Captain Charles Wilson and a small group of men from Her Majesty's Royal Engineers entered Jerusalem on October 2, 1865. They were there under private sponsorship to map the city, especially its ancient water system. With letters from Sir Moses Montefiore, one of the most influential Jewish figures in England, to Jerusalem's Jewish community, and with appropriate diplomatic permission (*firman*) from Izzet Pasha, the Turkish governor of the city, they had all the protection and passes they needed. Albeit a small endeavor compared to the Royal Engineers' surveys of England, Ireland, and India, their published report *Ordnance Survey of Jerusalem* was the impetus for creating the Palestine Exploration Fund (PEF), which was responsible for sending military survey teams to map all of Palestine. The Holy Land held a key position in British geopolitics and cultural geography. Not only was it a strategic location controlling access to land routes to India, it was also embedded in the nineteenth century's great search for the origins of languages, species, and cultures, accompanied by (or cutting against) the great guides of History and the Bible. Hence the survey work of Wilson's group intertwined imperialistic strategies with cultural meaning.[74]

But how did mapping an ancient water system get mixed up with photography? In the mid-nineteenth century Jerusalem still suffered from recurrent outbreaks of cholera and bubonic plague; the cause of disease was assumed to be the famous cisterns that had provided the city with water for centuries but which now received runoff from the cemeteries dotting the hillsides.[75] A Water Relief Committee, formed in England during 1864, declared its intent to make a complete survey of the water system and drainage of Jerusalem. Calling on the government to provide the engineers, the committee promised to subsidize the mission (Lady Angelina Georgina Burdett Courts actually provided the funds). The survey team traced the water system, identified the portions that had fallen into disarray, and proposed corrective procedures. But it accomplished much more before departing Jerusalem in July 1865. Not only did it produce a detailed map of Jerusalem with elevations and surrounding promontories clearly marked, but it surveyed the citadel where the Turkish soldiers were encamped, marking down the number and location of cannon, and conducted archaeological excavations.

Even though the three-volume *Ordnance Survey* contained eighty-seven photographs (all but three executed by Sergeant James McDonald), photographic explorations were still an adjunct to survey work. As Captain Wilson explained in the *Ordnance*, "Photography was not considered an essential part of the survey; the

73 Colonial rivalry between France and England left its mark on the East and would affect photography as well. This process began with Napoleon, who in July 1798 took control of the Red Sea route to India, denying England access to her richest colony. However, the route was liberated by Nelson in August 1798. Nelson destroyed the French fleet at Aboukir, ousted the Mamelukes, and turned over titular control of Egypt to the Ottoman Turks in 1802. Fighting continued as British troops aided the Ottoman Turks in driving out the Holy Land's Egyptian rulers in the 1830s. Furthermore, the Crimean War (1853–56) had as one of its secondary issues the control of Jerusalem's holy places. James Robertson and Felice Beato, photographers of the Crimean War, produced an album of photographs of Jerusalem in 1857 and 1862. Francis Belford and Felix Bonfils settled in Beirut in the 1860s and 1870s. Meanwhile, British army photographers James McDonald, H. Philips, and H. H. Kitchener took exploratory photographs of the Middle East. Napoleon III's expedition to Lebanon in 1860 and the British financing of the French-built Suez Canal in 1869 brought increasing geopolitical pressure to the region. Finally, the victory of England and France over the German-Turkish alliance during World War I enabled the first internationally acknowledged borders to be drawn around Palestine. Nir, 97.

Figure 15
Jerusalem from the City
Wall. Photo by Francis
Frith, 1857

Memories of Contention

74 Howe, 16–44.

75 Captain Charles Wilson wrote in the *Ordnance Survey*: "The city is at present supplied with water principally from the numerous cisterns under the houses in the city in which rain water is collected, but as even the water which, during the rains from December to March, runs through the filthy streets is also collected in some of these cisterns, the quality of the water may be well imagined, and can only be drunk with safety after it is filtered and freed from the numerous worms and insects which are bred in it." Captain Charles Wilson, *Ordnance Survey of Jerusalem* (1868). Quoted by Howe, 29.

76 Captain Charles Wilson, *Ordnance Survey of Jerusalem* (1868). Quoted by Howe, 30.

77 Lipman, "The Origins of the Palestine Exploration Fund," *Palestine Exploration Quarterly* 120 (1988), 58.

78 PEF Report of Proceedings (1865). Quoted by Lipman, 45.

views were taken at spare moments, and were intended to illustrate as far as possible the masonry of the walls and architectural details of the different buildings."[76]

Colonel Henry James, the director of the Ordnance Survey, was an enthusiastic supporter of the use of photography in copying maps. He was responsible for charging McDonald with photographing the most interesting places in and around Jerusalem. James subsequently sold prints of these views at the Ordnance office in Southampton (see Figure 17). These photographs were probably used not only to gain interest and support for the survey work but to acquire funds to excavate the exciting structures just beginning to be unearthed. Before the survey team returned to England in the fall of 1865, the Palestine Exploration Fund (PEF) had been established and Captain Wilson of the successful *Ordnance Survey* appointed as its director.[77] But what was the purpose of this "exploration"? The fund's founding member and chair, William Thompson, archbishop of York, proclaimed in June 1865:

> *This country of Palestine belongs to you and me, it is essentially ours . . . It is the land towards which we turn as the fountain of all our hopes; it is the land to which we may look with as true a patriotism as we do this dear old England which we love so much.*

> *Our object is strictly an inductive inquiry. We are not to be a religious society; we are not about to launch any controversy; we are about to apply the rules of science, which are so well understood by us in other branches, to an investigation into the facts concerning the Holy Land. . . . [This is to be] an expedition composed of thoroughly competent persons in each branch of research with perfect command of funds and time, and with all possible appliances and facilities, who should produce a report on Palestine which might be accepted by all parties as a trustworthy and thoroughly satisfactory document.[78]*

The PEF proposed a scientific investigation of the land of the Bible in an era when the authenticity of the scriptures was highly controversial. A brief history is as follows: In 1838 the scriptural geographer Edward Robinson began to debate the authenticity of sites in the Holy Land, arguing in his *Biblical Researches* that some were misplaced and others fraudulent. He considered all ecclesiastical tradition on ancient sites to be of no value, and with tape measure and compass as his aids he set about measuring and comparing until he declared that every shrine in Jerusalem was fallacious. Not long after, Darwin's theory of evolution (1859) dealt a blow to the unquestioned truthfulness of the Bible. Here now was the PEF, established in 1865 with the explicit intent of exploring the authenticity of biblical sites. George Grove, a well-known Biblical scholar and secretary of the famed Crystal Palace Company who would go on to achieve fame as an editor of *Grove's Dictionary of Music*, appears to have been the founder of the PEF. He was inspired by scholar and architect James Fergusson, who had written a skeptical account entitled *An Essay on the Ancient Topography of Jerusalem* (1847). Fergusson questioned the reliability of traditional holy sites, claiming that the Dome of the Rock was not an Islamic shrine but probably the original

Church of the Holy Sepulchre built by Constantine in the fourth century. Debate erupted as traditionalists insisted that the known sites were the correct sites. Grove supported Fergusson's view and began to compile a location index for every proper name in the Bible and an index of geographical names. His visits to Palestine in 1859 and 1861 convinced him of the paramount need for an accurate survey and map of the Holy Land.

More trouble flared up over the authenticity of holy sites. Upon reviewing Ermete Pierotti's 1864 account *Jerusalem Explored*, Grove concluded that parts of it were plagiarized. Pierotti's book was supposed to be a definitive and comprehensive compilation of the antiquities of Jerusalem, but Grove felt it borrowed rather liberally from the works of earlier explorers, altering them to support Pierotti's unshakable belief that the shrines of Jerusalem were the actual sites of Biblical events. Fergusson also saw Pierotti as a plagiarist, and threatened to sue the publishers for unauthorized use of one of his own illustrations.

Pierotti had been officially employed as architect and engineer by the pasha who governed Jerusalem and was given the task of repairing the water system of Haram al Sharif. He made a thorough investigation of its ruins, drew up maps and plans, and was even allowed to have a local photographer take pictures of the sacred enclosure. His plans of the Haram suggest that the Dome of the Rock, far from being Fergusson's Holy Sepulchre, was built above the remains of the altar of sacrifice of the Jewish Temple.[79] When Pierotti denied the charge of plagiarism, Fergusson suggested that the British Institute of Architects might settle the controversy. Eventually Grove and Fergusson found sufficient evidence to suggest that Pierotti was a scoundrel, and his book soon became the ridicule of English society. But questions lingered over the truth or falsehood of Biblical sites; the passion for authenticity still hung in the air. Grove gathered together some of his friends to discuss the shocking lack of knowledge about the Holy Land, and at one point exclaimed, "Why should we not found a society for the systematic exploration of Palestine?"[80]

Responding to a newspaper article proclaiming the glowing success of Captain Wilson's Jerusalem water survey and mapping project, Grove wrote a letter outlining four additional problems of Biblical geography that begged for accurate investigation and excavation.[81] Grove even suggested that the unspent balance of the Assyrian Excavation Fund, set up in 1853 by Layard, explorer of Nineveh, be diverted to archaeological projects in the Holy Land. Public response was enthusiastic, and funding was provided to continue Wilson's survey. Grove's enthusiasm for the Bible as the most interesting document in the world and his energetic interest in collecting facts united a group of men with a diverse set of opinions, both inside and outside of the Church, under the title "the Palestine Exploration Fund." This group declared itself constituted "for the purpose of investigating the archaeology, geography, geology and natural history of the Holy Land."[82]

79 Neil Asher Silberman, *Digging for God and Country: Exploration, Archeology, and the Secret Struggle for the Holy Land 1799–1917* (New York: Alfred A. Knopf, 1982), 73-78.

80 George Grove. Quoted by Lipman, 46. See also Silberman, 73–78.

81 These four problems were: the remains of the Frankish Mountain or the Herodium; the tombs of Tibneh; the Samaritan holy places; and the exact points at which the Wadi Serka and other torrents on the east side of the Jordan entered the river. PEF Report of Proceedings (1865). Quoted in Lipman, 51.

82 Lipman, 49.

Figure 17
Ordnance Survey of
Jerusalem. Photo by James
McDonald 1864.

Grove's formula for studying all aspects of the land of the Bible included five sections:
1 Archaeology (with a list of five sites to be studied)
2 Manners and Customs (to be reported on not by travelers but by competent persons after lengthy residences)
3 Topography (a complete survey to include the outlines of ancient roads and territorial subdivisions)
4 Geology
5 Natural Sciences

It was a matter of some reproach, Grove thought, that the Holy Land had been studied less than Greece, Italy, and even Assyria. Captain Wilson's task, with his accomplice Captain Warren, was to excavate the outer walls of Jerusalem to bedrock and to locate the outlines of the second wall of the ancient city and the foundations of the great temple. It was essential to ascertain the position of the second wall, for this would determine whether Christ's burial site was indeed that lying under the Holy Sepulchre.

Almost all of the survey teams sponsored by the PEF during the nineteenth century produced results important not only for later archaeological research but for establishing the frontiers of Mandatory Palestine. With the rise of imperialism and competing interests in the Middle East, religious enthusiasts and Biblical scholars formed a strange amalgam with military intelligence and geographic inquirers, all aspiring to survey, map, photograph, and explore hitherto unknown terrain.

Creating a Memory Book of Jerusalem

To use the history of photography and geography to explore the East as imagined by the West involves the examination of an intertwined crossover between travelers seeking spiritual fulfillment and explorers intent on scientific penetration—of curiosity and mass entertainment with scientific exploration and firsthand experience.
For both ancient pilgrims and those seeking verification of the literal truth of the Bible in the nineteenth century, travel to the East involved a process of longing, deferral, and disappointment. Medieval religious maps or pilgrimage routes were vehicles for figurative expression, marking in space a symbolic spirituality based on metaphysical concepts; Biblical proof-seekers harbored a similar longing for sacred visions and spiritual transcendence. And it would prove impossible either to achieve the stupendous spectacle of the pilgrimage vision or to verify the accurate location of Biblical narratives.[83]

European expansion and colonization entailed a different methodology: an epistemological imperialism. Beginning with Napoleon's twenty-two-volume *Description de l'Egypte*, the best scholars and military strategists were sent to the East to collect information on flora, fauna, customs, costumes, and racial types. They located towns, river basins, mountain ranges, and ruins by making rigorous field observations and

[83] Jas Elsner and Joan Pau Rubiés, *Voyages and Visions* (London: Reaktion Books, 1999), 1–56.

accurate measurements; they made geological and hydrological studies; they noted demographic movements and territorial boundaries. Precise measurements and objective depictions were the requirements of Western rationality as it explored and colonized the East. Maps were the base on which this information was located, the heart and soul of all the descriptive work that filled in the great white blanks on the geographical page of the East. But in doing so, this work eliminated the places of myth and mystery, of conjecture and imagination, replacing them with cartographic precision.

Photography, the recorder of direct exposures, abetted and enhanced the all-seeing, surveying eye of travelers and explorers. In the second half of the nineteenth century it ceased to be merely the handmaiden of associative memories and imaginary geographies and became a source of factual, material evidence, an accurate recorder of sights for the specialized work of architectural historians, archaeologists, anthropologists, and military engineers. Photographs illustrated the reports of surveyors, provided "scenographic" background, and offered a physiognomy of the East for the imperial archive.

Perhaps it was inevitable that the literal-minded, realistic photograph would erase the process of invention that a more open-ended memory entails. Or was it the geopolitics of rival empires, their scramble for the few "empty" spaces on the globe, that framed the Orient in a static unchanging mold?[84]

84 Tuathail, 21–55.

In the search for authenticity, the religious sites of the Holy Land inevitably became petrified in stone, embalmed in visual imagery, and marked on the map as a static containers of memories. They also became a cause of bitter disputes for the first time since the Crusades.

Detached from the vicissitudes of time and the manner in which time interacts with the spatial configuration of the city, the cult of authenticity delivered decisive blows to the very concept of authenticity it sought to validate. By freezing the past into an image, it created a fetish out of the view and protected it forever from change and renewal. Just at the moment when geopolitical concerns were ripping apart the fabric of the Middle East, the assumption that archaeological evidence would reveal historical truth arose to bolster the politics of the sacred and to protect the sites of memory from which three separate religions had taken their departure long ago. Memory, fixed once and for all in the temple, the tomb, and the nocturnal journey, had been withdrawn from the transitory and the experiential into nostalgia and the inauthentic. Yet in the past, each religion had appropriated the other's holy sites, banned the other from residence in the city, violently crushed and destroyed the terrain with armies, words, and architecture, forcing layers of memory to shift with time. The attempt to impose authentic fixity on the holy stones of Jerusalem—to found sacred meaning on the stones themselves, rather than the other way around—was doomed to self-defeat, as the fluid sacred history underlying those stones was exposed to the light of a "scientific" mind-set that could neither accept that history as valid nor change it for a more acceptable version.[85]

85 Carruthers, 35–40.

Conclusion

The sacred sites of the city and pilgrimage routes that engender remembering ought to be associated with discovery or creative thinking, not merely with the reiteration of stored material. What matters is the memory work, not the site as such; the latter only gives clues to thinking.

To highlight the difference between this associative, creative mode of sacred remembering and the static account of collective memory, Carruthers points to the Vietnam memorial in Washington, D.C.[86] It, too, has become a pilgrimage site for diverse publics: those who fought in the war and believed in its justice, and those who opposed it and are convinced of its illegality and immorality. Yet the names of the Americans who died in Vietnam, inscribed on the wall, have generated millions of memories for these and other publics visiting the site. There is nothing intrinsically meaningful about these names—that is, they tell no stories, in and of themselves— yet the wall *invites* storytelling, to oneself and others, and it is these stories that make the experience of visiting the wall memorable. In a shared activity of recollecting stories, various publics come together to reflect on the experience of the war. Some bring memory tokens to leave at the site; others take photographs or rubbings of particular names. These acts enable each individual to draw on this material, to translate it into personal stories, and turn these stories into new memories. This, it may be hoped, will be the future of the sacred stones of Jerusalem. Their authenticity lies not in what memories they contain, but in how they cue remembering, how they act as maps for thinking, responding, and reinventing. A community of different publics, focused on commonly shared and overlapping sites, can achieve awareness that remembering is a shared activity, that each is required to acknowledge another's acts of remembrance and incorporate them into their own.

86 The western engineers and archaeologists of the nineteenth century had almost exclusive rights to dig and survey the entire city of Jerusalem and did so under the noses of the Ottoman Turks, who were slow to connect archaeology with imperialism. Once the connection was made, archaeological exploration declined. Under Israeli control, the archaeologists' zeal and the magnetism of the holy returned, most notably in the conflict over the Temple Mount. It was believed that the objective study of archaeological evidence would reveal historical truth—that archaeological facts were transparent. In spite of the ascendancy of systematic archaeological inquiry in the twentieth century, however, it is assumed today that archaeology can thrown no direct light on the questions of authenticity that raged in the nineteenth century.

Concerning the tomb of Christ, Martin Biddle argues that everything learned about the site by modern archaeological and topographical investigation shows that this site could be authentic, but there is no proof (Biddle, 95). There is evidence of a large building of Roman date on the site now occupied by the Holy Sepulchre, a monumental public enclosure along the north side of what may have been the forum of Aelia. But there is no evidence that a temple was ever raised on the site of a tomb. Yet the former city archaeologist, Dan Bahat, commented in 1986: "We may not be absolutely certain that the site of the Holy Sepulchre Church is the site of Jesus' burial, but we certainly have no other site that can lay a claim nearly as weighty; and we really have no reason to reject the authenticity of the site" (quoted by Biddle, 103). The most significant archaeological work since the 1960s has thus increased knowledge about the northwestern quarter of Jerusalem and the site of the Holy Sepulchre and raised no serious obstacle to accepting local traditions of ancient date. A balanced assessment is that there is no harm in considering the authenticity of the site probable.

Furthermore, according to Dan Bahat, the walls of the Temple Mount, originally constructed by Herod, were rebuilt in the early Muslim period in order to support the erection of mosques on the Temple Mount. After the earthquake of 1033 damaged the walls they were reconstructed. Thus the location and names of sites on the Temple Mount were changed, making it difficult if not impossible to compare the location of Muslim monuments with relevant Jewish and Christian texts. Nor can the numerous Temple gates be identified precisely. The present-day Double Gate is probably the Gate of the Prophet, but nothing can be ascertained for certain. Dan Bahat, "The Physical Infrastructure," in *The History of Jerusalem*, 38–100.

Biographies

Ghiora Aharoni holds a bachelor of architecture from the City College School of Architecture and Environmental Studies, New York, and a master of architecture from Yale University School of Architecture. He is currently an architect with Polshek Partnership. His work has been exhibited in *100 Great Ideas for New York's Future: The City That Could Be*, at the Municipal Art Society of New York, and has been cited by architectural historian Victoria Newhouse.

Ariella Azoulay teaches visual culture and contemporary French philosophy at the Cultural Studies Program at Bar Ilan University and at the Camera Obscura School of Arts. Professor Azoulay is the author of *Death's Showcase* (2001) and *TRAining for ART* (2000, in Hebrew) and the director of two documentary films, *A Sign from Heaven* and *The Angel of History*.

Rasem Badran was born in Jerusalem in 1945 and was educated in the nearby town of Ramallah and later in Germany, where he graduated with a degree in architecture in 1970. Following his graduation, he worked in Germany for two years before returning to Jordan in 1973, where he has been practicing ever since. Mr. Badran was a recipient of the 1995 Aga Khan Award for Architecture, the 1997 Palestine Award for Architecture, and other awards. He is a permanent member in the Academic Council for the International Academy of Architecture in Sophia.

Moustafa Bayoumi is an assistant professor in the department of English, Brooklyn College, City University of New York. He is coeditor of *The Edward Said Reader* (2000), has received grants from the Mellon Foundation and the National Endowment for the Humanities, and has published widely on literature, culture, art, politics, architecture, and music in *Transition, The Yale Journal of Criticism, Souls, Documents*, and other publications.

Stella Betts and **David Leven** are partners at the Leven Betts Studio in New York City. They both hold master's degrees in architecture, Ms. Betts from the Graduate School of Design at Harvard University and Mr. Leven from the Yale University School of Architecture. Their work had been published in various architecture and design journals. They are currently working on projects in New York City and will be teaching an urban analysis and design workshop in Brasilia in the Fall of 2001.

M. Christine Boyer is the William R. Kenan Jr. Professor at the School of Architecture, Princeton University. She is an urban historian, city planner, and computer scientist who has written extensively about American and European urbanism. Her books include *Dreaming the Rational City* (1983), *Manhattan Manners: Architecture and Style* (1985), *The City of Collective Memory* (1993), and *CyberCities* (1995). Forthcoming are: *The City Plans of Modernism: Le Corbusier's Urban Rhetoric, Cinecities*, and *CyberCities II*.

Joan Copjec is Professor of English, Comparative Literature, and Media Study at the University at Buffalo, where she is also Director of the Center for the Study of Psychoanalysis and Culture. Professor Copjec is the author of *Read My Desire: Lacan Against the Historicists* (1994) and of *Counterglow* (2002). She has also edited several books, including Jacques Lacan's *Television* (1990),

Shades of Noir (1993), and *Giving Ground: The Politics of Propinquity* (1999; with Michael Sorkin).

Jerrilynn Dodds is an author, curator, and filmmaker. Professor Dodds is the author of *Architecture and Ideology of Early Medieval Spain* (1991), *Al Andalus: The Arts of Islamic Spain* (1992), and other works, including articles on the reconstruction of the historical center of Mostar in Bosnia. She has also curated and co-curated numerous exhibitions on the subject of cultural interchange as seen through art and architecture: *Al Andalus,* Metropolitan Museum (1992); *convivencia,* Jewish Museum (1992); *The Mosques of New York,* Society of American Archivists (1996); *Crowning Glory: Images of the Virgin in the Arts of Portugal,* Newark Museum (1997). A prize-winning filmmaker, Professor Dodds writes and directs films in conjunction with museum exhibitions (*Journey to St. James, An Imaginary East, NY Masjid*) and for public television (*Hearts and Stones: The Bridge at Mostar*). She is Professor of Architectural History and Theory at the School of Architecture of the City College of the City University of New York.

Keller Easterling is an architect, author, and associate professor at Yale. Her book *Organization Space: Landscapes, Highways and Houses in America* (1999) applies intelligence from information technologies to a discussion of American infrastructure and development formats. She is also author of *Call It Home* (1992), a laserdisc history of American suburbia from 1934 to 1960. In two Web sites she explores alternative methods for adjusting urban commercial space: *Wildcards: A Game of Orgman* (www.dmca.yale.edu/wildcards) and *The High Line: No Plans for NYC* (www.thehighline.com). She is currently working on a book entitled *Terra Incognita*, exploring the export of "U.S.-style" spatial formats to politically pivotal locations around the world.

Amir Sumaka'i Fink is a graduate student in the Department of Near Eastern Languages and Civilizations at the University of Chicago. He received his bachelor of arts. in archaeology from the Hebrew University, Jerusalem, and has assisted in the supervision of archaeological excavations in Tel Beit-Shean, Ein Gedi, Tel Kurdu, and Tel Rehov. He is the coauthor, with Jacob Press, of *Independence Park: The Lives of Gay Men in Israel* (1999).

Samira Haj is a history professor at City University of New York. Professor Haj is an Arab-American, born and raised in East Jerusalem. She earned her Ph.D. from the history department at the University of California at Los Angeles in 1988. Her interests include modern Middle East history, political economy, gender studies, and modern Islamic thought. She has published several articles on contemporary Iraq and Palestine. Her book *The Making of Iraq, 1900–1963: Capital, Power, and Ideology* was published in 1997. She is now writing her second book, *Reconfiguring Tradition: Islamic Reform, Rationality, and Modernity.*

Rassem Khamaisi is a senior lecturer in the Department of Geography, University of Haifa, and senior researcher and planner at the International Peace and Co-operation Center, East Jerusalem. Dr. Khamaisi has participated as staff member, head, or main planner in a number of local-, regional-, and national-scale Palestinian and Israeli urban-planning projects. Professor Khamaisi has published numerous academic paper in international journals in English, Arabic, and Hebrew.

Romi Khosla holds a B.A. in economics from Cambridge University and is a trained architect. After running his own practice in India for twenty-five years, he left to work for the United Nations on proposals for urban revitalization and job creation in beleaguered economies, including those of Bulgaria, Romania, and Cyprus. He has designed a number of large architectural complexes in India and Nepal and is presently working with the Palestine Authority to modernize the school system in the West Bank and Gaza. His publications include *Buddhist Monasteries in the Western Himalayas* (1979) and over fifty articles in various books and journals. He is presently at work on a second book, *The Loneliness of the Long-Distance Future*, concerning the future of architecture.

Thom Mayne received a bachelor of architecture from the University of Southern California and a master of architecture from Harvard University. He was a founder of the Southern California Institute of Architecture and has taught at many universities in both the U.S. and Europe, including Harvard, Yale, Columbia, Cornell, and Bartlett (London University). He is currently a professor at the University of California, Los Angeles. His firm, Morphosis, has won twenty Progressive Architecture Awards and thirty-eight American Institute of Architecture Awards. His work has been exhibited extensively in North and South America, Europe, and Asia and has been the subject of numerous publications and books, including three monographs by Rizzoli International Publications.

Deborah Natsios and **John Young** are New York architects and the operators of Cryptome.org and Cartome.org, online archives tracking the political and civil-liberties implications of new architectures and new technologies (including geoinformation technologies) in the global context of networked national security states. Natsios and Young teach architecture and urban design through Cryptome.org and Cartome.org, extending the institutional pedagogy of architecture programs they have been associated with at Columbia University, Pratt Institute, and the University of Texas. Their work has been presented at diverse forums, including the USENIX Advanced Computing Systems Security Symposium, the London Freedom Forum's panel on press freedoms versus national security, the American Museum of Natural History, the Asia Society conference on Korean Peninsula biodiversity, and the North American Cartographic Information Society.

Moshe Safdie is the principal of Moshe Safdie and Associates. He received his bachelor of architecture from McGill University and has taught at the Harvard University Graduate School of Design, Ben Gurion University, and the Yale School of Art and Architecture. He has completed a variety of projects in Israel, Canada, and the United States, and has exhibited his work in the United States and Canada. Safdie is the author of numerous books and articles on architecture, housing, and design, including *The Harvard Jerusalem Studio: Urban Designs for the Holy City* (1986) and *Jerusalem, the Future of the Past* (1989).

Mack Scogin is a principal in the firm of Mack Scogin Merrill Elam Architects, Inc., in Atlanta, Georgia. He is also Kajima Adjunct Professor of

Architecture at the Harvard University Graduate School of Design, where he was chairman of the Department of Architecture from 1990 to 1995. He has received the 1995 Academy Award in Architecture from the American Academy of Arts and Letters and the 1996 Chrysler Award for Innovation in Design. His work has been widely published, exhibited, and awarded numerous honors, including five American Institute of Architects Honor Awards and an award from *Progressive Architecture*. His work is the subject of a University of Michigan publication entitled *Mack & Merrill: The 1999 Charles and Ray Eames Lecture* (2000) and of a Rizzoli publication, *Scogin Elam and Bray: Critical Architecture/Architectural Criticism* (1992).

Efrat Shvily is a photographer living in Jerusalem. Her recent work includes two major projects, a series on the new Israeli urban landscape and a collection of portraits of Palestinian cabinet ministers. Her work has been exhibited in Israel, the U.S., and Europe at, among other places, the Israel Museum in Jerusalem, the Kunst Werke in Berlin, and the Lisson Gallery in London.

David Snyder holds a master's degree in architecture from the Yale University School of Architecture. He was a Fulbright Fellow in Warsaw and is currently pursuing a doctorate in architecture from Princeton University. He has worked and lived in Tel Aviv and currently resides in New York City.

Michael Sorkin is the principal of the Michael Sorkin Studio in New York City, a design practice devoted to both practical and theoretical projects on all scales with a special interest in the city. Sorkin is director of the Graduate Urban Design

Program at the City College of New York. His books include *Variations on a Theme Park* (1992), *Exquisite Corpse* (1991), *Local Code* (1993), *Giving Ground* (1998; edited with Joan Copjec), *Wiggle* (1998), *Some Assembly Required* (2001), *Other Plans* (2001), and *Work on the City* (forthcoming).

Achva Benzinberg Stein is an architect and a professor at the School of Architecture of the University of Southern California, where she is also the Director of the Landscape Architecture Program. A graduate of the Department of Landscape Architecture in the School of Architecture at Berkeley and the recipient of a master of landscape architecture from the Harvard University Graduate School of Design, Professor Stein has taught and practiced in the U.S., Europe, Israel, India, and China. She has won numerous awards in design and education. Her work and writings have been included in such publications as *Landscape Architecture, Landscape Journal, Architectural Record, Progressive Architecture, Arquitectura Viva, The New York Times Magazine*, and *The Los Angeles Times Magazine*.

Jafar Tukan received a bachelor of architectural engineering from the American University of Beirut in 1960. Since 1961 he has practiced continuously as an architect in Amman. His projects include mosques, hospitals, housing, schools, hotels, and office buildings. He has received the Palestine Award for Architecture (1999), the Arab Architect Award (1992), among others, and he has published articles in *Area, L'industria Delle Construzioni, Jordanian Engineer, The Architectural Review, Albenaa*, and other journals. He is a 2002 recipient of the Aga Khan Award for Architecture.

Dag Tvilde
Born in Norway, Dag Tvilde received his master of architecture from the ETH-Zürich in 1978. Influenced by teachers like Aldo Rossi and Paul Hofer, he now works mainly in urban planning and the design of complex urban areas. His specific focus has been on the structural transformations of cities. Tvilde worked in Palestine as project coordinator between the Palestinian Authority and the Norwegian Ministry of Planning. He has taught at numerous universities throughout Scandinavia and at Bir Zeit University.

Andrei Vovk, architect, was born in Moscow in 1962. In 1988 he received a master's degree in architecture from the Moscow Institute of Architecture. He joined the Union of Architects of Russia in 1990, winning a Grand Prix at the All Union Contest of Young Architects. He has participated in a number of international workshops on urban design and in competitions sponsored by the International Academy of Architecture. He taught design at the Moscow Institute of Architecture in 1991, and in 1992, shortly after collapse of the Soviet Union, emigrated to the United States. He has been associated with Michael Sorkin Studio since 1992 and presently teaches media and design at the Pratt Institute of Architecture and the City College of New York.

Eyal Weizman is an architect practicing in London and Tel Aviv. Since graduation from the Architectural Association in 1998, he has worked with Zvi Hecker in Berlin and has taught architecture at the University of Applied Arts in Vienna, at the Technion in Haifa, and at the NIA in Rotterdam, and is currently a unit master at the Bartlett School of Architecture, London University.

Weizman has published two books—*Random Walk* and *Yellow Rhythms* (2000)—and articles in such publications as *AAfiles, City Levels*, and *Architektur Aktuell*. Weizman's work has been exhibited at the Photographers' Gallery and Whitechapel Gallery in London, at the Kunstlerhaus in Vienna, and in Jerusalem, Berlin, and New York.

James Wines is head of the Pennsylvania State University Department of Architecture and president of the architecture and environmental-arts design firm SITE, founded by him in 1970 to explore a socially and environmentally responsive approach to the design of buildings, interiors, public spaces, and manufactured products. SITE buildings and interiors have been given twenty-one major design awards, including the 1995 Chrysler Award for Design Innovation. Professor Wines has written on art, architecture, design, and green issues for *Connaissance des Arts, L'Arca, Landscape Architecture, Architectural Record, Interior Design, Artforum*, and other publications in England, France, Spain, Italy, Korea, and Japan, and is the author of three books: *Architecture as Art* (1980), *De-architecture* (1987), and *Green Architecture* (2000).

Lebbeus Woods
Cofounder and codirector of RIEAeuropa and editor of the RIEAeuropa book series, Woods has concentrated on theory and experimental projects since 1976. He has exhibited, lectured, and published his work worldwide. Projects include Solohouse (1988), Berlin Free-Zone (1991), Havana Projects (1995–96), projects for the reconstruction of Sarajevo (1993–96), the installation *Hermitage* in Eindhoven, Holland (1999), and the *Future of Civilization* installation in Berlin (2000), as well as nine monographs, including *Anarchitecture:*

Architecture Is a Political Act (London, 1992), *Radical Reconstruction* (New York, 1997, 2001), and *Earthquake!* (New York and Vienna, 2001). Woods has received the Progressive Architecture Award for Design Research, the AIA Award for Design, and the Chrysler Award for Innovation in Design. He has taught at SCI-Arc, the Bartlett in London, and Harvard and Columbia Universities. He is currently a professor of architecture at the Cooper Union in New York City.

Oren Yiftachel teaches in the Departments of Geography and Politics, Ben-Gurion University, Beersheba, Israel. He has studied urbanism, urban planning and political geography at Australian and Israeli universities. His books include *Planning a Mixed Region in Israel: The Political Geography of Arab-Jewish Relations in the Galilee* (1992), *Urban Planning in Western Australia* (with D. Hedgcock; 1992), *Planning as Control: Policy and Resistance in a Divided Society* (1995), and *Ethnic Frontiers and Peripheries: The Politics of Development and Inequality in Israel/Palestine* (1998; edited with A. Meir).

Omar Youssef
Omar Youssef is an architect in Jerusalem. Youssef was educated at the Ion Mincu Institute in Romania and divided "West" Berlin. He is a visiting professor at Bir Zeit, Bezalel, Hebron Polytechnic, and the Technion Institute, and is a consultant for UNICEF. He is currently a member of the International Peace and Cooperation Centre and the Jerusalem-Berlin Forum.

Ali Ziadah
Ali Ziadah received his master's of architecture in

Amman, Jordan. He teaches Palestinian architecture and planning at Bir Zeit University. He is a founding member of Riwaq: Center for Architectural Conservation, a center to protect Palestinian architectural and cultural heritage. Ziadah is also a consultant to the Ministry of Planning and International Cooperation. Currently he has a private architectural practice and is a consultant in the fields of planning and conservation of Palestinian cultural sites.